ZOLAR'S
STARMATES

Other Books by *Zolar*

Zolar's Book of Dreams, Numbers & Lucky Days
Zolar's Book of the Spirits
Zolar's Compendium of Occult Theories & Practices
Zolar's Encyclopedia of Ancient and Forbidden Knowledge
Zolar's Encyclopedia & Dictionary of Dreams
Zolar's Encyclopedia of Omens, Signs, and Superstitions

ZOLAR'S
STARMATES

ASTROLOGICAL SECRETS
OF LOVE AND ROMANCE

PRENTICE HALL PRESS
New York   London   Toronto   Sydney   Tokyo

Prentice Hall Press
15 Columbus Circle
New York, New York 10023

Library of Congress Cataloging-in-Publication Data

Zolar.
    [Starmates]
    Zolar's Starmates : astrological secrets of love and romance.
      p. cm.
    ISBN 0–13–843145–0
    1. Astrology and sex. 2. Astrology and marriage. I. Title.
  BF1729.S4Z65   1989
  133.5'864677—dc20   89–31626
                                                  CIP

Designed by Irving Perkins Associates

Manufactured in the United States of America

10 9 8 7 6 5 4 3 2 1

First Edition

For two young lovers, Claire and
Eric, who prove daily "You are
only as old as you play and think."

I TELL THEE

There's not a pulse beat in the human frame that
Is not governed by the Stars above us.
The blood, in all its ebb and flow,
Is swayed by them as certainly as
Are the restless tides of the salt sea
By the resplendent Moon; and at thy birth,
Thy Mother's eyes gazed more steadfastly
On thee, than did the Stars that rule thy Fate.

M. Manilius,
The Astrologer Poet
(First Century, A.D.)

Contents

Introduction

A CHAT WITH ZOLAR

Here we are again, this time talking about Zolar's favorite subject . . . Love!

It has been said with truth that love is what makes the world go round. Love of God, love of another person, love of country, love of power, love of money—and sometimes even love of love.

What is this strange power that completely takes over our lives, our minds, our will and makes us foggy-eyed schoolchildren all over again? It seems to have nothing to do with age or sex, or race, or nationality, or physical appearance. None of these things matter to the loved or the lover!

Take a moment right now and think back to the very first time that you fell in love. How old were you? What did he or she look like? Where was it? How did you feel? Did you tell your parents? Did you tell the world?

Notice the way in which I described this first experience with the word "fell." Isn't it interesting that when we speak of love we often speak of "falling," suggesting we really have little to do with the who, why, where, and when we are tripped!

Once we are there, wherever there is, how do we stay there? In other words, how do we stay in love? Another great mystery, no doubt! Perhaps this is why some claim we "fall" in love and we "fall" out of love in the same way. But what really is the way?

Before I became an astrologer many, many years ago, I married my first wife. The marriage was from the start bumpy. Throughout its duration I always felt trapped, constricted, but never quite knew "why."

Once I became an astrologer and cast her horoscope chart, I discovered that Saturn (the planet of restriction) in *her* chart directly opposed the Sun (self) and Moon (feelings) in *my* chart. Then I knew why I always felt as I did, but had never quite been able to put my hands on the reason.

During the twenty years or so I have worked as a professional astrologer in New York and around this great country of ours, I had occasion to consult with thousands of persons whose primary concern was the outcome of either a personal or business relationship. Many were the times that couples stormed out of my office in a huff after being told that their relationship was not made in heaven, and that there would be stormy days ahead for various specific reasons. In almost every instance, I would later hear that these couples who were so certain that this relationship was "it," had parted for the very reasons I read in their horoscope charts.

Astrology is like gravity. You don't have to believe in it for it to be working in your life. Like gravity, you can't "see" the influence of the planets, but believe me it's there! It didn't take me long to realize that comparing one's horoscope with another's was not just another party game for adults.

Liken a horoscope chart to an X-ray in the hands of a skilled physician. Only in this case, it's a picture of your soul and not your body (although even the latter shows, too, in the hands of a good medical astrologer). Astrology, like chemistry, tells us which elements work together harmoniously and which form explosions.

And don't get the idea that astrology is something antireligious, because it's not!

If you remember the New Testament, the Magi came to worship the birth of Christ after seeing His star! The Magi were astrologers from Persia. In fact, some new translations of the Bible actually call them "astrologers."

Now what did they do when they got there? They brought gifts to Christ and worshipped Him. Thus, symbolically the authors of the New Testament show us that astrology is inferior to Christianity. But the story does not say that the Magi were wrong to use astrology to find Christ, or that they gave up astrology once they found Him.

A horoscope chart is a spiritual balance sheet. It tells you what your debits are and what credits you have brought with you into each incarnation. (Yes, astrologers do believe in reincarnation!)

Your chart is *your* business. And your business is to run your own life as best you can by turning scars into stars and lemons into lemonade. In other words, "Do what you can with what you have where you are *right now*!"

In the pages that follow I have tried to set down in a general way what astrology says about love, sex, and romance. What I have written is not meant to be a substitute for a one-to-one consultation with an astrologer who will accurately cast and interpret your very own horoscope. I encourage you to do this if you can.

But there are certain astrological principles which, like the laws that govern the universe, are *always true*! For instance, water and fire do not mix. Either the water will extinguish the fire, or the fire will boil the water. There is no exception to this!

For you to think you can beat the laws of God and Nature simply because you "want" to is somewhat foolish, akin to pushing a car uphill or rowing against the tide. Sure you might get to the shore, but at what price?

Sometimes, though, it is in the stars for someone to "grow" through a relationship which is star-crossed from the outset. Here, too, *Starmates* can be of great assistance to you inasmuch as you will know in advance what you are getting yourself into!

Ultimately, you are a free spirit and can even choose *not* to choose if you so wish. The stars impel. They never compel.

To make it easier for all of Zolar's loyal readers, I have divided this work into four distinct sections.

The first contains a general introduction to love and romance and will enable you to quickly determine whether your lover has the potential to be Mr. or Ms. Right!

The second section introduces you to the magical use of Venus and Mars to instantly discover what your relationship really is and what it can become!

The third section contains a special message regarding your individual potential for romance based on your particular birth day, according to astro-numerology.

Fourth, I have decided to share a number of actual case histories which illustrate exactly *how* astrology can be used successfully to deal with the many problems that falling in love sometimes brings. For the first time ever, you will sit behind the astrologer's desk!

Once again, thanks to Karen Fuson, my resourceful associate, for her assistance in the preparation of this manuscript.

Also, hats off to Sioux Rose for astute contributions to the Venus-Mars potentials and to Frank McCarthy for insight into astro-numerology.

And to my readers, follow my advice and take time to love someone today . . . even if the someone is yourself!

Blessings,
ZOLAR

I

YOUR ASTROLOGICAL GUIDE TO LOVE AND ROMANCE

ARIES

First Aries shines, and as he oft doth I see
His Fleece, and then as frequently renews,
'Twixt sudden Ruin, and a fair Estate
He gets, then loseth, then returns to Gain,
Then Loss steals in, and empties all his pain:
He rears new Lambs, he doth encrease the Fold,
And make the Rams to shine in native Gold;
Better the Wool, and whilst the Subject grows
He forms Mens Minds to use what he bestows;
To pick, to card, to spin, and weave, to deal
In Cloth with gain; to Buy, Exchange, and sell;
All useful Arts, whose constant Works supply
Mens real Want, not only Luxury;
This Pallas owns, nor doth disdain to claim
Arachne's conquest as her greatest Fame.
There are the manners, these the various Arts
Which Aries Rays, and secret force imparts;
To Anxious fears he troubled Minds betrays
And strong Desires to venture all for Praise.

Aries

THE RAM

MARCH 21–APRIL 20

An Aries man is basically a fundamentalist in many of his reactions, including sex. He knows that the world exists. He exists. Sex exists. He doesn't question this creative force in nature. He accepts it. He is as simple and direct in his sexual manifestations as the ram roaming over a hillside in spring. And, like the ram, he is filled with the exuberance and creative energy of the springtime. The mating season is approaching and he feels that stir in nature, that profound call of the universe, a force as mighty as that of swollen rivers crashing toward their union with the sea. He craves for the pure simplicity of nature in his own mating but he finds himself hedged about by conventions and manmade laws against which he inwardly chafes. He has discovered that his overflowing abundance of creative energy often surges upward into mental channels. He feels an urge to sally forth and conquer new worlds, to blaze new trails in the fields of literature, mechanics, engineering, or in whatever sphere of activity his brilliant mind carries him. But being virile and red-blooded, as all adventurers are, his sexual problems are always with him. Perhaps more than one born in any other sign of the Zodiac, he craves satisfying sexual expression so that he can be done with it, and be free to utilize his mental processes. He does not wish his progress to be hampered by pangs of sexual hunger. Perhaps the greatest problem of the Aries-born male lies in the distribution of his creative energies, his need for striking a happy medium between the sacred and the profane.

Regardless of how urgent his sexual requirements are, there is a pure, almost crystalline quality about him that usually refuses to resort to clandestine relationships. This is not so much a moral or religious issue, as it is one of cleanliness. Seldom do we find an Aries man haunting a questionable district or associating with people of ill-repute. In his eagerness for mental freedom, he doesn't want the corners of his memory cluttered with dark secrets, and he is always alert to the danger of physical contamination. To be sure, there are some who are dragged down into the gutter through reckless impetuosity, but there is always a spark of manhood left within the Arian that kindles a brighter fire (even though his self-contempt can surpass that which the world may have for him).

5

An Aries man is always at his best when married to a sexually responsive mate. But so warmhearted is he, so generous in his affections, that he is likely to rush headlong into a rash marriage that cannot bring anything but misery to one so dynamic. However, it is interesting to note that he nearly always weds a woman whose character is above reproach. She may be definitely unsuited to him, but he makes sure he woos a springtime flower that hasn't acquired any of summer's dust. He brings to his marital relationship idealism but not sentiment, purity but not romance. He is best suited to a woman who is affectionate and idealistic but one who accepts sex as a matter of course. A Leo, Sagittarian, or one born in his own sign of Aries is usually a harmonious choice. There are exceptions, of course, but a Taurus woman often proves too cold and matter of fact, a Cancer too romantic, a Piscean too reticent. Many Arians are attracted to Aquarians, whose capricious and complex natures no doubt stimulate and fascinate them.

The intelligent Aries man who is happily married remains faithful. If he is the typical ambitious and aggressive type, he seldom leads a mediocre or tabby-cat existence. Only by great diplomacy and fortitude on the part of his wife is the home kept on a stable foundation. His restlessness and wanderings are not compatible with an armchair by the fireside. If he finds himself unhappily married, he often resorts to separation or divorce as the most honorable way out of his difficulties. There is an occasional case where an Arian husband remains with his wife but seeks outside sex. However, like a homing pigeon, he usually returns to the nest. It is doubtful if he would have deserted his home in the first place had he not been thwarted in some emotional expression. In his headstrong, impulsive way, he is seeking that which he feels is rightfully his.

We often discover a strange quirk in the emotional side of an Aries man. So high are his ideals, that even though he seeks a clandestine alliance, he is determined that his paramour be of his own intellectual development, and if, perchance, he is the first man to erase the blush from the rose, so much the better. Then when the object of his desire has fallen from her pedestal, even though he was the cause of her descent from grace, he turns from her with repulsion, or perhaps it might be nearer the truth to say that he finds himself at odds with his own lack of self-respect. If married, he returns to his wife, in a vain attempt to rebuild his ego, which lasts until the "urge" overtakes him and he repeats the performance again.

We must not overlook one group of Arians, who appear to be the antithesis of the average type. We find this group among both men and women: timid, reserved, quiet figures, who not only embody fidelity, but are also lacking in strong sexual emotions. However, they are in the minority and are not typically Arian.

An Aries woman, although naturally warmhearted and amorous, may utilize so much of her creative energy in vocational and public activity that she has little left for physical expression. This is particularly true if she is unattached or if her marriage has failed. Rarely does she resort to illegitimate unions, regardless of how disillusioned she may be. Her inherent pride and her desire to appear well in the eyes of the world prohibits this. If we occasionally find an exception, we may be fairly certain that ambition has superceded pride, for so eager is the Arian to climb the ladder of success, that Aries women will sometimes become involved with men of power and position. There is probably no other type of woman who approaches sex with greater understanding, if she is happily married, than an Aries. She has none of the fear or inhibition that so often haunts women born in other signs. She is passionate, affectionate, and vital. She gives of herself with a simple abandonment that is as refreshing as a robin's first call.

GENERAL COMPARISONS

Aries have vital natures and varying moods that are very much like the weather: one day fair, the next stormy with thunder and lightning. It is easy for them to be strongly opinionated, and they will adopt a truculent attitude to press home a point. Often they are very quarrelsome and even seem to take a delight in stirring up trouble.

People are often amazed at their escapades and hare-brained schemes. Others gasp at the way they often live dangerously, for they are apt to take risks which more prudent people would avoid. But this readiness for adventure automatically equips them for leadership and for innovative roles. Thus, they are impulsive and forceful types. But to their credit it must also be said that they are ever ready to champion the cause of the underdog.

Being natural fighters, Arians do not shirk responsibility, but are remarkably strong-willed and simply do not give way to those opposed to their mode of thinking. Frequently they can become extremely despotic, and as such are likely to be unreasonable. They do not readily tolerate contradiction; their capacity for patience is by no means large.

Aries women have proud, generous natures, are high-spirited and buoyant, but often have quarrelsome dispositions. Marriages are frequently happy if they have accommodating husbands. But when they find it necessary to assert themselves, their spouse should accord a certain amount of latitude. He will certainly be most unwise if he does not.

Aries are very direct in speech, and fearlessly say what they mean. However, this is not always a virtue, for it can seem to indicate a lack of diplomacy. Furthermore, the revelations made by the tongue exposes them to the criticisms and spiteful talk of the gossip-mongers, among whom they are often a favorite topic of conversation. But let it be said that directness is their way of life, so much so that they love that same quality in others.

Aries and Aries

You will find a kindred soul in someone born in your own birth month. That is to say, you would both have instinctual, intuitive, and sympathetic understanding of the state of each other's feelings. Also your way of life is very similar. The only drawback will be the lack of contrasting characteristics. In consequence, neither of you would be particularly inspiring to the other, unless each is willing to sacrifice certain personal desires for the other.

Aries and Taurus

People born with the Sun in Taurus are warmhearted and as passionate as you are. Therefore, you would be well matched on the physical plane. But Taureans have a much slower tempo than you. Arians may find their phlegmatic ways exceedingly irritating, but remember it is useless to force Taureans. You will only be banging your head against a brick wall if you try. This is a type you cannot openly dominate; and the more you attempt to do so, the more you will find them stubborn, obstinate, and willful. And for goodness' sake refrain from losing your temper, for you have only to provoke a Taurus to realize just what blind rage is.

Aries and Gemini

Do not marry a Gemini unless you are prepared to offer your mate more than sex. The Gemini is looking for a congenial companion, one who is capable of measuring up to an intellectual standard of his or her choosing. Of course, it is very probable that if you are an Arian man you may succeed in sweeping a Gemini woman off her feet in an unguarded moment, thus gaining her consent to marriage. But you will certainly regret the venture should you subsequently prove uncongenial to her, if you try to bully her, or try her nerves with constant quarrels. Worse still, you will insult her intelligence and lose her respect by falling below the intellectual or artistic standards which she sees as ideal. There are also other reasons why an Aries should be wary of marrying a Gemini, especially if they happen to have the urges and instincts of a Casanova.

Aries and Cancer

Give a wide berth to Cancerians. If you do marry one, you are sure to experience very early the famous Cancerian moods. Cancers are extraordinarily sensitive and Arians are far too much of a diamond in the rough. Your Cancer mate would irritate you alarmingly, and you would loose your temper. It is this very temper which is the peril, since the memory of such quarrels would rankle the Cancerian, who normally finds it difficult to forgive and forget. Just because Cancers are habitually quiet and seem apparently tractable should not cause you to get the mistaken impression that they would be easily bent and molded to your will. Such an impression is a big mistake.

Aries and Leo

Your dashing romanticism and wild enthusiasms will blend well with the similar, though more reserved and dignified qualities of Leos. A Leo will understand your passionate nature and impetuous lovemaking. You will like the form of control which their dignified reserve and warm mannerisms will exert on your more tempestuous nature. You will be more inclined to tolerate their magnanimous condescension than you would from any other. But all the same you will do well not to take too much for granted in a Leo, or you may have a rude awakening. They are spirited people, too, and can be mighty stubborn. You also may be required to play second fiddle. Therefore, if you marry a Leo and wish for happiness, be prepared from the start to abandon any attempt to dominate. Yours must be reflected light and not self-radiation.

Aries and Virgo

Virgos likewise are "not the Arian type," so be cautious of marrying someone born under this sign. Such a marriage could ultimately deteriorate into a round of nagging, alternating with periods of acute boredom. Arians almost always rub Virgos the wrong way.

Aries and Libra

Librans would probably be the best choice an Arian could make, because this type has a warm temperament and passionate nature that makes a perfect foil for your own impulses. Marriage between you can be a great success provided you are careful to choose a mate of equivalent cultural standards.

Aries and Scorpio

Arians are not likely to find their ideal in the Scorpio types. You will find yourself up against a powerful, masterful nature calculated to provoke many disagreements. There is rarely room in one household for two dominant signs, unless one is a passive or subdued type.

Aries and Sagittarius

You are attracting a sagacious person when you seek a Sagittarian. The Sagittarius' passion and impulse can match your own, with equal directness and frankness. But in a manner similar to your own, the Sagittarian enthusiasms are rarely of any duration. You will find in your Sagittarius mate an adventurous spirit closely akin to your own, combined with a cheery, optimistic outlook which often produces a kind of tonic effect. The one great danger of matrimonial shipwreck, however, lies in the exceptional value which the Sagittarian places on liberty and freedom. Here once again you have to suppress your desire to dominate and run the show. If you want to live happily you have to follow the Sagittarius pattern in a realistic spirit, thus conforming to the requirements of pure comradeship. Given that degree of understanding, you will find here at least a partner of your own tempo who will have no difficulty in keeping pace with you.

Aries and Capricorn

Give the Capricorn a wide berth, too, for they may prove too much to handle in the long run. Arians are usually irked by people who sulk, and this sulkiness happens to be one of the most predominant symptoms of the Capricorn moods. To react roughly toward them will not help the situation. On the contrary, it will merely make them vengeful. It is true that the Capricorn may very well suit the passionate Aries nature in the matter of sex, but in no other respect are they likely to achieve true harmony.

Aries and Aquarius

It is inadvisable for Aries to marry Aquarians. That there are fewer obvious dangers is true, but such a union will make big demands without simultaneously yielding all they hope to find. Marriage would produce great disappointments for both partners, since the Aquarian outlook is so different from the Aries. One must have a stable temperament in order to please the Aquarius, combined with a tolerance that is foreign to the Arian nature. Attempts to dominate or bully will be met by a quiet, but firm resistance from the Aquarian. You will not get your way in the end, and this may not please your ego. On some occasions one does find an apparently good match between Aries and Aquarius; but a careful analysis will disclose that the price of such success is considerable self-sacrifice on both sides.

Aries and Pisces

Aries would do well to avoid the Sun in Pisces types. While these people are attractive and sympathetic, it is most unlikely that you will find complete happiness if married to a Pisces. If the Aries is a passionate lover and eager to prolong lovemaking preliminaries beyond a certain point, they will find the Pisces viewpoint is founded upon sentiment and not passion. Pisces have need of a romantic atmosphere and sense of languor in order to stimulate their sexual susceptibilities. Aries tend to affront them by accentuating virility and brevity. Furthermore, Aries people will find Pisces very cloying after a time, and may find the "clinging vine" tactics extremely irritating, and there may be a growing intolerance.

THE CUSPS

Persons born within three days of the beginning or the end of a sign will have some of the instincts and tendencies of the other sign. Such persons should read both charts to get a complete understanding of their dual characteristics. March 21–22–23, Aries with Pisces characteristics; April 18–19–20, Aries with Taurus characteristics.

LOVE AND EMOTIONS

You are by nature affectionate and crave the attention of others. Your sign indicates that there is going to be more than one outstanding love in your life. Generally speaking, sex matters and marriage are a naturally soothing and healing power, which makes the native of this sign a good partner for one with a high-strung nervous system.

Aries have an eminently practical nature; and the limitations which this practical outlook imposes on their otherwise passionate nature will, of course, yield observable effects. They are, therefore, less impulsive than calculating, and this in turn makes their reaction slower.

Of course, when they have made their final selection and have decided on a course, they are apt to let themselves go, and love wholeheartedly. They have a dominate, obstinate nature, and are imbued with the idea that what they say goes. Once they have made up their minds on a thing, they make sure they leave no stone unturned to achieve it.

They are conservative in their mannerisms and habits, and they like comfort and ease. But strangely enough, despite this conservative trait they often promise more than they deliver. Very often they make promises without having the slightest intention of fulfilling them. It is this idiosyncrasy which frequently makes them unpopular, because people resent being let down.

You Aries—males and females alike—are the real people who choose when seeking an affinity. The opposite number does not always know this; but you have definite ideas of what you like and your slower reactions enable you to gain the necessary time for a wise decision (as a rule). You are friendly and good-natured, but you are not the type to be easily thrown off balance. However, you may manage to choose wrongly for all that, owing to your tendency to pay too much attention to egotistical requirements. In short, you believe that what will suit you best is someone of fairly good circumstances who is probably able to satisfy your passionate nature. When you are satisfied on those points you believe that the bill is filled entirely. But in this you are often wrong. For there are a number of markedly inharmonious types who can apparently fill the bill in those ways but who are nevertheless capable of producing for you a lot of unhappiness.

HOW TO SEDUCE AN ARIES WOMAN

Flatter her, make her feel you want to take over her worries and relieve her of the burdens of independence. Send flowers. Shower her with gifts. Take her places where she will meet scintillating, intellectual people.

HOW TO SEDUCE AN ARIES MAN

Let him be the boss, flatter him and never criticize. Do not appear eager.

THE BEST PLACE TO MAKE LOVE

If you are a man, be sure your home is close to a big city. You are happiest if your dwelling is close to water and surrounded by trees. If you are a woman, you adjust easily to change, but you may overestimate your own ability to pay the bills. You are not a good housekeeper; you are energetic and creative, so get yourself a maid and be happy. The best places for you to live and promote love and sex harmony are, in the winter, a big city; in summer, the country. California is good for you. You should move around a lot. You like excitement and people of accomplishment, and your sex life is at its best when you are free to come and go as you please, but with the knowledge that you always have a home to come back to.

TAURUS

Dull, Honest Plowmen to manure the Field
Strong Taurus bears, by him the Grounds are till'd;
No gaudy things he breeds, no Prize for worth,
But Blesseth Earth, and brings her Labour forth;
He takes the Yoke, nor doth the Plough disdain,
And teacheth Farmers to manure the Plain;
He's their Example, when he bears the Sun
In his bright Horns, the noble toyl's begun;
The useful Plowshare he retrieves from Rust,
Nor lies at ease, and wants his strength in Dust
To him the Curij, and to him we owe
The brave Serrani, he i'th' Fields did Rods bestow,
And sent a great Dictator from his Plow,
Reserv'd, aspiring Minds, Limbs slow to move,
But strong in Bulk his powerful Rays improve,
And on his Surled Front fits wanton Love.

Taurus
THE BULL
APRIL 21–MAY 20

How a Taurus uses his abundant sexual forces depends greatly upon heredity, environment, and education. Born in the mating season, nature has endowed him with all the attributes of the most ardent lover, and he undoubtedly possesses the strongest passions of any of the twelve zodiacal types. He naturally inclines toward purely physical manifestations, whether it is a question of sex or a bountiful meal, for his animal nature is highly emphasized. The less educated Taurean may squander his intense creative energies in debauchery, although to his credit it must be said that he seldom does intentional wrong: He is led astray through his very strong sexual nature. As this is the sign symbolized by the bull, many Taureans regard sex merely as a biological function for the perpetuation of the species. They have few illusions about it, and seldom realize that it is the same creative force that writes a song or paints a picture. Yet paradoxically, many of the world's greatest musicians and artists are born in this sign. They seem to possess unlimited sexual powers, which they unconsciously sublimate for artistic purposes.

The favorite wife in an Oriental harem is frequently the Taurus. There is a healthy magnetism about her that is very appealing. She is usually attractive, with a genial vivid personality that makes her very fascinating. The voluptuous "kept" woman is often this type. Her Taurean love of ease and comfort, combined with the high regard all Taureans have for money, makes her an easy victim. Many young Taurus women are led astray through flattery, or they plunge into hasty and ill-advised marriages because of their lavish and sympathetic sexuality.

The highly developed, educated Taurean has his sexuality under excellent control, for in the same proportion as this sign bestows great sexual powers, it also provides the willpower to control them, once the Taurus native makes up his mind to do so. If married, there is a staunch loyalty that prohibits outside relationships. Furthermore, he feels that his security in life depends upon the good opinion of the world and he is careful not to forfeit it. Many married Taurus women, having very little romantic sentiment toward sex, regard it only as a marital duty and lose interest after children are born, and some women seem to be inhibited. They are still unconsciously clinging to the teachings of a Puritan past when sexual manifestations, even after marriage, were almost considered sinful. An unknown fear or sense of guilt encompasses them and they become negative and evasive instead of positive and yielding. They are often considered frigid and lacking in natural sexual impulses by their husbands. They have scant patience with those who commit indiscretions for they cannot seem to grasp the emotional value of sex. They seldom realize that to others it may mean more than a biological necessity, either for the purpose of propagation or as a husband-holding gesture. Neither do they pause to consider that those born in other signs may not be endowed with the Taurus willpower.

A Taurus husband often becomes so absorbed in his business and financial interests that he no longer cares for sexual gratification, particularly as he grows older. Yet both men and women of this sign demand personal contact. They want their loved ones by their side, even though they sometimes fail to appreciate this quiet, unspoken companionship. We recall one rather amusing case. A Taurus husband, in his late fifties, became so engrossed with business that he not only abandoned sex completely but decided to sever his home ties so that he could devote all his time to his precious vocation. His wife, a spunky little Capricorn, divorced him, and he found himself with the status he desired. But, like King Midas with his gold, everything was wrong. The very background of his life, the warp and woof from which he had woven the pattern of his days, was gone out from under him. After a few months of sleepless nights, he set about wooing his former wife with all the avidness of a young man. He promised her the world with a platinum fence, if she would only return to him. Wise little Capricorn kept him dangling until she was certain he had thoroughly learned his lesson, then they were remarried.

A youthful Taurean lover is never satisfied with courtship by "remote control." No amount of letters or telephone calls compensates him for the vital, living presence of his loved one. This may account for the fact that young Taureans are often led astray. The rapturous hugs and kisses that begin so innocently, with nothing but an overdose of love, lead to more amorous gestures. There is no other type of man more ardent and determined in his lovemaking that Taurus and none more loyal. Rarely would a Taurus man desert a woman with whom he has had a premarital relationship. He usually marries her, which was what he intended to do in the first place. Even in the most promiscuous cases, a Taurus lover seldom abandons a woman as ungraciously as men born in some of the lighter, more flirtatious signs.

The Taurus adolescent, not yet fully matured, needs careful guidance in sex matters. Many fine young men and women of this sign make mistakes that shadow their lives because their surplus sexual energy is misdirected. Nearly all Taureans, even very youthful ones, are so highly energized with the creative forces that they are exceedingly magnetic to the opposite sex. As this sign is closely correlated with the reproductive organs, much care should be taken so that dangerous habits are not formed. The reproductive processes should be explained in a sane, healthful way as soon as the Taurus youngster is old enough to understand.

GENERAL COMPARISONS

You are strong-willed and masterful. Yes, Mr. or Ms. Taurus, it is your portrait I am conjuring up. You are good-natured and have an easygoing disposition, but you do like to have your own way and can be resentful when contradicted.

You have a passionate nature and are very direct in your methods. But you will not brook being deceived, and nothing can arouse your anger more than to discover you have been the unwitting victim of insincerity.

You have the gift of patience; and you like sufficient time to complete a task. You are quiet and reserved, and you dislike being drawn into disputes. The only disputes you can tolerate are those of your own making!

The Taurus woman is divinely feminine. She loves good food, a very comfortable home, and an attentive mate. Given these things, she usually has what she wants.

The Taurus woman has a passionate nature, and is very sincere in her affections. She has little interest in serious flirtations, even though some of them are capable of trying out a variety of lovers to find the "one and only."

The Taurean woman makes a wonderful wife for the understanding husband—that is, the husband who understands it is a faux pas to interfere in any of her domestic arrangements.

However, you husbands with Taurus wives, reread the whole of the foregoing section which discloses the Taurus psychology. What I have told you there should aid in understanding your Taurus spouse.

Taurus and Aries

People born with the Sun in Aries have the passionate temperament that you appreciate. The only trouble is that you will have difficulty keeping pace with an Aries. He or she is really too busy for you and will not understand your lethargic ways. Arians tend to lose patience rapidly—a fact which naturally paves the way for many quarrels. Moreover, their natural tendency is to run the show, and this is something your dominant nature will not tolerate. Harmony can, however, be achieved if you both come to an understanding and draw up a domestic charter. Then, if your respective tempos can be adjusted to a common level, all will be satisfactory.

Taurus and Taurus

If you want someone who really understands your every mood and attitude, a Taurean of the opposite sex will be just that. Your personal comforts will be especially looked after, although reciprocity will naturally be expected. The two of you should get on well together in general, and it would be well for you to face all the facts at the outset; and one of the most important of these is that you are two very opinionated people.

If you were able to think alike, this would not be a great handicap; but if your thoughts and ideas clash, the results may be serious. One of you will have to give way if it comes to a dispute or an argument, but since both of you have unyielding natures it will be difficult. Therefore, I suggest you both discuss this problem before you get married. You should agree now on what concessions each will make.

Another factor each of you must understand is your mutual tendencies to be jealous. Something must be done about that too, otherwise there will surely be serious trouble should one of you ever attempt to flirt or wander from the hearth.

However, you are likely to be very much in love with one another on the physical level, and this should help tremendously.

Taurus and Gemini

If you are a Taurus man, a good housewife is essential if your comforts are to be served. The Gemini woman does not always make a good housewife (as a rule), for she has a restless, inquiring nature, and is far more interested in things which entertain the mind than in the more prosaic, boring routine of housework.

Furthermore, your two natures are basically at odds. While you may have settled habits and tend to be unchangeable in your ways and outlook, the Gemini is exceedingly changeable, capricious, and novelty-seeking.

Nor is the Gemini the ideal mate to promote the exercise of your passionate nature, for here again the basic conceptions of the respective parties on this subject are at total variance. You would need to know quite a bit about the Gemini way of looking at things to achieve proper sexual adjustment.

Taurus and Cancer

Provided you take the trouble to understand the moods of your Cancerian mate this should not be a bad match. The Crab, like yourself, likes a comfortable home and good living. The Cancerian woman makes a fine housewife. The passionate natures of the respective partners are also compatible.

The one thing you have to guard against is your tendency to dominate Cancer too openly. Your Cancer mate will resent any such attempt, and I must warn you that Cancerian feelings are hurt very easily. Therefore, Taurus would do well to unbend a little and try to understand the feelings of others. To do so will be to save yourselves a considerable amount of grief should you marry a Cancerian.

Taurus and Leo

Taureans are usually very strongly attracted to Leos. This is because there is more in sex appeal than meets the eye. You sense what you feel for each other; the physical qualities that promise gratifying results. Certainly your respective passionate natures are admirably suited to each other, and in this respect you are perfectly matched.

However, let me warn you: your Leo mate will expect much more attention than you feel inclined to bestow, for the simple reason that the Leo will feel himself (or herself) the superior partner. Yes, the Leo pride will tend to assert itself and will compel you to live up to the requirements of its ego if you want happiness.

Another important thing for you to remember is that it is very necessary for you to restrain your jealousies. You must be tolerant with the Leo on the basis of friendship, because if you show yourself mistrustful you will create a situation that may be difficult to overcome. As a general rule there should be little real justification for Taurus jealousy where the Leo is concerned; and it is the knowledge of this—plus an acute sense of injustice which accompanies it—that provides the Leo with a bitter sense of resentment. So do be careful.

Taurus and Virgo

If you marry a Virgo you can anticipate frequent criticisms from your spouse. At first you might take all this rather well, but after a time your conservative nature may rebel as you gradually find the criticisms becoming more aggravating.

What your Virgo mate will dislike in you most is your obstinacy and determined will (truly you want things your own way quite a lot).

However, the Virgo is usually remarkably attractive, and has a special way— a tantalizing, teasing, titillating appeal of a special order that arouses your expectations by promising you a great deal. Don't raise your hopes too high, however, you may be sorely disappointed.

If the Virgo will put a brake on the urge to criticize, and if the Taurus will loosen up a little from the conservative and rigid attitude, adjustment between the two types should not be too difficult to achieve.

Taurus and Libra

If you marry a Libra you will be satisfied—for a time. You should certainly have common interests, and a mutual appreciation of things musical and artistic. The danger is that the Libra may eventually come to regard you as too matter-of-fact. You are too easily contented, and the Libra wants to shake you up. This may cause disagreements. When such clashes occur they might very easily develop into large issues, because of obstinacy on both sides. When matters between a Taurus and a Libra reach this stage, there are rarely two such unforgiving and unrelenting personalities.

Taurus and Scorpio

You can be happily married to a Scorpio. By this I do not mean that your marriage would be free of quarrels or strife, since both of you are particularly strong and powerful characters, and could make formidable antagonists. But the qualities which make for compatibility reside in the fact that you have complementary characteristics which offset those of your partner and which arouse mutual admiration. All things being equal, Scorpio is one of the best signs that a Taurus could pick as a mate.

Taurus and Sagittarius

The Sagittarius is a type you should avoid. Sagittarians have too high a regard for personal freedom and independence to submit to your overlordship and dogmatism. The type is also far too unconventional to suit your conservative nature, and is, therefore, unlikely to agree with your views.

If you marry a Sagittarius, you may be letting yourself in for frequent and violent disputes. After a time you will fail to understand your mate altogether. Sagittarians need particularly careful handling. No one is going to change you, certainly, but don't make the mistake of imagining you will succeed in changing the Sagittarius by suggestion or by command. You will get a swift answer— and one you may not like—if you try.

Taurus and Capricorn

Union with a Capricorn is a fairly good match, and little need be said about mutual characteristics, since these blend remarkably well. The one necessity is that the Taurus should not take the Capricorn too much for granted. Capricorns need some encouragement, and unless they receive the attention they expect, they invariably feel lonely and misunderstood. No one is capable of feeling more sorry for himself than Capricorn, and if you prove an unreceptive channel for this self-pity, Capricorn can develop withdrawn habits, producing melancholia. However, marriage between Taurus and Capricorn holds forth distinct promise.

Taurus and Aquarius

The Aquarius is another bad match for you. True enough, the type has basic instincts akin to your own in desiring ease, comfort and a responsive counterpart. But these apparent suitabilities are actually snares. In the intimate association which marriage produces, the Aquarian would speedily come to the conclusion that you, the Taurean, are a "stick-in-the-mud." For your part you would come to the conclusion that the Aquarian is eccentric, neurotic, and hopeless.

The trouble is, of course, that the Taurus nature is fixed, whereas the Aquarius nature is dynamic. This constant restlessness would irritate your conservative habits intensely and a sharp division of interests would be discernible after a short time.

Taurus and Pisces

A Pisces might do worse than marry a Taurus. The Pisces has a sentimental nature which is by no means displeasing to the Taurus; and the Taurus will disclose qualities which increase rather than detract from the Pisces sentimentality. A Taurus-Pisces union usually works very well, and has a lot to recommend it.

THE CUSPS

Persons born within three days of the beginning or the end of a sign will have some of the instincts and tendencies of the other sign. Such persons should read both charts in order to get a complete understanding of their dual characteristics: April 21–22–23, Taurus with Aries characteristics; May 18–19–20, Taurus with Gemini characteristics.

LOVE AND EMOTIONS

Venus, your ruling planet, inclines you to romance and love. Being very sincere in your emotional desires, the companionship of a congenial mate is a definite part of your marital happiness. It is evident that self-restraint and control must be present if you are to avoid serious misunderstandings with your loved one. You find it difficult to take the first step when a love spat calls for reconciliation. Because of your inherent stubborn tendencies, there may be times when trifles are exaggerated (unless you are fortunate enough to have a mate who understands this idiosyncrasy of yours). These can become serious detriments to an otherwise very compatible marriage. Vanity is also one of your greatest enemies. Take care that it does not stand in the way of happiness.

True and sincere love gives you the inspiration and desire for material progress. You prefer a quiet home atmosphere and since Taurus is a "fixed" sign, you are not easily swayed from your habits and opinions. No doubt you will find that this innate trait of yours will be the cause of many disagreements in your home and in the social and business worlds. It is therefore essential that you be careful, if you have the choice, to select friends, associates or partners who do not have the same rigidities as you. You can be like the veritable "bull in a china shop," as the saying goes, when you encounter obstinate opposition to your pet ideas and plans. The ancient astrologers were very wise, when they gave the sign of the bull to Taurus as its symbol. Conditions permitting, you maintain a very artistic and luxurious home environment, for you greatly appreciate the finer things in life.

HOW TO SEDUCE A TAURUS WOMAN

Send flowers. Invite her for home-cooked meals in your bachelor quarters. Take her for quiet drives in the country. Find out what she collects and add to the collection. Speak quietly and look deeply into her eyes.

HOW TO SEDUCE A TAURUS MAN

Bide your time. Be neat and punctual. Be sweet, loving, charming, and cater to his mother. Cook for him.

THE BEST PLACE TO MAKE LOVE

If you are a man, you desire peace and harmony. Your house does not have to be a new one; remember you are handy and love to fix things. Carpentry, plumbing, electrical wiring, all these things are up your alley and you will thrive while doing them around your house. You dislike big cities, and will want to lead a quiet, relaxed existence away from the hullabaloo of life. Your home is all for your pleasure and your love life is at its best if you are able to secure a residence on a quiet street. If you are a woman, beauty in the home is important, as is your personal grooming. You are a wonderful housekeeper. You should live on the east side of the street, and if you can have a big garden and a pool, your sex and love happiness will be sublime.

GEMINI

Soft Gemini to easier Arts incline
For softer Studies fit an Infant Sign
They turn rough Words, or they incline to Sing,
To Stop the Pipe, or strike the speaking String;
Through reeds they blow the Natural Sound in
    Measure,
Gay their delight, and e'en their Pains are
    Pleasure;
Wars they avoid, Old Age they chase with Song,
And when Late Death o'ertakes them they are Young.
Sometimes to Heaven they mount, and trace the Stars,
Then fix in Globes, or turn the Signs in Spheres;
Their Wit reigns o'er their Nature, and refines
Its Powers; This is the influence of the Twins.

Gemini
THE TWINS
MAY 21–JUNE 21

Many Geminis never understand or experience the depths of sex emotion, which is not surprising when we consider that Gemini is not only a mental sign, but also one of the "air signs" of the Zodiac. Many Geminis do not possess the emotional depths of the water signs, the warmth of the fire signs, or the passionate instincts of the animal signs. A Gemini man may scatter his creative forces in many directions, usually mentally rather than physically. Unconsciously he is continually drawing upon these creative forces for new ideas, whether he is a businessman eager to improve his professional affairs or an artist who creates a masterpiece. Many of the world's great engineers, writers, designers, and musicians are born in this sign, usually becoming famous through a light, inspirational touch, keen imagination, and intelligence. Even the Gemini mother, designing her children's garments, adds this bit of creative originality. So active, both mentally and physically, are Geminis that there is little time for the regeneration of the life forces. Many Geminis renounce sex entirely and flee to the convent. Many Gemini men become priests, for deep within them lies a devout religious tendency, although this is not apparent from their light-hearted and sometimes frivolous surface appearance.

Geminis often regard sex lightly, with not much more than toleration, particularly Gemini women. We recall one Gemini woman who, after fifteen years of marriage, admitted that she hadn't learned what sex was all about. This may have been partially the fault of her husband who, either through selfishness or ignorance, had failed to bring the flower of love to full bloom. Another telling incident happened in a small group of women where sex was under discussion. We closely observed the reaction of a Gemini woman; and she did exactly what we thought she'd do: She looked at the group with big, wide eyes of amazement, blushed prettily, gasped, and sank into the nearest chair. It was beyond her understanding, yet she and her husband had celebrated their twenty-fifth wedding anniversary the week before. These women make very loyal and devoted wives—for it goes without saying that they are not easily tempted. There are probably some Gemini women more amorously inclined because of the position of Venus in their charts. Venus in Cancer causes them to be more loving, while Venus in Leo adds warmth and passion.

Gemini women are seldom immoral for the sake of sex itself, but some become gold diggers of the first magnitude. They are able to play upon a man's emotions in an impersonal and detached manner that is coolly fascinating, although it is extremely deplorable. Many Gemini women are nervous, restless, and high-strung. They indulge in every form of excitement that offers variety. This depletes their creative forces even if they have not indulged in sexual indiscretions.

A Gemini bachelor is often unfair to women, although he may be totally unaware of the fact. So debonair and attentive is he, so charming and courteous in manners that he easily sweeps women off their feet. Furthermore, since he lacks deep sexual emotions, he seldom offends a woman by overly-amorous approaches. This means that his current girlfriend feels that at last she has found the perfect man—a gentle, courteous soul but nevertheless one endowed with all desires peculiar to the male sex. She takes it for granted that he craves to possess her, and his great self-control endears him to her. Indeed, a perfect lover. In many cases, nothing could be farther from the truth. His feelings toward her may be as impersonal and sexless as those of an artist looking at an interesting painting. She has caught his fancy for the time being. He likes her and enjoys her companionship, and like a child with a new toy, he will remain captivated until another comes along. The only way to lead this man to the altar is to leave him dangling in mid air as soon as he has become interested in his new plaything, but before he has had time to investigate it. The wise woman will keep him guessing. She will play a game of hide and seek with him, each time edging a little nearer to the church and the parson. Even with the first strains of Lohengrin, she may not be entirely sure of him, for these men have a way of slipping out of anything that threatens their freedom. And so devoid is he of the grand passion, that even the anticipation of his wedding night may fail to lure him to the altar. As our Gemini is rarely carried away by passion, he is able to keep a cool head and a keen eye for an alliance that will be to his advantage. This may not mean that he doesn't marry for love but he makes sure that love's in the right direction.

The sensitive Gemini husband remains loyal after marriage, for he hasn't sufficient interest in sex to become involved in liaisons. If the marital relationship is satisfactory, he settles down with his business and his hobbies, and women become like birds of gay plumage to be admired momentarily and as quickly forgotten. He demands personal freedom but often is misjudged. He may be innocently playing pool with the guys while his wife is convinced he is parked with some cute blonde. However, the less sophisticated type may indulge in indiscreet flirtations, which not only prove a source of great irritation to his wife but frequently lead to divorce. It is usually flattery rather than keen emotional desires that lures these males away from established ties.

GENERAL COMPARISONS

You love gaiety, scenes and things of beauty, art and music and all things clever. You are eternally in search of the novel; and anything in the nature of an innovation will always interest you.

All these manifold interests leave you with very little time for any one thing, especially for anything in the domestic line. You abhor routine and soon become bored with the continuation of any one series of existing circumstances. That is just the trouble with courtship and marriage where you are concerned, and why it is so many of you Geminis are charged with being fickle.

You are no more fickle at heart than any other type, but you cannot for long stand the company of people who are perpetually dull, complacent, and uninspiring. You want someone full of life and surging enthusiasms. In short, someone capable of firing your imagination continuously.

The Gemini woman needs a congenial companion suited to her everchanging interests. A bohemian life without the hardships, penury, and sordidness usually associated with it would be her ideal existence. She would like to mingle with artistic personalities of all types, flitting from one to the other as the mood suited, or as her interests would dictate.

She likes new clothes and novelties of all kinds. She loves plays and all art forms.

The above are the lines on which she would like to plan her life in accordance with the ideal she envisages. But, of course, her idea of freedom is one that is very difficult to carry through to a logical conclusion. The Gemini—like all of us—frequently has to submit to her environment. Hence the Gemini woman frequently treads a difficult path; usually it happens that, tiring of the struggle, she ends up with a mate far different from the one she held as her ideal.

If you are in love with a Gemini and want to gain a realistic idea of their psychology, I would advise you to study the role of patience.

Yes, they are a magnet all right; and a particularly attractive one at that. But what you have to do if you hope to win them is not to turn yourself into a lump of iron, but transform yourself into an electric current and demagnetize them.

Gemini and Aries

If you are a Gemini who is married to (or thinking of marrying) an Aries there may be some hope for the match because there is likely to be some degree of accommodation between you.

However, the Gemini looks for change, novelty, and variety; and on the face of it one might think that these requirements are in line with the Aries character, too. But the fact is that the demands of the Gemini are likely to cost the Aries more than he is prepared to concede.

There is also a radical divergence between the mental aims and outlook of Gemini and Arian. Usually the cultural standard of the Gemini is superior to that of the Arian, with the consequence that after a time the former begins to find the latter boring. There is little doubt that eventually you would begin to get on each others' nerves seriously; and when quarrels begin the end is not very far off. Although the Aries may be the more aggressive and the strongest physically, it is the Gemini who is the ultimate victor.

Gemini and Taurus

For the Gemini to marry a Taurus is not too risky, for at least there will be a comfortable home (the Taurus wife will see to that). But the Gemini will also probably find the Taurus a particularly possessive partner, which may not be at all to their liking. There is rarely true harmony between Gemini and Taurus, and therefore it is a union that has its pitfalls.

The Gemini woman who is married to a Taurus soon finds that she is expected to be a particularly good housewife—something she may be least interested in. The Gemini woman expects domestic help to do housework, for she herself is rarely domesticated unless circumstances absolutely demand.

The odds are against true happiness for either party; the chances of grave incompatibility are very great.

Gemini and Gemini

In someone born under the same sign as yourself you have the chance of finding a kindred soul. You would certainly be able to understand each other, although of course there is always the danger of losing interest because of the lack of contrast.

The chief requisite for success is the development of mutual interests in some pursuit external to domestic life. The pursuit of a joint career, for example. By this I mean the kind of situation which is brought about when one partner is an artist and the other a model, a publicist or a salesman. Or where one is the lyricist and the other a composer.

Gemini and Cancer

The chances of success between yourself and a Cancer are borderline. There has to be considerable accommodation on either side in order to turn the balance.

The trouble usually is that the Cancer is a domesticated home-lover, whereas the Gemini must have outside interests.

The supreme danger arises when the Gemini has those acute restless urges and dominant desires to seek changes and new channels. It usually happens that these same symptoms and manifestations bring on the famous Cancer moods, which are not at all to the liking of the Gemini. Cancer resentment may play its part, too.

Much will depend upon the degree of understanding and mutual trust which may exist between respective partners. And it is because I am banking on the possibility of some such understanding existing between you, that I include

Gemini-Cancer among the "compatibles." At the same time such a union is certainly not devoid of considerable risks.

Gemini and Leo

The Gemini who marries a Leo is taking a chance, since the prospects of a successful and happy marriage are doubtful. You are both looking for different things and are unlikely to find them in each other. Superficially one might imagine you have many interests in common, since like you Leo is artistically inclined and is a lover of all things novel. Actually, however, your respective natures are at total variance, with scarcely any common ground between you at all. Emotionally, you may be far too unresponsive to suit the Leo zest for life and love; whereas the Leo is far too egotistical and "bossy" for your taste.

Gemini and Virgo

Here again we have two unsuited types, because Virgo and Gemini are both Mercurial. They would get on each other's nerves badly.

Gemini's cold, dispassionate, logical outlook would have little patience with Virgo's self-pity, and still less with Virgo's criticism.

Gemini's mental gymnastics would employ subterfuge against Virgo realism, which will invariably keep the Virgo guessing. Wordy battles would be frequent. Acute disharmony seems to exist between your respective basic natures.

Gemini and Libra

The Libra might not be at all a bad match for you. At least you both have similar mental attributes and artistic standards. Neither of you would be lost for want of conversation, since your logical mentality would be pitted against the balancing discernment of the Libra. Libras have the knack of taking the opposing point of view for the mere thrill of presenting you with counterarguments!

Gemini and Scorpio

If nothing else, a Scorpio would keep you alive! Their terrific energies would keep you on the move, especially if the activities took on intellectual form. In fact, your great difficulty might be keeping pace. You are probably more mentally alert than the Scorpio, but that fluidity is often discounted by lack of drive or sustaining force. The latter qualities, however, would derive from your Scorpio mate and could prove of remarkable reciprocal import if harnessed to aims and objects common to both of you.

The only real danger attached to a Gemini-Scorpio union occurs when an unusually restless and dissatisfied Gemini is married to a specially possessive or jealous Scorpio.

However, there are wide ranges between all types, and at least the average

Scorpio person has a high degree of understanding as befits his or her basically shrewd penetrating nature.

Gemini and Sagittarius

You have qualities that are reciprocal to, and complementary with, those of the Sagittarians. You will find a frank free nature in the Sagittarian; but you are likely to find them brusque on occasion, especially during the periods when you manifest acute restlessness.

You may find your Sagittarius mate hard to understand, because he or she rarely acts consistently—at least not in the way your logical mind comprehends.

You meet on common ground in your desire to roam; and if you plan frequent excursions together it will be tremendously helpful.

Gemini and Capricorn

You may not find the Capricorn person one with whom you blend easily. They do not as a rule get along too well with your sense of freedom. You may find the sign of the goat far too possessive for your temperamental nature. Your lack of patience may not be the virtue that the Capricorn is looking for. I am afraid that they will fall far short of the gay and exuberant type that you admire.

Gemini and Aquarius

You stand a good chance of finding a real affinity among the Aquarian types, for they have an outlook and mentality very similar to your own, with sufficient variety and scope to afford you constant stimulation and inspiration.

The Aquarian, like you, loves to roam and collect experiences. The chances are you will find an understanding and suitable mate in someone born under this sign.

Gemini and Pisces

You are not looking for the "clinging vine"; consequently, you should steer clear of an alliance with a Pisces. Indeed, such a union may produce unhappiness for both of you.

The Pisces can be mistrustful, and your subterfuges and possible fickleness would intensify that mistrust. This would manifest itself in changes of mood and general sulkiness which you would promptly resent. Your logical tongue would then sting through the sensitivities of the Pisces and make matters worse.

The Pisces is a sentimentalist, whereas you are a logician. Hence you would never meet on common ground and would fail to understand each other.

THE CUSPS

Persons born within three days of the beginning or the end of a sign will have some of the instincts and tendencies of the other sign. Such persons should read both charts in order to get a complete understanding of their dual characteristics. May 21–22–23, Gemini with Taurus characteristics, June 19–20–21, Gemini with Cancer characteristics.

LOVE AND EMOTIONS

Geminis are usually emotionally sensitive and have varied love emotions. They are inclined to be warm and affectionate one moment and cool and indifferent another. It appears that they are always at odds with their mind and emotional impulse. This often leads to a great deal of unhappiness. It is therefore advisable to use exceptionally good judgment in all matters of love and marriage, because the sign is an intellectual one. A person with patience who understands their dual personality, will be able to cope with their emotional idiosyncrasies.

In love and marriage, Gemini natives have the contrast of marvelous personalities and emotional reactions. The two qualities have little in common, because as lovers they are somewhat difficult. You seldom find them interested over a long period of time and even when attracted, there is always the possibility that other matters can draw their attention. As a husband, the Gemini is somewhat more satisfactory, because home ties mean a great deal to him, especially if he marries an intellectual companion. If, however, his wife is the nagging, possessive type the Gemini husband cannot endure it for long, because he is temperamentally unfit to stand constant pressure. Generally speaking, Gemini women are exceedingly refined. They have a rare, unapproachable delicacy, very attractive to the positive type of personality, particularly one who wishes to have a wife who reflects success.

HOW TO SEDUCE A GEMINI WOMAN

Propose marriage. This is the best ploy. If you can't do so in all good conscience, at least make it known you are looking to get married. Aside from that, stimulate her intellectually, allowing her to win arguments.

HOW TO SEDUCE A GEMINI MAN

Be up on current events. Ask his opinion on everything. Let him talk your ear off.

THE BEST PLACE TO MAKE LOVE

If you are a man, your house will be beautiful and clean if you have anything to say in the matter. If you are a woman, most likely your house is messy and the beds never made. Being a Gemini you are restless and easily bored, your duality and inconsistency will make you change houses (or wish to) as easily as others change clothes. By the time you buy and furnish a house or rent an apartment, you may be already thinking of a change. This may not be a bad idea if you are smart about real estate matters, but be careful of running your husband into debt otherwise. The best place for Gemini men and women to live for the harmonious love and sexual relations they desire is on the north side of the street.

CANCER

But Glowing Cancer (where the Summer sun
With Fiery Chariots bounds the Torrid Zone,
Drives fiercely up, then with a bending Rein
Sinks down, and runs the lower Rounds again),
As close in's Shell he lies, affords his Aid
To greedy Merchants, and inclines to Trade;
His births shall sail, through Seas and Dangers tost
To reap the Riches of a Foreign Coast,
What Thrifty Nature hath but thinly sown
In Many Countries, they shall bring to One;
Intent on gain ne'er heed the Poor's Complaint
But thrive on Scarcity, and live on Want:
For Wealth undaunted gather every Wind,
Out-sail good Fame, and Leave Repute behind,
And when their greedy Hands have seiz'd the Store
Of This, search other Worlds, and seek for more,
Or else at home prove griping Usurers,
Complaining at the slowness of the Years,
With swifter Suns, and set too vast a rate
On Time itself, to raise a quick Estate:
Their Bodies shall be strong, inur'd to Pain
Their Wits contriving, and intent to gain.

Cancer
THE CRAB
JUNE 22–JULY 22

There appear to be two distinct types of Cancers where sex is concerned. Some of the most moral and most immoral persons we have ever encountered were born in this sign. Sensitive, dreamy, romantic Cancer longs for an ideal mate more than one born in any other sign, with the possible exception of Libra. As this is the sign of parenthood, there may be a subconscious yearning for a home-loving mate, one worthy of perpetuating the species. But beyond this, there is an urge for emotional security. We find this tendency in the young man or woman who clings to the parental fireside long after his or her financial security has been assured. Nearly all Cancer women are the "clinging-vine" type, who yearn for the protecting arms of a dearly beloved. Even a Cancer man hopes, deep within his heart, that his sweetheart or wife will occasionally mother him, although not for the world would he admit this fact. The Cancer native is usually exceedingly responsive, sympathetic, and easily moved to tears. Undoubtedly, the reason for his great success on the stage or in the field of journalism lies in his profound emotional depths. He "feels" the joys and sorrows of the world regardless of how hard he tries to close the doors of his consciousness. It goes without saying that one so keenly responsive to the very heartthrobs of humanity would be highly sexed, as emotion goes hand in hand with the creative force.

However, there are undoubtedly many Cancerians who live a lifetime without realizing that sex should play an important part in their lives. This is because of the naturally repressive tendencies of the sign. Always sensitive, always shy, always fearful, the Cancer frequently lives out his life in a cloistered, secret spot within himself, which is vastly more important than anything the world has to offer. The intelligent Cancer woman who was reared strictly in an atmosphere of culture, and whose only knowledge of sex was sweet little stories about the birds and bees, approaches marriage poorly equipped. She is timid and embarrassed, and unless her husband is possessed with unusual wisdom, there may never be a satisfactory sex adjustment. Her modest, retiring nature may always feel a sense of shame or guilt, which results in a tense attitude entirely inimical

35

to a happy sexual relationship. This would be particularly true if she were married to an ardent, highly sexed Arian, Leo, or Sagittarian, who would never understand that the sex processes in others, particularly women, might not be as quickly responsive as his own. Yet, perhaps there is no other type of woman to whom sexual frustration is more harmful, and to whom sexual satisfaction is more of a blessing. When she is truly mated to an understanding husband, who is capable of comprehending and fulfilling her physical needs, she not only acquires emotional security but she utilizes the deep wells of emotion surging within her that might otherwise consume her. The difference between the woman who sings and the woman who weeps usually lies in the sexual equation. When a Cancer woman is happily married, she becomes a veritable "pillar of society," completely devoted to her husband, her children, and her community. Not for all the kingdoms of earth would she commit an indiscretion that would reflect on her family or friends.

A Cancer man reacts emotionally in much the same way as a Cancer woman. Although he yearns for marriage with all his heart, he is often fearful that he will fail his beloved. He is torn with doubts and fears that sometimes torment him to the point where he prefers to remain a bachelor. His natural shyness militates against him on his wedding night, particularly if his bride happens to be the dominant type. He may even wish he could run home to mother at the last minute. However, he makes his sexual adjustment much quicker than the Cancer woman. Once he is safely married the very reticence of his nature precludes any clandestine amours, and, like his Cancer sister, he is passionately devoted to his home and children. Furthermore, as he is determined to climb the ladder of success and prestige, he makes sure there are no skeletons in his closets to pop out at some inopportune time.

There are no half-way measures with an immoral Cancer woman. She "gives" with all the depths of her emotional nature. Nearly all women of this type are avid readers of sensational fiction, the kind that reeks with suppressed sex desires. So impressionable is she, that she sallies forth to live her dream story in reality. She often pounces on the first man who comes her way, invests him with all the glamorous qualities of the hero in the book, and settles down to a sensuous and fascinating love life. She easily attracts men, for she has a helpless, "poor-little-me" way about her that arouses a feeling of protection in the male, and from there on it is easy going. Furthermore, hidden under a soft flattering exterior she has crablike claws. It is not easy for a man to disengage himself from her clutches once she has attached herself. She is not exactly a gold digger, she is too romantic for that, but nevertheless the more favors she receives, the more convinced she becomes of her power over her lover, and a little extra cash comes in handy. Naturally vain, and craving admiration, she yearns for all the modish clothing, jewelry, and what-nots that make up the modern woman's ensemble. An immoral Cancer man follows much the same pattern as a Cancer woman;

however, he is more likely to woo one after another in a vain attempt to find a perfect love. He is convinced that somewhere lives a woman who would thoroughly understand his physical needs, and he is determined to find her.

GENERAL COMPARISONS

You have very deep but sensitive feelings, and consequently you are often hurt. Naturally, this sensitivity breeds indecision and tends to make you dilly-dally for fear of doing something that may hurt you.

The same pattern runs through your lovemaking and you are usually slow in coming to the point. Inwardly you love a considerable while before you reveal it, for fear you may encounter a rebuff. Often enough your erstwhile lover is deceived by these appearances, and despairing of making progress with you, turns to another and thus provokes your jealousy or leaves you with a severely aching heart.

You are not an easy mate for the average lover, because of your slow reactions. You just will not be swept off your feet, and therefore mistrust the ardent or whirlwind type of wooer. You need time in which to make an accurate appraisal first; but naturally a cool reception or a rebuff quickly chills the ardor of an incipient love and stifles it at the beginning.

What you need is someone to grow on you, and you on him or her. It is certain that when your own amorous feelings are aroused you surely do grow on the respondent with all the strength and tenacious hold that ivy exerts on a wall.

Only a patient lover can woo you successfully. But this fact certainly does provide a high degree of safeguard against alliance with certain of the more hopelessly inharmonious types.

The Cancer woman is the perfect housewife— affectionate, domesticated, quiet, and companionable. She likes a good table, understanding friends, and a man's shoulder for a pillow. Home and children are her central interests, and her plan of life is built around consideration of these things. They are requisite for her true happiness.

Cancer and Aries

If one of your suitors is an Aries, your passionate, sentimental nature will rise to the stimulation provided by the dashing romance of the equally passionate Aries. But be cautious, since your respective outlooks on life are certain to be at variance, and acute disharmonies can easily appear on the scene.

Your feelings are liable to be hurt by the Aries, but your moods will by no means help the situation. The transient Aries will arouse your jealousy, too, and thus some piquant situations are likely to develop.

Actually your respective basic characteristics are at such total variance that a happy match seems on the face of it unlikely—so be careful in pursuing the idea of marriage to an Arian.

Cancer and Taurus

Taurus would not make a bad partner for you. Physically you would be well mated, for the Taurus, like you, loves a comfortable home and a good table. Like you the Taurus has a warm and passionate nature. Thus conditions in the home would be comfortable and happy.

The possible source of friction would be your emotional reactions. You often have a habit of contradicting, and that is something the Taurus cannot bear. These people resent criticism, you know.

On the whole, however, the general run of your respective natures makes for harmony.

Cancer and Gemini

Marriage between you and Gemini is a borderline case, and it is not at all easy to decide whether it is going to turn out happily.

There are some hopes of success, if you are capable of controlling jealous reactions during the restless periods to which the Gemini is prone. For you have to remember that Geminis like social obligations far more than you do, and you may resent their interests in other people at your expense. The Gemini likes to go out and about more than you do and your mental interests will vary widely too.

However, the Gemini has discernment and if he or she is capable of forming a true estimate of the basic nature of your moods, all may be well. But if not, trouble may brew in the long run.

Cancer and Cancer

You would find a very understanding partner in one of your own sign, since your natures are very much akin and you instinctively understand each other.

I think that you would find complete happiness in such a match, for you would understand and sympathize with each other's moods.

Cancer and Leo

Physically you would be ideally suited for a Leo because you understand and greatly admire the Leonian romanticism and passionate nature.

However, your Leo mate will be a much more forceful type than you and may make big demands on your time. You will never have to stint your praise if you want to keep the Leo's interest. For your mate will insist on being the "life of the party" or nothing at all.

You two should have quite a considerable amount in common, and the union should prove quite compatible.

I do not, of course, promise you a life of freedom from disputes, because there are essential differences between your basic characteristics which may sometimes provoke quarrels and misunderstandings. However, you will find the Leo magnanimous and forgiving, and the moment your own moods "lift" sunshine will promptly be restored.

Cancer and Virgo

If you hope to find happiness in marriage, you should go easy with a Virgo, for you may not get on well together. The Virgo's criticisms will often wound your sensibilities and sting you into making unwise retorts. Your moods in turn will react badly with the Virgo who eventually may work up to a state of hysteria.

Your love natures, too, are at complete variance. You may be too shy, too reticent, and too sentimental at heart to please the Virgoan in the long run, for the Virgo prefers the direct approach and soon loses patience with those who hold back. They love to do all the talking, but are usually not so good at listening.

While Cancer-Virgo couples sometimes manage to make a go of it, all the same you will be wise to think about the risk entailed.

Cancer and Libra

The Libra is another type to check. Freedom seems to be an essential part of the Libra and consequently many of them seek the lighter side of life. Though you may think you like these things, too, your personal feeling will not intermesh properly with that of the Libran. You may probably be in the trough of depression when the other feels gayest—and you can imagine what sort of situation that is likely to create.

Moreover, though superficially considered exuberant, the Libra can be a very touchy type on occasion, and you do have an unfortunate knack of slighting people when you are in one of your moods.

You would very frequently find yourself at cross purposes with a Libra. Hence the reason for the caution I am giving you.

Cancer and Scorpio

You should be well suited to a Scorpion. The Scorpio will undoubtedly possess a more masterful demeanor than you. But you are fluid and adaptable and therefore mold well, provided the mold takes a form that is congenial to your way of thinking. At all times you should have little difficulty understanding one another.

The one great thing to guard against (and this applies equally to you both) is the demon jealousy. That alone could upset the apple cart.

Scorpio confers an excess of energy on those it influences. Provided this energy is properly employed, all will be well. But the "devil makes work for idle hands" will prove true in connection with this energy drive if proper use is not made of it; and that can be the fly in the Cancerian ointment if things get out of control.

Cancer and Sagittarius

Think twice—and if that is insufficient—think a third time before you marry a Sagittarius.

Sagittarians have very independent natures, and once you start with your moods they are finished. Moreover, their insistence upon personal freedom can become a fetish with them and their idea of freedom may by no means agree with your jealous disposition.

You are dissimilar personalities and may clash badly. I therefore mark Sagittarius as a sign-type that would be very difficult for you to get along with.

Cancer and Capricorn

You are the astrological opposite of Capricorn, but you also possess characteristics which are the complement of each other. Provided care is taken to adjust the phases of these characteristics the result should be a perfectly happy union.

Now, the Capricorn does not possess your sentiment; but that does not prevent him or her from appreciating your sentimental nature to the fullest, provided you do not lay it on too thick. Conversely, you must expect to find a more practical, material nature in a Capricorn. Their saving virtue is that they know how to look after your material welfare; and as you know, one cannot live on love alone—material needs also have to be considered.

You are the right soothing syrup for the "misunderstood" Capricorn. He or she will not feel so lonely while you are around.

Cancer and Aquarius

The Aquarius is another type with whom you may clash. Your respective ideals run in different channels. You are a home-bird, whereas the Aquarius prefers social life and worldly affairs. You have conservative tastes and interests, whereas the Aquarius is usually the opposite. With your moody nature on the one hand and the Aquarius' eccentric nature on the other, you will do well to ponder the implications.

Cancer and Pisces

Here is an ideal match for you! If you marry a Pisces you will be two sentimentalists together. Of course both of you will have your moody moments and during those periods the atmosphere may not be too pleasant. But as a rule you well understand the same things, and normally the disquieting situations simmer down to a blissful state after each turbulence.

You have very deep but sensitive feelings, and consequently you often are hurt. Naturally, this sensitivity inbreeds indecision and tends to make you dilly-dally for fear of doing something which may react and hurt you.

The same pattern runs through your lovemaking and you are usually slow in coming to the point. Inwardly you love a considerable while before you reveal it, for fear you may encounter a rebuff. Often enough your erstwhile lover is deceived by these appearances, and despairing of making progress with you, turns to another and thus provokes your jealousy or leaves you with a severely aching heart.

THE CUSPS

Persons born within three days of the beginning or the end of a sign will have some of the instincts and tendencies of the other sign. Such persons should read both charts in order to get a complete understanding of their dual characteristics. June 22–23–24, Cancer with Gemini characteristics; July 20–21–22, Cancer with Leo characteristics.

LOVE AND EMOTIONS

Generally speaking Cancer natives have a great capacity for self-control because they are reserved and do not show their emotions outwardly. This tendency at times may be the cause of many misunderstandings, especially in romantic affairs. While the average Cancer is tender and affectionate by nature, they are not overly sensuous. They treat love seriously and there is a tendency for jealousy which often upsets their normal composure. When their feelings are hurt, and they can easily be hurt, they can turn cold and unresponsive rather suddenly. This, of course, will be the cause of a great deal of unhappiness in their married life.

When their home life is not harmonious they will become restless and irritable. The Cancer native loves the great promise of a home, especially when he finds an intelligent and affectionate mate. They have a strong love for children and are much happier in the married state. While the Cancer husband may be fussy and exacting, he is always warm and affectionate. A Cancer wife may be moody and changeable, overfearful, and possessive in her demands on the time and efforts of her family, but she is also sincere, devoted, and her intensity is very genuine. The hearth is very important to the Cancer native, and marriage is a part of this department. It is treated seriously by both Cancer men and women. They live in the past a great deal and always remember the days of their childhood. In fact early environment has a greater bearing on Cancer's character than any other sign.

HOW TO SEDUCE A CANCER WOMAN

Be tender and protective. Tell her how you love children and introduce her to some. Go on outings together with children. Send flowers and give her everything to enrich her life.

HOW TO SEDUCE A CANCER MAN

Watch the moon. When it is on the rise make a strong play, on the wane sit it out. Show him what a homebody you are.

THE BEST PLACE TO MAKE LOVE

If you are a man, it will be very rare if you don't desire or already have a home of your own. Since Cancer men are the richest of the Zodiac, your house should be rich too, reflecting your success, with antiques, chandeliers, and paintings. Do not forget the importance of atmosphere: music, especially opera and the classics. You should live in a large city, but go to the sea for weekends. If you are a Cancer woman you need only to have a house with a big kitchen. Since you are a wonderful cook, you will spend a great deal of your time there. For a happy sex life, you should have the most comfortable surroundings, and a relaxed atmosphere.

LEO

What inclinations Leo's Rays dispense
Is quickly known, 'tis plain to Common Sense,
He gives his Own, for he the Woods Infests
The mighty Terror of the meaner Beasts:
He lives on Rapine, ranges all the Day
And sullenly at Night groans o'er his Prey.
Hence he inclines Mens Minds to Hunt, and fills
Our Nobles spacious Halls with grinning spoils;
There Skins and Horns do spread a dismal grace,
And stand as certain heralds of their Race.
This Beast was mine, and that my Father's game,
They cry, these are the Annals of their Fame;
That generous Youth which France and Spain did fear
Now prove the Humble Terror of a Deer.
Nay some in Towns pursue this wild delight,
They Barbarous grow, and breed up Beasts to fight;
Then bring them out for fight in Theatres,
And feast their Luxury with Brutish Wars;
Cruel in Sport; Their Posts are grac't with Spoyl,
And they get shameful Honour without Toyl.

Leo

THE LION
JULY 23–AUGUST 22

To our sunny, affectionate Leo, sex is the pot of gold at the end of the rainbow. Has he not followed Love's trail over hill and dale, even though the going has been rough in spots? Now, he expects to be rewarded. He brings in his sex life all the healthy, normal instincts of the lion in the jungle, and he is likely to roar if it isn't to his satisfaction. But perhaps more than one born in any other sign, he settles down in perfect bliss when he is wedded to a truly responsive mate. There is no other type of person so dependent upon love for his very existence as a Leo. No other so truly exalted if he has found real spiritual and physical companionship. No other so completely submerged if he finds himself allied to a nagging, unsympathetic mate, for it is rarely a Leo who seeks the panacea of a divorce. The lion's code of honor is magnificent. However, he is frequently enticed into an ill-advised marriage because of his ardent love nature, and the natural fixed tendencies of his sign. Propinquity is often the deciding factor. A Leo man goes out with the girl next door, even though he may not be particularly interested in her. He keeps on going because Leo is a creature of habit. In a rash moment, he proposes. Then his sense of honor and loyalty leads him to the altar, despite an inward conviction that she was never created for him. It has been said that a Leo seldom marries the one he could love the most. If he is an emotionally sensitive type, he remains faithful to her through life. If not, he still remains loyal as far as outward appearances are concerned, but he furtively casts about for more gratifying emotional channels. However, he makes sure there are no aspersions cast upon his honored wife. She is still the queen in his harem, as it were.

Leo men are great admirers of women, and with the less sophisticated type there seems to be an unholy yearning for forbidden fruit. Regardless of how happily married he may be, this type craves to possess every woman to whom he may be temporarily attracted. As appearance and personality count more with him than golden virtues, he is likely to fall often and hard for any pretty little miss who knows how to wield a lipstick. But he will go out of his way to make sure he isn't found out. There is a stealthy, leonine cunning about him that is often amusing to the person who sees through his camouflage. Those softly padded lion paws often leave an imprint. There is a certain type of Leo man who considers himself a connoisseur on the subject of sex. We recall one man who rather pompously admitted a large number of indiscretions before marriage. He was proud of his conquests. He dramatized himself as a hero in the eyes of the female contingent, and felt himself to be quite a man about town. Inconsistently, he eventually married a woman whose reputation was above reproach. It was a happy alliance and he reared his two sons by a strict code of conduct that utterly belied his previous pattern of behavior.

The Leo has no illusions about sex. He accepts it as a natural function and lets it go at that. He doesn't carry it to the heights of religious fanaticism or look askance at it as something of potential defilement. Perhaps this is the reason why Leo women seldom discuss this subject, even with their most intimate friends. It isn't that they are naturally more modest, but to their way of thinking there is nothing to be discussed. The sun shines, a tree grows, sex exists. However, there is undoubtedly no other type of woman more loving, more yielding, more responsive in the sexual relationship than the average Leo woman. Unless she is the cold, domineering type we occasionally encounter, she is naturally generous, affectionate, and vigorous and it goes without saying that these qualities would react beneficially on her emotional impulses. If she is happily married she asks for nothing greater in life than the privilege of living in loyal unison with her mate and rearing their children. If her marriage is a disappointment, she hides her misery from the world, plays up her husband's good points, lives for her children, and seldom deserts her mate, unless he becomes unbearable. Rarely does she seek outside companionship, but if she does she enshrouds the affair with such secrecy that it scarcely causes a ripple on the even tenor of her life. Her husband and children receive the same conscientious attention and not for one minute would she neglect them for her lover. We recall one case that covered a period of fifteen years, yet it is doubtful if three persons in her community were aware of the affair.

Despite the kindly warmth of a Leo man, he is often a marital disappointment to certain types of women (a romantic, sensitive Cancer, for example, or an emotional, idealistic Piscean). So simple and direct is he in his sexual manifestations that he forgets that the intoxicating wines of love should always precede the main issue. In fact, he doesn't always associate romance with sex. Both men and women of this sign retain their youthful vigor and sexual prowess until advanced age, and some appear younger as they grow older.

GENERAL COMPARISONS

You are egotistical. Why not admit it? For you feel (and think) you are really good—in fact, the model that all should follow.

You are proud and independent; but although many of you are prone to arrogance, as a rule you have a generous spirit coupled with it.

You do nothing by halves, and everything must be done in ceremonious style and with colorful window dressing.

You are a romanticist to the core of your being, and you know how to garnish and playact.

Yes, you are a born actor and with this talent goes a expansive mind; nothing petty or small will ever suit you.

True, your love of ostentation is certainly capable of brightening lives and adding color. Also it often achieves your purpose of gaining material ends. But it has its dangers, too. It often brings poverty and bankruptcy by virtue of the extravagance it engenders. It also causes some to place too high a value on their talents or services—considerably in advance of their real worth.

You Leo women love life well, with all the zest of spirited, impassioned warmheartedness. You are never dull company, for you have sparkling personalities and are forever seeking the brightest things life has to offer.

You are romantic, sincere lovers, and you expand toward those who understand and who are willing to cater for your special proclivities. But you are proud and quite easily affronted. Nothing must ever be allowed to disturb your dignity.

Leo and Aries

You will be well matched should you choose an Aries, at least in most respects. You may not perhaps receive all the deference due, but you will have a lover who can warm up to you. Naturally the direct approach will be tacitly admitted between you. But remember each of you is a person of surging enthusiasms and this means an ebbing as well as a flowing. So be prepared for periods during which love may cool off and don't go imagining that the end of the world has come when these periods arrive. It is then your business to set about reviving the love interest. This may be accomplished with complete satisfaction if you persevere. You are just as cool yourself, you know, in your "off" moments.

There is just one further point: Aries are really a great deal more "practical" than you. In any event, Aries like to assume that pose. Therefore, do not expect an overflow of sentiment from your mate. He or she will not love you any less; remember that the whisperings of sweet sentiments are not always the criterion of true love; deceivers can whisper them too—with their tongues in their cheeks!

Leo and Taurus

Your passionate nature would be admirably matched with that of a Taurus; hence a possible good marriage. But you have to remember that basically each of you is an obstinate and strong-willed person, and therefore quarrels are liable to be both numerous and heated. You have also to remember that in the Taurus you would have a jealous, possessive mate, and unless you understand the full significance and implications of these facts beforehand, you will most likely experience intolerable conditions in the years to come. You will have to forego a very considerable amount of your pride in order to make your marriage a success.

Leo and Gemini

From Gemini you will not get the deference which you consider your due, and you are likely to feel this keenly.

The Gemini is logically critical of the Leonian ego, and the appraisal is sometimes severe.

Of course, you will see very much to admire in each other, for each of you has qualities which are specially pleasing to the other. In fact, it is this mutual admiration that is the actual lure between you.

Sometimes Leo-Gemini marriages do work out favorably, but all the same I must caution you that the chances of ensuring love and happiness are quite problematical in the majority of cases because the normal Leo-Gemini union does not make for permanency.

Leo and Cancer

Provided you are an understanding, non-arrogant Leo, you could do worse than choose a Cancer. Cancers are sentimentalists at heart, and you would certainly find your mate "soulful," not to mention affectionate. Therefore, you will note that a Cancer will fill the bill from the point of view of your passionate and emotional requirements.

Your chief difficulty if you marry a Cancer will be that of accustoming yourself to the ever-changing Cancer moods. Hence you must be prepared to make allowances for this form of temperament. It would be a big mistake on your part to become forceful or exacting at such times. You are dealing with a very sensitive type and can do much damage unless you are understanding.

Your companion may seem very quiet; but he or she will invariably understand you well. Cancers have a special aptitude for adaptability and intuitive comprehensions. If your requirements are moderate and not exacting, you will find the perfect mate in the Cancer type.

Leo and Leo

Naturally you will have no difficulty in understanding a member of the opposite sex born under your own sign. What you have to be careful of is the danger of an all-consuming passion that may rapidly burn itself out. Therefore, if you marry a fellow Leo, take care to see that your love matters are accomplished in easy stages.

The chief difficulty that you are likely to encounter is the fact that the Leo mentality demands the central place in the family circle—the great light around which the lesser partner and resultant progeny will revolve. But two great Suns are apt to rob each other of light and glory. Gold is at its worst against a background of equal glitter. Hence there may have to be an agreed balance between you to resolve this problem.

Leo and Virgo

If you marry a Virgo you will have a mate of the semicompatible type. Therefore your mutual responsibility to ensure happiness in marriage will increase. You will find the Virgo exceptionally critical, and not easily impressed by your assumed belief in your own importance in the scheme of things. In other words, you have to be really good if you are to succeed in impressing the Virgo, for you may count on the unusual discernment and ability to see through pretexts.

To make a success of this marriage you will have to think less of yourself and more of your Virgo mate. Are you prepared to do this? Unless you can thoroughly convince yourself of this ability I would most strongly advise against marriage with a Virgo. On the other hand, there is much to be said in favor of this union. The Virgo is especially adaptable and will live up to any standard you set. You will not feel ashamed of your partner no matter to what station in life you might rise. In addition, Virgo normally retains youth and virility.

Leo and Libra

In a number of ways you might find yourself well suited with a Libra. But I am inclined to place Libras among the "inadvisable" types because of your unhappy knack of upsetting sensitive people. As a rule, you know, you are so wrapped up in yourself and in your special importance in the scheme of things, that you do not realize how bumptious you occasionally appear. Therefore, I am inclined to believe that you would frequently find your Libran mate unaccountably ill-tempered.

The Libran loves an argument. So do you, too, in your own special way, but your way is not the Libra way. What you say has to go—at least that is how you feel about it and want it. But the Libra will not view the matter quite like that.

Leo and Scorpio

There are great distinctions to observe in the case of Leonians married to Scorpios. As to basic characteristics there are many striking similarities. Each type has a remarkable personality. The best results are achieved when the couple is a Leo woman married to a Scorpio man. The results are far more problematical in the contrary case. Scorpio women appear to be less accommodating than Scorpio men, for some reason. Moreover, they are inclined to be more jealous, and frequently they can become very suspicious of their Leo husbands' behavior.

If, however, you are a Leo woman who is thinking of marrying a Scorpio you need have little fear of the outcome. You will find qualities in each other that will lead directly to reciprocal admiration.

Leo and Sagittarius

Your marriage to a Sagittarius stands an excellent chance of success. You will have common interests and your feelings will be on par. Both of you love change, novelties, and all the bright things life has to offer; both of you have great zest for life.

The one potential danger in this combination lies in your tendency to dominate the Sagittarian, whose independent spirit would be menaced by this. You will have to watch this, or it may easily lead to a parting of the ways.

Leo and Capricorn

If you marry a Capricorn I fear you will make a rather ill-sorted couple. Capricorn is taciturn as compared with your brighter, more carefree nature. The Capricorn is not a sentimentalist, and can be pretty matter-of-fact. There will be occasions when you may not like this; but take care how you react, because the Capricorn can be very vengeful when put out, and is remarkably slow to forgive. You can afford to be magnanimous; apparently, the Capricorn can not.

I am afraid, too, that your more sociable nature may become a factor which can arouse the spectre of jealousy in the Capricorn. This, in fact, constitutes one of the main dangers of this combination. This jealousy may not show itself in open animosity. Instead, the Capricorn mate will nurse a grievance and adopt an abused, misunderstood attitude. If this develops it can turn into something that is difficult to cope with.

Leo and Aquarius

Not all Leos mate happily with Aquarians, yet it is certainly true that the majority of such marriages can be successful. Given cultural balance, the union can prove very happy.

The trouble is usually based on the innate snobbishness of both Leo and Aquarius. Therefore if either "marries beneath their standard" (this phrase signifies cultural degree), a division is formed which can subsequently develop to exaggerated proportions.

Granted equality, this combination often proves unrivaled in matrimonial success.

Leo and Pisces

The Pisces is a sentimentalist, and this fact may lead you to conclude that you have much in common. But your character is too strong and vigorous for this person. Pisces people are ultra-sensitive, and arrogant behavior wounds them. Furthermore, they do not have your ambitious temperament. Your paths are therefore likely to diverge at quite an early stage. You have little patience with moodiness—something you might find more than a little trying in your Pisces mate on occasion.

While love lasts, the Pisces is happy enough. But it is the petty events of life, and the changing moods in people, that are the prime causes of love taking a back seat; and I am afraid this might be your experience in the long run.

You are egotistical. Why not admit it? For you feel (and think) you are really good—in fact, the model that all should follow.

You are proud and independent; but although many of you are prone to arrogance, as a rule you have a magnanimous generous spirit coupled with it.

You do nothing by halves, and everything must be done in ceremonious style and with colorful window dressing.

You are a romanticist to the core of your being, and you know how to garnish and playact.

Yes, you are a born actor (or actress) and with this talent goes a large-scale mind. Nothing petty or small will ever suit you.

True, your love of ostentation is certainly capable of brightening lives and adding color. Also it often achieves your purpose of gaining material ends. But it has its dangers, too. It often brings poverty and bankruptcy by virtue of the extravagance it engenders. It also causes some to place too high a value on their talents or services—considerably in advance of their real worth.

Leo women love life, with all the zest of spirited, impassioned warmhearted-ness. You are never dull company, for you have sparkling personalities and are ever seeking the brightest things life has to offer.

You are romantic, sincere lovers, and you expand toward those who under-stand and who are willing to cater for your special proclivities. But you are proud and quite easily affronted. Nothing must ever be allowed to disturb your dignity.

THE CUSPS

Persons born within three days of the beginning or the end of a sign will have some of the instincts and tendencies of the other sign. Such persons should read both charts in order to get a complete understanding of their dual characteris-tics. July 23–24–25, Leo with Cancer characteristics; August 20–21–22, Leo with Virgo characteristics.

LOVE AND EMOTIONS

Romance and love are especially important to Leos. They are generally quite passionate in their love affairs. However, their judgment in love is not always reliable. Unreasonable jealousy may mar some very tender romances. Obviously it is very important to be married to someone who is suited to your tastes and temperament, or you Leos can easily become very miserable. Economic diffi-culties, lack of appreciation, and disrespect are usually the principal causes for separation and divorce of Leos.

Persons born under this sign enjoy nice homes and pleasant surroundings. Although Leo is a fixed sign, its natives have a venturesome spirit. While loving your home, you like to travel, if only to avoid boredom. Your inherently charming personality will attract many friendships during your lifetime, which will not all be to your advantage. Your good heart will cause you to be the victim of many unscrupulous friendships. Beware of fair-weather friends, who heap flattery for no apparent reason. They expect you to pay dearly for their compliments. Leo is known as the natural pleasure sign of the Zodiac. There is sometimes a tendency to engage in many kinds of more or less risky social activities. Beware, a word to the wise should be sufficient.

HOW TO SEDUCE A LEO WOMAN

Buy her fabulous gifts: the best and most expensive of everything.

HOW TO SEDUCE A LEO MAN

Let him dominate. Never argue. Tell him he is the most macho man you've ever met. Let him talk all night, gaze admiringly at him.

THE BEST PLACE TO MAKE LOVE

All Leo men need a large home to be happy. When they are successful and living up to their image of themselves, their sex lives take on greater dimensions, greater fulfillment. As a Leo man you enjoy living near the mountains, rivers, and forests. The home should reflect prosperity, and be glamorous and dramatic. Leo women dislike housework, but can be good cooks. A Leo woman will be especially happy having a garden. For the greatest happiness in sex, a Leo woman should have a home close to a city, but away from the noise and movement of relentless life. The front door should face east.

VIRGO

But modest Virgo's Rays give prudish parts,
And fill Mens Breasts with Honesty and Arts:
No tricks for Gain, nor love of Wealth dispense,
But piercing Thoughts, and winning Eloquence;
With words persuasive, and with Rhetorick strong
They rule, and are e'en Monarchs by their Tongue.
Through Nature's Secrets too, they boldly press,
Tho' deeply hid, and meet a just success;
In Short-Hand Skill'd, where little Marks comprise,
Whole words, a Sentence in a letter lies:
And whilst Obedient hands their Aid afford,
Prevent the Tongue, and Fix the falling Word.
But bashful Modesty casts down their Eyes,
The best of Vices, yet 'tis still a Vice,
Because it stifles, checks or nips like Frost,
A blooming Vertue, and the Fruit is last,
Besides, through strange such Influence should come
From Virgo's Rays, she gives a fruitful Womb.

Virgo
THE VIRGIN
AUGUST 23–SEPTEMBER 22

In the crystal clear depths of Virgo, the purest of all signs, lie both its virtues and its weaknesses, so closely interwoven that the two may appear as one. For paradoxically, it is often the Virgo's search for purity which he can not find that leads him to the depths of degradation. We have attempted to analyze several cases involving Virgo men, whose indiscretions have become a matter of public scandal. Almost without exception, these men are possessed of a gentle courtesy, refinement, and a certain boyish eagerness not consistent with the usual blasé savoir-faire of the libertine. Probing deeply into these cases, we discovered that these men started out in life with the pure-minded, high ideals of the Virgo sign, but in every case marriage proved a failure. One was a young physician, intensely fond of children, who yearned for a family. His young, scatter-brained wife refused to bear him a child, and eventually deserted him for another man. It was at this point in his life that he began the downward trend that finally led to his moral and professional ruin.

Apparently, it is difficult for a Virgo man or woman to strike a happy medium. This is easily understood. He is so idealistic and discriminating that once he has become disillusioned and his ideals have been shattered, he has nothing to which to cling. Sexual excesses, liquor, or both, may be his outlet unless he has developed profound spiritual qualities. The same blow that completely disintegrates Virgo might cause one born in another sign to merely shrug his shoulders and turn the pages to the next chapter. It has been said that a Virgo man doesn't love, he worships. It is true that when a Virgo loses his mate it is nearly impossible for him to gather up the broken threads of his life. He may take refuge in work, but he doesn't forget. The picture of the one he has lost is always before him and it may be many years before he marries again, if ever. Many Virgos, particularly men, become recluses if they are disappointed in love or lose their mates.

It is doubtful that many Virgos know how to evaluate sex. It is incompatible with the very nature of this sign. Many nuns, priests, and holy men who lead a celibate life are born in Virgo. We have in mind one case where a marriage in name only existed between a Virgo husband and a Virgo wife. By mutual agreement their marriage was never consummated, for the thought of a sexual relationship was repellent to both. Virgo women do not place their affections easily and often go through life without the slightest desire for matrimony. Furthermore, they magnify every defect in their would-be suitors, and, as most men are made of mortal clay, our Virgo women never succeed in catching up with perfect ones. Some, like the Sleeping Beauty, may be awakened and roused by Love's sweet kiss, often late in life. If marriage is possible, all is well. If not, the Virgo woman either remains loyal to her sweetheart, in memory at least, or she engages in an endless search for another to replace him, whom she may never find because of her discriminating tendencies. Usually the commercial world claims her, and, as she has very little interest in sex, she lapses into a contented state of being unmarried.

Young Virgo men and women, who marry in the first flush of romantic youth, make very loyal and conscientious husbands and wives, but sex is accepted more or less as part of family routine. A Virgo man doesn't ask for a deeply romantic marriage, but he does want a satisfactory, smoothly running one. He brings to his honeymoon all the idealistic devotion and tenderness of a man who has not been satiated with sex, for very few Virgo men have premarital relationships. But after the honeymoon is over, he settles down with his business affairs, his books, and his radio. Women scarcely exist as far as he is concerned. The reason for this does not lie in the fact that he is deeply in love with his wife, but women do not interest him. Not having been endowed with an overabundance of passion to begin with, he is perfectly satisfied with his marital status, and being of an intellectual turn of mind, prefers a book any day to the most glamorous female. He enjoys the mental companionship of his wife as much as he does their physical relationship.

A Virgo wife reacts much the same way. So completely engrossed does she become in her children and household duties that sex is either relegated to the background or enjoys about the same dutiful status as Monday's laundry and Tuesday's ironing. Many Virgo men and women lose interest in sex entirely when they reach middle age. So highly mental are they that it apparently requires the vigor of youth to stimulate them physically. Many Virgo men are said to be sterile.

Virgo women are rarely led astray, for the instinct of chastity is strong within them, and they turn with repulsion from any immoral advances. They dislike morbid literature or risqué stories. Many of them are so coolly dispassionate that they marry for money or position rather than love. Seldom are they carried away by their emotions. If perchance a Virgo does join her "weak sisters," we may be sure that her indiscretions arise from an inordinate love of money and the finery it will purchase rather than from romantic, sexual instincts. To be sure, we find an occasional exception to these rules. In this event, we must examine closely the individual horoscope, with special emphasis on the position of Venus.

GENERAL COMPARISONS

You have a flirtatious disposition, brought about by buoyant spirits and by your curiosity to get to know those who intrigue you. Although you may not start a flirtation with the idea of love, you are, nevertheless, apt to be drawn into an affair. Certainly you do like to exercise your power of attraction to the opposite sex. You are very tantalizing to the opposite sex, for you have much that is appealing. You have a very cautious nature and usually know where to draw the line.

You are very difficult to please, you know, for your critical faculty makes you very selective. You are the real chooser in the resultant match. Because, if the "prospect" fails to measure up to your requirements, you certainly will not compromise yourself. With it all, your spirits are the liveliest. A note of gaiety permeates your demeanor, and your philosophy is the simplest.

The Virgo woman is intriguing, pretty, and bewitching. She knows how to get her man, but not necessarily how to hold him! She is too cautious to get hooked easily; but at the same time she loves to play with fire, and thus always runs the risk of getting burned.

You males have got to have something more than passion to captivate this woman for any length of time. She'll tease you to no end; but once she knows you well, she has little further interest—unless you have that "something else" about you to rekindle her interest and lead her on anew.

Her interest is centered on the study of your emotions and your mind. If she finds these commonplace, she is through with you. But if she can not get right to the bottom of them, you have turned the tables, for she will not be content until she has plumbed the depths. Therefore, if you want to woo a Virgo woman successfully, you should be very wary of becoming too obvious.

Virgo and Aries

You might hit it off well with an Aries partner. You like excitement and the Aries can provide that aplenty. You like change; therefore, Aries enthusiasms may keep you amused.

In the case of marriage between the Aries man and a Virgo woman, however, the results can be much more problematical and it would be safe to consider such a union incompatible.

Virgo and Taurus

You should get on very well with a Taurus mate provided you do not expect to find as volatile an individual as you. The Taurus nature is placid and easygoing, but for all that the Taurean makes a good listener, which is one of your essential needs.

Fundamental clashes are unlikely, though there may be frequent irritation over the stubborn nature of the Taurus. You will have to learn that nothing you can say or do is going to alter the Taurean; and once you have understood and digested that you can settle down comfortably.

Virgo and Gemini

If you marry a Gemini you will be mating with another Mercurial subject. But this would by no means be like the blessing it sounds, for most of the time you would get on each other's nerves. Both of you know how to talk, but Virgo will be far too "chatty" for the Gemini's liking. The Geminis are swift on the "uptake" and a lot of detailed explanation is wearisome and indescribably boring to them.

Though mental interests delight you both, there are often acute differences between you as to the nature of those interests.

There are many reasons why this would not be a happy match in the long run no matter how interesting your Gemini friend may seem to you at the moment.

Virgo and Cancer

A Cancer should be a good mate for you. Your only difficulty may be in coping with the Cancer moods. But it will be the frequency of these moods which will correct and adjust your impulses to criticize. The moment you sting the Cancer's sensitivity the moods will come to the surface. Therefore, you will be gradually schooled into what to avoid, since inevitably you are bound to find these moods unpleasant while they last. You will find you have many interests in common.

Virgo and Leo

Though Leos are charming, they may have little patience with your critical faculty, which is sure to sting the Leo's pride and create resentment. Leos are possessive and sure to be jealous of your flirtation and interest in others. Therefore, an alliance with a Leo would only be of the semicompatible type. If it is to be a happy marriage, a great deal will depend on you. You will have to restrain your habit of criticizing and you will also have to suppress your desire to flirt, which will mean that your interest in others will have to be confined to your spouse.

Virgo and Virgo

To make a real success of marriage to one of your own birth sign, you will need to have an all-consuming interest in common. Otherwise, it can be a commonplace relationship and may turn into a case of husband and wife talking each other into utter boredom.

Virgo and Libra

The Libra is another type that resents criticism. Libras are easygoing people and do not like being called to order frequently by a very meticulous partner. Life could become one infernal argument between you.

Virgo and Scorpio

There is usually much that is attractive about a Virgo-Scorpio match. That is to say, the Scorpio attracts you strongly, and vice versa.

I think your initial interest in Scorpio emanates from your curiosity. Scorpio has a strong character, and displays intriguing depths which you hope to explore. Further, the shrewd fending of the Scorpio provides the kind of intellectual excitement you love. You gain the idea that you could never be dull with such a person. Scorpio's forcefulness may often deter you, and perhaps even make you fearful.

Often you will be amazed at the ease with which the Scorpio penetrates your subterfuges, seeing through them far too clearly for your liking. Moral: Never attempt to practice deception on a Scorpio—you are sure to be found out despite your great cleverness.

Be careful not to wound Scorpio's pride, for if you do you will provoke a deep resentment, and Scorpios can be pretty vengeful.

Virgo and Sagittarius

If you choose a Sagittarius, you would be mated to another "semicompatible" type. I doubt if you could find the happiness you expect. You would be subjected to many tests, not the least of which would be the liberty the Sagittarius expects and demands. Some Sagittarians are extraordinarily touchy also; and reactions of that type are prone to upset your nerves badly. "Change" is an idea about which each of you holds conflicting opinions.

Virgo and Capricorn

Both you and the Capricorn have an element of self-pity in common. Hence you should be able to understand and sympathize with each other.

Virgo and Aquarius

Provided both of you are people with intellectual gifts or with mental interests of wide range, you might fare worse than marriage with an Aquarius. Both of you have a well-developed sense of curiosity, and this faculty should do much to keep a lively interest in each other.

The Virgo-Aquarius combination is not at all an easy one to analyze. How marriage between these heavily contrasting types will work out will depend a great deal on cultural levels and individual idiosyncrasies. It is like a vaccination; it either "takes" or it doesn't!

Virgo and Pisces

As a rule, people born under opposing signs usually have successful marriages; however, your tongue may get the better of a Pisces and friction is bound to ensue when your critical faculty gets going. There is little that is sentimental about your matter-of-fact ways.

The moods of the Pisces would get on your nerves too; for although you may be changeable yourself, you like consistency in others.

For you to contract marriage with a Pisces is to accept unusual responsibilities: you do not possess many of the qualities which a Piscean hopes and expects to find.

THE CUSPS

Persons born within three days of the beginning or the end of a sign will have some of the instincts and tendencies of the other sign. Such persons should read both charts in order to get a complete understanding of their dual characteristics. August 23–24–25, Virgo with Leo characteristics; September 20–21–22, Virgo with Libra characteristics.

LOVE AND EMOTIONS

Emotionally, Virgos are very sensitive and quite reserved. They prefer not to show their feelings if they can avoid it. In spite of this reserve, however, they are quite affectionate and tender to those that are near and dear to them. Certain types of Virgo individuals appear to be somewhat afraid when it comes to love and they are hesitant to tie up their emotional lives. When this is carried too far, their romantic affairs usually end in disillusionment because it is very difficult for them to assume a normal emotional equilibrium. Generally speaking, Virgos desire a good home amid pleasant surroundings.

As sweethearts and lovers, Virgos are usually engaging and considerate; however, as husbands or wives, this is not always the case. They can become very fussy, super-critical and difficult where marriage is concerned. The main reason appears to be because it is difficult for them to fully surrender themselves since they find it undesirable to give of themselves with abandon. Nevertheless, when the Virgo woman does marry, she becomes an excellent wife. She is usually capable of arranging her household routine smoothly. While her disposition may not always be the best, the Virgo wife guards the family responsibilities. The Virgo husband is willing to conduct his married life on a give-and-take basis only. He may not be too enthusiastic as a lover for a long period of time. While he safeguards his home, he does not necessarily have a deep approach toward the more intimate affairs of married life.

HOW TO SEDUCE A VIRGO WOMAN

Compliment her on her impeccable taste and conduct, admire her practicality, tell her she is special because she is not flighty like most women. Do not be eager at first, play it cool, and then move in like a panther.

HOW TO SEDUCE A VIRGO MAN

Be neat, punctual, fair, and honest about everything. Never allow him to see you in disarray, and make sure the house is spotless.

THE BEST PLACE TO MAKE LOVE

The Virgo man is constantly fearful of living beyond his means, or not being able to live up to his obligations. He cannot enjoy a purchase if he feels this way. Therefore, he should be careful to love modestly if this is the way his pocketbook dictates. If he tries to bite off more than he can chew, he can ruin his sex life from worry. Virgo women are excellent housekeepers. For a happy sex life the ideal Virgo home for both men and women should be spacious. There should be adequate room for all possessions. A fireplace, a big bay window, and fresh air will increase happiness and provide a center from which a happy sex life can grow.

LIBRA

Libra, whose Scales, when Autumn turns the Signs,
And ruddy Bacchus treads the juicy Vines;
In equal Balance, poise the Night and Day;
Teach how to measure, and instruct to weigh;
And Rival Polamed, (who numbers found,
And into Letters fram'd unpolisht sound;
To Him the Art of Words, and Speech we owe,
Till then Men only spoke, but knew not how)
Besides, he'll know the Niceties of Law,
What guard the Good, and what the Guilty Awe,
What Vengeance wait on Crimes, with Skill declare,
His Private Chamber, still shall be the Bar.
What He determines, that for Right shall stand,
As Justice weigh'd her Balance in his Hand.
This Ruled at Servius's Birth, who first did give
Our Laws a Being, rather than Revive;
The Tables seem'd old, Reverend Senseless Lines,
Meer Waxen Things, and sit to serve Designs
As Fools mistook, or Crafty Knaves would draw;
Till he infus'd a Soul, and made them law.

Libra

THE SCALES
SEPTEMBER 23–OCTOBER 22

To one born in this sign of the Zodiac, sex and love are synonymous. So pure in heart are our sons and daughters of Venus, that it is difficult for them to even think in terms of sex as far as its biological function is concerned. Nearly all Librans, particularly women, associate sex with all things beautiful and romantic. To a young woman of this sign reaching maturity, sex is mysteriously merged with moonlight magic, the perfume of roses clinging to a summer breeze; her dream-man, a magnificent Prince Charming approaching to woo her with music and sweet song. A Libra bride invariably insists upon a church wedding where her idealistic soul may reach the heights of romantic ecstasy among flowers, and candles, and prayer books. If she is congenially mated and her love nature is thoroughly aroused, she is capable of bestowing upon her mate that which very few persons in other signs are capable of giving, a romantic fire combined with a purity of affection that completely transcends any ordinary sex manifestation. To her, sex is an emotional experience of divine sweetness and inspiration. She becomes the essence of loyalty. She lives only for her loved one, closing the door of their sanctuary upon the outside world. However, woe be unto the husband who fails to understand her delicate sexual nature, and who approaches her with a masculine eagerness not consistent with her own ideas of loveliness. A caveman approach would not only be exceedingly repugnant to her, but it might sever forever all of that close, spiritual communion for which her soul yearns. She is best married to a man of gentleness and refinement, one who appreciates and shares in some measure her own high ideals.

The love life of a Libra man almost parallels that of a Libra woman. Perhaps being a man may add a little more aggression and ardor, but like his Libra sister, his love nature is aesthetic and romantic, and rarely purely sensual. If a Libran of either gender is unhappily married and becomes disillusioned, he or she is a pathetic soul indeed because this is the marriage sign of the Zodiac, and it is only through an alliance with another that the Libra fulfills or completes his or her own development. The Aquarian depends on friends for spiritual sustenance. The Cancerian is wrapped up in home and children. But Librans are not happy unless they have found a true mate, one who complements their own nature, and with whom they can settle down in peaceful union. If, in this disillusionment, the Libra appears to philander, he or she is really making a profound search for something that is vital. This probably accounts for the fact that there are many divorces among Librans. On the other hand, there are perhaps many Libra women who are so intellectual and daintily aesthetic that it is impossible for them to live up to the average husband's expectations, a fact which often leads to separation. This type seldom marries again but turns toward music, art, and literature for solace. It is claimed that there are more spinsters born in Libra than in any other sign (with the possible exception of Virgo), despite the fact that Libras express themselves best through marriage: They often place love and sex on such a high pedestal that these cannot easily be attained.

A Libra man with a strongly aspected or exalted Venus in his horoscope is likely to pour out his creative emotion in painting a beautiful picture or composing a lovely song. And many of the most intellectual types will sublimate emotionalism into religious fervor.

Among the less evolved types, we do find some "wandering Romeos." The very gentleness of a Libra man militates against him. He is an easy prey for any unscrupulous woman, for he doesn't like to appear ungracious or offensive. Furthermore, his vanity is easily tickled. There is a deep, underlying reason for what seems like a pronounced flirtatious tendency among Librans of either gender. They are born in the sign that hovers over the transition period between the gaiety and warmth of summer and the coldness of approaching winter. It comes at a time when the Sun crosses the equator and goes down into the dreary winter months, and Saturn, the planet of darkness, is exalted in Libra. A person born at this time is torn between two powerful magnets: He is drawn toward the cheerfulness of summer but is forced to accept the morose and melancholic tendencies of Saturn. Probably no one but a Libran can realize the mental suffering that these people undergo when Saturn has the upper hand and the Scales are tipped downward. The Libran loses self-confidence and feels that the world is antagonistic. They crave the approbation and flattery of the opposite sex as props to lift them out of this depression and to restore their self-confidence. The Scales tip upward in proportion to the number of romantic scalps they may attach.

Wherever we find a Libra Magdalene we look for either weakness, mental inefficiency, or disillusionment. Rarely, if ever, does a Libra woman degenerate morally because of sensual tendencies, neither does she prostitute herself for money or favors. If she is a woman of culture and refinement, we may be assured that she either loves with deep, emotional intensity, or that she has become so thoroughly disillusioned that she no longer cares about the opinions of others. The innocence of a young Libra woman is often her downfall. So gracious is she, so eager to please, that she is incapable of saying "No." She is in love with Love, and ready to sacrifice all on Love's altar. It is among the moronic type of Librans that we find our greatest moral turpitude, for at best this is not a sign of great moral strength, and when intelligence and education are lacking there are no props for the emotions.

GENERAL COMPARISONS

You have such a sociable nature that you can get along well with most people. But why accept the strains of the more incompatible types when there are so many others with whom you could agree so much better?

You are really an expert actor, and you do not need a director to teach you! Nature has taught you the art of pleasing. It is your hail-fellow-well-met attitude that most frequently causes others to misjudge your real intentions. Your easy mannerisms are liable to involve you in complications unless you take care and develop special techniques to meet each situation.

Having developed your sex appeal to a fine art, you can certainly be a very tender and considerate lover. Hence few who are attracted by your personality can resist you. In your heart of hearts you mean well, and you actually believe yourself sincere in your protestations of love and eternal fidelity. But, alas, the flesh is weak, and it should be noted that you are a person that loves and leaves. Numerous are the broken hearts credited to your record.

The Libra woman invariably has aesthetical qualities of high order as befits the daughter of Venus. But it must be said that she very often has the common accomplishment of vanity. They are aware of their power to attract, and they make the most of it.

They are often capricious and fanciful. And those who develop this particular trend are frequently very touchy and ultra-sensitive. It is a point they should watch, since the trait often makes them extremely unpopular with some people.

Those who seek to woo Libra women should not expect to find them too consistent in their affection: They can be exceedingly loving today, but quite cool tomorrow.

It would, of course, be grossly unfair to dub all Libra women the same. Nevertheless, it is true that a great many Libra women have one eye on money and the other on love. They want luxury and fine things, and they know that money is necessary to supply them. They invariably seek husbands who occupy a substantial position in the community. Life in a garret has little appeal for the Libran woman, even though they are found in bohemian circles.

Libra women are dainty, and you have to have "what it takes" if you hope to woo them successfully. Dress is frequently the magnet that attracts them; for the well-dressed man demonstrates that he probably has the wherewithal to satisfy the expensive tastes of one who has similar ideas about clothes and possessions.

Libra and Aries

The Aries is your astrological opposite. You would find this partner enlivening with many characteristics you enjoy. The Aries enthusiasms will keep you entertained even though it may subsequently develop into a case of follow-the-leader. You will have a partner who will delight in taking you out and about.

The Aries, of course, is not nearly as sentimental as you are. Once you are used to the brusque mannerisms, you will not mind this deficit very much, for the Aries will make up with passion what he or she lacks in politeness.

I don't say that this will be a problem-free marriage, because there is the Aries temper to deal with (and under some circumstances you are not always the spirit of sweet reasonableness yourself).

Libra and Taurus

The Taurus should make a good partner. However, don't expect someone quite as sprightly as you are, for the Taurus likes to take life serenely.

You will have much in common, for the Taurean is like you in the matter of being sociable, good-natured, and easygoing.

The Taurus, however, is more prone to jealousy than you are, and may resent your hail-fellow-well-met spirit toward others—especially if that spirit is directed to members of the opposite sex.

I know you love to argue but I offer you a word of advice: Try to avoid arguments with your partner. The Taurus just hates to be contradicted and you really won't achieve anything by trying it.

Libra and Gemini

A Gemini partner should suit you. He or she is just as artistically inclined as you are; and you both enjoy the brighter side of life.

You like change and novelty, sociable and interesting people. Because Geminis enjoy this side of life too, there should be much sympathetic understanding between you.

Do not try any form of subterfuge. Sometimes you can be rather deceitful and it should be pointed out that the Gemini can be a great schemer too. Hence it can be tragic if you both drift into the position of trying to outsmart each other.

Libra and Cancer

A Cancer has moods that may prove far too much of a problem for you. If you have married a Cancer, you are expected to be a handyman about the house, and that is simply not your bent. If you are a Libran woman married to a Cancer husband he will expect a domesticated housewife, which is not altogether in line with your ideas of the wife's role.

Cancers have many weaknesses which your character can not supplement or bolster, and this circumstance opens up many a danger.

Libra and Leo

You might be able to get along very well with a Leo partner since you would be married to quite an accommodating individual. But because there is something about you that sometimes seeks to impose on goodwill, I am obliged to regard this combination as somewhat incompatible. You would wound the Leo's pride; and if you did, the result would be very unpleasant.

Libra and Virgo

This is a semicompatible union, and much will depend upon what you expect from marriage.

You are a bit sensitive, and marriage to a Virgo means you will not escape criticism! Nor will you have too much sympathy for the Virgoan proclivity for self-pity.

However, the qualities you like about the Virgo are the mental fluidity, the great spirit, the restlessness, and the beauty and charm of the chatty Virgo. Would you like a dialogue? Well, the Virgo can talk too. And how! You'll have someone who can keep pace with you, and when and if it comes to flirtatiousness, the Virgo may even outpace you!

Libra and Libra

A mate born in your own birth month could also be a blessing. You will certainly understand each other very well, and if you make a point of studying each other's interests, there could be a devotion that will know no bounds. There is much to recommend in a Libra-Libra marriage.

Libra and Scorpio

It all depends on you when it is a case of marriage to Scorpio. If you play your part, the Scorpios will play theirs. Your partner will be a strong, masterful individual who won't tolerate being toyed with. Unless you understand this promptly, you will not find happiness: If you hurt the Scorpio's pride, all will not be well.

All things being equal, however, there is much to recommend the union for there are many sympathies in common. Both of you are strategists of the first order; and if the power which these gifts afford is wisely coordinated to common ends, the result could well be an unrivaled marriage. The Scorpio will understand you well.

Libra and Sagittarius

The spirit of freedom-loving Sagittarius will attract you, and you may be intrigued by your mate's impulsivity and frankness. But you may not find it easy to keep pace with the Sagittarius: Whereas you use your reasoning powers, the Sagittarian trusts more to instinct and intuition. That is the one important difference between you. The reasoning process is necessarily far slower than instinctual behavior. Thus the Sagittarian can prove extremely annoying to you on occasion.

Nevertheless, you will have an interesting and very exciting companion if you can make allowances for this trait. Your tastes will be very similar and you will see eye to eye on many things.

You might do worse than marry a Sagittarian. At the same time, if you fail to understand your partner, it is true the mixture may prove a little explosive at times.

Libra and Capricorn

Many Librans get along satisfactorily with Capricorn, yet it is a combination that is capable of developing far more disharmony than harmony.

No doubt the Libran is readily capable of interesting the Capricorn because of their geniality and gay spirits, which are the direct opposite of the Capricorn nature. But you may find the Capricorn distinctly boring. No matter how much your free-and-easy nature is admired before marriage, the Capricorn is sure to regard it with the profoundest distrust after marriage and your spirits would be sure to receive a letdown.

If the Capricorn does not like your friends or guests, you may be sure they will be insulted sooner or later, for Capricorns can be particularly rude and ill-mannered when resentful.

Libra and Aquarius

The Aquarius is just your type and so closely akin to you that little need be said concerning this combination. The sign is certainly one of the best of your astrological affinities. You will discover that you have married a very compatible partner.

Libra and Pisces

It is surprising how many Libra-Pisces couples are attracted to each other. Yet it seems to be a fatal attraction, for invariably there are great differences. You are most unlikely to meet the real needs of a Pisces, since the Pisces requires your exclusive company whereas you have need of outside social interests.

The brand of disharmony that will be generated may not perhaps affect you as badly as it will the Pisces, but you are pretty sure to react sooner or later. You can not make another person miserable indefinitely without eventually sharing in that misery.

THE CUSPS

Persons born within three days of the beginning or the end of a sign will have some of the instincts and tendencies of the other sign. Such persons should read both charts in order to get a complete understanding of their dual characteristics. September 23–24–25, Libra with Virgo characteristics; October 20–21–22, Libra with Scorpio characteristics.

LOVE AND EMOTIONS

Libras are emotionally affectionate, tender, sympathetic and loving. Their moods vary with their mental activity. They have poise and are reserved when conditions are ideal; however, under difficult circumstances they become highly sensitive. Their feelings are easily hurt in romantic affairs. The true expression of their nature is only found when harmonious conditions exist, but that nature is one of the most interesting in the Zodiac. The women, as a rule, have a delicate spiritual appeal; she is a fine mental companion, wise in the ways of partnership, and well able to bring harmony into the home. While the Libra husband is not easy to please, he is usually quite passionate, and a great respecter of tradition and the home.

Libra's mental and emotional needs can only be satisfied with a good mate and a nice home. The ideal mate for this sign, "that signifies Justice and Fair Play," is one who has an intellectual outlook as well as a sympathetic and affectionate nature.

Natives of this sign dislike a monotonous life, which may cause friction in the home. There is also an inherent desire to travel alone now and then. Too much absence can create a strain upon your marital affairs. The difficulties in life will not destroy your faith in the beauty of love; since this is the sort of faith that vindicates itself, you are likely to find more genuine happiness than you dared hope for.

The Libra female has a kind of Cinderella outlook on life; no matter how humble her position in life, she has a vision of herself in some degree of elegance, grace, and refinement. Be no more or less than your heart tells you to be and follow your instincts unfalteringly.

HOW TO SEDUCE A LIBRA WOMAN

Send flowers and gifts for the home. Give paintings, furniture, colorful knick-knacks. Take her to cocktail parties. Eat by candlelight.

HOW TO SEDUCE A LIBRA MAN

Ask his advice. Praise him, especially his beautiful taste and manner of dress, and be flatteringly romantic.

THE BEST PLACE TO MAKE LOVE

If you are a Libra man, beauty, harmony, and color are the first and foremost things your home must have. If you do not find harmony in the home your sex life will be miserable. As a Libra woman, you are gifted as a decorator, and have the ability to create lovely interiors, but don't forget that people must live in the house. Don't go overboard on blues and pinks, and take care to make your house a home, not a museum. For the sake of your sex life, the home should be comfortable and have a lived-in feeling. Learn to relax in your home, and do not be afraid of things getting messed up.

SCORPIO

Bright Scorpio Armed, with Poisonous tail prepares,
Mens Martial Minds, for Violence and Wars!
His Venom heats, and boils their bloods to Rage,
And Rapine spreads o'er the unlucky Age.
Yet 'tis not Prey they seek, as much as Blood,
For e'en in Peace they fiercely trace the Wood,
O'er Forest range, and every Plain infest,
Now Fight with Man, and now Engage with Beast,
To please the Crowd, they unprovok'd engage,
And sell their Lives, to the dishonest Stage:
And when calm Peace, doth Public Rest bestow,
Yet Still to Fight, each seeks himself a Foe.
They spend their Leisure Hours in fierce Alarms
And all their Recreation is in Arms.

Scorpio

THE SCORPION

OCTOBER 23–NOVEMBER 21

It is doubtful if there is another group of people so unfairly maligned where sex is concerned as the Scorpios, at least by those with only a smattering of astrological knowledge. Perhaps some of our books on this subject are largely to blame, as they emphasize the relationship between Scorpio and the reproductive or generative organs. To be sure, Scorpio does rule these parts of the anatomy, in the same way as Aries governs the head, Taurus the throat, and so on, but this fact doesn't necessarily imply that sex is of greater importance in the life of the average Scorpio than it is in the lives of many born in other signs. However, there is no doubt that Mars, the ruling planet of this sign, does endow our Scorpios with an extraordinary amount of energy or creative force, which in a deeper sense may be called the sexual force. Mars confers this same super-energy upon Aries, but there is a vast difference in the way these two groups of people utilize their forces.

The Aries direct their creative energies into constructive channels through mental processes. Everything must pass through the crucible of the Aries mind. If sexual gratification serves to make our Arian less restless, and if it clears the brain for mental objectives, all well and good. Otherwise, sex is a nuisance. But the creative forces of the Scorpio male lie deep within him and are not to be released through any amount of mental struggle. He doesn't "think," he "feels." The Aries uses the brain with which his Creator endowed him, but the higher type Scorpio quietly permits God-consciousness to flow through him, which it does in such tremendous volume that at times he is crushed beneath its weight. Only through his emotions can he channel these terrific creative energies surging within. He is often nearly consumed by these fires of passion, which may not have the slightest connection with sex in the commonly accepted meaning of the word. He may be fired by an inordinate ambition, which lashes him with all the fury of sexual love, and he may pursue it as avidly as a great Romeo his Juliet. This may lead to a renunciation of sex, and often does. We have known many Scorpio men and women who have dedicated their lives to some great service to humanity, and who have risen completely above all sexual desires. We have known Scorpio men with invalid wives, with whom a sexual relationship was impossible, to remain loyal to them over the years. We mustn't forget that this is a sign of strong willpower.

There is no way of accounting for what occurs sometimes in the deep, shadowy recesses of a Scorpio's heart. We have in mind a Scorpio man, who fell deeply in love with a woman whom he was unable to marry because of adverse circumstances. For a short time, they were blissfully happy. Suddenly, he was transferred to Hawaii, a few months before the fateful Japanese attack on Pearl Harbor. Every day he wrote to his sweetheart long, ardent letters that promised everything for which a woman's heart could yearn. On the day of the attack his letters ceased. In all these years since, she has never heard from him directly. But through other channels, she learned that he was alive, well, and engaged in a colossal and important undertaking. Over and over again, she implored him for a brief message that would assuage that terrible longing in her heart, but his silence was as vast as the Pacific. He wasn't tired of her, and he wasn't too busy to write. On that fateful day, amidst the black, enveloping horror of death, pain, and blood, some strange spirit of renunciation was born within him. Some ordinary sexual instinct was silenced by the roar of battle, and in its place arose the fire of patriotism. The work in which he was engaged was highly creative and of great importance to his country. All of his sexual and creative forces were bent in this direction.

It goes without saying that one so abundantly endowed with creative energy would naturally love with an all-consuming passion, not because he is more sexually inclined or more evil-minded than one born in another sign, but because his entire being is emotionally intense. There are no half-way measures with him. He loves, he hates, he works, he plays, with all the vim and vigor of his energetic nature. There is no doubt that what a Scorpio needs is a responsive mate. If happily married, he brings to the marital relationship the very depths of that passionate emotion which he feels so profoundly. To be met with coolness or disinterest must be a severe blow to both his pride and his love. We recall one case of a Scorpio man wedded to a Gemini woman. It was impossible for these two to find any common ground. He could not understand her cool indifference, she couldn't understand his fervent embrace.

The Scorpio doesn't place his affections easily. He regards matrimony as sacred, and usually remains loyal and devoted to his marriage partner. However, he may prove difficult to live with because of his exacting temperament. A Scorpio wife usually demands much attention, admiration, and praise. If her husband doesn't live up to her expectations in the more intimate phase of their marriage, she is likely to become suspicious and jealous. The average Scorpio has great respect for law and convention, and he wishes to appear well in the eyes of the world. However, once he has become bitter and disillusioned, there are no depths of degradation to which he may not descend. As usual, he does a thorough job. He apparently loosens all of his tremendous creative forces, which, without direction, follow primitive sex channels. It is then that he may indeed become a sex fiend although, being of a secretive nature, he takes every precaution to hide his misdemeanors from the world. As Scorpio rules the generative system, it is up to all Scorpios to control their sexual natures and conserve their life forces, for it is this part of the body that is most susceptible to weakness and disease. Scorpio adolescents should be taught the facts of life and the importance of sexual hygiene.

GENERAL COMPARISONS

Whether you are saint or sinner, there is no denying the strength and power of your personality. You have magnetic attractions and an air of mystery about you that is exceptionally intriguing to certain types, though it may frighten others.

You have a tendency to dominate, and this trait needs to be watched since it may so easily be to your detriment, especially in the matrimonial field if you are married to a Leo or a Taurus. Many domestic upheavals may be traced to that source. As a direct result of the rule-of-thumb methods of the Greeks who associated the individual signs of the Zodiac with the individual parts of the human anatomy, Scorpio has become associated in the minds of writers on popular astrology with sex, merely because the Greeks believed that Scorpio rules the sex organs.

But to infer that the average Scorpio is unduly passionate or sex-mad is an idea that may be far removed from the truth. Certainly you are ardent in temperament. But that springs from the rich generosity of your nature and your general warm-heartedness. You do not wear your heart on your sleeve.

Some of you may have possessive natures, and some may have very jealous dispositions, but it would be a mistake to impute either trait as a characteristic common to every Scorpion. It is a fact, however, that you have the makings of one of the world's great lovers.

Writers of popular astrology all seem to agree on dubbing the Scorpio woman a vamp. The sense of depth, the emotional wealth, the air of mystery, and the impression of intensity may convey to the uninitiated the constitution of a vamp. But usually the Scorpio woman is not a siren, nor is she necessarily as sexy as she would appear. Those who are foolish enough to believe that the Scorpio woman is easy game for a Casanova are likely to be disillusioned. She is far too level-headed and shrewd for that. She turns her brains and talents to much better account as a rule, because she rapidly finds that all too few males measure up to her own high standard.

It is not an easy matter to win the heart of a Scorpio woman, for she can see right through you! If you are not on the level you may be sure your motives will speedily reveal themselves to her practiced eye, for she is a born psychologist. She won't want anything to do with you if she senses that the attention you are paying her is not her own exclusive property.

She acts rightly, in accordance with her instincts, in doing this; because once she has given her heart she is usually heavily mortgaged. Hence she has to feel herself on sure ground before she bestows her affections.

She will make an exceptionally loyal partner, but she expects the same treatment from you; and her masterful nature will ensure that she gets it. Therefore let me caution the prospective wooer of a Scorpio woman: You are asking for trouble if you are setting out deliberately to deceive her. Eventually you'll be made to wish you hadn't. So don't start anything you cannot finish. Confine your activities to the flirts.

If, however, you want a real lover, why, here is the right woman for you. If you are the "right type" you will find her the very best of the lot.

Scorpio and Aries

These are the two signs that are ruled by Mars. If you know the laws of attraction and repulsion, you will know that two positives repel.

The Aries is often too ill-tempered to be tolerated by the masterful Scorpio. This trait is accentuated by the fact that the Aries seeks the leadership of the combination, irrespective of the fact that yours is the more dominant personality. It is likely that a struggle for supremacy will develop and life is likely to be one complete series of disputes and quarrels.

Scorpio and Taurus

A Taurus could make you a splendid mate, for here you would find the perfect reciprocator of your love. Very few others can compete with the Taurus in this respect. Yet, as you very well know, though love plays a great part—an immeasurable part—in the life of the average individual and is a prize greatly to be desired, it is nevertheless not everything; both you and the Taurus have other needs. The degree of success and happiness your partnership will achieve in marriage depends upon how these additional needs are met.

The Taurus has to rise above jealousy. You have to rise above the desire to force your will on your mate. You have to make the allowances for Taurean obstinacy, and be prepared to humor your mate when necessary. The urge to contradict must be consistently fought—and this may be a great effort on your part.

You should get to know your Taurus and grasp these points; then you will discover one of the finest mates possible in the Taurean.

Scorpio and Gemini

Your mental outlook will have a great impact on your degree of happiness if mated to a Gemini. It must be said that you greatly admire the Gemini intellect. You should get on very well with this type, but it will depend on your own cultural level and the direction in which your activities in life are taking you.

If pursuing a literary or artistic career, you have decidedly the type of personality that will appeal to the Gemini.

Scorpio and Cancer

Intrinsically, the Cancer should prove quite a harmonious type for you. But the fact remains that the Cancer nature is in many ways reminiscent of that of the Pisces; for Cancer, too, is a clinging vine.

You would not find happiness married to a Cancer unless your main interests are centered around the home.

The common bond between a Cancer and a Scorpio is fused in the emotional field. Go beyond that and the Cancer is rarely able to follow you. Your pace is too swift and your energies too great.

Scorpio and Leo

Marriage to a Leo holds within its promise most interesting possibilities. Many of the characteristics of both of you are parallel and complementary. You will admire the Leo's dignity and charm. The emotional qualities of the Leo will blend admirably with your own, and you will certainly experience a warm-hearted, affectionate response to your own lovemaking.

The snags are these: two dominant types are here united, and to achieve happiness and a successful marriage will require a mutual understanding of each other, combined with an accommodating spirit on both sides.

You must curb your critical impulses and avoid provoking Leonian obstinacy. You must live up to the gaiety and spontaneity of the Leo moods. The Leo must diminish "bossiness" to achieve success. This must be made an equal partnership in all fields and in all senses.

Scorpio and Virgo

The Virgo can make you a happy partner, too. The effervescent spirit of this type of partner is often a tonic to you, though you may sometimes get fed up when the mood changes, as the Virgo becomes plaintive, complaining, and self-pitying.

I do not think the Virgo trait to criticize will disturb you greatly. You understand the type too well for it to affect you. In fact you will habitually take from a Virgo the form of criticism that you would fiercely resent if coming from a person of any other sign.

Sometimes you may be apt to underrate the Virgo. It will be a mistake to do that, for the Virgo is clever and resourceful.

You will find a good mate in Virgo, but you must not expect to find all the qualities that go with your own.

Scorpio and Libra

The Libra has points of interest for you, too. The type is big-hearted, clever, and even-tempered. The main snag is that the Libra may be too much of a day-dreamer for your intense nature. The Libra skims the surface, whereas you go well below the line. Still, you'll find Libras very interesting people, and if what you want is a good time, well, doubtless you'll get it. But if you are one of the more serious Scorpios, you will find other types much more suitable.

Scorpio and Scorpio

There are very interesting possibilities in a Scorpio-Scorpio marriage, but, as in the matter of all couples who mate with one of their own sign, success will greatly depend upon their respective aims in life and their cooperative abilities.

Given a fully cooperative partnership, this can prove to be one of the most successful of all marriages, for there is sure to be great mutual understanding. It will not work out at all if an element of jealousy plays a part.

Completely allied, they make a formidable and a happy team. They can travel very far together.

Scorpio and Sagittarius

Marriage between a Scorpio and a Sagittarius is a combination that may be classed as doubtful, since there is more than a possibility of mutual distrust developing between the couple.

You cannot manipulate the Sagittarius temperament with the same expert certainty that you can handle some other types. For Sagittarians are much more temperamental and insist on more freedom.

This does not mean that you do not understand the Sagittarius character. Certainly you do. But you will have much greater difficulty in effecting adjustment with a Sagittarian mate unless you are willing to give them the reins.

Scorpio and Capricorn

In many respects a Capricorn may suit you. You may not find all the warm-heartedness or fundamental generosity that you expect, because basically the Capricorn is more matter-of-fact.

Of course, the Capricorn will safeguard your interests, up to a point. Your interests will be safeguarded just as long as the Capricorn feels that it is profitable to do so. The main snag, however, may occur in the emotional field. The moodiness of the Capricorn may sometimes get on your nerves, for you detest a sullen attitude. You are liable to react in a spiteful manner, and the situation can deteriorate rapidly.

Scorpio and Aquarius

The Aquarian types may not be your ideal from a temperamental point of view. They hold themselves too much in reserve, through a desire to preserve their genteel and sometimes snobbish demeanor. You see through them too clearly to please these people. You hate the mere pose of affections. Your instinct is also to criticize; but your criticism is driven by a desire to reconstruct and produce something better.

Your respective outlooks are essentially different. Friendships with Aquarius often prove a grand combination, but as lovers?

Scorpio and Pisces

You will probably see much to admire in the Pisces and no doubt you like the type when you encounter them socially. But here we are concerned with more intimate relationships—and in this regard the Pisces may not fit the bill. The love nature of Pisces is built upon their sensitivities and their swaying emotions; whereas the Scorpio has essentially a strong, masterful, and positive character— the exact antithesis. It is one thing to find the one who can respond to your feelings in a sympathetic sense and quite another being strangled by a clinging vine. I am afraid you would become dreadfully impatient with the Piscean moods, and with their habit of withdrawing into their shell. You are romantic, too, and you have no aversion to soft lights and sweet music when occasion offers. However, on the occasion when it is not possible to select such a location, you are still content. For your heart is set on a solid foundation and it is your mate you love—not the atmosphere. The Piscean, however, must have a dream world, and they want soft lights and sweet music at all times.

THE CUSPS

Persons born within three days of the beginning or the end of a sign will have some of the instincts and tendencies of the other sign. Such persons should read both charts in order to get a complete understanding of their dual characteristics. October 23–24–25, Scorpio with Libra characteristics; November 19–20–21, Scorpio with Sagittarius characteristics.

LOVE AND EMOTIONS

Natives of this sign as a rule have a passionate, profound but controlled response for a deep love, which must be satisfied to their individual standards. Sex is usually very important in your life. You are deeply aware of your environment and atmosphere. You love luxury, and some of you Scorpios have a garish taste in color and dress. Your personalities are made vivid by your emotional power. The directness and obvious sincerity of your reactions to social contacts frequently brings you the friendships you respect.

The Scorpion reproductive urge is directly linked with the self-preservation instinct, therefore they usually seek the fulfillment of their sexual instinct in marriage. But their desires are up against a strong urge to yield for pleasure, which sometimes replaces the love instinct with something more sensational that gratifies superficially, without demanding too much of their whole personality. Because self-justification joins with these deep primal instincts, you can be very suspicious, wary and among other things become a demon of jealousy. You must strive to compete with life on its own terms, and not to take yourself too seriously.

HOW TO SEDUCE A SCORPIO WOMAN

Allow her to win arguments. Praise her for her unusual personality, for her individuality. Take her to cultural events.

HOW TO SEDUCE A SCORPIO MAN

Make him think you are a complete individual but one who believes in male supremacy. Be honorable and straightforward.

THE BEST PLACE TO MAKE LOVE

If you are a Scorpio man, your home is your castle, where you can plant yourself and remain all your life. If your sex life is to reach its optimal fulfillment, you ought to get a house near water, on the shady side of the street. You dislike sunshine, and your home ought be enclosed and private, if possible in a small city. Scorpio women are not good housekeepers, but if married to certain men (such as Virgo) will have to learn to be or lose the man. In order to be happy in her sex life, a Scorpio woman really only needs a bed in any place, since sex is the most important thing in her life.

SAGITTARIUS

The double Centaur different Tempers breeds,
They break the horse, and tame the fiery Steeds;
They love the sounding Whip, the Race, the Rein,
And whirl the Chariot o'er the dusty Plain;
Nor is their Humor to the Fields confin'd
They range the Woods and tame the Savage Kind;
Young Bears they break, and Tygers heats aswage,
And hear Young Lions roaring without rage,
Discourse the Elephant, and Teach the Mass
A Mimick Action, and a decent Grace;
To Act in Plays, or raise the unwieldy load,
To Dance, and be the Darling of the Crowd.
For in the Frome, in doubt forms expressed;
The Man is uppermost, and rules the Beast!
His Bow full drawn implies, his Rays impart,
Strength to the Limbs, and Vigor to the Heart,
Quick active Motions, full of warmth and heat,
Still pressing on, unknowing to retreat.

Sagittarius
THE CENTAUR
NOVEMBER 22–DECEMBER 21

This is a sign of contradictions. There are no rules by which one may determine the emotional reactions of a Sagittarian. The reason for this undoubtedly lies in the fact that this sign is symbolized by the Centaur, half horse and half man. The enlightened Sagittarian, who reacts to the human instincts of this sign, has his emotions under excellent control. It is doubtful if one born in any other sign, with the exception of Virgo, is so completely the master of himself. But the Sagittarius deserves more credit than the Virgo, for he is endowed by nature with more amorous, fervent tendencies. It is easy for the average Virgoan to overcome emotional temptations for seldom is he greatly tempted, but it is only our Sagittarian's strong willpower and his sincere regard for moral propriety that keeps him on the conventional path. He is proud and can not endure the thought that the finger of shame could be pointed at him.

Perhaps there is another and more profound reason for his moral strength. So great are both his physical and mental activities that he utilizes a large portion of his creative or sex forces. Furthermore, he brings reason to bear upon all his problems, he weighs cause and effect to the last dot, and when he has decided that the righteous path produces the least thorns, he abides by his decision. He is eager to reduce life to its simplest terms in order that he may have sufficient freedom for his diversified activities. In this respect, he resembles an Aries. Sex can be a nuisance if it interferes with his more vital interests, for, like the Aries, he is seldom at ease. His brain functions constantly and his wandering feet may lead him anywhere, from a fishing expedition to a trip around the world.

He doesn't place his affections easily, and often prefers a life of single blessedness to an uncertain marital existence. However, once married, he is usually idealistic and devoted, although much depends upon his mate. A very sophisticated Sagittarius husband, who is happily wedded to a woman who understands and trusts his complex, yet childishly simple nature, will blossom into the kindest and most considerate of husbands, proud of his wife and devoted to his children. However, he does expect eager sexual response, for it is through the release of his emotions, that he has suppressed so carefully, that his whole nature expands. Perhaps more than any other type of man, our shy, proud Sagittarius needs a passionate, understanding mate, who will fan rather than repress his own ardent desires. For this reason, he usually mates best with one born in his own sign or in Leo or Aries, whose fiery, amorous nature would match his own. If he marries unhappily, he may remain loyal but he becomes cynical and sarcastic.

A Sagittarius wife demands much in the way of mental as well as physical companionship. Her husband must be a chum as well as a mate. She is direct, unaffected, and generous in her sex manifestations, although her attention may be easily diverted into other channels. If she becomes deeply engrossed in some fascinating subject, she can turn a deaf ear to the call of sex. However, if satisfactorily mated, she makes a very faithful and devoted wife.

Among the less sophisticated types of Sagittarians, those who follow the animal instincts of this sign, we find the strangest contradictions. We find many who are utterly incapable of understanding marriage and sex in its highest manifestation. The poet Shelley, for example, invited his abandoned wife to join him on a journey along with the woman with whom he had eloped. And less spectacular perhaps, but no less puzzling, were the recent cases of two Sagittarian bridegrooms, in no way related, who shortly after marriage insisted upon presenting former sweethearts with expensive gifts of jewelry. And another, who deserted a beautiful young wife, to marry one less attractive and many years his senior. One has only to observe Sagittarians to discover many unaccountable alliances, broken engagements, and divorces that follow in the wake of this unpredictable sign. Yet, strangely enough, the inconsistency of this type isn't occasioned by a sensual, philandering nature bent on sipping the sweetness of the rose then crushing it beneath his heel. It is born of a simple, childlike desire to be magnanimous to everybody, which really means that this type is fair to none. Furthermore, he resents the slightest curtailment of his liberty. This may mean that he doesn't marry at all, but flounders around in a genial, big-hearted way with various sorts of women, mostly those whom the world would not expect him to marry. If he marries and supports his family, he can find no reason why, with his wife and children well established, he should not resume the ways of his bachelorhood. He has very little jealousy and vindictiveness in his own nature and he can not understand it in others.

An unsophisticated type of Sagittarius woman is equally as unconventional. She is less harmful than some of her weaker sisters born in other signs, for she carries no deep ulterior motives. She is the breezy, hail-fellow-well-met type often found around racetracks and gambling marts. All that she asks is freedom to live her life according to the dictates of her nature. She is not a husband-snatcher, or a wrecker of homes, for it is rare that she loves with an intense, possessive passion. She may amuse an errant husband for a few hours but she lets it go at that. She prefers a coterie of men friends with whom she may associate in gay comradeship to any highly specialized romance.

GENERAL COMPARISONS

Your liberty-loving nature is no myth. For you do love your freedom. In itself, this urge is praiseworthy. It is identifiable with a cause for which people are prepared to fight and die.

But, remember, others have a right to freedom as well as you, and your intense desire for it does not give you any leave or license to encroach on the freedom of others. You must not seek your own freedom at the expense of your mate.

The enjoyment of freedom carries with it special responsibilities and it will be well for you to recognize this, since you are remarkably prone to shirk or avoid certain responsibilities on the ground that they tend to restrict your freedom.

You are a born optimist and you are usually a pronounced tonic to those with whom you associate. One never can be dull in your company.

You have a gay, generous nature, and are fond of bright company and kindred souls.

You are quite a stickler on points; and on matters wherein you may have definite views, you become very plainspoken and forthright.

Sagittarians tend to be rather generous in their lovemaking. There are times and when they think it safe to do so, they have little compunction about loving and leaving. The fact is that their passionate love nature frequently asserts itself, but they are held back by their equally powerful desire to preserve their independence. Because of this they have a proclivity to love and run away.

You are very temperamental, but bright, enthusiastic, and high-spirited.

It is the extreme value which you place on your personal freedom that makes you especially cautious where matrimonial ties are concerned.

Some of you are apt to treat your promises too lightly; perhaps this trait emanates from the amoral philosophy which always seems to accompany the extremist ideal of personal freedom. Or perhaps it occurs on account of a restless desire for change. But whatever the cause, the breaking of a promise or the failure to keep an appointment is undeniably aggravating to others. No wonder they set you down as unreliable.

Truth to tell, you have a complicated nature which you find difficult to understand.

Impulsiveness seems to be your second name and certainly you seem to have a craving for adventure.

Sagittarius and Aries

You would be well blended with an Aries for here you will find someone who is quite as devil-may-care as you. Someone who is as vital, eager, and enthusiastic as you, although perhaps somewhat more cautious. Someone who is as passionate as you and even more fiery-tempered. Someone who can use your romantic praise and flattery. Someone who will make a delightful traveling companion. Someone who will play you double or quits. Someone who will quarrel when you feel like it, with no hard feelings afterward. Someone who will help you burn the candle at both ends.

Sagittarius and Taurus

A Taurus certainly has capacity for charming you, but nevertheless this is not all you require. For one thing the Taurean is far too possessive; for another, you will be mated to a particularly obstinate person. You won't get your way so easily, and may have to stay put.

Sagittarius and Gemini

Here in the Gemini you will find the complementary other half of you. If you have come to the conclusion that physical love rates second (or even third) to mental interests, you have gone a long way already by choosing a Gemini, for you are striking the chord that may unite you both. True, the both of you are restless beings, but with proper understanding you can turn this very restlessness to a great advantage.

There is no certain promise of idyllic bliss as a result of this match. On the contrary, you are apt to explode occasionally. But if you achieve a common understanding, you should be able to get along together and continue to interest each other.

Sagittarius and Cancer

There is a vital difference between your tempo and that of a Cancer, therefore you will find that the Cancer may not keep pace with you. The Cancerian will be easily disappointed in you, for the Cancer is a homing-bird, which you are not; also a "clinging-vine" type, which you abhor.

Sagittarius and Leo

There is little doubt that the Leo is your type. Your attitudes toward life are invariably identical. You have the same tempo and the same rhythm. You have the same passionate sentimentality and romanticism. You have someone, in short, who may respond (or who at all events should be capable of responding) to your every mood. Someone who likes and expects the direct, romantic approach in which you specialize!

If you encounter a Leo I think your matrimonial fate will be signed, sealed, and delivered.

There is just one point, however: Beware of deceiving a Leo. Your Leo mate will forgive you anything except infidelity, which the Leo's pride never will forgive; so watch your step.

Sagittarius and Virgo

It is not at all easy to define why a marriage between you and a Virgo would not work out. At first glance it seems as if the two of you are akin, for you often think alike and in your respective general outlooks seem strikingly similar. Yet intimacy between you seems to work badly, because you soon begin to get on each other's nerves. Instinctively, you resent the Virgoan habit of criticizing; and the Virgo resents the amount of liberty you take in the exercise of your freedom.

In any case, neither of you find just what you had hoped for.

Sagittarius and Libra

You will find quite a harmonious type in the Libra and quite a charming mate. If you have even a spark of bohemianism about you, you can count upon a ready reciprocity. Here you have someone of equable temperament; but when I say "equable" I do not mean "placid." On the contrary, you may discover that your partner can be remarkably argumentative.

Mental and artistic talents will be the true bond uniting your respective interests; but you will be equally well blended in your passionate natures.

All will be well if you devote a little care to studying your mate, and provided you keep your personal activities within reasonable limits.

Sagittarius and Scorpio

I am rather dubious about the probable success of marriage should you wed a Scorpio. It could be a success, for you have many points in common, and your nature would be well understood by the Scorpio. The danger is that you are apt to evoke jealousy in the Scorpio to an unprecedented degree; and if you know anything at all of the Scorpio nature you know that this is dangerous in every sense of the word.

If you feel positive that your marriage is indeed going to mean the end of your amorous adventures, and that you intend to take it up as a serious business, all well and good. There will then be bright prospects for a wonderful marriage. But should you slip up at any time in this resolve, you will rue the day you ever married a Scorpio.

Sagittarius and Sagittarius

If you marry someone born in your own birth sign, you will have a partner who sees eye to eye with you in your theory of personal liberty and freedom of action. But don't forget that you have a mate who is equally as clever as you are and one who knows all the answers. You should be perfectly attuned in a passionate sense; but the danger is that this great burst of affection may not last for any considerable length of time unless you develop other mutual interests in life concurrently. The plain fact is that you both have to agree on a mutually acceptable formula. Given such an agreement, plus lines of common interest, you should have a wonderful partner in a Sagittarian.

Sagittarius and Capricorn

If you want to specialize in a type utterly unlike you, marry a Capricorn! For the Capricorn can be as pessimistic as you are optimistic; as taciturn as you are free-and-easy; as possessive as you are liberal; as restrictive as you are charitable.

You will have to make allowances for Capricorn's suspiciousness and innate distrust; and for the jealousy that is inherent in most Capricorns.

If you like playing with nitroglycerine, all well and good. You might get away with it.

Sagittarius and Aquarius

The Aquarius is another zodiacal type that may especially appeal to you. You will find many points about such a partner that you greatly admire. For here is the aristocratic, well-bred individual, possessed of artistic and intellectual talents. You will love your partner's eccentricities, as well as the bohemian spirit which seems part and parcel of the Aquarius make-up. The Aquarian also likes change and movement, and can readily fit into the mold of your moods.

Of course, with all the "mental" types, you will necessarily encounter periods of irritability, and during such times will be apt to get on each other's nerves. But all will be well, provided each of you preserves a sense of humor. And because each of you has the capacity for a real sense of humor, I am confident that the dangers will be negligible. Therefore, I recommend a Sagittarian-Aquarius wedding.

Sagittarius and Pisces

In several ways the Pisces is capable of charming you. For strangely enough you like sentiment. Even if you do not take it seriously yourself, at least you like it in others. Therefore you may find the Piscean remarkably "sweet."

What you will not like, however, will be the "clinging-vine" tactics, and the desire to lean on you consistently.

True, the Pisces may be less incompatible if you really desire to make certain personal sacrifices in your inherent make-up.

THE CUSPS

Persons born within three days of the beginning or the end of a sign will have some of the instincts and tendencies of the other sign. Such persons should read both charts in order to get a complete understanding of their dual characteristics. November 22–23–24, Sagittarius with Scorpio characteristics; December 19–20–21, Sagittarius with Capricorn characteristics.

LOVE AND EMOTIONS

The intensity of the Sagittarian feelings often varies with their moods. At times they can be very demonstrative and then at other times seem cool and apparently indifferent. During the first half of the Sagittarian's life, it appears that many of them will not feel happy and secure in their homes. While they love the hearth, they have a very active and adventurous nature that causes restlessness and a desire for change. After their thirtieth year they may become more settled and contented with a normal married existence; however, even then, there is always a danger of their kicking over the traces.

Many Sagittarians find the great love of the first weeks or months of marriage soon becomes subdued. Unless a strong personality shines forth, the strain on their marriage vows may become unbearable. Domestically a Sagittarian is not always a success because their attentions may be diverted to their greatly diffused interests. The sign shows that it does not usually value personal, possessive love as universally approved. While it is not a jealous sign, it does not appear to endure the continued supervision of domestic life over long periods of time. Too often the natives may decide to change partners and frequently you will find that many Sagittarians are engaged more than once during their early years.

It is not so much that they tire of the opposite sex as that their whole scheme of romantic love is to them a rather experimental divergence. Secret pastimes, and aspirations which they sometimes tend to keep from their intimate associations and loved ones, usually boomerang, with the result that many emotional and difficult situations bring about the termination of a long friendship or even a marriage. Their natural generosity is always a magnet for any who need their help. The Sagittarian wife is one of the best suited for real companionship to an ambitious husband. Since all outdoor life attracts her, she has a great deal in common with her mate. She is outspoken and not too tactful, so that both husband and children may expect to hear their errors and faults frankly discussed. While the Sagittarian man may not be entirely suited by nature for domestic life, he nevertheless makes a very interesting and exciting husband. The passions of the Sagittarian are lusty, sportive, and adventurous. They love humanity and take an absorbing interest in social progress. All the emotions accompanying this sign are high-strung, exciting, and demand action.

HOW TO SEDUCE A SAGITTARIUS WOMAN

Take her to sporting events, to the beach, on camping trips, interesting journeys, and other excursions. Be sure to always be on the move. Ask her to cook for you; then delight in her ability. She will be flattered.

HOW TO SEDUCE A SAGITTARIUS MAN

Allow him free rein. Try making him jealous. Don't be eager.

THE BEST PLACE TO MAKE LOVE

If you are a native of Sagittarius you should watch your step when buying a home. Better to live in an apartment or rent a home. Your mind is very changeable and you may lose materially by lack of proper planning, by impulsive buying. For a happy sex life you ought to have freedom, air, plenty of trees, and as little responsibility as possible.

CAPRICORN

But Sacred Vesta guards the fatal Fire,
And thence 'tis guess'd, what Minds thy
    Rays inspire,
Contracted Goat; by thee that Art's infus'd,
Which Fire assists, and where a Flame is us'd;
By thee the Miners burn the Womb of Earth,
And see the place of Metals' fatal Birth;
By thee they melt, by thee they work the Mould,
Refine, and Stamp it into mighty Gold:
By thee, the Silver, Iron, Gold, and Brass,
The Forge dissolves, and forms the easy Mass:
By thee, the Ovens heat, and Baths acquire,
And Happy Chymists blow enriching Fire;
Thy Cold (for thou o'er Winter Signs dost reign,
Pull'st back the Sin, and send'st Us Day again)
Makes Brokers Rich, for whilst you spread your Ice,
Their Ware go off, and they enchance the Price;
From thee our Youth unconstant tempers prove,
And eagerly pursue unlawful love,
'Cause Goat above; but these the Fish Behind
Corrects in Age, and fixes the soft Mind.

Capricorn
THE GOAT
DECEMBER 22–JANUARY 19

Here we find the true aristocrat of the Zodiac, whether it is a question of sex or hospitality. It is unfortunate, however, that many Capricorns, particularly women, reared by mothers who matured during the Prohibition and Depression Era, still regard sex according to the traditions of that period. Despite the fact that the world may have been gay in comparison with the puritanical era that preceded it, it was still hidebound regarding sex. Around our "not-so-young" Capricorn women today a "hush, hush" atmosphere prevails, and a firm conviction that sex should never be discussed in polite society. Naturally, this kind of suppression reacts detrimentally upon the more intimate phases of the conjugal state, especially if one is married to a man who isn't interested in how his grandmother lived. The younger generation are much more broad-minded but it is nearly impossible for a Capricorn woman to give herself in complete abandonment to any issue—sex or otherwise. Like the mountain goat, which symbolizes this sign, she picks her way through life so carefully, and she has so much respect for convention and authority that it is only at the end of long-range, thoroughly considered plans that she decides to enter any kind of an alliance with anyone.

It is rarely that a Capricorn woman would indulge in any clandestine or illegitimate arrangement, but when she does, the affair is almost never spur-of-the-moment. She may have been months weighing every possibility, and when she finally makes her decision, she enters her new relationship as conscientiously as a blushing bride approaching the altar. Every detail is planned ahead and the utmost secrecy insisted upon. To her credit, it must be said that usually she is loyal and seldom promiscuous. However, she is always wary and fearful. She mistrusts her lover at the slightest provocation, and becomes morbid and suspicious; but despite her many misgivings she clings to him through many vicissitudes, and only when every vestige of their romance has been torn to shreds will she completely lose her faith and abandon him. It is doubtful that many Capricorn women would be found in questionable districts, for they lack an indolent spirit. They are ambitious and willing to labor for every penny, but they have too much respect for law and authority to resort to a promiscuous life.

Once a Capricorn woman is married, she is devoted to her family and household duties. Sex is accepted as a natural component of the marital state but she refuses to become unduly excited about it. However, she may be incurably romantic and possessive. She demands much attention and affection from her husband, and, if there is the slightest hint of sexual coolness on his part, she immediately becomes suspicious and jealous. This may be traced to a Saturnine fear that she may lose her loved one, or perhaps it is nearer the truth that she fears the loss of her own security. Despite a pronounced ability to stand on her own feet, she always seeks protection in her mate, a quality that is very appealing to the male contingent. She frequently finds her greatest happiness with either a Virgo or Taurus mate, as men of these signs are usually faithful and the least likely to give her cause for jealousy. Furthermore, they share her interest in the home and her definite yearning for financial success and social prestige.

A Capricorn man easily accepts certain fixed standards of conduct and lives up to them. Seldom is he a betrayer of women. He is not aggressive. Even in courtship, he does not press his suit. He is discouraged by the slightest rebuff. However, when he has finally succeeded in leading a bride to the altar, he is the proudest of husbands. But so fearful is he of losing his treasure, that he often guards her very jealously and encompasses her with so many restrictions that he eventually loses, through his own fear, the one thing that he treasures most. Whether or not the marriage is successful through sex adjustment depends almost entirely on the wife. Her Capricorn husband awaits her pleasure. He hopes that she will welcome his approach with a tender, sympathetic response that will loosen that cold fear gripping at his heart. He yearns to warm himself at the fires of her love and devotion, but he will not intrude. Unless welcomed wholeheartedly, he turns away in sadness and buries himself in his social and business responsibilities. He does not easily resort to divorce, for the protective instinct is strong within him. He provides for the woman who bears his name. When happily married to a wife who has faith in him and spurs him on to fulfill the ambitions surging within him, he becomes a most devoted husband, eager for worldly success through which he may justify her faith.

Youthful Capricorns exhibit much self-consciousness in the presence of the opposite sex. It is difficult for them to appear natural and unrestricted. This may result in an awkward type of bashfulness or an exaggerated form of flirtatiousness, which is merely a coverall for fluttery sexual trepidation. Perhaps more than one born in any other sign, a youthful Capricorn possesses sexual curiosity. He is haunted by a feeling that it is something forbidden and unmentionable. He doesn't unfold as naturally and as free from inhibitions as youngsters born in other signs. The same Saturnine fear grips him that clutches a Capricorn woman at the psychological moment when she should be warm and yielding. The reproductive processes should be explained to these children early in life. Young Capricorn men and women readily conform to convention and law, and rarely become detrimentally involved in any scandalous affair.

GENERAL COMPARISONS

You certainly seem to know the importance of being earnest. You have a goal in view and have the power to concentrate on your objectives.

The sense of resentment is your chief failing, and is the one thing you should counteract. This comes to the fore especially whenever you feel you have been slighted in any way. Of course, it is only fair to say that part of the blame for this comes from those who arouse this resentment in you. For if they knew their Capricorn, they would know how to handle you. After all, you merely want the acknowledgment and appreciation which you know to be your due; and if only those few short words of praise were forthcoming, what a difference there would be! There would then be joy in your heart instead of that fiercely rankling feeling of injustice and growing spite.

Like the Virgo, you are subject to fits of depression, during which self-pity comes on and you feel very sorry for yourself.

You have the makings of the practical, economical mate, earnest and untiring, with an eye for a good bargain and for quality. You are sedate, reserved, and possibly shy.

It is by no means easy for you to express your feelings. But people should not imagine from this that you are incapable of feeling; for in actual fact your feelings are remarkably sensitive and are readily hurt.

The same reasoning applies to love. Because you may not be demonstrative and outwardly passive by no means implies that you are minus a passionate nature—quite the contrary, really. People do quite easily make many mistakes about you, and actually there is much justification at times for your growing conviction that you are "misunderstood." I repeat: The basis of this is to be found in your sheer inability to express outwardly the real state of your feelings in any other manner than resentfulness or self-pity. Try to develop a more positive approach.

You have sterling qualities which may be readily appreciated by those who really understand the basis of your restrictive nature and reserved mannerisms.

Capricorn and Aries

If you need to be convinced through practical experience that you are innately jealous, you should marry an Aries. You will certainly have your feelings stirred sooner or later if you do. But I do not promise you that this will be a pleasant experience, for I am inclined to believe there will eventually be ample grounds for your mistrust. This would be about the most hazardous alliance you could entertain. The Aries will not tolerate you for long; as for your own feelings, resentment would be a mild term to employ in describing your state.

Capricorn and Taurus

A Taurus should make a very good mate for you. True, both of you are greatly prone to jealousy, but unless either of you is unduly mistrustful a little mutual jealousy should act as a spur to your love. But do not make the great mistake of taking each other too much for granted. You have got to pay some degree of attention to the Taurus if you expect to receive attention. Furthermore, be on your guard against being too thin-skinned during occasional temperamental clashes—you are not being "misunderstood." Rather will it be a case of your lack of understanding. Drop some of your austerity on such occasions and act the part of the tender lover. It will pay off for you.

Capricorn and Gemini

I am afraid you fall a long way short of what a Gemini requires and expects to find. For you are not inherently a gay, exuberant type, and you are far too possessive for Gemini's liking. And, as for yourself, why, you have quite enough trouble with your own feelings to want to be tried still further by a temperamental mate. If you do marry a Gemini you will have only yourself to blame when you speedily learn the essential truth of the proverb that teaches patience is a virtue.

Capricorn and Cancer

The Cancer is your astrological opposite, but your psychological complement. There are good chances of success in this union provided you smooth down some of the edges of your rugged character. For you will be dealing with a mate who is extraordinarily sensitive. But the promise of compatibility resides in the fact that a Cancer is more contented with less than possibly any other type.

Here is one golden secret for you if you marry a Cancer. Take pains to be tender toward your mate. Treat him (or her) with affection, and at no time reject a demonstration of affection.

Unless you are prepared to follow that advice to the very letter, you may be in for many moody sessions.

Capricorn and Leo

You should be able to fit in rather well with a Leonian if you can first persuade one to marry you—which will not be easy! For your demeanor is usually a bit too taciturn to intrigue a Leo. Nor are you nearly as romantic as the Leo would like.

If and when you marry a Leo, you will have to remember two things: (1) never wound the Leo pride; (2) play up to the passionate Leonian nature in a truly romantic sense. If you can master those two points, you can make a success of it. But if you cannot, you may be sure that in due time you will feel greatly "misunderstood." More than that, you may find cause to be insanely jealous.

Capricorn and Virgo

You will not find it easy to understand a Virgo since your mercurial mate may often have you guessing. But if you marry one, you will have a talented, interesting partner. Certainly you could make a success of things between you, provided that your general aims in life are parallel.

There will be moments when each of you will be feeling very sorry for yourselves, but this is a trait which both will readily understand, which should make you tolerant of each other.

Capricorn and Libra

The Libra is another type that will try your patience. You will be jealous of your mate's social tendencies and interest in others. You will have the opinion that he (or she) is too easily led or influenced by others (which is not the case at all) and will therefore be tempted to put your foot down, thinking that a display of feeling on your part will restore your power to influence.

But what a mistake you will be making!

While you may not find the Libra difficult to get on with in the ordinary run of life, many traits of the Libra will run contrary to your basic nature and you may find it too much of a strain on your nervous system.

Capricorn and Scorpio

You might do worse than marry a Scorpio. You should remember that you are not dealing with a mild-mannered individual but with a mate who possesses a strong personality. So do not try to be too matter-of-fact in your dealings or approaches, for this simply will not do with a Scorpio.

You have to warm up to your mate wholeheartedly and do not try any stunts, because the Scorpio can see through them all too clearly.

For instance, when you feel determined to get your own way, you may have a habit of sulking, hoping to work on your mate's feelings. When this does not work, you tend to develop a "nobody-loves-me" act; or you may even go so far as to try out some melodramatic threat in the hope of provoking sympathy. But here you will be playing to a totally unsympathetic "gallery."

Capricorn and Sagittarius

The Sagittarian's principal trait is a certain excessive independence instigated by an inordinate love of personal freedom.

Try to reconcile that trait with your own very possessive nature if you can! You should certainly be able to see from the revelation of this one fact alone that your marriage to a Sagittarius would be a very difficult one.

Capricorn and Capricorn

You should get on well with a partner born in your birth sign and actually this combination may suit you very well. What will probably be lacking, however, will be an adequate foil for your periods of depression. As a result, a form of indifference may develop in the course of time.

Capricorn and Aquarius

The aristocratic bearing of the Aquarius may prove a strong attraction; and it is probable that your ambitions may be an equally powerful magnet for the Aquarius. But the fact is that each of you is cast from a totally different mold. Where the Aquarius is unpredictable, you are austere and mathematically minded.

The Aquarius wants all of the attention, and I fear it would literally mean having to turn yourself inside out to keep your mate satisfied.

Capricorn and Pisces

The Pisces is capable of making you an understanding mate, providing you do not show yourself too needy. Your moods may not be at all easy for the other to understand, and at times it will be difficult to obtain the slightest idea of the true causes which may be the basis of your petty quarrels.

When the Pisces feels the need of loving kindness try to build up a romantic atmosphere. You also need understanding, but your expectations take on a more practical form.

If you can manage to understand each other's idiosyncrasies you will go a long way toward comprehending the basis for an ideal marriage.

THE CUSPS

Persons born within three days of the beginning or the end of a sign will have some of the instincts and tendencies of the other sign. Such persons should read both charts in order to get a complete understanding of their dual characteristics. December 22–23–24, Capricorn with Sagittarius characteristics; January 17–18–19, Capricorn with Aquarius characteristics.

LOVE AND EMOTIONS

Because Capricorns are usually very sensitive, they seem to be rather timid at first. Yet they are very sympathetic and are loyal to those who sympathize with their high ideals. While the affections are deep, they are not necessarily demonstrative. In fact, at times they seem to be somewhat indifferent, which is really contrary to their inherent nature. When they fall in love with the wrong person, they suffer great disappointments and sometimes this marks their lives permanently. Because of their deep love nature they are inclined to be jealous, which is usually one of the primary sources of trouble in their domestic life. They are not really happy without a love mate so it is important that they select a partner who will harmonize with their rather restricted nature.

The Capricorn can adjust himself to any hardships to attain an end. They are usually very demanding in their home life and expect a great deal of attention and respect from their family. The Capricorn woman is a strange mixture of dependence and independence. She is capable, faithful, dependable, and sympathetic. She is always very ambitious for the success of her loved ones. Encouragement and affection will call forth her deep sense of loyalty and she will become an efficient housekeeper, with scrupulous integrity.

The male of this sign may fall in readily enough with the domestic scheme, but usually adds very little to its spiritual success; as husbands, they make good providers, but they do not allow their wives too much freedom of action. The Capricorn husband is usually very dictatorial as well as conservative, and lays down hard and fast rules when it comes to the family budget. He may be found very demanding and suspicious in all domestic matters. His passions are strong and quick, usually on the selfish side. There are, however, a great many Capricorns who are embellished by softer moods, making, of course, a much more agreeable person.

HOW TO SEDUCE A CAPRICORN WOMAN

Impress her with your ambition and material success. Tell her you'll go even further with a smart woman behind you, and this is what you're looking for now.

HOW TO SEDUCE A CAPRICORN MAN

Talk to him about his job. Tell him how important he is and how successful. Compliment him on how he dresses and his art collection.

THE BEST PLACE TO MAKE LOVE

If you are a Capricorn man, tradition must be a part of your home, and your sex life will be at its fullest when this is observed in your choice of dwelling. As a Capricorn woman you will be happy knowing you have gotten a good bargain in your choice of home. Happiest sex relations for Capricorn are achieved when their home is close to a city and west of a river.

AQUARIUS

Aquarius pouring out his Urn, imparts
An useful knowledge in resembling Arts,
To find out Springs, and with new Streams supply
The Barren Countries, and refresh the dry;
To raise in Pipes, or to extend in Beams,
And in high Rooms imprison Foreign Streams;
Affront the Sea, for State, not use, restrain
The Waves with Moles, and curb the raging Main;
Or Engine raise, whence Waters mount above,
And mix the lower, with the higher Jove.
A thousand other Arts, which Waters sway,
As Channels lead, or else as Pipes convey,
Depend upon the Influence of his Ray,
And to his Births the World oblig'd shall owe,
Spheres, Cycles, Orns, and turn New Skies below.
Soft, easie Tempers, loving Coin for use,
Not sordid, but inclin'd to be profuse;
Not pincht, nor yet to swelling in Estate;
Thus flows the Urn, and fixes this for Fate.

Aquarius

THE WATER BEARER
JANUARY 20–FEBRUARY 18

This is a sign of paradoxes and inconsistencies. There is no yardstick by which one may measure the emotional depths of an Aquarius. One may only guess from observation and trust that he is correct. The average Aquarian male functions on a remote plane, which may be interwoven with the real world, yet he remains detached. Tradition and convention mean nothing to him. Just because a condition has never existed is no reason (to him) that it shouldn't exist. He is a law unto himself. If it suits him to conform to authority, all well and good. If not, he defies it. However, he doesn't cast convention aside from a rebellious or belligerent point of view. He doesn't ask that the world agree with his opinions or change its laws or its principles for his sake. But he does ask, in fact, he demands, that the world let him go his way in peace, with his head among the stars. Naturally, this attitude toward life is reflected in his creative, sexual emotions.

One of the strangest paradoxes about an Aquarius man is his attitude toward marriage. Undoubtedly, the sanctity of marriage means less to him than to any other type of man, yet he is usually loyal to his marriage vows. However, he would feel as completely united to a paramour as to a legal wife. He may live happily and contentedly over a period of years or for a lifetime in an illegitimate union. Furthermore, he has as much respect for his alliance and for the woman involved as he would have for marriage and a legal wife. If the time arrives when he abandons this arrangement, it is not because of any contempt he feels for it, it is merely that he has outgrown this particular phase of his life, and he is ready to go on to new experiences.

If the next episode happens to be a satisfactory marriage, he settles down and is the most loyal of husbands. Yet, his hobbies usually come first, and if it suits him to proffer a hand of deep friendship to another woman, he will do so, although it may be strictly a platonic hand. Nearly all Aquarian men are passionate but not sensual, loyal but not affectionate. The wife of an Aquarian man seldom complains that their marital relationship is not what it should be; in fact, there is likely to be a tendency toward overindulgence on his part, which is difficult to understand in a sign so highly mental. It may be that he becomes so absorbed in his own interests that he neglects his wife, then, when his conscience awakens him, he hastens to make amends, and to reveal his love for her through sexual expression, since he is usually tongue-tied when it comes to flowery speeches. Or it may be that he seeks frequent sexual contact because of an inherent loneliness within him. By uniting with another, he may experience a warm, rosy glow of companionship that cheers him. He often has a tender, wholesome consideration for his conjugal ties that is very appealing.

If an Aquarius man finds himself unhappily married, he often detaches himself. He may seek legal separation or he may continue to live with his wife in name only and it is very difficult for him to mate with one who is not in perfect harmony. However, unless he is the unsophisticated type, he makes certain his wife and children are financially secure. It is often difficult for him to stabilize his affections because of his universal and platonic interest in all people, women included. We have in mind one Aquarian man, who has been married and divorced three times. At present, he is living illegitimately with his second-divorced wife, but occasionally writes letters of endearment to his third-divorced wife. Definitely, he is not an evil person; he is a likeable chap with many fine qualities, but he is unable to stabilize his affections because of his Aquarius heritage.

It is rare that an Aquarius marries the one he loves the most. There is nearly always a broken heart among his souvenirs. The middle-aged Aquarian women who live with their cats and their memories are legion. However, they are usually to blame for this state of affairs. An Aquarius man procrastinates so long before "popping the question" that his sweetheart, weary of waiting, abandons him for a more ardent lover. It is nearly impossible for an Aquarius woman to make up her mind. So analytical is she, that she finds it difficult to find a man who fulfills all her ideals.

There is one type of Aquarius man who never marries. He is so fastidious and impeccable in his tastes that it is impossible for him to find a woman who measures up to his standard. Furthermore, unless he is very well-off financially, he needs all his resources to maintain his own precious ego.

The emotional, creative urges of an Aquarius woman are fathoms deep, and sometimes never appear on the surface. There are some who claim they have never experienced sexual desires. Whether this is because they have never been sufficiently awakened, or whether they have evolved out and beyond the physical aspects of sex, remains a mystery. Yet, paradoxically, these women "love to be loved." They derive much satisfaction from caresses and close personal contact.

There is another type of Aquarius woman who appears to be ardently passionate, although we are not certain that she is seeking romance and affection more than sexual satisfaction. Apparently, an Aquarius woman can not endure frigidity. If she is wedded to a man who is cold and unresponsive, she very likely will seek clandestine liaisons, for like her Aquarius brother, she has little regard for convention. To her way of thinking, it is more sinful to live with a man whom one does not love, than it is to live in illicit relationship with one who is adored. But if she is happily wedded, her loyalty knows no bounds. There is no sacrifice too great for her to make for her family, but her husband should remember that the caveman's method of possession should be confined to the "movies." Despite a certain rugged exterior, there is a delicate, artistic daintiness about nearly all Aquarius women that is easily repelled by uncouth advances. Her "romantic moments" should be enjoyed in an exotic boudoir with flowers, perfume, soft lights, and a husband as chivalrous as a Victorian prince.

It goes without saying that a group of people so unmindful of convention and tradition would produce some wayward characters. Perhaps there is no more pathetic sight than an Aquarius woman who has joined the "weak sisterhood." One man is as popular as another as far as she is concerned, which usually means one man right after another. There is a cool, synthetic sparkle about her that holds a fatal fascination for men—she is strangely intriguing. Some Aquarius men follow much the same pattern, and being naturally vacillating and changeable, leave a trail of broken hearts and homes behind.

GENERAL COMPARISONS

Your appraisal of others is very critical, and in the majority of people you contact, you find points of which you disapprove. Your outlook and your way of life is very liberal. Thus you tend to generate a certain aloofness from the general public.

You dislike emotionalism in others, but are not averse to a certain amount of sentimentality—especially when the latter is directed toward you.

You place a high value on personal liberty, and for that reason are wary of entering into a marriage very rapidly. Yet you have a gregarious nature, and in particular you like to circulate among liberal circles either as a humanitarian or an exponent of some movement.

Aquarian women like to feel, and be thought of, as uncommon. You have a fondness for uncommon things and uncommon people. That is one reason why you are apt to develop eccentricities. You desire to prove yourself superior to your fellows.

You are not too romantic as a rule, for you cultivate a kind of psychology that raises something of a barrier against a purely emotional appeal. Though it is certainly true that many Aquarian women greatly prefer masculine company to that of their own sex.

The man of your choice has to be exceptional. In your eyes he has to be something of a genius. Outstanding accomplishments alone succeed in attracting you. If you are not fortunate enough to marry someone who fulfills your inherent expectations, you are never truly happy. When you get fed up with a person or a situation, you suddenly kick over the traces without any warning.

Aquarius and Aries

An Aries is an unsuitable type because your respective natures and outlooks tend to be at such variance. The Aries is often a cruder person than you are, and the resultant mannerisms accordingly call forth disapproving criticism from you. Also you are an independent spirit and will resent attempts at domination.

Aquarius and Taurus

The chief objection to marriage to a Taurus would seem to be your dislike of an overpossessive mate. You have social interests which go beyond the confines of home and a purely domestic realm. In pursuit of these you would not get the Taurus to follow you. Instead, you would find an impediment to your plans. You would have to surrender a very large part of your personal freedom. If you did not, you would rapidly bring on jealous reactions.

Furthermore, you do love a debate or an argument; and really you could hardly choose a worse type than the Taurus with whom to indulge that luxury. Just try the experiment of contradicting a Taurus, and you will speedily discover the truth of this assertion.

Aquarius and Gemini

You would have a splendid mate in a Gemini because mental interests predominate. In other words you have the type of mentality that interests the other. You both like novelty and change. You both have artistic aptitudes and inclinations.

My opinion is that if you could not get along with a Gemini, you would not get along with anybody!

Aquarius and Cancer

Very many of the considerations taken into account in my analysis of the Aquarius-Taurus combination hold true here. Thus the Cancer is an unsuitable type, a homing-bird, whereas you are not. Hence you would encounter antipathy toward any of your social activities.

You are a lover of change and progress; whereas the Cancer lives in the past, revealing the essential divergence of your respective ways.

It is useless for you to expect the Cancer to live up to your special tempo. Often the Cancer attempts to do so in the initial stages (especially during courtship and in the early days of the marriage), but the effort is predestined to be short-lived. It is not merely a question of self-sacrifice, but rather one of natural incapacity. If adjustment in that particular way is to be effected, the self-sacrifice will of necessity have to come from your side.

Aquarius and Leo

You have your opposite zodiacal partner in the Leo and you will find plenty to admire.

You may not always see eye to eye with the Leo; in fact, you may very well quarrel violently—often over the merest trifles. But in the Leo you will have a partner who will understand and who will want to share your desire for social activities and your interest in the outside world.

The Leo, however, is more conventional than you are, and you should take note of that fact. Moreover, you will have to give your mate more attention than you might otherwise be inclined to. Here you have someone who simply will not be ignored.

If you want a mate who will supply all your needs and then take a back seat, don't marry a Leo! Because if that is your idea it will not be long before you are made to realize your mistake.

Aquarius and Virgo

You could make a very good match with a Virgo or a very bad one. Usually there are no half measures. You either like immensely the chatty, friendly, intellectual Virgo, or you hate the catty, spiteful, overcritical Virgo.

Therefore, before you marry a Virgo, make sure you have dispelled all illusions. Convince yourself that it is the type that can spout honey or vinegar, so be prepared.

You will not find everything you want in a Virgo, and there are sure to be some traits which will displease you. (I'll not specify what these are, for you are the type of person who is best left alone to find your own ammunition.)

The best Aquarian-Virgo marriages are those in which the Virgo is slightly superior to the Aquarius either in intellectual achievements or in social status. The other way is usually calamitous.

Aquarius and Libra

If you marry a Libra you probably will not have made a bad choice at all. You should have many things in common, for the Libra has quite a number of characteristics which are reminiscent of you. Hence you should harmonize admirably in regard to your joint way of life and respective aims. You both like the bright things of life, and enjoy good company. The Libra will support your aristocratic outlook.

Aquarius and Scorpio

If you marry a Scorpio you will be wedded to a very masterful mate. You will not be the controller, but the controlled! It would be wise for you to recognize the fact from the start, since by doing so you will save yourself a lot of trouble. Scorpios will not cease until you have surrendered.

The Scorpio may be very similar to the Taurus in regard to jealousy, because the Scorpio—especially the Scorpio woman—can be very possessive.

Remember, too, that you will have a mate who is quite as obstinate as you are. Should you come to cross-purposes, you may easily lock horns permanently.

Aquarius and Sagittarius

Again in the Sagittarius you may discover "just your type." Of course, the Sagittarius is more fiery than the Libra, but you will be inclined to put that down to spirit. Anyway, you do appreciate the need for the preservation of independence and are therefore less likely than most to tread on the Sagittarian's tenderest corn.

Personally, I think you are both capable of understanding each other perfectly. Though each of you is certainly not averse to going off the deep end at times, you should be able to get along very well together.

Aquarius and Capricorn

While it is not impossible for you to find true happiness with a Capricorn, your requirements as an Aquarius demand an optimistic outlook because you have little understanding and perhaps less sympathy with moods of depression. True, you are adaptable and a hope resides in the possibility of your ability to fall into line with the Capricorn view of things. For this reason I would not rule out the Capricorn as a possible mate for you.

Aquarius and Aquarius

Of course you will understand a mate who was born in your own birth month; and quite possibly this could prove the best of all marriages for you, since you are both independent of emotional pull. It would be either a marriage of intellect or a marriage of convenience, and I think you would agree perfectly both in tastes and talents. If your respective eccentricities follow a similar channel, the match should be perfect.

Aquarius and Pisces

The chances of a successful marriage to a Pisces are excellent.

It is true that the Pisces is sometimes unduly sensitive, but yours is a personality with a smooth surface and the chances of acute friction are accordingly much diminished. The only rather discordant factor is the undue insistence of the Pisces on the sentimental value of things. Usually you know how to play up to this all right, but now and again you will doubtless find it wearisome.

The Pisces moods are sometimes a disturbing factor for you too, for you are also given to emotionalism and therefore some trying situations can develop.

All the same you will like the sentimental spirit of the Pisces and it should not be difficult for you to make the grade together.

THE CUSPS

Persons born within three days of the beginning or the end of a sign will have some of the instincts and tendencies of the other sign. Such persons should read both charts in order to get a complete understanding of their dual characteristics. January 20–21–22, Aquarius with Capricorn characteristics; February 16–17–18, Aquarius with Pisces characteristics.

LOVE AND EMOTIONS

Your emotional sensitiveness may cause many complications in your intimate affairs. Perhaps your greatest weakness is an uncontrollable tendency to be unreasonably jealous of the object of your affections. You also have a knack of misinterpreting what others say or do, because you do not seem to realize the depths of your highly emotional senses.

Love and marriage will play an important part in your life and will stimulate your desire to accomplish your cherished ambitions.

While loving adventure, you are also adaptable to a proper domestic home life. If you have the means with which to travel, you will want a place to return to that you know as home. While there are times you like to be alone, undisturbed by outside influences, you can be gay and congenial in a crowd that meets with your approval. Otherwise you find it difficult to relax and enjoy yourself.

You are the type of person that makes an excellent friend, because you are willing to give a great deal of yourself. You will choose your mate for certain qualities that will appeal to you and your comforts.

You are not easy to please in domestic life and respond only to the one who has mutual interest in your activities and idiosyncrasies. You love to entertain and at times are liable to collect some pretty peculiar companions, who will no doubt take advantage of your humanitarian principles.

Emotionally the Aquarius woman is responsive, but her intellect seems to rule her actions, and while she is appreciative when married to a man she is proud of, she does not always stick to conventions when married to someone she feels is mentally or socially inferior.

The Aquarius husband is usually kind and generous, but may not be too ardent a lover. He is kind, gracious, and sociable, and accepts marriage as a part of the domestic scheme. If you marry an Aquarius man, you must be prepared to accept a husband who may appear to take his marriage in an impersonal light. This is because his interests are universal, and he has a difficult time with a mate who is too possessive.

The Aquarius usually makes a good parent, because it is a very human sign, the qualities are ideal for raising children. They guide and encourage their young ones, spurring them on to excel without boastfulness and show. They command respect, because of their intelligent guidance and reasonable qualities of censorship. While the Aquarius child is treated with great affection, he is not deluged with sentimentality. The Aquarius always tries to create mental appreciation, believing that this will endure long after the emotional diffusions are spent.

HOW TO SEDUCE AN AQUARIUS WOMAN

Give many gifts, be romantic and flattering, sincere and kind. Be sure you are well-informed and make no blunders. Be suave and continental.

HOW TO SEDUCE AN AQUARIUS MAN

Be up on his interests. Flatter him and praise him with your sincere interest. Be able to converse on his level or keep silent. Be romantic and lovely.

THE BEST PLACE TO MAKE LOVE

If you are a native of Aquarius, your home should be like a space rocket, since you belong to the New Age. Aquarius women like the new and modern, also originality and touches of foreign influence: Chinese rooms, French eighteenth-century chairs, Tibetan bells. The Aquarius men fall into two categories: One who lives in a tiny room and eats hamburgers, worrying about money all the time, and the true Aquarius, rich, modern, with a sense of savoir-faire, and money in his pocket. For the first type, since he is the unfortunate slave of his mind, a one-room house is enough, and his sex life will be as limited as his surroundings. The second type of Aquarius will have a home which is his castle, with paintings, statues, period furniture, and a sex life as expansive as his mind and talent, and a charming Aquarius or Aries wife to enjoy. The correct surroundings are extremely important to Aquarius in order to fully enjoy his sexual potential.

PISCES

Last Double Pisces, from their shining scale
Spread wat'ry influence, and incline to Sail:
To trust their lives to Seas, to plow the Deep,
To make fit Rigging, or to build a Ship,
In short, what e'er can for a Fleet be fram'd,
A thousand Arts, too numerous to be nam'd.
Beside to steer, observe the Stars, and guide
As they direct, and never lose the Tide;
To know the Coasts, the Winds, the Ports, and Shores
To turn the Helm, or ply the bending Oars;
To sweep smooth Seas with Nets, to drag the Sand
And Draw the leaping Captives to the Land,
Lay cheating Wires, or with unfaithful bait,
The Hook conceal, and get by the deceit;
To fight at Sea, to stain the Waves with blood,
Whilst War lies floating on the unstable flood;
Fruitful their Births, of Pleasure fond, engage
In Love, are quick, but changing with their Age.

Pisces

THE FISHES

FEBRUARY 19–MARCH 20

This is one of the most difficult of the twelve signs to interpret, whether in the matter of sex or otherwise. The lights and shadows that play upon the profound inner sanctuary of a Pisces are ever-changing and evasive, yet as beautiful and penetrating as sunlight mottling through a virgin forest. Like Virgos, whose weaknesses are often their virtues upside down, Pisces possess a fine idealism which may carry them to the heights of emotional bliss when happily married or lead them to the depths of social degradation when disappointed or disillusioned. The heavens may fall but the Pisces are determined to live their own lives at any cost. They will follow the dictates of the heart, though they prove will-o'-the-wisps that lead to the brink of ruin. The immature Pisces man often attaches himself to a woman of questionable desirability, places a halo around her head, and then worships her with as much idealistic sexual abandonment as Don Quixote his Dulcinea. Not for a single instant does he feel any pang of conscience or regret. Mentally, he has sublimated her into his ideal woman and he dwells with her in a dream world which exists, if not exactly in the shadow of the pearly gates, in close proximity thereof. To him, the convention of marriage is no reason to restrain oneself from aiding any woman in distress, no matter where or when, or what the circumstances. There is little tolerance for an irate wife who may not share this Piscean philosophy.

From his viewpoint, at least, our Pisces lives a more honest life than the law-abiding citizen whose conduct is outwardly above reproach but who inwardly chafes at society's restrictions. To his credit, it must be said that he always endeavors to do right but in his eagerness to be true to himself, he is frequently at variance with convention and man-made laws. An unattached Pisces is often very inconsistent and unfair to a woman he courts. So idealistic, tender, and thoughtful is he that he dramatically lifts her to the very heights of matrimonial expectancy. She can almost feel the wedding band upon her finger. Perhaps a week later, she isn't sure that he even loves her, and neither is he. Like the two fishes that symbolize this sign, each swimming in opposite direction, our poor

115

Pisces is bewildered and is never sure which fish to follow. It is difficult for him to stabilize his affections.

Despite his sympathetic, affectionate nature, it is doubtful if sex in its mere physical manifestation means as much to him, even the most unsophisticated type, as it does to those born in many other signs. It is the emotional outlet the Pisces seeks. The gold digger, with the hard luck story, the forlorn widow with small children, the poor little woman whose husband has abandoned her, can always make a romantic and financial hit with a Pisces man casting about for an idealistic haven for his misunderstood affections. If he is married, his wife may be the soul of virtue, the very core of domestic efficiency, but her matter-of-fact practicality may be the very factor that pushes our dreamy, romantic Pisces out of the nest, particularly if she is the dominating, exacting type that insists upon strict observance of the rules of life.

A very enlightened Pisces man, with his emotional and sexual nature under control, is one of the world's finest specimens of manhood. Like his astrological opposite Virgo, he often prefers the celibate or monastic life. But if he marries (and if his affections are firmly grounded), the union is usually one of those marriages made in heaven. He brings to the marital relationship all of that tender consideration and idealism for which he alone of all the twelve types is peculiarly capable. He feels a sense of completion, a unity of mind as well as body, for a very sophisticated Pisces is so mentally pure that he becomes almost passionless. It is only his great capacity for love, and his need for emotional absorption, that stimulates any interest whatsoever in sex. This is particularly true of a mature Pisces woman. So innately refined is she, so highly sensitized, that it is nearly impossible for her to fulfill her marriage obligations unless she meets with spiritual responsiveness and love's persuasion. The man who regards sex merely as a biological pleasure was never made for her, as he soon discovers by her cool, remote reticence. Neither can a husband who has been unfaithful ever hope to rekindle that divine spark that bloomed so beautifully for him on his honeymoon. Once the lovely idealism of a Pisces woman has been shattered, no power on earth can cement the fragments. She may forgive, for that is her nature, but her dreams seek new channels. They may turn toward books, art, or music, for seldom is she unfaithful, regardless of how disillusioned she may be. She clings stoutly to conventional integrity, which no doubt is good for her soul, and for society, but not so favorable for her physical well-being, for the Pisces woman, who is frustrated sexually, many times resorts to a tearful, self-pitying attitude toward life. However, when she is harmoniously mated, she represents the best in a wife. Generous, companionable, and tolerant, she blends her lovely soul qualities with a host of homemaking accomplishments.

The less sophisticated Pisces woman lives in an illusionary world, without rhyme or reason, often stimulated by and seeking narcotics, alcohol, or food. Her determination to possess what she covets is only superceded by her desire. She believes as her birthright that anything or anyone she desires should be hers.

This is often true of the men she meets. If she meets someone she likes, she never questions the existence of any previous alliance he may already have. Whether he is already married or has a flock of children is of no consideration. The fact that she is attracted to him is all that matters. He will be hers, regardless! Since the Pisces woman is often endowed with a certain mesmeric quality, she will often get "her" man. Whether or not she will keep him is another issue!

As such a Pisces is often curiously indolent, she too frequently seeks the easy road to fulfill her romantic aspirations. In short, she craves the luxuries of life and sees little reason why she can not have them with a little skillful manipulation.

GENERAL COMPARISONS

You are receptive and easily influenced. Too easily influenced. But having a dual nature you become readily mistrustful. As a result, you are very much a worrying type of person. For you want to be convinced, but at the same time you mistrust your own judgment, and remain poised between two negatives—uncertain and undecided.

You have a very dependent nature and feel compelled to rely upon others, especially for moral support. Thus you develop affectionate, loving tendencies. But because of your extreme sensitivity, you often surprise a lover who is seeking to move you with protestations of love by reason of your sudden reactions—caused by your undecided actions. Yes, you will probably lose many a lover as a result of this.

Your deep sympathies are your winning asset, and it is the true awakening of sympathy in you that will win your love where all other means would fail. This, then, is the real secret to be learned by the lover who seeks to woo you and win you. Your sympathetic nature is readily vulnerable.

You Pisces women are truly feminine. Your softness gives the impression of feminine sweetness par excellence. When you smile the attractive possibilities are enhanced to their highest degree and you take on the appearance of seductive charm with a central nucleus of irresistible sweetness wrapped around a mystery. No wonder men find you intriguing. Add to this all the arts and crafts which can be supplied by an inherently sentimental nature, and all the atmospheric trimmings that can be imagined, and one can then form a complete picture of you as a glamorous, ravishing, languorous creature.

You would be a winner the whole way in the love stakes were it not for the dual qualities of your nature, which produce a kind of interior tug-of-war. Thus, where your seductive charm compells, your revulsions of feeling repell! No wonder you often become edgy and a prey to curious moods—which the would-be swain finds puzzling to an extreme. These are capable of swiftly damping even a very promising romance. No wonder many of you frequently develop alarming neurasthenic symptoms and even nervous breakdowns. It will not be at all easy for you to control these conflicting phases of your nature; and yet it is this very element which is capable of introducing tragic factors into many Piscean lives.

Tragedy often enters into Pisces lives. Possibly to a far greater extent than any other zodiacal type. Yet the majority of such devastating happenings seem traceable to the very symbol of the sign, which is two fish joined together, one headed upstream and the other downstream.

Pisces and Aries

Aries seem to have a special predilection for Pisces; and if it is happiness in marriage they are seeking, they could not possibly marry anyone better calculated to jeopardize that happiness.

During the courtship period they will probably find the Aries ideal, though perhaps too aggressive in the mode of making love. But this is just the trouble—the Aries tempo is far too swift for them to keep pace; and the Pisces is too languid and phlegmatic to sustain the Aries' interest permanently.

Pisces and Taurus

In the Taurus you have a partner who is like you to a great degree. The Taurus is less sentimental than you, and perhaps more passionate, but it should not be difficult to make the proper adjustments.

Anyway, you will have an easygoing, pleasant partner who will be interested in your ways and views, and there is little doubt you will get along well together.

Pisces and Gemini

A Gemini blends with your artistic aptitudes and will be your bait, for you have the type of personality which is really the latter's bane.

Natives of Gemini, however, do not like anyone to lean on them. They detest the idea of being transformed into a moral prop. They want self-reliant and resolute mates. Hence, happiness with a Gemini would be problematical.

Pisces and Cancer

The Cancer will probably make you the best match of all. For here is someone who has a kindred sentimental nature and who will be a very pleasant companion indeed.

The only trouble (and each of you is affected by the same complaint) resides in your moody tendencies. Fortunately, both you and the Cancer understand moods and know how to cope with them.

Pisces and Leo

The Leo is a dangerous attraction, while the Pisces sentimental outlook combined with the Leo's romanticism may cause them both to think of each other as the world's perfect lover, it may only last for the courtship period. For the Leo is intolerant of moods and will display marked impatience when you begin to show them; the more your moods develop, the worse the Leo's arrogance will hurt you.

The one redeeming feature here is the Leo's ready forgiveness by an emotional appeal of tenderness. If you can master your moods sufficiently to make a fuss over your Leo mate, the chances for a happy marriage will be greatly enhanced.

Pisces and Virgo

Sometimes a Pisces-Virgo couple makes a good match; and certainly this zodiacal type is not inharmonious. A Virgo could produce the happiness you expect, but the Virgo does not have your degree of sentiment and is often markedly matter-of-fact.

What the Pisces produces by moods, the Virgo makes up for in nerves. This makes for a very explosive mixture when these two manifestations collide.

Pisces and Libra

Of all the zodiacal types, the Libra is probably the most difficult.

If a Pisces woman wants a husband who "works late at the office," marry a Libra; or if a Pisces man wants a wife who always seems to be out visiting friends when he comes home tired, then marry a Libra. You are not likely to find in the Libra the homey, reciprocal partner you conjured up in your dreams. There is little need to elaborate; take this tip on incompatibility.

Pisces and Scorpio

Marriage between you and a Scorpio is presumed to have harmonious possibilities. However, one must take pains to understand the complicated nature of Scorpio. A moody Pisces would prove intolerable to the Scorpion.

Some Scorpios may be able to understand and make allowances for your moods, but that degree of toleration can not be conceded for the majority.

Pisces and Sagittarius

The Sagittarius is harmonious only under the proper planetary conditions.

Although it is true that in some respects you do harmonize, you still have to control your jealousy, because here you will have someone who has a high regard for personal freedom and one who does not easily tolerate the possessiveness of a clinging partner. This is the principal snag.

Pisces and Capricorn

You could do worse than marry a Capricorn but don't expect to find a sentimentalist. Therefore, if sentiment is your greatest need, remember this point and guide yourself accordingly.

Although you have many points of similarity, you both will discover a practical, helpful partner by way of compensation.

Pisces and Aquarius

Marriage between you and an Aquarius may produce more good for the Aquarius than it would for you.

Though you may not find the deep emotions and sentimental values that you hope for, you will measure up to the expectations of the Aquarius in many respects.

Pisces and Pisces

Needless to say, if you marry a partner born in your own birth month, you will have a mate who understands you thoroughly. Both of you, then, will be able to enjoy a state of sentimentality, and will be able to warm up to each other in the same tempo.

This is the kind of marriage that should suit you very well. It is also the one that would really be the best for you. However, as is usually the case, you may seek the more illusive types who seemingly offer something "different" rather than turn to the one quarter where you would be both safe and satisfied.

THE CUSPS

Persons born within three days of the beginning or the end of a sign will have some of the instincts and tendencies of the other sign. Such persons should read both charts in order to get a complete understanding of their dual characteristics. February 19–20–21, Pisces with Aquarius characteristics; March 18–19–20, Pisces with Aries characteristics.

LOVE AND EMOTIONS

The Pisces native is very sympathetic, affectionate, and sensitive in all love matters. When they are able to overcome their natural reserve they can also become quite demonstrative. They are inherently kind and unusually devoted and considerate. There is a tendency here to display great jealousy and impulsive, emotional tantrums when they suspect they are being betrayed or neglected. Their nature demands a great deal of attention and affection and naturally when this is denied they do not hesitate to show their displeasure. There is sometimes a tendency to hide their oversensitivity about love and if this is carried to a great extent, it can cause much misunderstanding between the natives and their loved ones. Pisces take a great deal of pride in properly furnishing their homes according to their financial means and are very fastidious about the appearance of their person as well as those with whom they are in love.

Any lack of sympathy and mutual understanding between a Piscean and their loved one usually brings about some very distressing domestic scene. Most men and women under the sign of Pisces love domestic life and they are most willing to carry out the romantic legend of lover and sweetheart throughout their married life. They show great affection in the home and flatter mates with little gestures of affection. Usually a Pisces woman makes a very kind, loving, and devoted wife. She is extremely responsive and tends to make her man a very satisfied husband because she is adaptable and experimental, and her concept of sex ties in beautifully with her mate, far above the average.

The Pisces husband seeks a great deal of sympathy and response to his physical nature. He is the type of man for whom sexual satisfaction is important, and he seeks it persistently throughout his life. Generally speaking he is one of the most loving and attentive of men, considerate, thoughtful, the eternal escort showing his wife courtesy and attention. On the negative side the Pisces can have a big problem: His notions and dreams are more real to him than the difficulties of living and so he is apt to drift along in a phantom world. Of course these qualities in a husband are most distressing, especially when there is a struggle for existence facing the family household. The main fault here lies in a lack of stability, strength, and realism.

HOW TO SEDUCE A PISCES WOMAN

Compose poetry or copy it if you must, but send it, together with roses. One at a time will do. Tell her you want to penetrate her inner core.

HOW TO SEDUCE A PISCES MAN

Never put him down. Always build up his confidence. Show you are empathetic and sympathetic.

THE BEST PLACE TO MAKE LOVE

A Pisces native, for a happy and complete sex life, should live in a spacious and comfortable home. Being a water sign, the best location for the home is close to trees and water. The beach, in particular, is the ideal place where the rhythms of the sea can become fused in the sexual rhythm of the Pisces native. An old house with verandas, if found close to the beach, will bring about complete ecstasy in sexual relations.

II

WHO TURNS YOU ON? YOUR VENUS-MARS FACTOR

An Introduction to Venus and Mars

Venus and Mars was painted by Boticelli. When I stood before this painting in London's National Gallery, I was struck by how timid the god Mars looked in comparison with the earthy sensuality of Venus. She was presented as an irresistable earth force, the grip of matter and flesh combined. Her completely effortless magnetism seemed to exude the force of Love itself. Mars was no challenge to her.

Venus normally has that power to attract passively, while Mars is what we desire and actively pursue. Some ancient astrologers suggested that polarities shift with the gender of the person so that in a man's chart, Venus would represent the women drawn to him (their type and perhaps sign) and Mars would represent the women he would actively pursue. In a woman's chart, Venus might represent how she acted to attract the men of her choice, whereas Mars might represent the men naturally in pursuit of her.

After the sexual revolution of the 1970s—as Uranus, planet of revolution and change of custom, passed through the sexual sign of Scorpio—I don't think Venus-Mars factors can any longer be easily defined by gender. Carlos Castaneda's teacher, Don Juan (*Separate Reality, Tales of Power,* etc.) suggested that people were *born* with different sexual quotients, based in part on the moment of conception and the degree of passion therein. (If you've always been a live wire, that's saying something rather personal about your parents, now isn't it?)

Many people take the Mars force of *Desire* and *Vril* (virility) and channel it into work, sports, and adventure. Many take the Venus force of beauty, love, and sensuality and channel it into art, music, food preparation, home decor, etc. We are multifaceted beings and while Venus-Mars forces aptly describe a great deal about our sexual preferences and natural attractions, other factors are involved.

First, we will discuss Mars in each element, then we will discuss how Venus works in each element. If elements are missing in your chart, or that of your prospective mate, a discussion about missing elements should follow. If you know your Mars position and aspects it makes in your chart, you may want to review the "Mars guide." Similarly, if you know your Venus position and the aspects it makes, you can review your "Venus guide." These are simplified guides for understanding your needs. Then we will embark upon the journey of discussing the 144 possibilities that exist between twelve sign potential placements of Venus and twelve sign potential placements of Mars.

This guide will give you some very strong insights into all combinations and as to how one might overcome the potential weaknesses of a coupling which may not follow the traditional "laws" of harmony and compatibility. Karmically, we all have different lessons to learn; that being the case, we don't all choose harmonious relationships. This guide may give you insight into that which you are seeking to fulfill through your relationship and its karmic undertones.

In case you have forgotten, the horoscope is divided into four groups of elements: Earth, Air, Fire, and Water, with three astrological signs comprising each.

MARS IN ELEMENTS

Mars is the life force, the sexual force, the vril of the organism. Astrologically, it is linked to Aries, the primal force of spring where all life forms surge into concrete expression.

1. **Fire:** Aries, Leo, Sagittarius
   Pure impulse, the sheer joy of action synthesized instantaneously with thought into bursts of movement. Action without time for judgement or analysis, pure instinct coupled with inspiration. Spontaneity. (Your best bill-payers don't fall in this group.)
2. **Earth:** Taurus, Virgo, Capricorn
   These are the builders, the ones who move rock to make buildings. These persons work with tangibles or turn ideas to money; they are the pragmatists. They may have a strong sexual stamina but frequently turn that stamina to work-related projects and can be workaholics. (This is not the romanticist who would follow you across the country to prove love.)
3. **Air:** Gemini, Libra, Aquarius
   These are the experimenters; their assertiveness shows in communications. They are clever strategists who play the game of life. They are the sales-

people who sell you on the image they promote of themselves. They are human chess players, politicians, wits. (They are not always honest because like air, their direction of commitment can quite easily change.)

4. **Water:** Pisces, Cancer, Scorpio
   These people do without doing; they use the inner power to draw things unto themselves. They let God's will be done. They are the passive mystics or sometimes escapists. Not usually the aggressive movers and shakers of the world, their energy may be expressed on the soul level, i.e., writers, artists, dancers, mystics. (Even if you don't understand yourself, they'll read right between your lines to your core!)

VENUS IN ELEMENTS

Associated with comfort and the development and utilization of *all* of the physical senses, Venus gives the capacity to respond to beauty, taste, smell, touch, and sound. Strong Venus in a chart can bring artistic expression through one of these sensory channels. Venus is also about pleasure, body adornment, making one irresistible. Venus has to do with hair care, body lotions, body massage, and beautiful clothing.

1. **Fire:** Aries, Leo, Sagittarius
   This position seeks to dazzle and sees the sexual as an urge toward purification. Venus's fire is impulsive in love, falls in love with beauty or through beauty is romanced into love. Venus's fire can do the bizarre, the dangerous, the questing for love. Or Venus's fire can channel unrequited love into works of creative energy—art, music, dance, writing. Venus's fire is attracted to impulsive types.

2. **Earth:** Taurus, Virgo, Capricorn
   This Venus makes a home, makes love so comfortable that the partner will never want to leave. He/she is the cook, the one who makes her own cushions, blankets, quilts; the one who prepares the holiday table in a step-by-step fashion. (Or if he/she is a modern earth sign, his/her worldly status affords him able helpers to do all that.) This Venus admires the successful, practical mate.

3. **Air:** Aquarius, Gemini, Libra
   This Venus flirts with love, approaching it from a intellectual level. Experimenting with words, movements, and appearances that elicit specific loving responses from others, they plot their actions to invoke the feelings of others. Through the love of others, they gradually learn about feelings and themselves. These are the cool types, ones who love several at once and spread their attentions about; not necessarily capable of experiencing all the words and ideas. This Venus is drawn to the witty, entertaining types.

4. **Water:** Pisces, Cancer, Scorpio

    You can't lie to this one, as every tributary of every stream must eventually return home to the water table and make its journey back to the source. Water is life's common denominator. Water recognizes what others feel— themselves connected to the wellspring awareness of *the* source itself. They are the empathetic, caring, mothering, psychic, nurturing types. Love is awesome; two become one. There are no barriers.

MISSING ELEMENTS

A good relationship acts as a kind of mirror. If we sense we have something missing, and someone we love has a lot of that quality, we can't help but see some of it reflected back to us. Akin to the psychological technique of "behavior modification" (B. F. Skinner), over time we absorb the behaviors we think we have become. Thus we learn to overcompensate for missing elements and largely through imitation, learn the skills relevant to the missing element.

1. **Lack of Earth**—These people are often immoderate with money. They may lack ambition or the wherewithal to get on with worldly goals. This person has difficulty seeing the long-term effect of immediate actions and choices. Not your practical, down-to-earth type. They may draw a mate: Virgo, Taurus, Capricorn who may compensate for their shortcomings.
2. **Lack of Fire**—They may be very concise and hard working, but there is a certain spark of enthusiasm missing for life and much else. This person has difficulty visualizing what *could* be and isn't motivated by faith alone. They often lack creative inspiration. They may attract Aries, Leo, Sagittarius to make up for their lack.
3. **Lack of Water**—They may tend to intellectualize what others feel; they can be great logicians, mathematicians, and strategists yet somehow miss the great human element, flawed as it may be. They may lack a capacity for real blended integration (oneness) with another human being which is the basis for transcendent love. They may attract Pisces, Cancer, and Scorpio to help fill this "void" in them.
4. **Lack of Air**—They may not be a great communicator. They may have difficulty looking at facts and reality, and being impartial in judgment. Emotions, impulse, or excessive practicality may create imbalance in their beliefs. They may be drawn to Gemini, Libra, or Aquarius to help them objectify their experience.

Venus and Mars most aptly refer to sexual potentials and male-female animal attractions. However, let us look briefly at other factors in the great puzzle of human interaction.

SUN AND MOON

Sun: The light of our conscious perception of ourselves in this lifetime.
Moon: The "print out" of what was reflected to us about ourselves through early family experiences, socialization.

Sun and Moon are a couplet, representing the self and the self's early relation to others, thus creating our basis for how we react to relationships and often who we choose to play the part with.

PLANETS

Venus: Our search to love and be loved; our pleasure and creative instincts.
Mars: Our life force, our passion, our desires; also our capacity for assertiveness and self-preservation.
    Even if your Venus/Mars expresses a fine tuning of your sensual nature, the conscience speaks through all planets and can, for some, offset natural leanings with conditioned guilt or repression.
Mercury: Rules our ideas, method of communication, our beliefs.
Jupiter: Symbolizes our faith and capacity to act on vision.
Saturn: Symbolizes our doubts, guilt, fear—sense of void where we often overcompensate.
Uranus: Represents rebellion against conventional standards and an openness to the unexpected.
Neptune: Symbolizes the collective unconscious and our inner search; the bond to the self above and beyond the conscious ego.
Pluto: The capacity for totally starting anew, being born again.

SYNASTRY

There are many "laws" in astrology. Some of us respond to the law of opposites and choose relationships that are highly charged and magnetized. There are struggles within such a tie (in chemistry, ionic bonding). Others seek harmony and are drawn to harmonious ties. Each partner brings something more or less equal to the relationship (in chemistry, covalent bonding.) Still others choose mates for convenience. They may simply feel it is time to marry. There are no deep, transcendental forces at work (van der Waals force).
    Still, in any union, the two become more than the sum of separate parts and through alchemy, a new entity, "the relationship," is born.
    Synastry is the name given to the relationship between one individual's planets and those of another. There are nine planets plus the Sun and Moon. We also use the Moon's Node (and this is a karmic symbol) as well as the Ascendant. Therefore approximately twelve positions from one chart aspect and twelve from

another gives a potential for 144 major contacts! Added to this is the fact that these contacts vary in strength and quality and we see that there are actually many thousands of points of contact between any two individuals. This can explain why and how both strong feelings of love *and* strong feelings of disharmony can exist within one relationship!

The following is a guide to all possible relationships between Mars and Venus. Once you have a better understanding of this aspect of your relationship, you should be ready to study other interwoven planetary elements in what is known as synastry.

Here is a short overview of how the various planets speak to and respond to each other.

VENUS AND MARS IN COMPARISON

Between two persons, the qualities emphasized will be an important element of the relationship. Within a single chart, the interblend represents *a* facet of character. The stronger the relationship (by angle, aspect) between the planets involved, the more important this quality will be to the relationship or, in the case of a single chart, the individual.

Venus Aspects

1. **Sun:** A strong identification with beauty, pleasure, sensuality; sometimes laziness will follow. Love can be used to attract "the good life."
2. **Moon:** A feminine tendency to sensitivity, intuition, blending occurs. There is a strong need to nurture; feelings flow easily. Domestic sharing or domestic needs are emphasized.
3. **Venus:** Similar sensual needs are shown between partners. Both seek a sensual, artistic connection or outlet.
4. **Mercury:** There will be a gift for language, communication arts, beautiful expressions. There may be interest in crafts and hobbies, too.
5. **Jupiter:** One expects much of love; there is a large capacity for pleasure and an appetite for the good things in life. There is joy and generosity over love. Sensuality is easily expressed.
6. **Saturn:** Commitment is taken seriously in love; there are old-fashioned values; love develops slowly. Artists patiently cultivate technique. The loved one may be older, more mature.
7. **Uranus:** Love is impulsive and experimental; love is sought as an electrifying experience, a way out of conventional life. The couple is subject to strange meetings at strange intervals; on again/off again.
8. **Neptune:** Love is sought at the soulmate level; there is poetry, mysticism, a loss of personal ego. Intuition and the arts are favored.
9. **Pluto:** Love is an all or nothing proposition, relationships come to punctu-

ate an old way of life. There are many endings and new beginnings during the course of loving. A memorable, turning-point relationship.

Mars Aspects

1. **Sun:** There is a sense of bravado, adventure, independence, willingness to take risks. Both rebel together; each learns to compromise.

2. **Moon:** The home will be volatile or agitated in some way; there can be many changes of residence or the need to work off steam with physical labor (i.e., construction work) at home. There may be some rebellion against traditional domestic ties.

3. **Mercury:** A quick mind, quick intellectual exchanges are shown; each arouses the others' intellect. Both may press each other on to intellectual achievements.

4. **Mars:** Creative competitiveness keeps each on their toes. They may participate in sports together, fitness contests, explorations, or other tests of independence and courage to some degree.

5. **Jupiter:** There will be a great expansive sense of adventure, a personal faith that can stand many tests. This would indicate a person who loved to hunt for unusual experiences. Between individuals, a love of exploration and personal liberties. They may take on more in life than they can handle: overly optimistic.

6. **Saturn:** An individual could regulate activity with amazing stamina and self-discipline or they could feel resentment for life's restraints. A relationship may feel tested by timing, each meeting at a "bad" time for the other. There are karmic lessons or limitations inherent in this tie.

7. **Uranus:** An individual would manifest unusual physical aptitudes and an attraction to danger. An individual might feel as though he/she were a law unto themselves. There may be great physical agility. Couples feel a sudden, inexplicable attraction to one another and their relationship might reflect a theme of rebellion to established norms of conduct in one way or another.

8. **Neptune:** Actions may stem from spiritual, intuitive planes. The individual might be interested in yoga, t'ai chi, or meditative arts. Action may come from unconscious planes. A couple could experience this as a quest for inner truth; then they might even practice Tantric sex. They might also draw each other into drugs or negative escapisms.

9. **Pluto:** An individual might have amazing physical prowess and a very developed sexual drive. This person might also have a means to justify the ends (or vice versa) attitude. The person could use sex to manipulate others. Violence and sexuality may link up somehow. Between two persons, sex can be a very strong element of the relationship and one partner could manipulate the other through sex. On its most positive, hopeful note, it could mean that both explore healing methodologies or represent an important turning point in each other's lives.

How to Find Your Venus-Mars Potential for Love and Sex

To find your very own Venus-Mars potential, consult the following tables. First, look up your own year of birth. Then, find your date of birth under Venus and note the sign in which it is placed. Now do the same thing with Mars and again note the sign in which it is placed. This gives you *your* Venus-Mars potential.

Now, look up the year of birth of your lover and find his or her Venus-Mars placements.

If you are a woman, first consult the text for *his* Mars and *your* Venus. This represents the primary influence on your partnership. To find the secondary influence, consult the text for *your* Mars and *his* Venus.

Last, to find the tertiary influence, consult the text for both *your own* Venus-Mars combination and *his* Venus-Mars combination.

When examined in this manner, you will have before you all the influences at work here.

If you are a man, first consult the text for *your* Mars and *her* Venus. Next, *her* Mars and *your* Venus. Last, consult the text for your own Venus-Mars combination and her own as well.

CHILDREN, PARENTS AND THE BOSS!

Besides using the Venus-Mars potential for a lover, one can also do the same for a parent of either sex, a child, or one's employer!

The main thing to remember is to take into consideration the sex of the partner as explained above. For example, should a daughter wish to find out her relationship with her father, she would begin with his Mars placement and her Venus. On the other hand, should a daughter wish to find out her relationship with her mother, she would use the Mars position of whoever is dominant, she or her mother!

By using the positions in this way, endless combinations are possible.

1900

Venus

Jan.	1–Jan. 19	Aquarius
Jan.	20–Feb. 13	Pisces
Feb.	14–Mar. 10	Aries
Mar.	11–Apr. 5	Taurus
Apr.	6–May 5	Gemini
May	6–Sep. 8	Cancer
Sep.	9–Oct. 8	Leo
Oct.	9–Nov. 3	Virgo
Nov.	4–Nov. 28	Libra
Nov.	29–Dec. 22	Scorpio
Dec.	23–Dec. 31	Sagittarius

Mars

Jan.	1–Jan. 22	Capricorn
Jan.	23–Feb. 28	Aquarius
Mar.	1–Apr. 7	Pisces
Apr.	8–May 16	Aries
May	17–June 26	Taurus
June	27–Aug. 9	Gemini
Aug.	10–Sep. 26	Cancer
Sep.	27–Nov. 22	Leo
Nov.	23–Dec. 31	Virgo

1901

Venus

Jan.	1–Jan. 15	Sagittarius
Jan.	16–Feb. 9	Capricorn
Feb.	10–Mar. 5	Aquarius
Mar.	6–Mar. 29	Pisces
Mar.	30–Apr. 22	Aries
Apr.	23–May 16	Taurus
May	17–June 10	Gemini
June	11–July 4	Cancer
July	5–July 29	Leo
July	30–Aug. 23	Virgo
Aug.	24–Sep. 16	Libra
Sep.	17–Oct. 12	Scorpio
Oct.	13–Nov. 7	Sagittarius
Nov.	8–Dec. 5	Capricorn
Dec.	6–Dec. 31	Aquarius

Mars

Jan.	1–Mar. 1	Virgo
Mar.	2–May 10	Leo
May	11–Jul. 13	Virgo
July	14–Aug. 31	Libra
Sep.	1–Oct. 14	Scorpio
Oct.	15–Nov. 23	Sagittarius
Nov.	24–Dec. 31	Capricorn

1902

Venus		
Jan.	1–Jan. 11	Aquarius
Jan.	12–Feb. 6	Pisces
Feb.	7–Apr. 4	Aquarius
Apr.	5–May 6	Pisces
May	7–Jun. 3	Aries
June	4–June 29	Taurus
June	30–July 25	Gemini
July	26–Aug. 19	Cancer
Aug.	20–Sep. 12	Leo
Sep.	13–Oct. 7	Virgo
Oct.	8–Oct. 30	Libra
Oct.	31–Nov. 23	Scorpio
Nov.	24–Dec. 17	Sagittarius
Dec.	18–Dec. 31	Capricorn

Mars		
Jan.	1	Capricorn
Jan.	2–Feb. 8	Aquarius
Feb.	9–Mar. 18	Pisces
Mar.	19–Apr. 26	Aries
Apr.	27–June 6	Taurus
June	7–July 20	Gemini
July	21–Sep. 4	Cancer
Sep.	5–Oct. 23	Leo
Oct.	24–Dec. 19	Virgo
Dec.	20–Dec. 31	Libra

1903

Venus		
Jan.	1–Jan. 10	Capricorn
Jan.	11–Feb. 3	Aquarius
Feb.	4–Feb. 27	Pisces
Feb.	28–Mar. 23	Aries
Mar.	24–Apr. 17	Taurus
Apr.	18–May 13	Gemini
May	14–June 8	Cancer
June	9–July 17	Leo
July	8–Aug. 17	Virgo
Aug.	18–Sep. 6	Libra
Sep.	7–Nov. 8	Virgo
Nov.	9–Dec. 9	Libra
Dec.	10–Dec. 31	Scorpio

Mars		
Jan.	1–Apr. 19	Libra
Apr.	20–May 30	Virgo
May	31–Aug. 6	Libra
Aug.	7–Sep. 22	Scorpio
Sep.	23–Nov. 2	Sagittarius
Nov.	3–Dec. 11	Capricorn
Dec.	12–Dec. 31	Aquarius

1904

Venus			*Mars*		
Jan.	1–Jan. 4	Scorpio	Jan.	1–Jan. 19	Aquarius
Jan.	5–Jan. 29	Sagittarius	Jan.	20–Feb. 26	Pisces
Jan.	30–Feb. 23	Capricorn	Feb.	27–Apr. 6	Aries
Feb.	24–Mar. 19	Aquarius	Apr.	7–May 17	Taurus
Mar.	20–Apr. 12	Pisces	May	18–June 30	Gemini
Apr.	13–May 7	Aries	July	1–Aug. 14	Cancer
May	8–May 31	Taurus	Aug.	15–Oct. 1	Leo
June	1–June 25	Gemini	Oct.	2–Nov. 19	Virgo
June	26–July 19	Cancer	Nov.	20–Dec. 31	Libra
July	20–Aug. 12	Leo			
Aug.	13–Sep. 6	Virgo			
Sep.	7–Sep. 30	Libra			
Oct.	1–Oct. 24	Scorpio			
Oct.	25–Nov. 18	Sagittarius			
Nov.	19–Dec. 12	Capricorn			
Dec.	13–Dec. 31	Aquarius			

1905

Venus			*Mars*		
Jan.	1–Jan. 7	Aquarius	Jan.	1–Jan. 13	Libra
Jan.	8–Feb. 2	Pisces	Jan.	14–Aug. 21	Scorpio
Feb.	3–Mar. 5	Aries	Aug.	22–Oct. 7	Sagittarius
Mar.	6–May 8	Taurus	Oct.	8–Nov. 17	Capricorn
May	9–May 27	Aries	Nov.	18–Dec. 27	Aquarius
May	28–July 7	Taurus	Dec.	28–Dec. 31	Pisces
July	8–Aug. 5	Gemini			
Aug.	6–Sep. 1	Cancer			
Sep.	2–Sep. 26	Leo			
Sep.	27–Oct. 21	Virgo			
Oct.	22–Nov. 14	Libra			
Nov.	15–Dec. 8	Scorpio			
Dec.	9–Dec. 31	Sagittarius			

1906

Venus

Jan.	1	Sagittarius
Jan.	2–Jan. 25	Capricorn
Jan.	26–Feb. 18	Aquarius
Feb.	19–Mar. 14	Pisces
Mar.	15–Apr. 7	Aries
Apr.	8–May 1	Taurus
May	2–May 26	Gemini
May	27–June 20	Cancer
June	21–July 15	Leo
July	16–Aug. 10	Virgo
Aug.	11–Sep. 7	Libra
Sep.	8–Oct. 8	Scorpio
Oct.	9–Dec. 15	Sagittarius
Dec.	16–Dec. 25	Scorpio
Dec.	26–Dec. 31	Sagittarius

Mars

Jan.	1–Feb. 4	Pisces
Feb.	5–Mar. 16	Aries
Mar.	17–Apr. 28	Taurus
Apr.	29–June 11	Gemini
June	12–July 27	Cancer
July	28–Sep. 12	Leo
Sep.	13–Oct. 29	Virgo
Oct.	30–Dec. 16	Libra
Dec.	17–Dec. 31	Scorpio

1907

Venus

Jan.	1–Feb. 6	Sagittarius
Feb.	7–Mar. 6	Capricorn
Mar.	7–Apr. 1	Aquarius
Apr.	2–Apr. 27	Pisces
Apr.	28–May 22	Aries
May	23–June 16	Taurus
June	17–July 10	Gemini
July	11–Aug. 3	Cancer
Aug.	4–Aug. 28	Leo
Aug.	29–Sep. 21	Virgo
Sep.	22–Oct. 15	Libra
Oct.	16–Nov. 8	Scorpio
Nov.	9–Dec. 2	Sagittarius
Dec.	3–Dec. 26	Capricorn
Dec.	27–Dec. 31	Aquarius

Mars

Jan.	1–Feb. 4	Scorpio
Feb.	5–Apr. 1	Sagittarius
Apr.	2–Oct. 13	Capricorn
Oct.	14–Nov. 28	Aquarius
Nov.	29–Dec. 31	Pisces

1908

Venus			Mars		
Jan.	1–Jan. 20	Aquarius	Jan.	1–Jan. 10	Pisces
Jan.	21–Feb. 13	Pisces	Jan.	11–Feb. 22	Aries
Feb.	14–Mar. 9	Aries	Feb.	23–Apr. 6	Taurus
Mar.	10–Apr. 5	Taurus	Apr.	7–May 22	Gemini
Apr.	6–May 5	Gemini	May	23–July 7	Cancer
May	6–Sep. 8	Cancer	July	8–Aug. 23	Leo
Sep.	9–Oct. 7	Leo	Aug.	24–Oct. 9	Virgo
Oct.	8–Nov. 2	Virgo	Oct.	10–Nov. 25	Libra
Nov.	3–Nov. 27	Libra	Nov.	26–Dec. 31	Scorpio
Nov.	28–Dec. 22	Scorpio			
Dec.	23–Dec. 31	Sagittarius			

1909

Venus			Mars		
Jan.	1–Jan. 15	Sagittarius	Jan.	1–Jan. 9	Scorpio
Jan.	16–Feb. 8	Capricorn	Jan.	10–Feb. 23	Sagittarius
Feb.	9–Mar. 3	Aquarius	Feb.	24–Apr. 9	Capricorn
Mar.	4–Mar. 28	Pisces	Apr.	10–May 25	Aquarius
Mar.	29–Apr. 21	Aries	May	26–July 20	Pisces
Apr.	22–May 16	Taurus	July	21–Sep. 26	Aries
May	17–June 9	Gemini	Sep.	27–Nov. 20	Taurus
June	10–July 4	Cancer	Nov.	21–Dec. 31	Aries
July	5–July 28	Leo			
July	29–Aug. 22	Virgo			
Aug.	23–Sep. 16	Libra			
Sep.	17–Oct. 11	Scorpio			
Oct.	12–Nov. 6	Sagittarius			
Nov.	7–Dec. 5	Capricorn			
Dec.	6–Dec. 31	Aquarius			

1910

Venus

Jan.	1–Jan. 15	Aquarius
Jan.	16–Jan. 28	Pisces
Jan.	29–Apr. 4	Aquarius
Apr.	5–May 6	Pisces
May	7–June 3	Aries
June	4–June 29	Taurus
June	30–July 24	Gemini
July	25–Aug. 18	Cancer
Aug.	19–Sep. 12	Leo
Sep.	13–Oct. 6	Virgo
Oct.	7–Oct. 30	Libra
Oct.	31–Nov. 23	Scorpio
Nov.	24–Dec. 17	Sagittarius
Dec.	18–Dec. 31	Capricorn

Mars

Jan.	1–Jan. 22	Aries
Jan.	23–Mar. 13	Taurus
Mar.	14–May 1	Gemini
May	2–June 18	Cancer
June	19–Aug. 5	Leo
Aug.	6–Sep. 21	Virgo
Sep.	22–Nov. 6	Libra
Nov.	7–Dec. 19	Scorpio
Dec.	20–Dec. 31	Sagittarius

1911

Venus

Jan.	1–Jan. 10	Capricorn
Jan.	11–Feb. 2	Aquarius
Feb.	3–Feb. 27	Pisces
Feb.	28–Mar. 23	Aries
Mar.	24–Apr. 17	Taurus
Apr.	18–May 12	Gemini
May	13–June 8	Cancer
June	9–July 7	Leo
July	8–Nov. 8	Virgo
Nov.	9–Dec. 8	Libra
Dec.	9–Dec. 31	Scorpio

Mars

Jan.	1–Jan. 31	Sagittarius
Feb.	1–Mar. 13	Capricorn
Mar.	14–Apr. 22	Aquarius
Apr.	23–June 2	Pisces
June	3–July 15	Aries
July	16–Sep. 5	Taurus
Sep.	6–Nov. 29	Gemini
Nov.	30–Dec. 31	Taurus

1912

Venus			Mars		
Jan.	1–Jan. 4	Scorpio	Jan.	1–Jan. 30	Taurus
Jan.	5–Jan. 29	Sagittarius	Jan.	31–Apr. 4	Gemini
Jan.	30–Feb. 23	Capricorn	Apr.	5–May 27	Cancer
Feb.	24–Mar. 18	Aquarius	May	28–July 16	Leo
Mar.	19–Apr. 12	Pisces	July	17–Sep. 2	Virgo
Apr.	13–May 6	Aries	Sep.	3–Oct. 17	Libra
May	7–May 31	Taurus	Oct.	18–Nov. 29	Scorpio
June	1–June 24	Gemini	Nov.	30–Dec. 31	Sagittarius
June	25–July 18	Cancer			
July	19–Aug. 12	Leo			
Aug.	13–Sep. 5	Virgo			
Sep.	6–Sep. 30	Libra			
Sep.	31–Oct. 24	Scorpio			
Oct.	25–Nov. 17	Sagittarius			
Nov.	18–Dec. 12	Capricorn			
Dec.	13–Dec. 31	Aquarius			

1913

Venus			Mars		
Jan.	1–Jan. 6	Aquarius	Jan.	1–Jan. 10	Sagittarius
Jan.	7–Feb. 2	Pisces	Jan.	11–Feb. 18	Capricorn
Feb.	3–Mar. 6	Aries	Feb.	19–Mar. 29	Aquarius
Mar.	7–May 1	Taurus	Mar.	30–May 7	Pisces
May	2–May 30	Aries	May	8–June 16	Aries
May	31–July 7	Taurus	June	17–July 28	Taurus
July	8–Aug. 5	Gemini	July	29–Sep. 15	Gemini
Aug.	6–Aug. 31	Cancer	Sep.	16–Dec. 31	Cancer
Sep.	1–Sep. 26	Leo			
Sep.	27–Oct. 20	Virgo			
Oct.	21–Nov. 13	Libra			
Nov.	14–Dec. 7	Scorpio			
Dec.	8–Dec. 31	Sagittarius			

1914

Venus		Mars	
Jan. 1–Jan. 24	Capricorn	Jan. 1–May 1	Cancer
Jan. 25–Feb. 17	Aquarius	May 2–June 25	Leo
Feb. 18–Mar. 13	Pisces	June 26–Aug. 14	Virgo
Mar. 14–Apr. 6	Aries	Aug. 15–Sep. 28	Libra
Apr. 7–May 1	Taurus	Sep. 29–Nov. 10	Scorpio
May 2–May 25	Gemini	Nov. 11–Dec. 21	Sagittarius
May 26–June 19	Cancer	Dec. 22–Dec. 31	Capricorn
June 20–July 15	Leo		
July 16–Aug. 10	Virgo		
Aug. 11–Sep. 6	Libra		
Sep. 7–Oct. 9	Scorpio		
Oct. 10–Dec. 5	Sagittarius		
Dec. 6–Dec. 30	Scorpio		
Dec. 31	Sagittarius		

1915

Venus		Mars	
Jan. 1–Feb. 6	Sagittarius	Jan. 1–Jan. 29	Capricorn
Feb. 7–Mar. 6	Capricorn	Jan. 30–Mar. 9	Aquarius
Mar. 7–Apr. 1	Aquarius	Mar. 10–Apr. 16	Pisces
Apr. 2–Apr. 26	Pisces	Apr. 17–May 25	Aries
Apr. 27–May 21	Aries	May 26–July 5	Taurus
May 22–June 15	Taurus	July 6–Aug. 18	Gemini
June 16–July 10	Gemini	Aug. 19–Oct. 7	Cancer
July 11–Aug. 3	Cancer	Oct. 8–Dec. 31	Leo
Aug. 4–Aug. 28	Leo		
Aug. 29–Sep. 21	Virgo		
Sep. 22–Oct. 15	Libra		
Oct. 16–Nov. 8	Scorpio		
Nov. 9–Dec. 2	Sagittarius		
Dec. 3–Dec. 26	Capricorn		
Dec. 27–Dec. 31	Aquarius		

1916

	Venus			*Mars*	
Jan.	1–Jan. 19	Aquarius	Jan.	1–May 28	Leo
Jan.	20–Feb. 13	Pisces	May	29–July 22	Virgo
Feb.	14–Mar. 9	Aries	July	23–Sep. 8	Libra
Mar.	10–Apr. 5	Taurus	Sep.	9–Oct. 21	Scorpio
Apr.	6–May 5	Gemini	Oct.	22–Dec. 1	Sagittarius
May	6–Sep. 8	Cancer	Dec.	2–Dec. 31	Capricorn
Sep.	9–Oct. 7	Leo			
Oct.	8–Nov. 2	Virgo			
Nov.	3–Nov. 27	Libra			
Nov.	28–Dec. 21	Scorpio			
Dec.	22–Dec. 31	Sagittarius			

1917

	Venus			*Mars*	
Jan.	1–Jan. 14	Sagittarius	Jan.	1–Jan. 9	Capricorn
Jan.	15–Feb. 7	Capricorn	Jan.	10–Feb. 16	Aquarius
Feb.	8–Mar. 4	Aquarius	Feb.	17–Mar. 26	Pisces
Mar.	5–Mar. 28	Pisces	Mar.	27–May 4	Aries
Mar.	29–Apr. 21	Aries	May	5–June 14	Taurus
Apr.	22–May 15	Taurus	June	15–July 27	Gemini
May	16–June 9	Gemini	July	28–Sep. 11	Cancer
June	10–July 3	Cancer	Sep.	12–Nov. 1	Leo
July	4–July 28	Leo	Nov.	2–Dec. 31	Virgo
July	29–Aug. 21	Virgo			
Aug.	22–Sep. 16	Libra			
Sep.	17–Oct. 11	Scorpio			
Oct.	12–Nov. 6	Sagittarius			
Nov.	7–Dec. 5	Capricorn			
Dec.	6–Dec. 31	Aquarius			

1918

Venus			Mars		
Jan.	1–Apr. 5	Aquarius	Jan.	1–Jan. 10	Virgo
Apr.	6–May 6	Pisces	Jan.	11–Feb. 25	Libra
May	7–June 2	Aries	Feb.	26–June 23	Virgo
June	3–June 28	Taurus	June	24–Aug. 16	Libra
June	29–July 24	Gemini	Aug.	17–Sep. 30	Scorpio
July	25–Aug. 18	Cancer	Oct.	1–Nov. 10	Sagittarius
Aug.	19–Sep. 11	Leo	Nov.	11–Dec. 19	Capricorn
Sep.	12–Oct. 5	Virgo	Dec.	20–Dec. 31	Aquarius
Oct.	6–Oct. 29	Libra			
Oct.	30–Nov. 22	Scorpio			
Nov.	23–Dec. 16	Sagittarius			
Dec.	17–Dec. 31	Capricorn			

1919

Venus			Mars		
Jan.	1–Jan. 9	Capricorn	Jan.	1–Jan. 26	Aquarius
Jan.	10–Feb. 2	Aquarius	Jan.	27–Mar. 6	Pisces
Feb.	3–Feb. 26	Pisces	Mar.	7–Apr. 14	Aries
Feb.	27–Mar. 22	Aries	Apr.	15–May 25	Taurus
Mar.	23–Apr. 16	Taurus	May	26–July 8	Gemini
Apr.	17–May 12	Gemini	July	9–Aug. 22	Cancer
May	13–June 7	Cancer	Aug.	23–Oct. 9	Leo
June	8–July 7	Leo	Oct.	10–Nov. 29	Virgo
July	8–Nov. 8	Virgo	Nov.	30–Dec. 31	Libra
Nov.	9–Dec. 8	Libra			
Dec.	9–Dec. 31	Scorpio			

1920

Venus			*Mars*		
Jan.	1–Jan. 3	Scorpio	Jan.	1–Jan. 31	Libra
Jan.	4–Jan. 28	Sagittarius	Feb.	1–Apr. 23	Scorpio
Jan.	29–Feb. 22	Capricorn	Apr.	24–July 10	Libra
Feb.	23–Mar. 18	Aquarius	July	11–Sep. 4	Scorpio
Mar.	19–Apr. 11	Pisces	Sep.	5–Oct. 18	Sagittarius
Apr.	12–May 6	Aries	Oct.	19–Nov. 27	Capricorn
May	7–May 30	Taurus	Nov.	28–Dec. 31	Aquarius
May	31–June 23	Gemini			
June	24–July 18	Cancer			
July	19–Aug. 11	Leo			
Aug.	12–Sep. 4	Virgo			
Sep.	5–Sep. 30	Libra			
Sep.	31–Oct. 23	Scorpio			
Oct.	24–Nov. 17	Sagittarius			
Nov.	18–Dec. 11	Capricorn			
Dec.	12–Dec. 31	Aquarius			

1921

Venus			*Mars*		
Jan.	1–Jan. 6	Aquarius	Jan.	1–Jan. 4	Aquarius
Jan.	7–Feb. 2	Pisces	Jan.	5–Feb. 12	Pisces
Feb.	3–Mar. 6	Aries	Feb.	13–Mar. 24	Aries
Mar.	7–Apr. 25	Taurus	Mar.	25–May 5	Taurus
Apr.	26–June 1	Aries	May	6–June 18	Gemini
June	2–July 7	Taurus	June	19–Aug. 2	Cancer
July	8–Aug. 5	Gemini	Aug.	3–Sep. 18	Leo
Aug.	6–Aug. 31	Cancer	Sep.	19–Nov. 6	Virgo
Sep.	1–Sep. 25	Leo	Nov.	7–Dec. 25	Libra
Sep.	26–Oct. 20	Virgo	Dec.	26–Dec. 31	Scorpio
Oct.	21–Nov. 13	Libra			
Nov.	14–Dec. 7	Scorpio			
Dec.	8–Dec. 31	Sagittarius			

1922

Venus			*Mars*		
Jan.	1–Jan. 24	Capricorn	Jan.	1–Feb. 18	Scorpio
Jan.	25–Feb. 16	Aquarius	Feb.	19–Sep. 13	Sagittarius
Feb.	17–Mar. 12	Pisces	Sep.	14–Oct. 30	Capricorn
Mar.	13–Apr. 6	Aries	Oct.	31–Dec. 11	Aquarius
Apr.	7–Apr. 30	Taurus	Dec.	12–Dec. 31	Pisces
May	1–May 25	Gemini			
May	26–June 19	Cancer			
June	20–July 14	Leo			
July	15–Aug. 9	Virgo			
Aug.	10–Sep. 6	Libra			
Sep.	7–Oct. 10	Scorpio			
Oct.	11–Nov. 28	Sagittarius			
Nov.	29–Dec. 31	Scorpio			

1923

Venus			*Mars*		
Jan.	1	Scorpio	Jan.	1–Jan. 20	Pisces
Jan.	2–Feb. 6	Sagittarius	Jan.	21–Mar. 3	Aries
Feb.	7–Mar. 5	Capricorn	Mar.	4–Apr. 15	Taurus
Mar.	6–Mar. 31	Aquarius	Apr.	16–May 30	Gemini
Apr.	1–Apr. 26	Pisces	May	31–July 15	Cancer
Apr.	27–May 21	Aries	July	16–Aug. 31	Leo
May	22–June 14	Taurus	Sep.	1–Oct. 17	Virgo
June	15–July 9	Gemini	Oct.	18–Dec. 3	Libra
July	10–Aug. 3	Cancer	Dec.	4–Dec. 31	Scorpio
Aug.	4–Aug. 27	Leo			
Aug.	28–Sep. 20	Virgo			
Sep.	21–Oct. 14	Libra			
Oct.	15–Nov. 7	Scorpio			
Nov.	8–Dec. 1	Sagittarius			
Dec.	2–Dec. 25	Capricorn			
Dec.	26–Dec. 31	Aquarius			

1924

Venus			Mars		
Jan.	1–Jan. 19	Aquarius	Jan.	1–Jan. 19	Scorpio
Jan.	20–Feb. 12	Pisces	Jan.	20–Mar. 6	Sagittarius
Feb.	13–Mar. 8	Aries	Mar.	7–Apr. 24	Capricorn
Mar.	9–Apr. 4	Taurus	Apr.	25–June 24	Aquarius
Apr.	5–May 5	Gemini	June	25–Aug. 24	Pisces
May	6–Sep. 8	Cancer	Aug.	25–Oct. 19	Aquarius
Sep.	9–Oct. 7	Leo	Oct.	20–Dec. 18	Pisces
Oct.	8–Nov. 2	Virgo	Dec.	19–Dec. 31	Aries
Nov.	3–Nov. 26	Libra			
Nov.	27–Dec. 21	Scorpio			
Dec.	22–Dec. 31	Sagittarius			

1925

Venus			Mars		
Jan.	1–Jan. 14	Sagittarius	Jan.	1–Feb. 4	Aries
Jan.	15–Feb. 7	Capricorn	Feb.	5–Mar. 23	Taurus
Feb.	8–Mar. 3	Aquarius	Mar.	24–May 9	Gemini
Mar.	4–Mar. 27	Pisces	May	10–June 25	Cancer
Mar.	28–Apr. 20	Aries	June	26–Aug. 12	Leo
Apr.	21–May 15	Taurus	Aug.	13–Sep. 28	Virgo
May	16–June 8	Gemini	Sep.	29–Nov. 13	Libra
June	9–July 3	Cancer	Nov.	14–Dec. 27	Scorpio
July	4–July 27	Leo	Dec.	28–Dec. 31	Sagittarius
July	28–Aug. 21	Virgo			
Aug.	22–Sep. 15	Libra			
Sep.	16–Oct. 11	Scorpio			
Oct.	12–Nov. 6	Sagittarius			
Nov.	7–Dec. 5	Capricorn			
Dec.	6–Dec. 31	Aquarius			

1926

Venus			*Mars*		
Jan.	1–Apr. 5	Aquarius	Jan.	1–Feb. 8	Sagittarius
Apr.	6–May 6	Pisces	Feb.	9–Mar. 22	Capricorn
May	7–June 2	Aries	Mar.	23–May 3	Aquarius
June	3–June 28	Taurus	May	4–June 14	Pisces
June	29–July 23	Gemini	June	15–July 31	Aries
July	24–Aug. 17	Cancer	Aug.	1–Dec. 31	Taurus
Aug.	18–Sep. 11	Leo			
Sep.	12–Oct. 5	Virgo			
Oct.	6–Oct. 29	Libra			
Oct.	30–Nov. 22	Scorpio			
Nov.	23–Dec. 16	Sagittarius			
Dec.	17–Dec. 31	Capricorn			

1927

Venus			*Mars*		
Jan.	1–Jan. 8	Capricorn	Jan.	1–Feb. 21	Taurus
Jan.	9–Feb. 1	Aquarius	Feb.	22–Apr. 16	Gemini
Feb.	2–Feb. 26	Pisces	Apr.	17–June 5	Cancer
Feb.	27–Mar. 22	Aries	June	6–July 24	Leo
Mar.	23–Apr. 16	Taurus	July	25–Sep. 10	Virgo
Apr.	17–May 11	Gemini	Sep.	11–Oct. 25	Libra
May	12–June 7	Cancer	Oct.	26–Dec. 7	Scorpio
June	8–July 7	Leo	Dec.	8–Dec. 31	Sagittarius
July	8–Nov. 9	Virgo			
Nov.	10–Dec. 8	Libra			
Dec.	9–Dec. 31	Scorpio			

1928

	Venus			*Mars*	
Jan.	1–Jan. 3	Scorpio	Jan.	1–Jan. 18	Sagittarius
Jan.	4–Jan. 28	Sagittarius	Jan.	19–Feb. 27	Capricorn
Jan.	29–Feb. 22	Capricorn	Feb.	28–Apr. 7	Aquarius
Feb.	23–Mar. 17	Aquarius	Apr.	8–May 16	Pisces
Mar.	18–Apr. 11	Pisces	May	17–June 25	Aries
Apr.	12–May 5	Aries	June	26–Aug. 8	Taurus
May	6–May 29	Taurus	Aug.	9–Oct. 2	Gemini
May	30–June 23	Gemini	Oct.	3–Dec. 19	Cancer
June	24–July 17	Cancer	Dec.	20–Dec. 31	Gemini
July	18–Aug. 11	Leo			
Aug.	12–Sep. 4	Virgo			
Sep.	5–Sep. 28	Libra			
Sep.	29–Oct. 23	Scorpio			
Oct.	24–Nov. 16	Sagittarius			
Nov.	17–Dec. 11	Capricorn			
Dec.	12–Dec. 31	Aquarius			

1929

	Venus			*Mars*	
Jan.	1–Jan. 5	Aquarius	Jan.	1–Mar. 10	Gemini
Jan.	6–Feb. 2	Pisces	Mar.	11–May 12	Cancer
Feb.	3–Mar. 7	Aries	May	13–July 3	Leo
Mar.	8–Apr. 19	Taurus	July	4–Aug. 21	Virgo
Apr.	20–June 2	Aries	Aug.	22–Oct. 5	Libra
June	3–July 7	Taurus	Oct.	6–Nov. 18	Scorpio
July	8–Aug. 4	Gemini	Nov.	19–Dec. 28	Sagittarius
Aug.	5–Aug. 30	Cancer	Dec.	29–Dec. 31	Capricorn
Aug.	31–Sep. 25	Leo			
Sep.	26–Oct. 19	Virgo			
Oct.	20–Nov. 12	Libra			
Nov.	13–Dec. 6	Scorpio			
Dec.	7–Dec. 30	Sagittarius			
Dec.	31	Capricorn			

1930

Venus			Mars		
Jan.	1–Jan. 23	Capricorn	Jan.	1–Feb. 6	Capricorn
Jan.	24–Feb. 16	Aquarius	Feb.	7–Mar. 16	Aquarius
Feb.	17–Mar. 12	Pisces	Mar.	17–Apr. 24	Pisces
Mar.	13–Apr. 5	Aries	Apr.	25–June 2	Aries
Apr.	6–Apr. 30	Taurus	June	3–July 14	Taurus
May	1–May 24	Gemini	July	15–Aug. 27	Gemini
May	25–June 18	Cancer	Aug.	28–Oct. 20	Cancer
June	19–July 14	Leo	Oct.	21–Dec. 31	Leo
July	15–Aug. 9	Virgo			
Aug.	10–Sep. 6	Libra			
Sep.	7–Oct. 11	Scorpio			
Oct.	12–Nov. 21	Sagittarius			
Nov.	22–Dec. 31	Scorpio			

1931

Venus			Mars		
Jan.	1–Jan. 3	Scorpio	Jan.	1–Feb. 16	Leo
Jan.	4–Feb. 6	Sagittarius	Feb.	17–Mar. 29	Cancer
Feb.	7–Mar. 5	Capricorn	Mar.	30–June 10	Leo
Mar.	6–Mar. 31	Aquarius	June	11–Aug. 1	Virgo
Apr.	1–Apr. 25	Pisces	Aug.	2–Sep. 16	Libra
Apr.	26–May 20	Aries	Sep.	17–Oct. 30	Scorpio
May	21–June 14	Taurus	Oct.	31–Dec. 9	Sagittarius
June	15–July 9	Gemini	Dec.	10–Dec. 31	Capricorn
July	10–Aug. 2	Cancer			
Aug.	3–Aug. 26	Leo			
Aug.	27–Sep. 20	Virgo			
Sep.	21–Oct. 14	Libra			
Oct.	15–Nov. 7	Scorpio			
Nov.	8–Dec. 1	Sagittarius			
Dec.	2–Dec. 25	Capricorn			
Dec.	26–Dec. 31	Aquarius			

1932

Venus			Mars		
Jan.	1–Jan. 18	Aquarius	Jan.	1–Jan. 17	Capricorn
Jan.	19–Feb. 12	Pisces	Jan.	18–Feb. 24	Aquarius
Feb.	13–Mar. 8	Aries	Feb.	25–Apr. 2	Pisces
Mar.	9–Apr. 4	Taurus	Apr.	3–May 11	Aries
Apr.	5–May 5	Gemini	May	12–June 21	Taurus
May	6–July 12	Cancer	June	22–Aug. 4	Gemini
July	13–July 27	Gemini	Aug.	5–Sep. 30	Cancer
July	28–Sep. 8	Cancer	Oct.	1–Nov. 13	Leo
Sep.	9–Oct. 6	Leo	Nov.	14–Dec. 31	Virgo
Oct.	7–Nov. 1	Virgo			
Nov.	2–Nov. 26	Libra			
Nov.	27–Dec. 20	Scorpio			
Dec.	21–Dec. 31	Sagittarius			

1933

Venus			Mars		
Jan.	1–Jan. 13	Sagittarius	Jan.	1–July 6	Virgo
Jan.	14–Feb. 6	Capricorn	July	7–Aug. 25	Libra
Feb.	7–Mar. 2	Aquarius	Aug.	26–Oct. 8	Scorpio
Mar.	3–Mar. 27	Pisces	Oct.	9–Nov. 18	Sagittarius
Mar.	28–Apr. 20	Aries	Nov.	19–Dec. 27	Capricorn
Apr.	21–May 14	Taurus	Dec.	28–Dec. 31	Aquarius
May	15–June 8	Gemini			
June	9–July 2	Cancer			
July	3–July 27	Leo			
July	28–Aug. 21	Virgo			
Aug.	22–Sep. 15	Libra			
Sep.	16–Oct. 10	Scorpio			
Oct.	11–Nov. 6	Sagittarius			
Nov.	7–Dec. 5	Capricorn			
Dec.	6–Dec. 31	Aquarius			

1934

Venus			Mars		
Jan.	1–Apr. 5	Aquarius	Jan.	1–Feb. 3	Aquarius
Apr.	6–May 5	Pisces	Feb.	4–Mar. 13	Pisces
May	6–June 1	Aries	Mar.	14–Apr. 22	Aries
June	2–June 27	Taurus	Apr.	23–June 2	Taurus
June	28–July 23	Gemini	June	3–July 15	Gemini
July	24–Aug. 17	Cancer	July	16–Aug. 30	Cancer
Aug.	18–Sep. 10	Leo	Aug.	31–Oct. 17	Leo
Sep.	11–Oct. 4	Virgo	Oct.	18–Dec. 10	Virgo
Oct.	5–Oct. 28	Libra	Dec.	11–Dec. 31	Libra
Oct.	29–Nov. 21	Scorpio			
Nov.	22–Dec. 15	Sagittarius			
Dec.	16–Dec. 31	Capricorn			

1935

Venus			Mars		
Jan.	1–Jan. 8	Capricorn	Jan.	1–July 29	Libra
Jan.	9–Feb. 1	Aquarius	July	30–Sep. 16	Scorpio
Feb.	2–Feb. 25	Pisces	Sep.	17–Oct. 28	Sagittarius
Feb.	26–Mar. 21	Aries	Oct.	29–Dec. 6	Capricorn
Mar.	22–Apr. 15	Taurus	Dec.	7–Dec. 31	Aquarius
Apr.	16–May 11	Gemini			
May	12–June 7	Cancer			
June	8–July 7	Leo			
July	8–Nov. 9	Virgo			
Nov.	10–Dec. 8	Libra			
Dec.	9–Dec. 31	Scorpio			

1936

Venus			Mars		
Jan.	1–Jan. 3	Scorpio	Jan.	1–Jan. 14	Aquarius
Jan.	4–Jan. 28	Sagittarius	Jan.	15–Feb. 21	Pisces
Jan.	29–Feb. 21	Capricorn	Feb.	22–Apr. 1	Aries
Feb.	22–Mar. 17	Aquarius	Apr.	2–May 12	Taurus
Mar.	18–Apr. 10	Pisces	May	13–June 25	Gemini
Apr.	11–May 4	Aries	June	26–Aug. 9	Cancer
May	5–May 29	Taurus	Aug.	10–Sep. 26	Leo
May	30–June 22	Gemini	Sep.	27–Nov. 14	Virgo
June	23–July 17	Cancer	Nov.	15–Dec. 31	Libra
July	18–Aug. 10	Leo			
Aug.	11–Sep. 3	Virgo			
Sep.	4–Sep. 28	Libra			
Sep.	29–Oct. 22	Scorpio			
Oct.	23–Nov. 16	Sagittarius			
Nov.	17–Dec. 11	Capricorn			
Dec.	12–Dec. 31	Aquarius			

1937

Venus			Mars		
Jan.	1–Jan. 5	Aquarius	Jan.	1–Jan. 5	Libra
Jan.	6–Feb. 1	Pisces	Jan.	6–Mar. 12	Scorpio
Feb.	2–Mar. 9	Aries	Mar.	13–May 14	Sagittarius
Mar.	10–Apr. 13	Taurus	May	15–Aug. 8	Scorpio
Apr.	14–June 3	Aries	Aug.	9–Sep. 29	Sagittarius
June	4–July 7	Taurus	Sep.	30–Nov. 11	Capricorn
July	8–Aug. 4	Gemini	Nov.	12–Dec. 21	Aquarius
Aug.	5–Aug. 30	Cancer	Dec.	22–Dec. 31	Pisces
Aug.	31–Sep. 24	Leo			
Sep.	25–Oct. 19	Virgo			
Oct.	20–Nov. 12	Libra			
Nov.	13–Dec. 6	Scorpio			
Dec.	7–Dec. 30	Sagittarius			
Dec.	31	Capricorn			

1938

Venus

Jan.	1–Jan. 22	Capricorn
Jan.	23–Feb. 15	Aquarius
Feb.	16–Mar. 11	Pisces
Mar.	12–Apr. 5	Aries
Apr.	6–Apr. 29	Taurus
Apr.	30–May 24	Gemini
May	25–June 18	Cancer
June	19–July 13	Leo
July	14–Aug. 9	Virgo
Aug.	10–Sep. 6	Libra
Sep.	7–Oct. 13	Scorpio
Oct.	14–Nov. 15	Sagittarius
Nov.	16–Dec. 31	Scorpio

Mars

Jan.	1–Jan. 30	Pisces
Jan.	31–Mar. 11	Aries
Mar.	12–Apr. 23	Taurus
Apr.	24–June 6	Gemini
June	7–July 22	Cancer
July	23–Sep. 7	Leo
Sep.	8–Oct. 24	Virgo
Oct.	25–Dec. 11	Libra
Dec.	12–Dec. 31	Scorpio

1939

Venus

Jan.	1–Jan. 4	Scorpio
Jan.	5–Feb. 5	Sagittarius
Feb.	6–Mar. 5	Capricorn
Mar.	6–Mar. 30	Aquarius
Mar.	31–Apr. 25	Pisces
Apr.	26–May 20	Aries
May	21–June 13	Taurus
June	14–July 8	Gemini
July	9–Aug. 2	Cancer
Aug.	3–Aug. 26	Leo
Aug.	27–Sep. 19	Virgo
Sep.	20–Oct. 13	Libra
Oct.	14–Nov. 6	Scorpio
Nov.	7–Nov. 30	Sagittarius
Dec.	1–Dec. 24	Capricorn
Dec.	25–Dec. 31	Aquarius

Mars

Jan.	1–Jan. 28	Scorpio
Jan.	29–Mar. 20	Sagittarius
Mar.	21–May 24	Capricorn
May	25–July 21	Aquarius
July	22–Sep. 23	Capricorn
Sep.	24–Nov. 19	Aquarius
Nov.	20–Dec. 31	Pisces

1940

Venus			Mars		
Jan.	1–Jan. 18	Aquarius	Jan.	1–Jan. 3	Pisces
Jan.	19–Feb. 11	Pisces	Jan.	4–Feb. 16	Aries
Feb.	12–Mar. 8	Aries	Feb.	17–Apr. 1	Taurus
Mar.	9–Apr. 4	Taurus	Apr.	2–May 17	Gemini
Apr.	5–May 6	Gemini	May	18–July 2	Cancer
May	7–July 5	Cancer	July	3–Aug. 19	Leo
July	6–July 31	Gemini	Aug.	20–Oct. 5	Virgo
Aug.	1–Sep. 8	Cancer	Oct.	6–Nov. 20	Libra
Sep.	9–Oct. 6	Leo	Nov.	21–Dec. 31	Scorpio
Oct.	7–Nov. 1	Virgo			
Nov.	2–Nov. 26	Libra			
Nov.	27–Dec. 20	Scorpio			
Dec.	21–Dec. 31	Sagittarius			

1941

Venus			Mars		
Jan.	1–Jan. 13	Sagittarius	Jan.	1–Jan. 4	Scorpio
Jan.	14–Feb. 6	Capricorn	Jan.	5–Feb. 17	Sagittarius
Feb.	7–Mar. 2	Aquarius	Feb.	18–Apr. 1	Capricorn
Mar.	3–Mar. 26	Pisces	Apr.	2–May 15	Aquarius
Mar.	27–Apr. 19	Aries	May	16–July 1	Pisces
Apr.	20–May 14	Taurus	July	2–Dec. 31	Aries
May	15–June 7	Gemini			
June	8–July 2	Cancer			
July	3–July 26	Leo			
July	27–Aug. 20	Virgo			
Aug.	21–Sep. 14	Libra			
Sep.	15–Oct. 10	Scorpio			
Oct.	11–Nov. 5	Sagittarius			
Nov.	6–Dec. 5	Capricorn			
Dec.	6–Dec. 31	Aquarius			

1942

Venus			Mars		
Jan.	1–Apr. 6	Aquarius	Jan.	1–Jan. 11	Aries
Apr.	7–May 5	Pisces	Jan.	12–Mar. 6	Taurus
May	6–June 1	Aries	Mar.	7–Apr. 25	Gemini
June	2–June 27	Taurus	Apr.	26–June 13	Cancer
June	28–July 22	Gemini	June	14–July 31	Leo
July	23–Aug. 16	Cancer	Aug.	1–Sep. 16	Virgo
Aug.	17–Sep. 10	Leo	Sep.	17–Nov. 1	Libra
Sep.	11–Oct. 4	Virgo	Nov.	2–Dec. 15	Scorpio
Oct.	5–Oct. 28	Libra	Dec.	16–Dec. 31	Sagitarius
Oct.	29–Nov. 21	Scorpio			
Nov.	22–Dec. 15	Sagittarius			
Dec.	16–Dec. 31	Capricorn			

1943

Venus			Mars		
Jan.	1–Jan. 7	Capricorn	Jan.	1–Jan. 26	Sagittarius
Jan.	8–Jan. 31	Aquarius	Jan.	27–Mar. 8	Capricorn
Feb.	1–Feb. 25	Pisces	Mar.	9–Apr. 16	Aquarius
Feb.	26–Mar. 21	Aries	Apr.	17–May 26	Pisces
Mar.	22–Apr. 15	Taurus	May	27–July 7	Aries
Apr.	16–May 10	Gemini	July	8–Aug. 23	Taurus
May	11–June 7	Cancer	Aug.	24–Dec. 31	Gemini
June	8–July 7	Leo			
July	8–Nov. 9	Virgo			
Nov.	10–Dec. 7	Libra			
Dec.	8–Dec. 31	Scorpio			

1944

Venus			Mars		
Jan.	1–Jan. 2	Scorpio	Jan.	1–Mar. 27	Gemini
Jan.	3–Jan. 27	Sagittarius	Mar.	28–May 22	Cancer
Jan.	28–Feb. 21	Capricorn	May	23–July 11	Leo
Feb.	22–Mar. 16	Aquarius	July	12–Aug. 28	Virgo
Mar.	17–Apr. 10	Pisces	Aug.	29–Oct. 12	Libra
Apr.	11–May 4	Aries	Oct.	13–Nov. 25	Scorpio
May	5–May 28	Taurus	Nov.	26–Dec. 31	Sagittarius
May	29–June 27	Gemini			
June	28–July 16	Cancer			
July	17–Aug. 10	Leo			
Aug.	11–Sep. 3	Virgo			
Sep.	4–Sep. 27	Libra			
Sep.	28–Oct. 22	Scorpio			
Oct.	23–Nov. 15	Sagittarius			
Nov.	16–Dec. 9	Capricorn			
Dec.	10–Dec. 31	Aquarius			

1945

Venus			Mars		
Jan.	1–Jan. 5	Aquarius	Jan.	1–Jan. 5	Sagittarius
Jan.	6–Feb. 1	Pisces	Jan.	6–Feb. 13	Capricorn
Feb.	2–Mar. 10	Aries	Feb.	14–Mar. 24	Aquarius
Mar.	11–Apr. 7	Taurus	Mar.	25–May 2	Pisces
Apr.	8–June 4	Aries	May	3–June 10	Aries
June	5–July 7	Taurus	June	11–July 22	Taurus
July	8–Aug. 3	Gemini	July	23–Sep. 7	Gemini
Aug.	4–Aug. 30	Cancer	Sep.	8–Nov. 11	Cancer
Aug.	31–Sep. 24	Leo	Nov.	12–Dec. 26	Leo
Sep.	25–Oct. 18	Virgo	Dec.	27–Dec. 31	Cancer
Oct.	19–Nov. 11	Libra			
Nov.	12–Dec. 5	Scorpio			
Dec.	6–Dec. 29	Sagittarius			
Dec.	30–Dec. 31	Capricorn			

1946

Venus			Mars		
Jan.	1–Jan. 22	Capricorn	Jan.	1–Apr. 22	Cancer
Jan.	23–Feb. 15	Aquarius	Apr.	23–June 19	Leo
Feb.	16–Mar. 11	Pisces	June	20–Aug. 9	Virgo
Mar.	12–Apr. 4	Aries	Aug.	10–Sep. 24	Libra
Apr.	5–Apr. 28	Taurus	Sep.	25–Nov. 6	Scorpio
Apr.	29–May 23	Gemini	Nov.	7–Dec. 16	Sagittarius
May	24–June 17	Cancer	Dec.	17–Dec. 31	Capricorn
June	18–July 13	Leo			
July	14–Aug. 8	Virgo			
Aug.	9–Sep. 6	Libra			
Sep.	7–Oct. 15	Scorpio			
Oct.	16–Nov. 7	Sagittarius			
Nov.	8–Dec. 31	Scorpio			

1947

Venus			Mars		
Jan.	1–Jan. 5	Scorpio	Jan.	1–Jan. 24	Capricorn
Jan.	6–Feb. 5	Sagittarius	Jan.	25–Mar. 4	Aquarius
Feb.	6–Mar. 4	Capricorn	Mar.	5–Apr. 11	Pisces
Mar.	5–Mar. 30	Aquarius	Apr.	12–May 20	Aries
Mar.	31–Apr. 24	Pisces	May	21–June 30	Taurus
Apr.	25–May 19	Aries	July	1–Aug. 13	Gemini
May	20–June 13	Taurus	Aug.	14–Sep. 30	Cancer
June	14–July 8	Gemini	Oct.	1–Nov. 30	Leo
July	9–Aug. 1	Cancer	Dec.	1–Dec. 31	Virgo
Aug.	2 Aug. 25	Leo			
Aug.	26–Sep. 18	Virgo			
Sep.	19–Oct. 13	Libra			
Oct.	14–Nov. 6	Scorpio			
Nov.	7–Nov. 30	Sagittarius			
Dec.	1–Dec. 24	Capricorn			
Dec.	25–Dec. 31	Aquarius			

1948

Venus			Mars		
Jan.	1–Jan. 17	Aquarius	Jan.	1–Feb. 11	Virgo
Jan.	18–Feb. 11	Pisces	Feb.	12–May 18	Leo
Feb.	12–Mar. 7	Aries	May	19–July 16	Virgo
Mar.	8–Apr. 3	Taurus	July	17–Sep. 3	Libra
Apr.	4–May 6	Gemini	Sep.	4–Oct. 16	Scorpio
May	7–June 28	Cancer	Oct.	17–Nov. 26	Sagittarius
June	29–Aug. 2	Gemini	Nov.	27–Dec. 31	Capricorn
Aug.	3–Sep. 8	Cancer			
Sep.	9–Oct. 6	Leo			
Oct.	7–Oct. 31	Virgo			
Nov.	1–Nov. 25	Libra			
Nov.	26–Dec. 19	Scorpio			
Dec.	20–Dec. 31	Sagittarius			

1949

Venus			Mars		
Jan.	1–Jan. 12	Sagittarius	Jan.	1–Jan. 4	Capricorn
Jan.	13–Feb. 5	Capricorn	Jan.	5–Feb. 11	Aquarius
Feb.	6–Mar. 1	Aquarius	Feb.	12–Mar. 21	Pisces
Mar.	2–Mar. 25	Pisces	Mar.	22–Apr. 29	Aries
Mar.	26–Apr. 19	Aries	Apr.	30–June 9	Taurus
Apr.	20–May 13	Taurus	June	10–July 22	Gemini
May	14–June 6	Gemini	July	23–Sep. 6	Cancer
June	7–July 1	Cancer	Sep.	7–Oct. 26	Leo
July	2–July 26	Leo	Oct.	27–Dec. 25	Virgo
July	27–Aug. 20	Virgo	Dec.	26–Dec. 31	Libra
Aug.	21–Sep. 14	Libra			
Sep.	15–Oct. 9	Scorpio			
Oct.	10–Nov. 5	Sagittarius			
Nov.	6–Dec. 5	Capricorn			
Dec.	6–Dec. 31	Aquarius			

1950

Venus			*Mars*		
Jan.	1–Apr. 6	Aquarius	Jan.	1–Mar. 28	Libra
Apr.	7–May 5	Pisces	Mar.	29–June 11	Virgo
May	6–June 1	Aries	June	12–Aug. 10	Libra
June	2–June 26	Taurus	Aug.	11–Sep. 25	Scorpio
June	27–July 22	Gemini	Sep.	26–Nov. 5	Sagittarius
July	23–Aug. 16	Cancer	Nov.	6–Dec. 14	Capricorn
Aug.	17–Sep. 9	Leo	Dec.	15–Dec. 31	Aquarius
Sep.	10–Oct. 3	Virgo			
Oct.	4–Oct. 27	Libra			
Oct.	28–Nov. 20	Scorpio			
Nov.	21–Dec. 14	Sagittarius			
Dec.	15–Dec. 31	Capricorn			

1951

Venus			*Mars*		
Jan.	1–Jan. 6	Capricorn	Jan.	1–Jan. 22	Aquarius
Jan.	7–Jan. 30	Aquarius	Jan.	23–Mar. 1	Pisces
Jan.	31–Feb. 24	Pisces	Mar.	2–Apr. 9	Aries
Feb.	25–Mar. 20	Aries	Apr.	10–May 21	Taurus
Mar.	21–Apr. 14	Taurus	May	22–July 3	Gemini
Apr.	15–May 10	Gemini	July	4–Aug. 17	Cancer
May	11–June 6	Cancer	Aug.	18–Oct. 4	Leo
June	7–July 7	Leo	Oct.	5–Nov. 23	Virgo
July	8–Dec. 7	Libra	Nov.	24–Dec. 31	Libra
Dec.	8–Dec. 31	Scorpio			

1952

Venus			*Mars*	
Jan.	1	Scorpio	Jan. 1–Jan. 19	Libra
Jan.	2–Jan. 26	Sagittarius	Jan. 20–Aug. 26	Scorpio
Jan.	27–Feb. 20	Capricorn	Aug. 27–Oct. 11	Sagittarius
Feb.	21–Mar. 16	Aquarius	Oct. 12–Nov. 20	Capricorn
Mar.	17–Apr. 8	Pisces	Nov. 21–Dec. 29	Aquarius
Apr.	9–May 3	Aries	Dec. 30–Dec. 31	Pisces
May	4–May 28	Taurus		
May	29–June 21	Gemini		
June	22–July 15	Cancer		
July	16–Aug. 8	Leo		
Aug.	9–Sep. 2	Virgo		
Sep.	3–Sep. 26	Libra		
Sep.	27–Oct. 21	Scorpio		
Oct.	22–Nov. 15	Sagittarius		
Nov.	16–Dec. 9	Capricorn		
Dec.	10–Dec. 31	Aquarius		

1953

Venus			*Mars*	
Jan.	1–Jan. 4	Aquarius	Jan. 1–Feb. 7	Pisces
Jan.	5–Feb. 1	Pisces	Feb. 8–Mar. 19	Aries
Feb.	2–Mar. 14	Aries	Mar. 20–Apr. 30	Taurus
Mar.	15–Mar. 30	Taurus	May 1–June 13	Gemini
Mar.	31–June 4	Aries	June 14–July 29	Cancer
June	5–July 6	Taurus	July 30–Sep. 14	Leo
July	7–Aug. 3	Gemini	Sep. 15–Nov. 1	Virgo
Aug.	4–Aug. 29	Cancer	Nov. 2–Dec. 19	Libra
Aug.	30–Sep. 23	Leo	Dec. 20–Dec. 31	Scorpio
Sep.	24–Oct. 18	Virgo		
Oct.	19–Nov. 11	Libra		
Nov.	12–Dec. 5	Scorpio		
Dec.	6–Dec. 29	Sagittarius		
Dec.	30–Dec. 31	Capricorn		

1954

Venus

Jan.	1–Jan. 21	Capricorn
Jan.	22–Feb. 14	Aquarius
Feb.	15–Mar. 10	Pisces
Mar.	11–Apr. 3	Aries
Apr.	4–Apr. 28	Taurus
Apr.	29–May 23	Gemini
May	24–June 17	Cancer
June	18–July 12	Leo
July	13–Aug. 8	Virgo
Aug.	9–Sep. 6	Libra
Sep.	7–Oct. 22	Scorpio
Oct.	23–Oct. 26	Sagittarius
Oct.	27–Dec. 31	Scorpio

Mars

Jan.	1–Feb. 9	Scorpio
Feb.	10–Apr. 12	Sagittarius
Apr.	13–July 2	Capricorn
July	3–Aug. 23	Sagittarius
Aug.	24–Oct. 21	Capricorn
Oct.	22–Dec. 3	Aquarius
Dec.	4–Dec. 31	Pisces

1955

Venus

Jan.	1–Jan. 5	Scorpio
Jan.	6–Feb. 5	Sagittarius
Feb.	6–Mar. 4	Capricorn
Mar.	5–Mar. 29	Aquarius
Mar.	30–Apr. 24	Pisces
Apr.	25–May 19	Aries
May	20–June 12	Taurus
June	13–July 7	Gemini
July	8–July 31	Cancer
Aug.	1–Aug. 25	Leo
Aug.	26–Sep. 18	Virgo
Sep.	19–Oct. 12	Libra
Oct.	13–Nov. 5	Scorpio
Nov.	6–Nov. 29	Sagittarius
Nov.	30–Dec. 23	Capricorn
Dec.	24–Dec. 31	Aquarius

Mars

Jan.	1–Jan. 14	Pisces
Jan.	15–Feb. 25	Aries
Feb.	26–Apr. 10	Taurus
Apr.	11–May 25	Gemini
May	26–July 10	Cancer
July	11–Aug. 26	Leo
Aug.	27–Oct. 12	Virgo
Oct.	13–Nov. 28	Libra
Nov.	29–Dec. 31	Scorpio

1956

Venus			Mars		
Jan.	1–Jan. 17	Aquarius	Jan.	1–Jan. 13	Scorpio
Jan.	18–Feb. 10	Pisces	Jan.	14–Feb. 28	Sagittarius
Feb.	11–Mar. 7	Aries	Feb.	29–Apr. 14	Capricorn
Mar.	8–Apr. 3	Taurus	Apr.	15–June 2	Aquarius
Apr.	4–May 7	Gemini	June	3–Dec. 5	Pisces
May	8–June 22	Cancer	Dec.	6–Dec. 31	Aries
June	23–Aug. 3	Gemini			
Aug.	4–Sep. 7	Cancer			
Sep.	8–Oct. 5	Leo			
Oct.	6–Oct. 31	Virgo			
Nov.	1–Nov. 25	Libra			
Nov.	26–Dec. 19	Scorpio			
Dec.	20–Dec. 31	Sagittarius			

1957

Venus			Mars		
Jan.	1–Jan. 12	Sagittarius	Jan.	1–Jan. 28	Aries
Jan.	13–Feb. 5	Capricorn	Jan.	29–Mar. 17	Taurus
Feb.	6–Mar. 1	Aquarius	Mar.	18–May 4	Gemini
Mar.	2–Mar. 25	Pisces	May	5–June 20	Cancer
Mar.	26–Apr. 18	Aries	June	21–Aug. 7	Leo
Apr.	19–May 12	Taurus	Aug.	8–Sep. 23	Virgo
May	13–June 6	Gemini	Sep.	24–Nov. 8	Libra
June	7–July 1	Cancer	Nov.	9–Dec. 22	Scorpio
July	2–July 25	Leo	Dec.	23–Dec. 31	Sagittarius
July	26–Aug. 19	Virgo			
Aug.	20–Sep. 13	Libra			
Sep.	14–Oct. 9	Scorpio			
Oct.	10–Nov. 5	Sagittarius			
Nov.	6–Dec. 6	Capricorn			
Dec.	7–Dec. 31	Aquarius			

1958

	Venus			*Mars*	
Jan.	1–Apr. 6	Aquarius	Jan.	1–Feb. 3	Sagittarius
Apr.	7–May 4	Pisces	Feb.	4–Mar. 16	Capricorn
May	5–May 31	Aries	Mar.	17–Apr. 26	Aquarius
June	1–June 26	Taurus	Apr.	27–June 6	Pisces
June	27–July 21	Gemini	June	7–July 20	Aries
July	22–Aug. 15	Cancer	July	21–Sep. 20	Taurus
Aug.	16–Sep. 9	Leo	Sep.	21–Oct. 28	Gemini
Sep.	10–Oct. 3	Virgo	Oct.	29–Dec. 31	Taurus
Oct.	4–Oct. 27	Libra			
Oct.	28–Nov. 20	Scorpio			
Nov.	21–Dec. 13	Sagittarius			
Dec.	14–Dec. 31	Capricorn			

1959

	Venus			*Mars*	
Jan.	1–Jan. 6	Capricorn	Jan.	1–Feb. 10	Taurus
Jan.	7–Jan. 30	Aquarius	Feb.	11–Apr. 9	Gemini
Jan.	31–Feb. 24	Pisces	Apr.	10–June 1	Cancer
Feb.	25–Mar. 20	Aries	June	2–July 19	Leo
Mar.	21–Apr. 14	Taurus	July	20–Sep. 5	Virgo
Apr.	15–May 10	Gemini	Sep.	6–Oct. 20	Libra
May	11–June 6	Cancer	Oct.	21–Dec. 3	Scorpio
June	7–July 8	Leo	Dec.	4–Dec. 31	Sagittarius
July	9–Sep. 19	Virgo			
Sep.	20–Sep. 24	Leo			
Sep.	25–Nov. 9	Virgo			
Nov.	10–Dec. 7	Libra			
Dec.	8–Dec. 31	Scorpio			

1960

Venus		Mars	
Jan. 1	Scorpio	Jan. 1–Jan. 13	Sagittarius
Jan. 2–Jan. 26	Sagittarius	Jan. 14–Feb. 22	Capricorn
Jan. 27–Feb. 20	Capricorn	Feb. 23–Apr. 1	Aquarius
Feb. 21–Mar. 15	Aquarius	Apr. 2–May 10	Pisces
Mar. 16–Apr. 8	Pisces	May 11–June 20	Aries
Apr. 9–May 3	Aries	June 21–Aug. 1	Taurus
May 4–May 27	Taurus	Aug. 2–Sep. 20	Gemini
May 28–June 21	Gemini	Sep. 21–Dec. 31	Cancer
June 22–July 15	Cancer		
July 16–Aug. 8	Leo		
Aug. 9–Sep. 2	Virgo		
Sep. 3–Sep. 26	Libra		
Sep. 27–Oct. 21	Scorpio		
Oct. 22–Nov. 15	Sagittarius		
Nov. 16–Dec. 9	Capricorn		
Dec. 10–Dec. 31	Aquarius		

1961

Venus		Mars	
Jan. 1–Jan. 4	Aquarius	Jan. 1–May 5	Cancer
Jan. 5–Feb. 1	Pisces	May 6–June 28	Leo
Feb. 2–June 5	Aries	June 29–Aug. 16	Virgo
June 6–July 6	Taurus	Aug. 17–Oct. 1	Libra
July 7–Aug. 3	Gemini	Oct. 2–Nov. 13	Scorpio
Aug. 4–Aug. 29	Cancer	Nov. 14–Dec. 24	Sagittarius
Aug. 30–Sep. 23	Leo	Dec. 25–Dec. 31	Capricorn
Sep. 24–Oct. 17	Virgo		
Oct. 18–Nov. 10	Libra		
Nov. 11–Dec. 4	Scorpio		
Dec. 5–Dec. 28	Sagittarius		
Dec. 29–Dec. 31	Capricorn		

1962

Venus			*Mars*		
Jan.	1–Jan. 21	Capricorn	Jan.	1–Feb. 1	Capricorn
Jan.	22–Feb. 14	Aquarius	Feb.	2–Mar. 11	Aquarius
Feb.	15–Mar. 10	Pisces	Mar.	12–Apr. 19	Pisces
Mar.	11–Apr. 3	Aries	Apr.	20–May 28	Aries
Apr.	4–Apr. 27	Taurus	May	29–July 8	Taurus
Apr.	28–May 22	Gemini	July	9–Aug. 21	Gemini
May	23–June 16	Cancer	Aug.	22–Oct. 11	Cancer
June	17–July 12	Leo	Oct.	12–Dec. 31	Leo
July	13–Aug. 8	Virgo			
Aug.	9–Sep. 6	Libra			
Sep.	7–Dec. 31	Scorpio			

1963

Venus			*Mars*		
Jan.	1–Jan. 6	Scorpio	Jan.	1–June 2	Leo
Jan.	7–Feb. 5	Sagittarius	June	3–July 26	Virgo
Feb.	6–Mar. 3	Capricorn	July	27–Sep. 11	Libra
Mar.	4–Mar. 29	Aquarius	Sep.	12–Oct. 24	Scorpio
Mar.	30–Apr. 23	Pisces	Oct.	25–Dec. 4	Sagittarius
Apr.	24–May 18	Aries	Dec.	5–Dec. 31	Capricorn
May	19–June 11	Taurus			
June	12–July 6	Gemini			
July	7–July 31	Cancer			
Aug.	1–Aug. 24	Leo			
Aug.	25–Sep. 17	Virgo			
Sep.	18 Oct. 11	Libra			
Oct.	12–Nov. 4	Scorpio			
Nov.	5–Nov. 28	Sagittarius			
Nov.	29–Dec. 23	Capricorn			
Dec.	24–Dec. 31	Aquarius			

1964

Venus

Jan.	1–Jan. 16	Aquarius
Jan.	17–Feb. 9	Pisces
Feb.	10–Mar. 6	Aries
Mar.	7–Apr. 3	Taurus
Apr.	4–May 8	Gemini
May	9–June 16	Cancer
June	17–Aug. 4	Gemini
Aug.	5–Sep. 7	Cancer
Sep.	8–Oct. 4	Leo
Oct.	5–Oct. 30	Virgo
Oct.	31–Nov. 24	Libra
Nov.	25–Dec. 18	Scorpio
Dec.	19–Dec. 31	Sagittarius

Mars

Jan.	1–Jan. 12	Capricorn
Jan.	13–Feb. 19	Aquarius
Feb.	20–Mar. 28	Pisces
Mar.	29–May 6	Aries
May	7–June 16	Taurus
June	17–July 29	Gemini
July	30–Sep. 14	Cancer
Sep.	15–Nov. 5	Leo
Nov.	6–Dec. 31	Virgo

1965

Venus

Jan.	1–Jan. 11	Sagittarius
Jan.	12–Feb. 4	Capricorn
Feb.	5–Feb. 28	Aquarius
Mar.	1–Mar. 24	Pisces
Mar.	25–Apr. 17	Aries
Apr.	18–May 11	Taurus
May	12–June 5	Gemini
June	6–June 30	Cancer
July	1–July 24	Leo
July	25–Aug. 18	Virgo
Aug.	19–Sep. 13	Libra
Sep.	14–Oct. 8	Scorpio
Oct.	9–Nov. 5	Sagittarius
Nov.	6–Dec. 6	Capricorn
Dec.	7–Dec. 31	Aquarius

Mars

Jan.	1–June 28	Virgo
June	29–Aug. 19	Libra
Aug.	20–Oct. 3	Scorpio
Oct.	4–Nov. 13	Sagittarius
Nov.	14–Dec. 22	Capricorn
Dec.	23–Dec. 31	Aquarius

1966

Venus

Jan.	1–Feb. 5	Aquarius
Feb.	6–Feb. 25	Capricorn
Feb.	26–Apr. 6	Aquarius
Apr.	7–May 4	Pisces
May	5–May 31	Aries
June	1–June 25	Taurus
June	26–July 21	Gemini
July	22–Aug. 15	Cancer
Aug.	16–Sep. 8	Leo
Sep.	9–Oct. 2	Virgo
Oct.	3–Oct. 26	Libra
Oct.	27–Nov. 19	Scorpio
Nov.	20–Dec. 13	Sagittarius
Dec.	14–Dec. 31	Capricorn

Mars

Jan.	1–Jan. 29	Aquarius
Jan.	30–Mar. 8	Pisces
Mar.	9–Apr. 17	Aries
Apr.	18–May 28	Taurus
May	29–July 10	Gemini
July	11–Aug. 25	Cancer
Aug.	26–Oct. 12	Leo
Oct.	13–Dec. 3	Virgo
Dec.	4–Dec. 31	Libra

1967

Venus

Jan.	1–Jan. 6	Capricorn
Jan.	7–Jan. 30	Aquarius
Jan.	31–Feb. 23	Pisces
Feb.	24–Mar. 19	Aries
Mar.	20–Apr. 13	Taurus
Apr.	14–May 9	Gemini
May	10–June 6	Cancer
June	7–July 8	Leo
July	9–Sep. 8	Virgo
Sep.	9–Oct. 1	Leo
Oct.	2–Nov. 9	Virgo
Nov.	10–Dec. 6	Libra
Dec.	7–Dec. 31	Scorpio

Mars

Jan.	1–Feb. 11	Libra
Feb.	12–Mar. 30	Scorpio
Mar.	31–July 19	Libra
July	20–Sep. 9	Scorpio
Sep.	10–Oct. 22	Sagittarius
Oct.	23–Dec. 1	Capricorn
Dec.	2–Dec. 31	Aquarius

1968

Venus		Mars	
Jan. 1	Scorpio	Jan. 1–Jan. 8	Aquarius
Jan. 2–Jan. 26	Sagittarius	Jan. 9–Feb. 16	Pisces
Jan. 27–Feb. 19	Capricorn	Feb. 17–Mar. 27	Aries
Feb. 20–Mar. 15	Aquarius	Mar. 28–May 8	Taurus
Mar. 16–Apr. 8	Pisces	May 9–June 20	Gemini
Apr. 9–May 2	Aries	June 21–Aug. 5	Cancer
May 3–May 27	Taurus	Aug. 6–Sep. 21	Leo
May 28–June 20	Gemini	Sep. 22–Nov. 8	Virgo
June 21–July 15	Cancer	Nov. 9–Dec. 29	Libra
July 16–Aug. 8	Leo	Dec. 30–Dec. 31	Scorpio
Aug. 9–Sep. 1	Virgo		
Sep. 2–Sep. 26	Libra		
Sep. 27–Oct. 20	Scorpio		
Oct. 21–Nov. 14	Sagittarius		
Nov. 15–Dec. 9	Capricorn		
Dec. 10–Dec. 31	Aquarius		

1969

Venus		Mars	
Jan. 1–Jan. 3	Aquarius	Jan. 1–Feb. 24	Scorpio
Jan. 4–Feb. 1	Pisces	Feb. 25–Sep. 20	Sagittarius
Feb. 2–June 5	Aries	Sep. 21–Nov. 4	Capricorn
June 6–July 6	Taurus	Nov. 5–Dec. 15	Aquarius
July 7–Aug. 2	Gemini	Dec. 16–Dec. 31	Pisces
Aug. 3–Aug. 28	Cancer		
Aug. 29–Sep. 22	Leo		
Sep. 23–Oct. 17	Virgo		
Oct. 18–Nov. 10	Libra		
Nov. 11–Dec. 4	Scorpio		
Dec. 5–Dec. 27	Sagittarius		
Dec. 28–Dec. 31	Capricorn		

1970

Venus			*Mars*		
Jan.	1–Jan. 20	Capricorn	Jan.	1–Jan. 24	Pisces
Jan.	21–Feb. 13	Aquarius	Jan.	25–Mar. 6	Aries
Feb.	14–Mar. 9	Pisces	Mar.	7–Apr. 18	Taurus
Mar.	10–Apr. 2	Aries	Apr.	19–June 1	Gemini
Apr.	3–Apr. 27	Taurus	June	2–July 17	Cancer
Apr.	28–May 22	Gemini	July	18–Aug. 2	Leo
May	23–June 16	Cancer	Aug.	3–Oct. 19	Virgo
June	17–July 12	Leo	Oct.	20–Dec. 6	Libra
July	13–Aug. 7	Virgo	Dec.	7–Dec. 31	Scorpio
Aug.	8–Sep. 6	Libra			
Sep.	7–Dec. 31	Scorpio			

1971

Venus			*Mars*		
Jan.	1–Jan. 6	Scorpio	Dec.	1–Dec. 22	Scorpio
Jan.	7–Feb. 5	Sagittarius	Dec.	23–Mar. 11	Sagittarius
Feb.	6–Mar. 3	Capricorn	Mar.	12–May 3	Capricorn
Mar.	4–Mar. 29	Aquarius	May	4–Nov. 6	Aquarius
Mar.	30–Apr. 23	Pisces	Nov.	7–Dec. 26	Pisces
Apr.	24–May 18	Aries	Dec.	27–Dec. 31	Aries
May	19–June 11	Taurus			
June	12–July 6	Gemini			
July	7–July 30	Cancer			
July	31–Aug. 24	Leo			
Aug.	25–Sep. 17	Virgo			
Sep.	18–Oct. 11	Libra			
Oct.	12–Nov. 4	Scorpio			
Nov.	5–Nov. 28	Sagittarius			
Nov.	29–Dec. 22	Capricorn			
Dec.	23–Dec. 31	Aquarius			

1972

Venus			Mars		
Jan.	1–Jan. 16	Aquarius	Jan.	1–Feb. 10	Aries
Jan.	17–Feb. 9	Pisces	Feb.	11–Mar. 26	Taurus
Feb.	10–Mar. 6	Aries	Mar.	27–May 12	Gemini
Mar.	7–Apr. 3	Taurus	May	13–June 28	Cancer
Apr.	4–May 10	Gemini	June	29–Aug. 14	Leo
May	11–June 11	Cancer	Aug.	15–Sep. 30	Virgo
June	12–Aug. 5	Gemini	Oct.	1–Nov. 15	Libra
Aug.	6–Sep. 7	Cancer	Nov.	16–Dec. 30	Scorpio
Sep.	8–Oct. 4	Leo	Dec.	31	Sagittarius
Oct.	5–Oct. 30	Virgo			
Oct.	31–Nov. 24	Libra			
Nov.	25–Dec. 18	Scorpio			
Dec.	19–Dec. 31	Sagittarius			

1973

Venus			Mars		
Jan.	1–Jan. 11	Sagittarius	Jan.	1–Feb. 11	Sagittarius
Jan.	12–Feb. 4	Capricorn	Feb.	12–Mar. 26	Capricorn
Feb.	5–Feb. 28	Aquarius	Mar.	27–May 7	Aquarius
Mar.	1–Mar. 24	Pisces	May	8–June 20	Pisces
Mar.	25–Apr. 17	Aries	June	21–Aug. 12	Aries
Apr.	18–May 11	Taurus	Aug.	13–Oct. 29	Taurus
May	12–June 5	Gemini	Oct.	30–Dec. 23	Aries
June	6–June 29	Cancer	Dec.	24–Dec. 31	Taurus
June	30–July 24	Leo			
July	25–Aug. 18	Virgo			
Aug.	19–Sep. 12	Libra			
Sep.	13–Oct. 8	Scorpio			
Oct.	9–Nov. 5	Sagittarius			
Nov.	6–Dec. 7	Capricorn			
Dec.	8–Dec. 31	Aquarius			

1974

Venus			*Mars*		
Jan.	1–Jan. 29	Aquarius	Jan.	1–Feb. 26	Taurus
Jan.	30–Feb. 28	Capricorn	Feb.	27–Apr. 19	Gemini
Mar.	1–Apr. 6	Aquarius	Apr.	20–June 8	Cancer
Apr.	7–May 4	Pisces	June	9–July 27	Leo
May	5–May 30	Aries	July	28–Sep. 12	Virgo
May	31–June 25	Taurus	Sep.	13–Oct. 27	Libra
June	26–July 20	Gemini	Oct.	28–Dec. 10	Scorpio
July	21–Aug. 14	Cancer	Dec.	11–Dec. 31	Sagittarius
Aug.	15–Sep. 7	Leo			
Sep.	8–Oct. 2	Virgo			
Oct.	3–Oct. 26	Libra			
Oct.	27–Nov. 18	Scorpio			
Nov.	19–Dec. 12	Sagittarius			
Dec.	13–Dec. 31	Capricorn			

1975

Venus			*Mars*		
Jan.	1–Jan. 5	Capricorn	Jan.	1–Jan. 21	Sagittarius
Jan.	6–Jan. 29	Aquarius	Jan.	22–Mar. 2	Capricorn
Jan.	30–Feb. 22	Pisces	Mar.	3–Apr. 11	Aquarius
Feb.	23–Mar. 19	Aries	Apr.	12–May 20	Pisces
Mar.	20–Apr. 13	Taurus	May	21–June 30	Aries
Apr.	14–May 9	Gemini	July	1–Aug. 14	Taurus
May	10–June 5	Cancer	Aug.	15–Oct. 16	Gemini
June	6–July 8	Leo	Oct.	17–Nov. 25	Cancer
July	9–Sep. 2	Virgo	Nov.	26–Dec. 31	Gemini
Sep.	3–Oct. 3	Leo			
Oct.	4–Nov. 9	Virgo			
Nov.	10–Dec. 6	Libra			
Dec.	7–Dec. 31	Scorpio			

1976

Venus

Jan.	1	Scorpio
Jan.	2–Jan. 25	Sagittarius
Jan.	26–Feb. 19	Capricorn
Feb.	20–Mar. 14	Aquarius
Mar.	15–Apr. 7	Pisces
Apr.	8–May 2	Aries
May	3–June 20	Gemini
June	21–July 14	Cancer
July	15–Aug. 7	Leo
Aug.	8–Sep. 1	Virgo
Sep.	2–Sep. 25	Libra
Sep.	26–Oct. 20	Scorpio
Oct.	21–Nov. 13	Sagittarius
Nov.	14–Dec. 9	Capricorn
Dec.	10–Dec. 31	Aquarius

Mars

Jan.	1–Mar. 18	Gemini
Mar.	19–May 15	Cancer
May	16–July 6	Leo
July	7–Aug. 23	Virgo
Aug.	24–Oct. 8	Libra
Oct.	9–Nov. 20	Scorpio
Nov.	21–Dec. 31	Sagittarius

1977

Venus

Jan.	1–Jan. 4	Aquarius
Jan.	5–Feb. 1	Pisces
Feb.	2–June 5	Aries
June	6–July 6	Taurus
July	7–Aug. 2	Gemini
Aug.	3–Aug. 28	Cancer
Aug.	29–Sep. 22	Leo
Sep.	23–Oct. 16	Virgo
Oct.	17–Nov. 9	Libra
Nov.	10–Dec. 3	Scorpio
Dec.	4–Dec. 27	Sagittarius
Dec.	28–Dec. 31	Capricorn

Mars

Jan.	1–Feb. 8	Capricorn
Feb.	9–Mar. 19	Aquarius
Mar.	20–Apr. 27	Pisces
Apr.	28–June 5	Aries
June	6–July 17	Taurus
July	18–Aug. 31	Gemini
Sep.	1–Oct. 26	Cancer
Oct.	27–Dec. 31	Leo

1978

Venus			Mars		
Jan.	1–Jan. 20	Capricorn	Jan.	1–Jan. 25	Leo
Jan.	21–Feb. 13	Aquarius	Jan.	26–Apr. 10	Cancer
Feb.	14–Mar. 9	Pisces	Apr.	11–June 13	Leo
Mar.	10–Apr. 2	Aries	June	14–Aug. 3	Virgo
Apr.	3–Apr. 26	Taurus	Aug.	4–Sep. 19	Libra
Apr.	27–May 21	Gemini	Sep.	20–Nov. 1	Scorpio
May	22–June 15	Cancer	Nov.	2–Dec. 12	Sagittarius
June	16–July 11	Leo	Dec.	13–Dec. 31	Capricorn
July	12–Aug. 7	Virgo			
Aug.	8–Sep. 6	Libra			
Sep.	7–Dec. 31	Scorpio			

1979

Venus			Mars		
Jan.	1–Jan. 6	Scorpio	Jan.	1–Jan. 20	Capricorn
Jan.	7–Feb. 4	Sagittarius	Jan.	21–Feb. 27	Aquarius
Feb.	5–Mar. 3	Capricorn	Feb.	28–Apr. 6	Pisces
Mar.	4–Mar. 28	Aquarius	Apr.	7–May 15	Aries
Mar.	29–Apr. 22	Pisces	May	16–June 25	Taurus
Apr.	23–May 17	Aries	June	26–Aug. 8	Gemini
May	18–June 11	Taurus	Aug.	9–Sep. 24	Cancer
June	12–July 5	Gemini	Sep.	25–Nov. 19	Leo
July	6–July 30	Cancer	Nov.	20–Dec. 31	Virgo
July	31–Aug. 23	Leo			
Aug.	24–Sep. 16	Virgo			
Sep.	17–Oct. 10	Libra			
Oct.	11–Nov. 3	Scorpio			
Nov.	4–Nov. 28	Sagittarius			
Nov.	29–Dec. 22	Capricorn			
Dec.	23–Dec. 31	Aquarius			

1980

Venus			Mars		
Jan.	1–Jan. 15	Aquarius	Jan.	1–Mar. 11	Virgo
Jan.	16–Feb. 9	Pisces	Mar.	12–May 3	Leo
Feb.	10–Mar. 6	Aries	May	4–July 10	Virgo
Mar.	7–Apr. 3	Taurus	July	11–Aug. 28	Libra
Apr.	4–May 12	Gemini	Aug.	29–Oct. 11	Scorpio
May	13–June 4	Cancer	Oct.	12–Nov. 21	Sagittarius
June	5–Aug. 6	Gemini	Nov.	22–Dec. 30	Capricorn
Aug.	7–Sep. 7	Cancer	Dec.	31	Aquarius
Sep.	8–Oct. 4	Leo			
Oct.	5–Oct. 29	Virgo			
Oct.	30–Nov. 23	Libra			
Nov.	24–Dec. 17	Scorpio			
Dec.	18–Dec. 31	Sagittarius			

1981

Venus			Mars		
Jan.	1–Jan. 10	Sagittarius	Jan.	1–Feb. 6	Aquarius
Jan.	11–Feb. 3	Capricorn	Feb.	7–Mar. 16	Pisces
Feb.	4–Feb. 27	Aquarius	Mar.	17–Apr. 24	Aries
Feb.	28–Mar. 23	Pisces	Apr.	25–June 4	Taurus
Mar.	24–Apr. 16	Aries	June	5–July 17	Gemini
Apr.	17–May 11	Taurus	July	18–Sep. 1	Cancer
May	12–June 4	Gemini	Sep.	2–Oct. 20	Leo
June	4–June 29	Cancer	Oct.	21–Dec. 15	Virgo
June	30–July 24	Leo	Dec.	16–Dec. 31	Libra
July	25–Aug. 18	Virgo			
Aug.	19–Sep. 12	Libra			
Sep.	13–Oct. 8	Scorpio			
Oct.	9–Nov. 5	Sagittarius			
Nov.	6–Dec. 8	Capricorn			
Dec.	9–Dec. 31	Aquarius			

1982

Venus		Mars	
Jan. 1–Jan. 22	Aquarius	Jan. 1–Aug. 2	Libra
Jan. 23–Mar. 1	Capricorn	Aug. 3–Sep. 19	Scorpio
Mar. 2–Apr. 6	Aquarius	Sep. 20–Oct. 31	Sagittarius
Apr. 7–May 4	Pisces	Nov. 1–Dec. 9	Capricorn
May 5–May 30	Aries	Dec. 10–Dec. 31	Aquarius
May 30–June 25	Taurus		
June 26–July 20	Gemini		
July 21–Aug. 13	Cancer		
Aug. 14–Sep. 7	Leo		
Sep. 8–Oct. 1	Virgo		
Oct. 2–Oct. 25	Libra		
Oct. 26–Nov. 18	Scorpio		
Nov. 19–Dec. 12	Sagittarius		
Dec. 13–Dec. 31	Capricorn		

1983

Venus		Mars	
Jan. 1–Jan. 5	Capricorn	Jan. 1–Jan. 17	Aquarius
Jan. 6–Jan. 29	Aquarius	Jan. 18–Feb. 24	Pisces
Jan. 30–Feb. 22	Pisces	Feb. 25–Apr. 5	Aries
Feb. 23–Mar. 18	Aries	Apr. 6–May 16	Taurus
Mar. 19–Apr. 12	Taurus	May 17–June 28	Gemini
Apr. 13–May 8	Gemini	June 29–Aug. 13	Cancer
May 9–June 5	Cancer	Aug. 14–Sep. 29	Leo
June 6–July 9	Leo	Sep. 30–Nov. 17	Virgo
July 10–Aug. 27	Virgo	Nov. 18–Dec. 31	Libra
Aug. 28–Oct. 5	Leo		
Oct. 6–Nov. 8	Virgo		
Nov. 9–Dec. 6	Libra		
Dec. 7–Dec. 31	Scorpio		

1984

Venus		Mars	
Jan. 1–Jan. 25	Sagittarius	Jan. 1–Jan. 10	Libra
Jan. 26–Feb. 18	Capricorn	Jan. 11–Aug. 17	Scorpio
Feb. 19–Mar. 14	Aquarius	Aug. 18–Oct. 4	Sagittarius
Mar. 15–Apr. 7	Pisces	Oct. 5–Nov. 15	Capricorn
Apr. 8–May 1	Aries	Nov. 16–Dec. 24	Aquarius
May 2–May 26	Taurus	Dec. 25–Dec. 31	Pisces
May 27–June 19	Gemini		
June 20–July 13	Cancer		
July 14–Aug. 7	Leo		
Aug. 8–Aug. 31	Virgo		
Sep. 1–Sep. 25	Libra		
Sep. 26–Oct. 19	Scorpio		
Oct. 20–Nov. 13	Sagittarius		
Nov. 14–Dec. 8	Capricorn		
Dec. 9–Dec. 31	Aquarius		

1985

Venus		Mars	
Jan. 1–Jan. 3	Aquarius	Jan. 1–Feb. 2	Pisces
Jan. 4–Feb. 1	Pisces	Feb. 3–Mar. 14	Aries
Feb. 2–June 5	Aries	Mar. 15–Apr. 25	Taurus
June 6–July 5	Taurus	Apr. 26–June 8	Gemini
July 6–Aug. 1	Gemini	June 9–July 25	Cancer
Aug. 2–Aug. 27	Cancer	July 26–Sep. 9	Leo
Aug. 28–Sep. 21	Leo	Sep. 10–Oct. 27	Virgo
Sep. 22–Oct. 16	Virgo	Oct. 28–Dec. 14	Libra
Oct. 17–Nov. 9	Libra	Dec. 15–Dec. 31	Scorpio
Nov. 10–Dec. 3	Scorpio		
Dec. 4–Dec. 26	Sagittarius		
Dec. 27–Dec. 31	Capricorn		

1986

Venus			*Mars*		
Jan.	1–Jan. 19	Capricorn	Jan.	1–Feb. 1	Scorpio
Jan.	20–Feb. 12	Aquarius	Feb.	2–Mar. 27	Sagittarius
Feb.	13–Mar. 8	Pisces	Mar.	28–Oct. 8	Capricorn
Mar.	9–Apr. 1	Aries	Oct.	9–Nov. 25	Aquarius
Apr.	2–Apr. 26	Taurus	Nov.	26–Dec. 31	Pisces
Apr.	27–May 21	Gemini			
May	22–June 15	Cancer			
June	16–July 11	Leo			
July	12–Aug. 7	Virgo			
Aug.	8–Sep. 6	Libra			
Sep.	7–Dec. 31	Scorpio			

1987

Venus			*Mars*		
Jan.	1–Jan. 6	Scorpio	Jan.	1–Jan. 8	Pisces
Jan.	7–Feb. 4	Sagittarius	Jan.	9–Feb. 20	Aries
Feb.	5–Mar. 2	Capricorn	Feb.	21–Apr. 5	Taurus
Mar.	3–Mar. 28	Aquarius	Apr.	6–May 20	Gemini
Mar.	29–Apr. 22	Pisces	May	21–July 6	Cancer
Apr.	23–May 16	Aries	July	7–Aug. 22	Leo
May	17–June 10	Taurus	Aug.	23–Oct. 8	Virgo
June	11–July 5	Gemini	Oct.	9–Nov. 23	Libra
July	6–July 29	Cancer	Nov.	24–Dec. 31	Scorpio
July	30–Aug. 23	Leo			
Aug.	24–Sep. 16	Virgo			
Sep.	17–Oct. 10	Libra			
Oct.	11–Nov. 3	Scorpio			
Nov.	4–Nov. 27	Sagittarius			
Nov.	28–Dec. 21	Capricorn			
Dec.	22–Dec. 31	Aquarius			

1988

Venus			Mars		
Jan.	1–Jan. 15	Aquarius	Jan.	1–Jan. 8	Scorpio
Jan.	16–Feb. 9	Pisces	Jan.	9–Feb. 21	Sagittarius
Feb.	10–Mar. 5	Aries	Feb.	22–Apr. 6	Capricorn
Mar.	6–Apr. 3	Taurus	Apr.	7–May 21	Aquarius
Apr.	4–May 17	Gemini	May	22–July 13	Pisces
May	18–May 26	Cancer	July	14–Oct. 23	Aries
May	27–Aug. 6	Gemini	Oct.	24–Nov. 1	Pisces
Aug.	7–Sep. 6	Cancer	Nov.	2–Dec. 31	Aries
Sep.	7–Oct. 4	Leo			
Oct.	5–Oct. 29	Virgo			
Oct.	30–Nov. 23	Libra			
Nov.	24–Dec. 17	Scorpio			
Dec.	18–Dec. 31	Sagittarius			

1989

Venus			Mars		
Jan.	1–Jan. 10	Sagittarius	Jan.	1–Jan. 18	Aries
Jan.	11–Feb. 3	Capricorn	Jan.	19–Mar. 10	Taurus
Feb.	4–Feb. 27	Aquarius	Mar.	11–Apr. 28	Gemini
Feb.	28–Mar. 23	Pisces	Apr.	29–June 16	Cancer
Mar.	24–Apr. 16	Aries	June	17–Aug. 3	Leo
Apr.	17–May 10	Taurus	Aug.	4–Sep. 19	Virgo
May	11–June 4	Gemini	Sep.	20–Nov. 3	Libra
June	5–June 28	Cancer	Nov.	4–Dec. 17	Scorpio
June	29–July 23	Leo	Dec.	18–Dec. 31	Sagittarius
July	24–Aug. 17	Virgo			
Aug.	18–Sep. 12	Libra			
Sep.	13–Oct. 8	Scorpio			
Oct.	9–Nov. 4	Sagittarius			
Nov.	5–Dec. 9	Capricorn			
Dec.	10–Dec. 31	Aquarius			

1990

Venus		
Jan.	1–Jan. 16	Aquarius
Jan.	17–Mar. 3	Capricorn
Mar.	4–Apr. 5	Aquarius
Apr.	6–May 3	Pisces
May	4–May 29	Aries
May	30–June 24	Taurus
June	25–July 19	Gemini
July	20–Aug. 13	Cancer
Aug.	14–Sep. 6	Leo
Sep.	7–Oct. 1	Virgo
Oct.	2–Oct. 24	Libra
Oct.	25–Nov. 17	Scorpio
Nov.	18–Dec. 11	Sagittarius
Dec.	12–Dec. 31	Capricorn

Mars		
Jan.	1–Jan. 29	Sagittarius
Jan.	30–Mar. 11	Capricorn
Mar.	12–Apr. 20	Aquarius
Apr.	21–May 30	Pisces
May	31–July 12	Aries
July	13–Aug. 30	Taurus
Aug.	31–Dec. 13	Gemini
Dec.	14–Dec. 31	Taurus

1991

Venus		
Jan.	1–Jan. 4	Capricorn
Jan.	5–Jan. 28	Aquarius
Jan.	29–Feb. 21	Pisces
Feb.	22–Mar. 18	Aries
Mar.	19–Apr. 12	Taurus
Apr.	13–May 8	Gemini
May	9–June 5	Cancer
June	6–July 10	Leo
July	11–Aug. 21	Virgo
Aug.	22–Oct. 6	Leo
Oct.	7–Nov. 8	Virgo
Nov.	9–Dec. 5	Libra
Dec.	6–Dec. 31	Scorpio

Mars		
Jan.	1–Jan. 20	Taurus
Jan.	21–Apr. 2	Gemini
Apr.	3–May 26	Cancer
May	27–July 15	Leo
July	16–Aug. 31	Virgo
Sep.	1–Oct. 16	Libra
Oct.	17–Nov. 28	Scorpio
Nov.	29–Dec. 31	Sagittarius

1992

Venus			Mars		
Jan.	1–Jan. 24	Sagittarius	Jan.	1–Jan. 8	Sagittarius
Jan.	25–Feb. 18	Capricorn	Jan.	9–Feb. 17	Capricorn
Feb.	19–Mar. 13	Aquarius	Feb.	18–Mar. 27	Aquarius
Mar.	14–Apr. 6	Pisces	Mar.	28–May 5	Pisces
Apr.	7–May 1	Aries	May	6–June 14	Aries
May	2–May 25	Taurus	June	15–July 26	Taurus
May	26–June 18	Gemini	July	27–Sep. 11	Gemini
June	19–July 13	Cancer	Sep.	12–Dec. 31	Cancer
July	14–Aug. 6	Leo			
Aug.	7–Aug. 31	Virgo			
Sep.	1–Sep. 24	Libra			
Sep.	25–Oct. 19	Scorpio			
Oct.	20–Nov. 13	Sagittarius			
Nov.	14–Dec. 8	Capricorn			
Dec.	9–Dec. 31	Aquarius			

1993

Venus			Mars		
Jan.	1–Jan. 3	Aquarius	Jan.	1–Apr. 27	Cancer
Jan.	4–Feb. 2	Pisces	Apr.	28–June 22	Leo
Feb.	3–June 5	Aries	June	23–Aug. 11	Virgo
June	6–July 5	Taurus	Aug.	12–Sep. 26	Libra
July	6–Aug. 1	Gemini	Sep.	27–Nov. 8	Scorpio
Aug.	2–Aug. 27	Cancer	Nov.	9–Dec. 19	Sagittarius
Aug.	28–Sep. 21	Leo	Dec.	20–Dec. 31	Capricorn
Sep.	22–Oct. 15	Virgo			
Oct.	16–Nov. 8	Libra			
Nov.	9–Dec. 2	Scorpio			
Dec.	3–Dec. 26	Sagittarius			
Dec.	27–Dec. 31	Capricorn			

1994

Venus			*Mars*		
Jan.	1–Jan. 19	Capricorn	Jan.	1–Jan. 27	Capricorn
Jan.	20–Feb. 12	Aquarius	Jan.	28–Mar. 6	Aquarius
Feb.	13–Mar. 8	Pisces	Mar.	7–Apr. 14	Pisces
Mar.	9–Apr. 1	Aries	Apr.	15–May 23	Aries
Apr.	2–Apr. 25	Taurus	May	24–July 3	Taurus
Apr.	26–May 20	Gemini	July	4–Aug. 16	Gemini
May	21–June 14	Cancer	Aug.	17–Oct. 4	Cancer
June	15–July 10	Leo	Oct.	5–Dec. 11	Leo
July	11–Aug. 7	Virgo	Dec.	12–Dec. 31	Virgo
Aug.	8–Sep. 7	Libra			
Sep.	8–Dec. 31	Scorpio			

1995

Venus			*Mars*		
Jan.	1–Jan. 6	Scorpio	Jan.	1–Jan. 22	Virgo
Jan.	7–Feb. 4	Sagittarius	Jan.	23–May 25	Leo
Feb.	5–Mar. 2	Capricorn	May	26–July 20	Virgo
Mar.	3–Mar. 27	Aquarius	July	21–Sep. 6	Libra
Mar.	28–Apr. 21	Pisces	Sep.	7–Oct. 20	Scorpio
Apr.	22–May 16	Aries	Oct.	21–Nov. 30	Sagittarius
May	17–June 10	Taurus	Dec.	1–Dec. 31	Capricorn
June	11–July 4	Gemini			
July	5–July 29	Cancer			
July	30–Aug. 22	Leo			
Aug.	23–Sep. 15	Virgo			
Sep.	16–Oct. 9	Libra			
Oct.	10–Nov. 2	Scorpio			
Nov.	3–Nov. 27	Sagittarius			
Nov.	28–Dec. 21	Capricorn			
Dec.	22–Dec. 31	Aquarius			

1996

Venus			*Mars*		
Jan.	1–Jan. 14	Aquarius	Jan.	1–Jan. 7	Capricorn
Jan.	15–Feb. 8	Pisces	Jan.	8–Feb. 14	Aquarius
Feb.	9–Mar. 5	Aries	Feb.	15–Mar. 24	Pisces
Mar.	6–Apr. 3	Taurus	Mar.	25–May 2	Aries
Apr.	4–Aug. 6	Gemini	May	3–June 12	Taurus
Aug.	7–Sep. 6	Cancer	June	13–July 25	Gemini
Sep.	7–Oct. 3	Leo	July	26–Sep. 9	Cancer
Oct.	4–Oct. 28	Virgo	Sep.	10–Oct. 29	Leo
Oct.	29–Nov. 22	Libra	Oct.	30–Dec. 31	Virgo
Nov.	23–Dec. 16	Scorpio			
Dec.	17–Dec. 31	Sagittarius			

1997

Venus			*Mars*		
Jan.	1–Jan. 9	Sagittarius	Jan.	1–Jan. 2	Virgo
Jan.	10–Feb. 2	Capricorn	Jan.	3–Mar. 8	Libra
Feb.	3–Feb. 26	Aquarius	Mar.	9–June 18	Virgo
Feb.	27–Mar. 22	Pisces	June	19–Aug. 13	Libra
Mar.	23–Apr. 15	Aries	Aug.	14–Sep. 28	Scorpio
Apr.	16–May 10	Taurus	Sep.	29–Nov. 8	Sagittarius
May	11–June 3	Gemini	Nov.	9–Dec. 17	Capricorn
June	4–June 28	Cancer	Dec.	18–Dec. 31	Aquarius
June	29–July 23	Leo			
July	24–Aug. 17	Virgo			
Aug.	18–Sep. 11	Libra			
Sep.	12–Oct. 7	Scorpio			
Oct.	8–Nov. 4	Sagittarius			
Nov.	5–Dec. 11	Capricorn			
Dec.	12–Dec. 31	Aquarius			

1998

Venus			*Mars*		
Jan.	1–Jan. 9	Aquarius	Jan.	1–Jan. 24	Aquarius
Jan.	10–Mar. 4	Capricorn	Jan.	25–Mar. 4	Pisces
Mar.	5–Apr. 5	Aquarius	Mar.	5–Apr. 12	Aries
Apr.	6–May 3	Pisces	Apr.	13–May 23	Taurus
May	4–May 29	Aries	May	24–July 5	Gemini
May	30–June 24	Taurus	July	6–Aug. 20	Cancer
June	25–July 19	Gemini	Aug.	21–Oct. 7	Leo
July	20–Aug. 12	Cancer	Oct.	8–Nov. 26	Virgo
Aug.	13–Sep. 6	Leo	Nov.	27–Dec. 31	Libra
Sep.	7–Oct. 24	Virgo			
Oct.	25–Nov. 17	Scorpio			
Nov.	18–Dec. 11	Sagittarius			
Dec.	12–Dec. 31	Capricorn			

1999

Venus			*Mars*		
Jan.	1–Jan. 4	Capricorn	Jan.	1–Jan. 25	Libra
Jan.	5–Jan. 28	Aquarius	Jan.	26–May 5	Scorpio
Jan.	29–Feb. 21	Pisces	May	6–July 4	Libra
Feb.	22–Mar. 17	Aries	July	5–Sep. 2	Scorpio
Mar.	18–Apr. 12	Taurus	Sep.	3–Oct. 16	Sagittarius
Apr.	13–May 8	Gemini	Oct.	17–Nov. 25	Capricorn
May	9–June 5	Cancer	Nov.	26–Dec. 31	Aquarius
June	6–July 12	Leo			
July	13–Aug. 15	Virgo			
Aug.	16–Oct. 7	Leo			
Oct.	8–Nov. 8	Virgo			
Nov.	9–Dec. 5	Libra			
Dec.	6–Dec. 30	Scorpio			
Dec.	31	Sagittarius			

Mars Aries

Mars Aries/Venus Aries

Equal energies meet. The quest of conquest emanating from Mars Aries meets a challenging equal in Venus in Aries. Both exchange roles; neither partner is always the aggressor. Mating may involve spice, a touch of danger, and often a quality of experimentation. There's a creative competition here between the sexes that can motivate both partners on to greater personal achievements, or in less compatible combinations (based on other chart aspects) may leave both rivals for years to come.

Mars and Venus coupled in Aries within a single chart suggests a very passionate and fiery nature. Such people allow no constraints on them, especially regarding their pursuit of romance. This individual would be drawn to a very individualistic, and hopefully a patient mate who could balance his/her penchant for impulsive (even dangerous) behavior. Quite a libido!

Mars Aries/Venus Taurus

Fire and earth can be compatible if earth (Venus Taurus) is willing to play a constant nurturing role to fire. It is the nature of fire (Mars Aries) to constantly seek "new fuel" and in their pursuit of the new, they traverse many miles and many life situations. Venus Taurus is content with home, comfort, family. How can these differences of life-style be reconciled? (Other earth in the chart of the Mars Aries person can help). Venus in Taurus has a very intuitive sense of love and sensual pleasure, this can be a giant magnet to one with the passions of Mars in Aries. The solution then would be for Venus in Taurus to become an irresistible magnet of sensual power, always drawing the volatile Mars in Aries home.

Within a single chart the combination suggests a great deal of physical energy (Mars in Aries) coupled with artistic sensitivities. Here the Mars in Aries can anchor itself to creative projects and find a haven of inner balance. Otherwise, there can be inordinate lust, caught in an ambivalent state—both wanting its independence and its passionate oasis (stability) as well.

Mars Aries/Venus Gemini

Gemini represents curiosity and intellectual pursuits and Aries *is* the sign of the head. This couple can enjoy great debates, literary pursuits, and adventures into consciousness (if both are ready and accessible to mental growth). If not, the passions of Mars Aries can dominate and overwhelm the more airy, less sensual quality of a Venus in Gemini. Basically, with Venus in a divided (the twins) sign, the capacity for fidelity isn't strong, and Mars in Aries will bear no competition. Any major planets in Aries represent a soul that not only wants to be number 1, in fact the person "HAS TO BE NUMBER 1." So unless a great deal of mental stimulation is shared (as in hobbies, travel, educational options together), this is not the best fusion of energy.

In a single chart the combination can represent a mind that can't rest. Such a person ought to be a lover of words and ideas. This person can be successful in communications ventures or in engineering equipment of a communications nature. Much brightness and original thinking is shown.

Mars Aries/Venus Cancer

In as much as Aries is a very masculine archetype and Mars in Aries can indicate something of a super-male ego, Venus, a feminine planet is quite comfortable in the nurturing maternal sign of Cancer. Therefore, while both elements are not traditionally compatible, they are symbolic of ancient archetypes. If the male has Mars in Aries, he may be somewhat of an adventurer, who gets his competitive energies out in the world of business or ideas. His partner, with Venus in Cancer could be content to run a home. Many persons with Venus in Cancer use home skills in professional manners or run businesses out of their homes. If the woman has Mars in Aries, she's likely to work and her mate might then be a house husband (with Venus in Cancer). Fire and water are not easy elements to blend, but there is a good deal of attraction here, largely based on the idea that opposites do attract. Mars Aries will, over time, learn sensitivity from Venus Cancer while Venus Cancer may learn not to take the world's opinions so seriously.

In a single chart the combination represents a deep inward duality. Part of the self longs for independence, adventure and no binding roots. Another part of the self wants home, family, and security. Unless the balance is worked out from within, different partners will be chosen at different intervals in life and something vital will always seem to be missing; turning love into a bloodbath of broken hearts. When the inner vision is cleared, the harmonious partner (reflecting balanced needs) will arrive.

Mars Aries/Venus Leo

This can be a match made in heaven. You wouldn't want the hotel room next to this duo, unless you're a deep sleeper! Passion galore flows from one to the other, revitalizing each. Love and sex can blend well as fire understands fire and both are warm and spontaneous. In fact, the romantic aspect makes each feel so good that the good feelings can spill over into other areas of life and make each more successful as a result of having met. There's healthy alchemy here and little can put out this eternal flame. (Both are a bit vain and strut like peacocks.)

Within a single chart there is a built-in harmony. These persons will know what they want and "go for it." Such persons lack patience, expect the best, but have many creative faculties which will fulfill their desires. This combination favors creative minds that build new, artistic, and dramatic projects.

Mars Aries/Venus Virgo

Linda Goodman suggests that the attraction between Aries/Virgo is based on a kind of innocence which each shares with the other. Venus Virgo can put aside self-interest to help the loved one and Mars in Aries can be very self-centered. In a relationship where one devotes his life to helping the other fulfill her ambitions can work. It is not totally different from the Mars Aries/Venus Cancer concept of old socialized values. Mars in Aries has a huge libido and Venus in Virgo does not. However, Venus in Virgo likes to please others and in the vein of the *I Ching* youthful folly (14), perhaps the Mars in Aries will take pleasure in initiating the Venus Virgo into the art of lovemaking. If both are tolerant of each other, it can work.

In a single chart there is great skill and ability with engineering, matters that involve precision measurement and detail; and a possible attraction to military (or another very regimented) life-style.

Mars Aries/Venus Libra

Venus and Mars are natural counterparts and symbolize a relationship of opposites. When they are in opposite signs, their essential qualities are magnified and each exerts a powerful magnetic pull on the other. This could represent the kind of relationship where a couple meets and each person has a sense of immediate dislike for the other, and yet they can't get each other out of their minds. Eventually, their reserve (felt as fear and dislike originally) melts and they find they can feel like soulmates and blend powerfully together, especially via love and sex.

Mars in Aries has something rough and primitive about itself, while Venus in her own sign, Libra, is a master of charm, diplomacy, art, and sensitivity. Venus in Libra tames the wilds of Mars in Aries and gives him a very comforting outlet for expressing his libido forces.

In a single chart the combination favors physical expression through dance, yoga, t'ai chi, and the martial arts. There's a very powerful combination of muscle power and grace and rhythm. This can also symbolize a person who is diplomatic enough to get their original plans across.

Mars Aries/Venus Scorpio

As human knowledge grows, "new" planets are discovered which represent new vortexes of power and energy. Until 1930, it was thought that Mars ruled both Aries and Scorpio; yet after Pluto's discovery, most astrologers agreed that Pluto was ruler of Scorpio. An ancient bond exists between these signs. Aries is the surge of life force clearly projected at the time of the vernal equinox as spring and the bursting forth of greenery. Scorpio links to autumn where a crimson crescendo rises up in all plant life as a splendid climax prior to a mini-death (winter). In mythology, Pluto was said to have made captive the daughter of the goddess of agriculture. Agriculture (life plan) closed down when this occurred. Eventually Pluto allowed his captive to return to the world, yet he would take her back every year for six months. So when Persephone came to the world, life flourished as spring and summer (Aries) and when Persephone returned to the underworld with Pluto, life "declined" (Scorpio). Both of these signs symbolize major turning points in the natural order of our organic world. Yet Aries wants to surge forward and Scorpio holds power within. Thus between these signs exists a challenging, but compelling relationship. Aries tries to analyze mystery, while Scorpio thrives on the preservation of that intrigue. Both may play sleuth with each other for a while. It's not an easy bond. Each will try to control the other.

In a single chart there is something fated. This person may begin personal projects and be shocked at where they lead. This individual has a very strong sex drive and may be drawn to persons he can mold. Dangerous jobs, hospital work, construction work, or military-related careers are often associated with this position (as could be prostitutes).

Mars Aries/Venus Sagittarius

This is a very positive combination wherein each person has a love of travel and adventure and is likely to pursue these common interests as mutual love and respect develop out of these shared interests. Both positions often favor sports and a love of physical activity and herein can lie a major feature of bonding. Each needs plenty of room to experience his/her own ideals, goals, and sense of freedom, and both should understand and accept this. There will be tremendous honesty between both partners and fidelity, only if chosen, as neither need be too possessive (although usually it's Mars in Aries that is the more possessive). This relationship can imply a long-term bonding with both lives made more colorful by this interaction.

In a single chart this combination shows a very active person. This individual might be a professional in sports, might be an archaeologist, a researcher, an art historian, or someone involved with the airlines or travel-related fields. I would expect excellent physical health here (unless other chart factors imply karmic lessons in that area) and a very active life-style.

Mars Aries/Venus Capricorn

We have elements here that do not harmonize. I believe that all relationships exist for a purpose and teach us something; therefore even when bonds don't traditionally imply an easy love, something of value can always develop if both parties are willing to work toward that goal. Basically, it takes Venus in Capricorn a long time to open up to love and especially to *trust* love. Mars in Aries is an impulsive character and so may not regard Venus Capricorn as responsive to his/her love. If Mars Aries is willing to take on a challenge, something can grow here. Venus Capricorn tends to equate love with the mate's capacity to be successful and provide Venus with the bounties of life's successes. Mars in Aries can be ambitious, especially if he/she loves an earthy mate that grounds him/her. So there are qualities here. Besides, Capricorn (Venus) can be a stick in the mud and can benefit from Aries' youthful vitality and willingness to simply try new things for the pure joy of trying. Mars could stand to gain some patience from this Venus type.

In a single chart there will be a rocky rhythm in life pursuits until the person learns where to direct impulse (new starts) and where and when to hold back and patiently approach a goal. If the individual does harness patience, skill in business and creative work (as well as management related leadership) is shown.

Mars Aries/Venus Aquarius

The less conventional the person with Mars Aries, the better chances of this tie working out. Venus in Aquarius tends to be in love with people, not *a* person. This Venus is quite popular and his/her time will be divided among many social activities. Can the ego of Mars in Aries bear with it? Only if Mars Aries has a very active and fulfilling personal life of his/her own. The more space these two give each other, the better; and when they're together, plan on unusual and exotic activities. Both have enormous curiosity and both want to try just about everything in life. They can be two adventurers, platonic buddies, who occasionally indulge in sex. A tighter bond between these two is bound to be explosive as neither will yield to possessiveness easily. The choice is two free birds not necessarily flying in the same direction.

In a single chart it would describe a person who was a navigator or involved with delicate forms of communication or transportation. This person could exhibit both unconventionality and genius. There's something of a dare devil here and it could represent a person with a "love in every port."

Mars Aries/Venus Pisces

This is a challenging couplet in that Venus in Pisces feels everything and has a capacity for unlimited empathy and Mars in Aries can ride roughshod over others needs and feelings in an attempt to reach his/her goal. Venus Pisces would have to be a saint or martyr to be willing, over the course of a lifetime, to gradually modify and refine the behavior and sensitivity of Mars Aries. Now Venus in Pisces can be a dreamer and a procrastinator and Mars in Aries (kind of like the morning reveille bell going off at a military camp) can trigger Venus Pisces to get moving toward some objective. The teary-eyed sensitivity of Venus Pisces can melt down the tendency for Mars in Aries to have surges of ambitious movement, where a review of effects has never been undertaken. In other words, Venus in Pisces gives Mars in Aries the rudiments of conscience which were never felt this way before. This slows down the natural impetuous tendencies of Mars Aries and may be difficult for Mars to accept. Each might lose their sense of identity into the other and this would by no means be a smooth transition and is not recommended.

In a single chart it can be useful. The person's emotional sensitivities (capacity to empathize with the differing or dilemmas of others) can help them to act (Mars Aries) on behalf of others. This can symbolize a religious leader, a human-rights activist, a special education or physical-fitness teacher, etc. It can also represent a person who escapes the sense of his own errors through drugs or alcohol. But spiritual purification and meditation can be a strong asset—an inborn quality to such a person.

Mars Taurus

Mars Taurus/Venus Aries

An unusual blending of personalities occurs here. Mars is in the sign ruled by Venus, while Venus is in the sign ruled by Mars. Each is a tenant in the house of the opposite. Together, a kind of "mutual reception" occurs allowing each to be somewhat telepathic with the other. There can be role reversals and fate or karma may play a strong role in the meeting of these two persons. Passion can be exquisite precisely because each is reading the other on an unconscious or intuitive level. Mars in Taurus (if a man) can have enormous sexual stamina and Venus in Aries is often spontaneous with her affections and sexuality. These two can have a very dynamic and at times transcendental sexual interchange.

In a single chart the "mutual reception" idea is strong and this individual may become suddenly inspired with ideas that take a long, creative effort to work through. It would favor occupations involving engineering, buildings construction, and also innovative artistic forms such as sculpture. An interesting blend of spontaneity and perseverance exists—interplaying together, or taking turns to affect the individual.

Mars Taurus/Venus Taurus

Ancient astrological texts speak of the blending of Venus and Mars as a cosmic marriage. This is a highly sensual combination and indicates a couple who has a tendency to rely exclusively on the body comforts and material joys of life. Each would be quite possessive of the other, and hopefully their joint income is a good one since they would enjoy jacuzzis and beautiful homes with gardens and lavish furniture. (There are some woodchuck-like Taurus natives who, like Jeremiah Jones, opt for all handmade wood items and the rustic life; but they are a rare breed today!) This couple is likely to meet about food, money (banks), or about real estate matters. If each learns to share their possessions, their thoughts, and feelings it can be a wonderful coupling. However, each has a tendency to think in terms of "mine" not "ours" and that might bring lessons for both.

In a single chart we have an artist. This person can have a melodic singing voice, a developed sense of touch (massage therapist), and a brilliant sense of harmony for sound or color. Interior decorators, persons who have the Midas touch for land and real-estate investments, and sometimes people who love money more than love will have this combination. If the individual heeds the higher call of Venus, ruler of Taurus, they can be a "Rock of Gibraltar" who others turn to for advice, stability, and solace. And let's not forget, they can be brilliant chefs and cooks; their senses are extremely sharp and tasteful.

Mars Taurus/Venus Gemini

Life has many twists and turns and not all of us are destined for smooth bonds of love. This combination will be rocky at best. Mars in Taurus (anything major in Taurus!) wants stability and roots and a good deal of structure in their life. Venus in Gemini wants to try almost anything once, and generally abhors stability and finds it stultifying. How can these two with such opposite needs negotiate a relationship? Sometimes Taurus yearns for the unreachable, the exotic "possession" and Venus in Gemini will seem like a shimmering strand of air, incapable of being possessed. The challenge of Venus Gemini may spur Mars in Taurus' resolve to—with time and patience—conquer the Venus in Gemini. Once conquered, however, you'd either have a very frustrated bull (unable to cope with Gemini's nagging, if he/she is trapped) or a very out-of-element Venus Gemini, trapped and out of touch with his/her own identity. I think the trade-off here is too costly for both—*unless* other chart factors are so scintillatingly promising, that they overpower this challenging elemental interplay.

In a single chart the versatile hands of Venus in Gemini can yield interesting crafts or creative projects if Mars in Taurus keeps the persevering resolve to work on a project until its completion. Because within a single individual there co-exist a very flighty, uncommitted part of the character, coupled with a part that demands results—or else! Patience and attention to creative detail can indicate an individual with a rare command of a particular skill.

Mars Taurus/Venus Cancer

If other factors concur, these two will never "leave the nest" and that's probably the worst that can be said of them! Both love home; family pursuits and endeavors; and eating. By mid-life, their marital harmony will show by corpulent proportions. They both tend toward being conservative and acquisitive of things. They'll need to periodically go through closets and cupboards and learn to let go of yesterday's objects as well as thoughts. Both can nurse resentment and small grudges and possibly, if both agree on where the grudge is directed, they can become a small mutual admiration society which shuts the world out. Just as easily, this couple could learn to extend their love and harmony and take in a foster child or two. Their home is likely to be stable and caring.

In a single chart the individual ought to go into home repair, real estate, sales of home products, architecture (if Libra figures prominently through other planetary positions), or floristry and plant sales. This person will be much affected by early environmental conditions and personal moods and attitudes will be highly affected by the type of home and family situations he/she is able to build in adult life. This can indicate a very down-to-earth person who wants the "American Dream."

Mars Taurus/Venus Leo

While both are equal to the other in passion, their basic needs and method of personal expression are vastly different. Mars in Taurus carries a great deal of sexual power which usually gets partially sublimated into long-term projects of a professional nature. Mars in Taurus desperately wants the luxuries and "good things of life." So does Venus in Leo and therein lies part of their possible attraction to each other. Venus in Leo is a very outgoing, ostentatious person who can enjoy having the romantic favors (or at least flirtations) of several suitors. Mars in Taurus believes that which he/she loves is equivalent to a possession and will abide no rivals! Venus Leo likes to spend money, often on whim and Mars in Taurus saves money for that huge purchase. These two will clash over many things and can have storms which discharge their emotional and mental differences; and then sunny, warm passionate moments of love. It would be rather like a gothic novel and is not recommended for those with weak knees.

In a single chart there is a strong need for money, passion, and pleasure in such a person. They may have some ruthlessness about getting what they want and might twist morals a bit, using people to reach their aims. The chart can indicate a person with a flare for nightclub work, show business, or a touch of glamour. It can also indicate a person who sells luxury products: fancy cars, jewelry, Persian rugs, or other high-premium goods at an inflated profit!

Mars Taurus/Venus Virgo

Here is a combination where both are likely to meet at work, through friends from work, or at a supperclub/bar near their workplace. Both will admire the workaholic tendencies that each has. In fact, a large portion of their attraction to each other is the life they envision from pooling resources and mutual labors toward a common end—a nice home. Generally, Mars in Taurus is more passionate than Venus Virgo; but Taurus has a conservative side and might be secretly grateful that Venus in Virgo is not more seasoned in the art of sexual love! Slowly, their sexual natures can unfold; but unless there are many placements in Leo-Scorpio, these two are more interested in what kind of life they can build together and how they can fulfill personal (or joint) ambitions, rather than what kind of orgasm they achieve in bed.

In a single chart familiarity and persistence are the keywords in such a person. Ever present is the underlying need to clarify and record each and every moment of pleasure. Although slow to get started, once involved in a relationship, this native craves regularity both in partner and performance. This is an excellent placement for someone who would actually derive income from matchmaking or arranging liaisons for others. "Show me" rather than "tell me" is an often recurring theme.

Mars Taurus/Venus Libra

Somewhat akin to what was mentioned earlier (Mars Taurus/Venus Aries) we have a mutual reception here, again. This combination is mixed. In certain ways, Mars Taurus is drawn to the beauty or beauty instincts of Venus in Libra. But Venus in Libra (like Venus Leo) is somewhat vain and really wants to be the center of the party. Mars in Taurus could feel unloved by what to Mars in Taurus seems like the flightiness and lack of commitment on the part of Venus Libra. Venus in Libra will love Mars in Taurus for his/her efforts at pleasing Venus. But Venus in Libra is just as happy to be the center of a newcomer's luncheon, or the beauty queen at the prom. Venus in Libra needs to constantly do things with another in partnership. Since most marital partners spend a third of their time at work, Venus in Libra will seek other forms of partnership elsewhere. She can also shop constantly. The needs of Mars in Taurus are to have a beautiful home and possibly a beautiful life partner; but security comes first and Taurus might misconstrue Libra's attempts at social interaction as a threat to security. This is going to be a rough ride, and Libras want peace.

In a single chart there is a great sense of beauty, which can manifest as one who does interior design, designs clothing, designs jewelry, or one who sings and composes music. This individual ought to be connected with the arts in some form or with products that enhance the senses. A person who is an entertainment director for large corporations might have this planetary signature.

Mars Taurus/Venus Scorpio

This is an unforgettable connection. Even if the two of you were to later split, this would be the relationship you'd pull out of your "X-rated mental video file" and review the gourmet moments of love and passion. Mars Taurus can be very ambitious and channel that awesome libido into work; and Venus in Scorpio loves his/her privacy. Both should give each other space and neither of these two is known for trust, particularly in relationships—both being highly possessive. BUT if both can relinquish the deathly grip each has on the other, they will enjoy years of fulfillment. It's like what Shakespeare said: Don't let the love be "consumed by that which it was nourished by." Too much filet mignon at once renders that delicacy a rather banal occurrence. I think you understand me. The key is to give the other enough space so that your very ample desire for one another wells up and each meeting is volcanic. Too much of a close tie (based on lack of trust and fear of losing the other) will result in burning the whole affair up—before it has had time to root. This can be marvelous; it will test the self-control of each party. (Something rather obsessive, compulsive could exist between you two.)

In a single chart the person would be somewhat of an extremist. If the chart is very off balance, this could represent the type of person that still pursues a loved one, long after the tie is over. It can also indicate someone who can have meaningless sexual encounters and never really experience the wonder of intimacy and loss of ego. Occupationally, this person could be drawn to the military, construction work, demolition work, ecological work, military factory work, or other extreme conditions (i.e., sanitation work).

Mars Taurus/Venus Sagittarius

Each of these individuals has a very clear idea of the kind of life they wish to create. Venus in Sagittarius usually would like to be surrounded by fine art, travel opportunities, and an expanse of natural splendor—hopefully the backyard. Mars in Taurus shares Venus' love of beauty and certainly has the ambitious wherewithal to make it happen. The trouble is, Mars is patient and willing to work for it and Venus more or less expects it to happen as a result of creative visualization or luck. Venus would like to travel in the meanwhile; but Mars in Taurus plugs along on a set and persevering course. They could lose each other in the means (on the way) before they get to the ends (goal). This can be an interesting short-term tie. Both can take time off from work (Mars Taurus, that is) and hike, mountain climb, camp out, or take evening classes in art (a love they both share) at a local university. Mars in Taurus will thoroughly enjoy the sexual abandon and animal-like freedom of Venus Sagittarius' sexual expression. This appears to me to be more an affair, than a marriage; but other ties can strengthen it.

In a single chart the individual could be involved with historical art preservation, museum work, or in the travel industry. Additionally, this person could become an illustrator, sports enthusiast, or even someone involved with the financial accounts of international commercial firms.

Mars Taurus/Venus Capricorn

Two very ambitious souls meet under these astrological rays and hopefully both are sufficiently mature, seasoned by life experience. Their meeting can be a turning point for both. They can love each other in a quiet, deep way. Each will be highly supportive toward the goals and professional strivings of the other. Together they could quite possibly build an empire. Much of their passion is diverted from self and the body, toward (sublimated form) the outer world and climbing toward ambitions. Lovemaking can be slow and involve a slow burn, rather than a passionate explosion. This slow burn can last a very long time. Each needs privacy and each has a self-covenant about personal satisfaction in the outside world. If their professional strivings complement each other, this bonding can work out well.

In a single chart there is a strong emphasis on earth which denotes practicality, a capacity for hard work, and very strong ambitions. This individual would likely work in business, commerce, accounting, or even in government and would strive toward a high position—even if it involved a twenty-year plan!

Mars Taurus/Venus Aquarius

Mars in Taurus tends to be conservative and Venus in Aquarius is anything but! Many with Venus in Aquarius have experimented with bisexuality, dated someone of a different race, or had several relationships at the same time; Mars in Taurus would be very threatened by this unless Mars in Taurus just broke out of a stultifying marriage and was ready to taste the bizarre and put on mock wings and fly (never fitting for an earth sign in the long run). It is bound to be an interesting interaction, and as in alchemy each is bound to change the other somewhat through their interaction. However, in time, both will return to their more set ways. Compromises can endure, but not usually for a lifetime. The need of Mars Taurus is roots and security; the need of Venus in Aquarius is to know all of God's creatures and their bohemian, (unusual) pathways as well. Mars Taurus will explode one day when Venus Aquarius has the living room full of local street people—too many differences for the long term.

In a single chart this person can express unconventional skills and ideas in a way that can impress others. If the Mars Taurus can be harnessed to work hard with the creative inspirational ideas of Venus Aquarius, this individual could produce film, writing, art, and fashion that really is ahead of its time and highly unique. The character has opposing forces of reckless individualism and a need for conformity and security. An interesting life will be produced by such an individual seeking to reconcile his own interior conflicts and contradictions.

Mars Taurus/Venus Pisces

This is a beautiful potential bond. The visionary quality of sensitivity, possessed by one with an exalted Venus enables them to intuit the needs of anyone they care to love. Venus in Pisces is mutable and adaptable, and like water can fit any vessel. This person can adapt to the demands and fixity of one with the sometimes rigid nature endowed by Mars in Taurus. Mars in Taurus, in turn, provides the safe, secure vessel which Venus Pisces requires so that he/she can reenter his own poetic world and bring pearls of inspiration up for skeptical Mars Taurus to see. Mars in Taurus is likely to be successful over time and can eventually put the pool in the backyard, buy the boat, or the condo on the sea which Pisces (on the soul level) continually yearns for. All fish need to return to the sea, sooner or later. They can have a very interesting union. To an outsider, it might seem that Venus Pisces concedes to every urge of Mars Taurus; but Mars, when pleased, builds an empire to fill every whim of Venus Pisces. (Both could eat and drink a bit too much at times.)

In a single chart we see one involved with boat building; or building homes near water. This person will combine the artistic power of Mars Taurus with the visionary, imaginative power of Venus Pisces. It could indicate a therapist who uses dreams to help the client. This can also favor a musician, especially one who works with wind instruments. Such a person could actually model and design wooden musical instruments. Ability with artistic crafts that involve inspiration and patient attention to detail is shown.

Mars Gemini

Mars Gemini/Venus Aries

This couple will be mighty active together. Between Mars in Gemini's eternal, unquenchable curiosity and Venus in Aries' spontaneous brainstorms of adventurous outings, there will be no time to get bored with each other. Both are likely to live mainly through the mind, intellect, and mental pursuits. Likely they will meet while attending classes, seminars, or perhaps while bike riding around the community. Both will strike up conversations easily and have a ready flow of ideas; in fact, they will be drawn to one another through their capacities to articulate effectively.

If there is passion, it will come like bubbles and fly away just as quickly. Unless there is a lot of Taurus, Scorpio or Leo, these two will have a relationship where the great high involves exploring life's ideas and lessons—more than each other. They may have his and her computers or wave as they pass each other on the way to their respective adult-education classes. Each can never get enough "education" and might pursue doctors, head to head.

In a single chart the combination brings mental agility and often is the mark of an idea person: teacher, writer, copy writer, newspaper reporter, or salesperson. There is a need to expose one's self to many terrains of the world and the intellect. This person constantly strives to grow mentally, and would be very restless in anything that is routine.

Mars Gemini/Venus Taurus

While not traditionally compatible, there can be compensating factors between these two. Mars in Gemini is often somewhat of a jack-of-all trades or entrepreneur. Mars Gemini's life hangs in a creative balance of simultaneous activities that keep him/her rushing, like a mad hatter from project to project. Venus Taurus wants a home, food on the table, and a comfortable chair, bed, and bath. If Venus in Taurus likes a mate who scurries about while he/she stays home, all comfy-cozy, it can work. At rare intervals Mars will take time out and move into the exotically sensual world of Venus, just for the sheer mental adventure of it. But if Venus in Taurus grows possessive or wants more of Mars' time, battle will result. The needs of each are vastly different; only strongly compensating factors between Saturn/Venus or Sun/Moon could help offset the inevitable.

In a single chart the Mars Gemini can give manual dexterity while Venus in Taurus gives sensitivity to beauty, color, and artistic composition. This can manifest as a person with artistic or musical aptitudes. Such an individual will learn to balance his/her need for near-constant momentum with moments of velvet relaxation and sensuality.

Mars Gemini/Venus Gemini

What a great deal of mental activity these two would share. In fact, sex is largely a collection of games, fantasies, or mental flights of fancy. Neither is sexual on a physical level; both are infinitely curious and might try anything (I mean anything) once. Together they are really two sets of twins which means they hear each others' conversations in stereo and meanings get lost in the shuffle. They can alternately see each other clearly and then misread. Those two sets of twins can be quite slippery and difficult to define. The combination is challenging. Each sees his reflection through the mirror of the partner and when two reflections (twins) mirror two more reflections, there's a strange complexity to the relationship. While it can be highly confusing at times, each feels so inextricably bound up with the other that it's difficult to break such a tie. Future relationships would seem dull (possibly much more sane) by comparison.

In a single chart the person can be an expert who can speak on many topics. Such a person needs to cultivate a reputation of honesty since each twin can present a different, cogent point of view! Since Gemini rules the hands, manual dexterity runs high here and such an individual might be good with line drawings, carvings, and special skills that involve manual dexterity (cutting diamonds, designing jewelry). Computer work or math is also favored.

Mars Gemini/Venus Cancer

This is going to be a challenging combination. Mars in Gemini loves word games and battles of wit. Venus in Cancer is highly sensitive, sentimental, and easily hurt. The basic nature of Mars Gemini is teasing and banter (good-natured or not) and the basic nature of Cancer is to absorb those barbs and nurse the wounds for a long time. Inherent problems within the nature of each make this a problem. Breaking up alternating with making up could bind this couple for a while, but it has shades of sado-masochism and is not a good steady diet for long-term ties.

In the charts of what might be termed highly evolved individuals, the Mars Gemini over time could bring a touch of the power of the analytic to balance Venus Cancer's emotionalism. And Venus Cancer could hopefully bring some of the water element's empathy to the cool, calculating pattern of Mars Gemini.

In a single chart sensitivity and delicacy move to the head of the class. You are an apt pupil when it comes to learning both the science and art of lovemaking. Communication of one's feelings is a necessity. You can go long periods without lovemaking only to find yourself exploding once a partner and opportunity arises. This often happens because you do not easily express your highly emotional and somewhat vulnerable nature. The danger here is that you may very well destroy the love you seek the most by squeezing it too tightly. Beware lest you become dependent and a slave of love!

Mars Gemini/Venus Leo

This duo will be both dynamic and active. Mars Gemini basically wants to be in the know concerning community events, films, and theatrical productions (anything that is new, really!). Venus in Leo loves to be involved with the local events, particularly those that have an element of glamor or a royal touch of class. So common interests can bring these two together. Mars Gemini would have command of the language and know how to verbally seduce the romantic Venus in Leo. However, while one twin is spinning a irresistible tale of love, the other may be looking on humorously. There's always a bit of a split, when planets are in Gemini. Venus in Leo will put up with Gemini's offbeat humour *if* he is attentive, fills her need to be told flattering things, and doesn't keep her waiting often. Neither is particularly patient and each can be a master of charm. If they take turns taking the spotlight for their various literary and other talents, it could work out.

In a single chart the combination brings a deep skill with language. This person could be a writer, art critic, movie critic, or a novelist. Mars Gemini gives an incessant flow of words and Venus Leo seeks to explore human psychology and the ever-changing kaleidoscope of complex human interactions. Such an individual could also be a lay or professional psychologist and would be an observer of all the "sins that flesh is heir to."

Mars Gemini/Venus Virgo

Each of these individuals is a bit of a perfectionist and because of the square angle between Gemini and Virgo, their petty qualities are going to be intensified by this relationship. Each may have some little neurotic way of doing things that gets on the nerves of the other and both are masters of criticism. If as children, each had a very verbally critical parent, they might find a continuance of that unhealed pattern through this adult-life mate! If each directs his acid wit critically at other things it could possibly be a very intellectually stimulating relationship. Each would force the other to see another side of the coin they weren't willing to look at earlier. Direct the critical tendencies toward professional critical writing, or fixing antiques, restoring old furniture, editing manuscripts, running a domestic home or a rug-cleaning service! Or better yet, an animal groomer!

In a single chart this combination favors some of the trades just mentioned. It can be the mark of a person with a lack of self-respect and a tendency to rely on witty analysis of what's wrong with everything. It probably stems in part from early childhood patterns of socialization. Yet from a karmic perspective, we "choose" (soul, not conscious ego level) our parents and therefore are karmically destined to work through various patterns. Such an individual would probably have a quick metabolism and might want to stay away from cigarettes as the condition of the lungs and respiratory system can be sensitive to many things—including allergies. Once critical thoughts are transcended, health resonates more harmoniously.

Mars Gemini/Venus Libra

Both are good communicators and could meet through social relations, public relations, the legal field, or sales-related endeavors. If not careful, both could become professional social butterflies. Each thoroughly enjoys a new environment filled with new people to converse with. Air can be superficial and after all, is detached. By remaining socially active, and together, neither gets bored with the other and both of these can get bored rather quickly (a quality of air is essential movement and change) like the wind. Each is more mental than physical in nature, though many a soul with Venus Libra has earned his/her charm by playing courtesan in another life. The artistic instincts of lovemaking can be coaxed out of the soul memory to one with Venus Libra. Mars Gemini is often a hobbyist or craftsperson and any lack of talent on the part of Venus in Libra would be quickly and easily compensated by his/her bounty of creative ideas (Then Mars Gemini can build upon those ideas). An interesting blend of outer world activities keep these two together; left at home together, boredom could set in.

In a single chart the combination brings success with diplomatic communications. This favors a diplomat, ambassador, sales representative, product demonstrator. This individual would be an apt communicator, very flexible with words and would carry much charm. If artistically inclined, the combination could be one who makes delicate instruments, clocks, or tools.

Mars Gemini/Venus Scorpio

Venus in Scorpio communicates in the way most Scorpios do, nonverbally. Scorpio is the sign of sexual co-mingling, resulting in the transcendental third party: the alchemical relationship of two blended as one. But Mars Gemini relies on the verbal and is essentially a creature of mind. A brief entanglement could be interesting in that Venus Scorpio seldom has any sexual inhibitions and Mars Gemini is sexually curious. Finally he/she has found a partner who might play games in bed or act out fantasies. But because this is experimental for Mars Gemini, Venus in Scorpio might sense the lack of depth or commitment and feel somewhat betrayed. The natures of each are vastly different and as mentioned earlier, unless very strong Sun-Moon or Venus-Saturn ties exist, the bond is likely to be ephemeral.

In a single chart the combination could represent a person who researches details. It would fit police work, detective work, certain kinds of medical technology, chemistry, pharmaceutical work, and the technical research necessary for major communications and computer systems. This person might be very sexual *and* very detached at the same time. They could alternate between being sensitive and brutally detached, or they could learn to integrate their sexual nature with trusting another person and learning to verbalize their feelings. It takes much personal work to balance this integration of influences.

Mars Gemini/Venus Sagittarius

This is an interesting blend of factors. Gemini and Sagittarius are opposites on the wheel of astrological reference and opposites always bring something to the relationship which the other seems to lack. Together they can have a synergistic wholeness which is profound and emotionally dynamic. Both like to be active and each is likely to give the other plenty of room to grow and do his/her own thing. The key to the success of this relationship is for each to bring their personal freedom to the relationship and learn to be two free birds together! Mars is rather active mentally, and Venus Sagittarius loves physical sports and the great outdoors. If Venus Sagittarius goes with Mars Gemini to his seminar, then perhaps Mars will go with Venus to her favorite picnic spot in the mountains, hiking, and all. Timing sometimes conspires with opposite signs and it may just when Mars has a critical appointment when Venus wants him/

her to take a weekend off and backpack in Colorado. Again, each must give the other space and reserve spaces for creative togetherness. A world of knowledge opens to each as each opens his/her treasure chest of accumulated experiences to the other. Real wholeness is possible here.

In a single chart the combination produces a love of words and literary achievements. There is also great appreciation (often talent in languages, communications, the arts). This individual can be a dynamic debater, salesperson, and a good communicator able to come up with solutions to problems rather quickly. The nature is chameleon-like and able to adapt to a wide variety of environments. This can be a Henry Kissinger, Indiana Jones, or Orville Wright.

Mars Gemini/Venus Capricorn

It is likely that these two would meet at a political convention, top insurance sales convention, or other career event in which they mistake their novel circumstances with grounds for romance. Anything is possible, but in and of itself there is virtually no compatibility in this tie. It could be a very cool and detached arrangement where each has a separate room to work with their notes, computers, and clients. They might create together a better economic base than apart. Yet Venus Capricorn primarily is in love with his/her work and Mars in Gemini is often too detached for the kind of love that demands day-to-day nurturing and commitment. As an arrangement, of sorts, to those of a psychology tepid enough to be satisfied by this, it could work. The mechanics of this workability are not grounds for a great tale of love, however.

In a single chart the makings of a great mechanic exist. There is manual dexterity coupled with a great insight into technically detailed systems. A computer programmer or analyst might well have these planets. This person is going to need to love work and might enjoy hobbies like ham-radio operations or building unique inventions in the backyard! The capacity for love and intimacy might come later in life, but is not strongly inborn as pure passion.

Mars Gemini/Venus Aquarius

Here two free spirits meet and create a relationship which might be open-ended and highly unconventional, but it may well be tailor-made to their own needs. Mars in Gemini is somewhat of a rebel as is Venus Aquarius. Together they will find mutual acceptance of their separate idiosyncrasies and much humor, at that. When understanding fails, each will amuse, entertain, or humor the other into a very accepting friendship which has its moments of sexuality as well. The keynote here is friendship. Aquarians don't necessarily separate sex from friendship and that's what could keep this tie alive. Neither may define it too possessively and each remains vitally open to whatever spontaneous possibilities exist between the two—moment by moment. Both can be very clever and might brainstorm new projects, product lines, or figure out other ways of doing things together. This can be a very interesting bond that lasts for years where both families sound like a chorus: "So when are you getting married?" The secret to the longevity is the fact that neither seeks to possess the other. They trust that what they have will remain, and move through life's vicissitudes just fine.

In a single chart we have a very inventive mind coupled with manual dexterity. This person could be a creator, inventor, or one who designs things that involve mass communications or transportation or that which is yet to come. This person will have a great ability to talk to and make friends with people, but will cut loose from any shackles, prizing freedom and individuality first and foremost. Marriage ought to come in later life, since fidelity is not this individual's strong suit.

Mars Gemini/Venus Pisces

Borrowing from the comments made under Mars Gemini/Venus Cancer this is a tough tie. Venus Pisces is capable of much devotion in love and self-sacrifice and some with this placement too easily slip into the martyr role. Mars Gemini can be cruel in that they don't (unless much water is seen elsewhere in their chart) understand why others feel "hurt" just because they made a critical, but objective statement. Mars Gemini is very good at critical statements and Venus Pisces can feel hurt for a long time. Unless the two individuals *need* to play some pseudo-sadomasochistic vignette where one repeatedly hurts the other, this will be a painful bond. Gemini naturally is in a tense relationship with Pisces. I could see artistic projects between the two on an *impersonal* level. Venus Pisces has a fabulous imagination and can come up with situations which Mars Gemini can sketch into comic form. If each worked at the therapeutic part of the tie and learned to project their conflict onto paper as a comic or as an educational device, there's grounds for hope—but not much.

In a single chart the individual would be a Houdini. Such a person could be a thief, a plagiarist, and an impressionist (like Robin Williams). Until the individual is full of self-respect *and* honest with others, life will reflect a lot of broken engagements and unfulfilled ambitions. Too many branches of the tree are sent out at once and without enough definition, self-discipline, and direction.

Mars Cancer

Mars Cancer/Venus Aries

Mars in Cancer is moody and irritable and quite sensitive. This Mars position is seeking a home that makes for feelings of security so that Mars can let down his/her guard and experience his/her rainbow of emotions. Venus in Aries loves passion and certainly *some* of Mars-Cancer's moods will suit those passions of Venus Aries. But Venus Aries really wants personal independence *and* the independence of the partner, unless this Venus has Capricorn (fathering) elsewhere in the chart. This would be a challenging bond, and one that is bound to be interesting. Mars can learn more about independence and self-reliance from this Venus individual; and the Venus individual would learn more about becoming sensitive to the ever-changing feelings of another human being. Each would struggle for domination in this bond. If Mars Cancer is allowed to be the "boss of the home domain," while Venus in Aries conquers some aspect of the outer world (or his/her own colorful creative potential), it could work—at times.

In a single chart the drive toward personal freedom and independence is in conflict with the need to create secure roots and a supportive home base. Conflict exists *within* this individual about the issue of independence. Learning to trust one's own intuition can allow a kind of biological compass to evolve, guiding this individual toward constructive behaviors and powerfully enhancing life choices.

Mars Cancer/Venus Taurus

This might be one of those matches that relatives say were, "made in heaven." There is much support between individuals who possess this cosmic rapport. Mars in Cancer finds his/her needs for a home-loving mate, who is also a "Rock of Gibraltar" in Venus Taurus. Many with Venus Taurus do work at home or are marvelous with food, home decorating, and stretching the family budget by recycling anything from food to clothing. A very sexual sensitivity evolves between these two who benefit from each other's passions. Mars in Cancer can be very sexual, especially when the calm seductive magnetism of a Venus Taurus hits him/her. This isn't fireworks, but it is grounds for a long-lasting attachment where love grows because of inner compatibility and mutual tolerance, not anything flimsy or surface oriented. Both will probably enjoy cooking and family occasions; they might be advised to entertain friends at home, just to add some new elements to their own nearly perfectly balanced equation!

In a single chart there is a strong aptitude for sales or construction of home or family products. The food or restaurant business is apt to be a strong area of intuitive expertise as well. This individual will have powerful emotions (Mars Cancer) which will be well centered and modulated by the balancing effect of Venus Taurus. Some artistic skill is also likely.

Mars Cancer/Venus Gemini

Because Mars Cancer's quest is for personal and family security, Venus Gemini is not the best choice for providing that. If Venus Gemini has a predominance of Taurus-Cancer influence elsewhere, then perhaps he/she will use the Venus Gemini to do professional writing, editing, or handiwork at home. Otherwise, Venus in Gemini's emotional needs are ever-changing and the moody Mars Cancer will feel threatened and off-center from this. Mars Cancer may spend a good deal of time trying to please and/or capture, the flightiness of Venus Gemini, but to no avail. This could become a marriage of quiet desperation for both as water reaches out to air, only to get occasional bubbles. It's not a strong enough contact for long-term bonding. However, during the time frame of relating, Venus may learn more about *pure* feeling from Mars while Mars begins to learn to analyze and verbalize emotional *needs*.

In a single chart it will be difficult to know what one wants (and is indeed searching for) emotionally. Mars Cancer creates an inner insecurity about home, family, and domestic ties, and Venus Gemini wants to try everything or everyone once! This doesn't make for much stability. Job-wise, the individual can be a jack of all trades or a person who moves uncommitted from one job to another; it would be OK for a rock star!

Mars Cancer/Venus Cancer

This synergistic fusion arouses many emotions and may express *all* of them. To the two persons involved, they may be amazed at how well they ride their emotional whirlwinds next to each other—without either disappearing or falling from the wave! To outsiders, they both appear a little (or a lot) crazy! Each has a great need to express emotion and the emotion, much like the engine on a plane, empowers the movements of these individuals in other areas of their lives. If the man has Mars Cancer he will want to dominate the home which might be harmonious for some women with Venus in Cancer. Venus Cancer is quite feminine and usually is searching for a "macho" man. Both can also work around the home doing jobs that involve food, household, crafts, other goods, or channeling emotions into writing, music, and art. Sexually, there is a tremendous blending as both feel a blending into oneness, each identifying strongly with the water element. Because of the vicissitudes of emotional ups and downs, this relationship will probably never be boring. If both persons have a lot of earth planets as well, theirs may be a long-term match.

In a single chart the combination produces someone who loves home and hearth (and possibly mother) too much. This individual will be quite sensitive to the abrasions of the other world and will prefer working from his own womb-like residence. This individual can channel emotions into work and it can favor a writer, counselor, teacher, guru, or someone interested in food—perhaps marketed from home!

Mars Cancer/Venus Leo

There is an interesting co-mingling here with the Mars in the Moon's sign, ever circling the Sun. With Venus in the Sun's sign, an unusual affinity exists. Mars Cancer may be somewhat of a fan to Venus Leo and Venus Leo can be a real proud peacock when it comes to love! I would expect that Mars Cancer would do a good deal of the housework (or provide funds for a maid or cleaning service) while Venus Leo did some showy work in the world. Mars Cancer has a strong libido and Venus in Leo can be a very tempting creature as he/she prunes himself for the great stage of life. This person wants to look good and feel like a treasure and Mars Cancer will jealously guard his/her treasures. To an outsider, it might seem that one worships the other; in essence, like fire to wood, both need each other. Relatively speaking, they thrive on each other's roles. Mars Cancer can usually provide a very attractive, comfortable home and Venus Leo can thrive on being the hostess with the "mostess." This will be an interesting bond; each more drawn to the role implied by the other, more than the essence of the other, like the moon reflecting the illusion of solar light.

In a single chart the individual might be very artistic and work behind the scenes, but enjoy the limelight of his/her creations when viewed by the public. The Cancer mothering capacity couples up with the Venus Leo love of children and some of the world's better educators (counselors) have this chart significator.

Mars Cancer/Venus Virgo

While it is unlikely to my thinking that Venus Virgo can meet the sexual power surges of Mars Cancer, the relationship has other supportive qualities that can perhaps fill the gaps, so to speak. Venus Virgo will try to please his/her mate and Mars Cancer can be very childish in demands. Mars Cancer is always testing to see how much security he/she has at home and does this by testing his/her authority around the home front. Venus Virgo can put up with everything, except messes and sloppiness. Mars Cancer can learn to put his clothes away; hang up his wet towel, and clean his nails. Virgo *can* respond to cleanliness. Venus Virgo can give Mars Cancer very specific directions for anything from making brownies to passing a successful interview with a Fortune 500 company. Mars Cancer can use a little direction; feeling that something in the way of mothering was missing and is an eternal gap in his/her make-up. This can appear as a mother-son or father-daughter relationship to onlookers.

In a single chart there is good skill in handiwork and attention to detail. The detail work would favor marketing, market research, products from home and family, construction work, real estate, and pharmaceutical product sales.

Mars Cancer/Venus Libra

There will be some scintillating sexual attraction between these two, as sometimes very unfamiliar substances have a magnetic pull to each other's exotic compositions. Each may try to figure the other out. Mars Cancer loves anything or anyone who is beautiful; and many with Venus Libra have refined beauty and culture (as well as manners) to an art! Mars Cancer will want to possess Venus Libra. Now some Mars Cancer types are super-achievers who can give Venus Libra the good life he/she desires. But Venus Libra does want more than romance, having seen evidence to her power to choose in much the same way Scarlet O'Hara did in *Gone with the Wind.* Venus Libra likes harmony and wants life to flow, more or less, on an even keel. Mars Cancer has tantrums; and mood swings and Venus Libra (remember it is air and borrows from air a definite detachment) really doesn't want to be bothered with smoothing out someone else's emotional problems. Perhaps in the beginning, if love seems fresh and promising, Venus Libra will play "social worker" to this Mars. But on a long-term basis, this tie will be tenuous.

In a single chart there is the need for a stable partnership. The individual may not work through his/her own complex emotional contradictions and will instead seek a partner who he/she can project on. This person wants the partner to be their savior and will tend to create unstable partnerships until they take personal responsibility for who they are and what they are creating. There is a lot of artistic sensitivity and may reveal musical leanings. The individual will also enjoy the catering business, nightclub work, bar tending, etc.

Mars Cancer/Venus Scorpio

This is a compelling and almost sexually intoxicating position. Very possibly, neither has had so deep a sexual involvement as that which this relationship brings to both. Water recognizes itself (both are water signs) at highly instinctive and telepathic levels and blending of a transcendental type may occur. Each will be a bit compulsive about possessing the other (unless each is older on the level of soul maturity). There is immense fertility here and this can indicate potential for a large family. Both can be dedicated to the family ideal. Each loves mystery and intrigue and both can create it spontaneously for the other's enjoyment and arousal as a byproduct of what each brings to the other. If other chart factors show that they also *like* each other, added to this deeply unifying love tie, they can have a long-lasting marriage. If there is a break-up, both carry the scars from this one until spiritual forgiveness and healing is practiced.

In a single chart the individual has a great insight into human nature and also has strong sexual magnetism. Even if not conventionally attractive, this person will always have a choice of love-sex partners. Such an individual would be wise in matters of scientific research, occult research, working with hypnosis to remedy other's negative habits, or working in high psychology.

Mars Cancer/Venus Sagittarius

It would be hard for me to imagine what would draw these two together in the first place? Venus Sagittarius loves nature, fitness, freedom, and the great outdoors; while Mars Cancer loves home, possessing each other in relationship, and leisurely pursuits. What would give them grounds for a relationship? If Mars Cancer has a huge country home where Venus Sagittarius could take long morning walks, and work out outside . . . maybe it could work. If Venus Sagittarius studied art or literature by home study, maybe the possessive needs of Mars Cancer would be sated. But the needs of each of these individuals is so vastly different that sooner or later each would complain about the compromises. Water (Mars Cancer) should not be allowed to put out Fire (Venus Sagittarius). There are some things simply unethical in love. Neither should compromise their nature to the point of exhaustion or extinction. This bond could ask for just that.

In a single chart Mars needs to have home and security is in conflict with the Venus need to set out on pilgrimages to see the world. Perhaps this individual would spend time at home, meditating, and then gather strength to set sail and see the world. This individual could be a historian or "set sail" into his/her own interior realms and bring forth some great material for writing or philosophy. Such a person might also become a gourmet cook of exotic foods or design homes of unusual (international themes) architecture.

Mars Cancer/Venus Capricorn

There's always an attraction between opposites because each ideally yearns for an inner sense of completion and feels that the other might provide this (this is not a conscious process, but something sensed from within). Mars Cancer really wants to feel secure in a home or family situation and Venus Capricorn is a natural boss, commander, or advisor. Venus Capricorn can be a bit cold-blooded as Venus, in Saturn's sign, tests love until it finally accedes to it. Mars Cancer is a more trusting sort, who blindly follows his/her emotions and rides the waves of life in the process. Mars brings rain to Venus' dry sign, and rain means "feelings." In return, Venus Capricorn brings a measure of order, discipline, and ambition to Mars' sometimes too emotional whirlwind world. Over time, each one's rhythms will fall in sync with the other. Mars Cancer wants assurance and love *now;* Venus Capricorn says "wait." This is a relationship which reminds me of wine, it needs time to mature and gets better with age.

In a single chart the individual may have a "mother complex" or "father complex." This individual might repeatedly date persons who are a lot younger or older than him/herself. Career-wise, the person can have skills such as carpentry, which require feelings and patience coupled together. This individual might like to live far from the maddening crowd in a quiet rural setting.

Mars Cancer/Venus Aquarius

Although this is a very challenging interplay of astrological factors, I must say that from 1949–1956 the planet Uranus, ruler of Aquarius, passed through the sign of Cancer and has had a big influence on Cancers (or Mars Cancer individuals) born in those years. To the reader with Mars Cancer born from 1949–1956 you will be attracted to Venus Aquarius because both of you are exploring new family relationships as part of the Aquarian Age of revolution of values that is currently taking place. This relationship will be highly off-beat. You could live together in a commune, have a child out of wedlock, or otherwise take variations on the theme of "nuclear family." In persons not born in those years, the relationship will be too rocky for your "dietary" needs. As mentioned previously, Mars Cancer wants a secure home and the secure knowledge that what is his at home, is his (or hers). Venus Aquarius loves the world and easily mixes with platonic associations. Venus Aquarius has difficulty differentiating between the purely platonic and the much-more-so which will only inspire the wrath of Mars Cancer . . . which is rated "high wrath" in anybody's book! The needs of this duo are vastly different. As an in-college "affair," it could prove both passionate and fascinating. It's quite off-key for marriage, however.

In a single chart the person is going to have incredible mood swings which will yield very impulsive behavior. Part of the individual wants home, family, and security, while another part wants to impulsively explore the dating field; and "what's out there." The individual can run from one relationship to another or confuse him/herself as to what he/she really wants. This favors getting involved with New Age meditation groups and possibly going into careers with holistic healing or health food sales.

Mars Cancer/Venus Pisces

This bond represents a mystical meeting of near soulmates. Each brings quiet magnetism and inner knowledge to the other resulting in an indisputable feeling of *oneness*. Possibly, they eat, drink, and use drugs too much and water signs (propensity to addictions, since water has no shape of its own) need to stay away from addictive substances. Venus Pisces can read into the thoughts and feelings of anyone and Mars Cancer will be so gratified that another person can read his/her complicated feelings. Very little verbal communication is necessary to these two who walk, move, and make love in a silent cocoon of easy oneness. This combination is very fertile and hopefully the female will take precautions so that a child does not come in before the young couple is ready for that added dimension to their relationship. Should other factors give stability (i.e., earth signs), this can represent a long-term bond. Each can be the "spiritual ally" to the other.

In a single chart there is fantasy, imagination, inspiration, poetry, sensitivity, and musical aptitude. Such an individual could be involved in psychic work, animation, art, music, New Age therapies, foot reflexology, and New Age food preparation. The individual would be extremely psychic and compassionate.

Mars Leo

Mars Leo/Venus Aries

The benevolent, and at times volatile Mars Leo will find an independent, equally fiery mate in Venus Aries. These two can go places together and enjoy the relative light of each other's presence. Both will at times dominate and each will learn to take turns with center stage. Each is a very proud type person, and they will learn to use passion to smooth over the minor injuries of hurt pride that erupt from time to time as each seeks to be leader or "the chosen one." In the vein of a mutual admiration society, these two will enjoy each other's company. It's likely that when they meet, each will be striving toward some personal objective. The success of the relationship lies in each one learning to support the other's life quest. There is a lot of passion inborn in each of these fiery persons and they may at times project that creative flame toward creative works; whereas it may become the center of joyous sexual interchange at other times. Neither will be very good at ordering the other about and respecting each other's liberties would be another prerequisite to the continuation of this tie.

In a single chart the combination brings a measure of strength and athleticism to showmanship and could easily be the mark of a professional sports figure, a theatrical celebrity, or a politician. This individual will strive toward showmanship or leadership in some way. They are apt to nurse wounded pride should their great love be rejected.

Mars Leo/Venus Taurus

Mars Leo, possessing a fair measure of "Divine Right of King" mentality believes that what is loved in a sense, is owned. Venus Taurus is also very possessive so this entanglement will be an interesting tug-of-war which might be titled, "Who Owns Who?" Additionally, both Mars Leo and Venus Taurus are sexually powerful and will meet a compatible bedmate in this union. Traditionally, squares (90 degree angles between planets) are considered difficult in chart comparison, but squares bring the kind of abrasion, which keeps the passionate embers burning. Mars Leo is very proud about his/her sexual performance and Venus Taurus essentially feels "the more the merrier," and so may develop the knack for egging on greater and greater "performances" from Mars Leo. In fact, the most compatible thing about this relationship may be its horizontal (rather than vertical) moments! If other planets present harmonious ties, this relationship could be more than a very passionate, sexual love affair.

In a single chart there will be a very sensuous, pleasure-loving nature that can render the individual a romantic, constantly seeking love *or* a pleasure-addict. This individual will want the best in life and if his/her own creative efforts don't warrant receipt of "the best," then love partners may be used as means to ends of financial (and other) gratification. There may be an aptitude for modeling, show business, burlesque, and even prostitution, or organized crime! (Something of the bully can appear.)

Mars Leo/Venus Gemini

The Mars in Leo individual will be tantalized by the game-playing and imagination of the person with Venus Gemini. If Mars in Leo is secure, this tie can work out. Mars in Leo has to understand that his/her passions run a lot deeper than do those of Venus Gemini who may appear to be "playing at" (rather than directly experiencing) the experience of love. Both can be youthful together and humor may provide for fillers where deep passion is absent. Mars Leo will undoubtedly be the aggressor and may enjoy constantly needing to pursue and conquer Venus in Gemini, again and again, simply because with Venus in Gemini, there is no real constancy and commitment in love. Of course, the proud Mars Leo could also get rather bored with the game of constant and repetitive captivation . . . and simply move on to a partner with more constancy and personal magnetism. Venus in Gemini is not above using flattery to con the Mars Leo out of his/her generous favors, either. If Mars Leo feels used, that will injure the trust of this relationship for a long time.

In a single chart the individual would be a master spokesperson, charismatic speaker, salesperson, advertising agent, writer, teacher, or "born" communicator. They would have to train their fidelity, since there would be a tendency for many romantic conquests and a fear of one.

Mars Leo/Venus Cancer

Again, Leo relates to the Sun and Cancer to the Moon so when planets occupy their respective signs, there is a powerful joining effect. The Moon and the Sun are cosmically bound, eternally. Mars Leo will feel that Venus Cancer is his/her counterpart. This works better (due to socialized sex roles) when Venus is the female partner and Mars the male. But Mars will be able to show strength and power to this very feminine and receptive Venus Cancer. When roles are reversed, the woman will tend to overpower the man. If he wants to be a "house husband" and she likes the ambitious outer world field, it could be an extraordinarily symbiotic tie.

Mars moves to a masculine, aggressive "Yang beat" while Venus receives in the most feminine Yin way. The complimentariness here can bring a very binding and mutually supportive relationship. Venus Cancer can create a beautifully harmonious home, while Mars in Leo uses personal bravado to fulfill career ambitions that put steak or tofu (whichever) on the table! This can be a bond of lifelong helpmates.

In a single chart there will be moments of aggressive pushiness in an attempt to meet external goals; and at other times, the most disarming of warmth and generosity displayed. Male and female qualities abound and like a kaleidoscope, often manifest in new patterns. The best occupations might be working with the public in nurturing fields where the individual plays a maternal or paternal role. Leadership, management, theater, and other creative pursuits also are suggested.

Mars Leo/Venus Leo

These two show-offs are very concerned with how they play their parts on the "world stage." Probably attracted to each other's image or reputation, or status, they may be compliments to each other's images more than souls—unless each has done some soul-searching and hard work of his/her own. Both want the good things in life and both have a tendency to "pay homage" to others. Leo carries an unconscious "Divine Right of Kings" attitude; that is, Leos of either sex! Together, they form a mutual admiration society. Both require a lot of praise and flattery and it might appear phony when each one reciprocates a compliment to the other, to the observation of onlookers. Fire signs want everything quickly and this combination has to be careful not to consume the love "by that which it was nourished by" too quickly. They might both be in the entertainment field, one way or another, anyhow. The relationship is volatile; there's a lot of narcissism and each relates to the other on the basis of this narcissism.

In a single chart this is a born entertainer. This individual wants a great deal of attention and may be a creative artist and *will* be a performer . . . even if the performance involves working in a beauty salon with hair styling! There is bound to be something ostentatious about this person. They can also be very generous to those select few on whom they bestow the royal rites of attention.

Mars Leo/Venus Virgo

Mars in Leo will do anything for whomever he/she loves, if it doesn't interfere with his or her other demands. Venus Virgo sees love as an extension of serving the needs of another and has no problem with self-sacrifice and devotion (most of the time). In this arrangement, Venus Virgo may play servant to the fickle whims of Mars Leo's tendency to play king or queen. Each of us in the world has his/her own peculiar psychology and it's possible that such a master-servant relationship can be adequate for some. Mars in Leo will bring to Venus Virgo a measure of warmth and passion otherwise unknown to Venus Virgo and perhaps that is the "trade-off." Mars Leo can have very creative ideas and Venus Virgo may have the patience and attention for detail to carry these out so that mutual artistic projects may flourish between the two. I said "may." Generally, methinks this is not the ultimate love for either.

In a single chart the individual may have a rare ability to combine deep animal magnetism with a soft, kind, devotional attention to the object of his/her affections. Creatively speaking, the vast inspiration given to fiery Mars Leo can find technical form and expression through Venus Virgo. This could be the chart of an amazing artisan-craftsman, a master educator, a salesperson of technical materials, or an administrator.

Mars Leo/Venus Libra

This combination is an interesting one that merits harmony. Mars Leo likes to be seen with the jet set or beautiful people and so does Venus in Libra. Mars Leo impresses with tales of bravado and Venus Libra just has to be there, be beautiful (which has been a gift to many with Venus in her own natural sign, Libra). Socially, they are a splendid match and frequently an impressive-*looking* couple. They both want ceaseless flattery, however, and unless each is willing to handle the ego needs of the other, both are apt to seek followers or fans elsewhere. Both of these individuals have powerful, creative or artistic urges in addition to vast social needs. In all probability, they would have met at an art show, theatrical event, big party or other social-artistic occasion. They can learn to team up and pool their creative drives and ambitions. Both really want similar things in life and each has many good raw materials to allow this relationship to grow and flourish. The central snag is the maturity of each individual, soul-wise. Both have to learn to be equals and enjoy some humility, not just ego reinforcement.

In a single chart there is a natural capacity for showmanship, playing the role of master of ceremonies, party planner, talent agency owner, model, actor, singer, or sales representative for a big company that entitles him/her to a big expense account (I mean BIG!).

Mars Leo/Venus Scorpio

There are no shades of gray within this dynamic union. Each will unconsciously compete with the other to see who feels more, and who sexually overcomes the other. Venus in Scorpio will not be passive with Mars Leo. Both will feel an enormously strong magnetism, one to the other and sex roles will be extraneous. Each is possessive with perhaps Venus Scorpio more so. This could almost be a relationship of sex slaves, and each will even outdo themselves in trying to create a sexual hold on the partner. In a bond such as this, it would be difficult to separate love from sex because the very nature of the bond is mindless passion. Both individuals *might* have little in common, but they will find themselves irresistibly drawn together. The square aspect between these two very sexual placements makes it difficult for these individuals to ignore each other. An apt scene comes to mind from "The Night Porter," wherein a Nazi officer and a beautiful concentration camp inmate have an affair. Likely, this Venus/Mars was the cross-over aspect of their connection.

Should this relationship end for other reasons (like the need for people to get out of bed and go to work); each will take a long time in mending the wounds left from the depth of passion that gave each, at times, a very deep and binding sense of oneness.

In a singular chart the person will be ruled by passion—unless a lot of practical earth signs dominate elsewhere. This individual will use his/her sexuality, even subtly, in whatever career they take on. The aspect fits someone involved in body contact sports such as wrestling; it can fit a sex counselor; a nightclub owner; a paid call-girl or an "American gigolo."

Mars Leo/Venus Sagittarius

This somewhat playful combination allows for the Mars Leo to feel older and very benevolent while the Venus Sagittarius plays uncommitted and allows the best chase of the lion to unfold. Venus Sagittarius falls in love with sports, ideas, foreign cities, and art. This position is not usually prone to addictive romances. Love is felt in many places and many ways to this versatile, life-loving Venus. Mars Leo is the ego of the lion, king of the jungle, when it comes to sex and romance. No one dares to turn down his/her advances; Leo, the king/queen expects to get what he/she wants! Now if Venus Sagittarius likes Mars Leo, a kind of game will emerge wherein over time, he/she may find that Leo's magnanimous generosity is worth sticking around for. Each has a different approach to life but each is highly capable (if willing) to blend into a compatible relationship together. Both highly praise and enjoy the arts and therein may be grounds for shared activities that enable each to grow closer together. Both may also enjoy physical sports and activities and that can lead to sexual abandon, frequently, in the great outdoors!

In a single chart the individual will have an expansive sense of personal freedom and probably a great deal of physical, athletic power. This person can be a visionary of sorts and may project that quality into writing, theater, the arts, or music. This individual would be a capable executive who traveled to represent his/her company and did it all with vast charm.

Mars Leo/Venus Capricorn

Both of these individuals seeks ambition. Capricorn needs to reach the top of the mountain and Venus Capricorn will consciously (or unconsciously) set up relationships to aid his/her career or social standing. Mars in Leo pursues love and sex for the pure joy of sensation, and especially conquest. Should Mars Leo have something in the way of status to offer Venus Capricorn, then possibly Mars will conquer that Venus and begin a relationship that has much to teach each. Mars in Leo can benefit from the cool, calculating approach of Venus Capricorn. After all, Mars Leo (if accompanied by more water or fire in the overall chart) just wants to dive in and assess the damages (or successes) later. Pure impulse governs much about Mars Leo's demeanor. Whereas Venus Capricorn can play strategic waiting games with anything to do with a life pursuit or goal. So Venus brings Mars patience and the capacity to review one's actions; Mars brings this Venus more spontaneity and pure abandon. Can they accept their differences on a long-term basis? It probably has to do with how patient Venus Capricorn really is. For Venus Capricorn, good things take time to develop and he/she will not feel *all* of his/her feelings at once. Mars Leo takes for granted that love will be felt at more or less the first meeting and from there on, it's simply a matter of diving in. So their timing in love's process of unfolding is quite different. Both wish to achieve other things in life and each can aid the other where the other is lacking; a kind of symbiosis of a positive sort can emerge.

In a single chart the combination is ambitious and shrewd. The individual sees him/herself as a winner and often has high self-esteem and the indomitable feeling that anything he/she does will eventually result in success. There is management ability, leadership ability, the arts and a patient attention to detail. This person could work for major corporations or government and seek status and recognition for work well done.

Mars Leo/Venus Aquarius

Opposites have a natural polarity, one to the other, and like a cat chasing its own tail, the two come together often to seek some kind of closure and wholeness. In this case, Mars Leo is a great "conquistador" who lives to pursue love and enjoy its delicious conquest. It's not that Venus can't be caught (in Aquarius), it's that this Venus constantly *is* caught, but remains aloof and self-contained at every meeting thereafter. Venus Aquarius is in love with personal liberty and finds love among many individuals and because of that, has great difficulty with traditional fidelity—or doesn't bother with it at all. That will be very hard on the ego of Mars Leo. Yet there's no question that Mars Leo turns on Venus Aquarius and Venus Aquarius' electric, intangible magnetism is a challenging thrill to "the big cat." This cross-over of volatile energy is more likely to mean a love affair, rather than a marriage unless one or both parties has a career linked to frequent travels and the separations allow for the on-again/off-again rhythm that will emerge with this heavy overload of basic human electricity. Sexually, the blending is strong and mystical; it's just that their getting together and finding their moods in sync won't always be easy.

In a single chart the person is a natural entertainer, master of ceremonies, a center of attention. This person would be a natural game show host (or talk show host) and has a flair for drama and public relations of all kinds. In sales work, such an individual would be hard sell and probably quite successful.

Mars Leo/Venus Pisces

There is some empathy here. Mars Leo pursues love with grandeur and generous gifts of love. Venus Pisces could be so moved by the gracious gestures that he/she would allow him/herself to fall in love, even if he/she wasn't initially attracted to Mars Leo. Venus Pisces is a water sign (very sensitive) and mutuable (adapts to situations). If Venus Pisces responded to the favors of Mars Leo and Mars Leo genuinely loved Venus Pisces; then Venus Pisces would be "in good hands" because Mars would chase away all their fears and take on a kind of protective role. Mars Leo can be professional and quite bossy. Venus Pisces has ways to get what he/she wants and the classic term for that way is "manipulation."

Mars Leo can be very generous and hardly knows he/she is being manipulated, if ever. Both are romantics; both are interested in the fine arts and both have an aptitude for educating the young. In fact, if other chart factors concur, they could found a school for special children or work together in fields that cater to the recreational needs of the young. Mars Leo probably has a stronger sex drive than Venus Pisces; but remember, Venus Pisces can adapt to anything and might be an ideal mate for the passionate instincts of Mars Leo.

In a single chart there may be deep aptitude for dance, gymnastics, yoga, t'ai chi, or the basic marital arts. The individual joins sexual bravado with spiritual sensitivity. There's probably no sacrifice that this person wouldn't make for the one he/she loves. The love force can be projected toward the so-called less fortunate and such an individual could work with handicapped children; autistic children; children with addictive patterns or emotional problems. Psychologists with these planets would have both love and rare intuitive insight into their patient's needs.

Mars Virgo

Mars Virgo/Venus Aries

Venus in Aries is a creature of whimsy and impulse and good-natured fun, much like Charlie Chaplin. Mars in Virgo believes vehemently that there's a right way to do everything—including "having sex." When Venus Aries feels down on his/her luck after repeated attempts at allowing impulse to rule, a Mars Virgo might seem like a salvation. Suddenly there is this person who can remember where the keys are; who pays bills on time; who can fix the car starter or fix just about anything else. A marriage made in heaven then? Mars in Virgo can be a nag and generally finds things to be critical about, even when there aren't any. Venus is in Mars (Aries) sign, which is, incidentally, the sign of "war." These two can argue and bicker back and forth and Venus Aries can be a quick learner and Mars Virgo will eventually tell him/her how to do everything, short of "blowing his nose." This combination reminds me of "My Fair Lady." The professor was forever teaching Liza how to speak! Venus Aries is capable of a strong passionate response and while Mars Virgo can be a connoisseur of the delicate *details* of sex, his/her sex drive is apt to be sublimated into little jobs about the house or the office. Much compromise would be required of each to let this relationship endure.

In a single chart the combination brings engineering skills and manual dexterity. This individual can work with delicate mechanical or other engineering systems or perhaps experiment with new technologies that might include bacteriology, microscopy, or pharmaceutical testing. This person has a very strong sense that his/her way is *the* right way and can be intolerant and high-strung. They may, however, have a sense of humour as a pressure release on their character!

Mars Virgo/Venus Taurus

Because both are of the earth element, both understand a great deal instinctively about one another's natures. This will give them a good deal of tolerance for one another and attraction as well. Venus Taurus can be a lazy, sensualist, the kind of wife we see in movies who emerges from bed at noon with a shimmering, gorgeous silk nightgown and robe floating off her sensual body. Mars Virgo would have been up at 7 A.M. doing odd jobs around the house; including mowing the lawn (to the dismay of more luxury-loving neighbors). Mars in Virgo likes to please and Venus Taurus has a nearly insatiable sexual drive. At times, I would think, Mars in Virgo would engage in sex simply to seek to fulfill the unverbalized sexual demands of Venus Taurus. Venus Taurus also loves to eat and many with Mars Virgo (anything in Virgo, really) make excellent cooks. Venus Taurus enjoys the luxury of a comfortable, beautiful home and can take things of relatively little value and paint them, fix them, change them so that they have decorator appeal. Mars Virgo will be very proud of this instinct for beauty and resourcefulness which is part and parcel of the Venus Taurus make-up. There will be some compromises here, but generally, it is a compatible bond capable of long-term sharing.

In a single chart there is a flare for designing home products; selling real estate; working with the earth, or in ecological pursuits; in fact, it also favors archaeologists and anthropologists and those who study and catalog aspects of nature. These individuals may also have a flare for farming, food preparation, and natural foods preparation.

Mars Virgo/Venus Gemini

This relationship reminds me of Phyllis Diller and her husband or any comedy duo. Both love to play with words since both Gemini and Virgo come under the rulership of the planet Mercury, the trickster who represents all forms of communication. Mars Virgo likes to tell others what to do and how to do it: the born critic. Venus in Gemini loves satire and is quick to analyze and poke fun at others' critical flaws. These two can go back and forth endlessly with verbal banter. Others would wonder what they see in each other because their remarks can be rude and insulting. However, they both secretly appreciate that finally there is an accomplished player to their verbal ping-pong matches! Neither position is particularly in or of the body, flesh, sensuality (unless there is much Taurus-Scorpio-Leo elsewhere), and so sex is not the tie that binds here. Both are mental sorts who seek fusion through a common plane of ideas to which they both can freely enter and express. Venus Gemini would be playful about sex and experiment with various kinds of role-playing or techniques and Mars Virgo loves to master technique. They could go to bed with a manual or video projector. If they enjoy each other's verbal assaults and their own capacity for rebuttal, they might stay together simply because they never bore each other.

In a single chart you have the born critic who might write for newspapers or movie reviews, play reviews, art or music reviews. This is a good position for a possibly obnoxious reporter who never lets up on getting the last word from celebrities. But there is a coldness here and a definite lack of insight into others feelings. This individual could be so caught up on the intellectual plane, that they totally lack awareness of *love,* sensitivity, empathy, *feelings.* It can represent the chart of a criminal—particularly good at writing bad checks, stealing, or embezzling funds.

Mars Virgo/Venus Cancer

Mars Virgo will be less sharp and critical when around Venus Cancer who gives a kind of melt-down to the acid criticism of Virgo's usual way. There is a good merging of energies here as earth and water draw together as inexorably as the pull of the sea to land. Mars Virgo will help to give Venus Cancer a sense of security. The two can build a very comfortable home together. Mars Virgo can work in his/her workshop or office while Venus Cancer works in the kitchen or garden. Separate, but compatible interests enable these two to team up and produce some splendid results. Venus in Cancer is a very feminine and nurturing position and has ample emotions and usually a positive expression of these. Mars Virgo is dry, earthy, and requires the watery flow of Venus Cancer's emotions in order to link up with this "great thing called love." Venus Cancer is one of the few positions that can relax Mars Virgo into a posture where the rudiments of loving and pure feeling are felt! Mars Virgo has to be careful not to be overly critical to the sensitive (grudge-holding) Venus Cancer on his/her "off" days.

In a single chart we have the makings of a *chef extraordinaire*. This person will work well with home products, cleaning services, gardening services, pet grooming services, or kitchen products, and catering. Floristry and the like may also be favorites for such an individual. There is a strong capacity to provide a nurturing home base for the loved ones.

Mars Virgo/Venus Leo

Mars in Virgo is often compulsive and needs to constantly do small, useful jobs (and we're talking about Sundays and holidays here). Venus in Leo borrows from royalty and would really like to have a retinue to fulfill his/her whims. Mars Virgo is elected! Mars Virgo gets to do constant small jobs in a "servant" capacity to the whims and demands of Venus Leo. If each person's psychology can handle this type of thing, who knows, the relationship might work. Basically, Venus Leo will not be appreciative because he/she will simply feel that a servant is a servant and not befitting to the great king or queen. Mars Virgo may try harder to please the *"enfant terrible"* for a while, only to quit and go on. Virgo is, after all, a mutable sign and will change with change. Venus Leo will miss his/her loyal servant and may decide retrospectively that love was indeed present. Venus Leo has a healthy appetite for both lust and flattery, neither of which runs high with Mars Virgo. I am afraid this pairing is not for the ultimate fulfillment of either.

In a single chart a certain flair for beauty, drama, creativity (Venus Leo) couples with the necessary muscle and physical skill to capture the vision in a tangible way. This combination therefore favors artists, writers, and visionary creators. Film animation would be a very good way to use both energies, as would fashion design. This individual could fall in love easily (Venus Leo), only to tear apart the partner with criticism (Mars Virgo). Tough to live with!

Mars Virgo/Venus Virgo

This couple will, in all probability, have the cleanest house, car, and body on the block. If "cleanliness is next to godliness," they'll have a spot waiting for them in heaven! Their best sexual experiences will probably occur in the bath, shower, or jacuzzi. They are nearly obsessed with bodily hygiene and probably never found a person who met their high standards until they crossed each others' paths. Neurotic to the world, together, they create their own high society. They will both be involved with precision, detail, and critical acumen toward the world around themselves—yet together, criticism can ebb away and they get lost in the sheer pleasure of finding someone who thinks as they do. In this coupling, each will sense that he belongs to and is, in fact, definitely a part of the other. They will be surprisingly attentive and sensitive to each other's needs. As long as neither feels shortchanged, each will inordinately tone down their natural tendency to criticize, when in the company of the other. Sexually, neither position is known to be a Don Juan, but they will have a definite magnetic tug on one another which will manifest in sexual relations far more frequently than either of them would have experienced in any other tie. When Mars and Venus meet, there is instinctive fusion. A good meeting of minds is the rule here, not the exception.

In a single chart this person will be a perfectionist and might enjoy work as a magazine editor, cleaning product salesperson, safety products tester, health hygienist, dental hygienist, or medical researcher. The person would be exceptionally finicky and probably possessed of a sex drive that was sublimated to work instead of pleasurable pursuits.

Mars Virgo/Venus Libra

Mars Virgo likes life, the home, the office, and people to run according to his/her view of "the right way." Picky at times and striving toward perfection, they are bound to experience high stress. Venus Libra likes life to balance (as an equation) also, but is usually far more calm and easygoing than Mars Virgo. If other factors bring these two together, it is possible that Mrs. Virgo will work hard to create a clean and organized environment which Venus Libra will try to keep that way. Both can be highly fastidious and too concerned with appearances or the opinions of others. Probably Mars Virgo will cater to the Venus Libra pleasure-loving whims, since planets in Virgo often *serve* the needs of the partner. Venus Libra has a good deal of intuition about the art of love and may find the secret way to soothe the tension in a Mars Virgo. They can also work together on projects that improve their mutual environment. This is not my personal favorite in terms of Mars-Venus contacts, but there is mild compatibility.

In a single chart the individual will have a great need for beauty and order around him/herself. This can make it difficult to work in office situations where there are bound to be smokers and inefficient people. Mars Virgo is quite intolerant, while Venus Libra puts a sugar coating of diplomacy over the very critical perceptions of this Mars. This person would work well alone on architecture, accounting, clerical work, or editing.

Mars Virgo/Venus Scorpio

In the *I Ching,* the hexagram of "youthful folly" depicts (for me) this planetary relationship. If Mars Virgo is willing to be led into the joys of sex by expert Venus Scorpio, then a rather beautiful unfolding of intimacy is possible. However, Mars Virgo is usually somewhat prudish and may find certain bodily acts "immoral," whereas Venus Scorpio is very much at home in the body and enjoys *all* manner of sexual interactions. Generally, Venus Scorpio will "outsex" Mars in Virgo and this can prove to be very unfulfilling over time. However, Mars Virgo is usually a good student and as mentioned earlier, if willing to take the lead from Venus Scorpio, some order of relationship could evolve. Each of these signs is interested in respecting privacy and each has a deep capacity for loyalty. If

Miss Virgo has Taurus-Leo-Scorpio prominent in her chart, she could couple up nicely with this Venus.

In a single chart this configuration would be excellent for a researcher in the medical or scientific fields. It also favors demolition and construction work. Other occupations include: police work, detective work, firefighting, forestry, and mortuary work.

Mars Virgo/Venus Sagittarius

Venus Sagittarius has the optimism and love of freedom reminiscent of a positive Walt Disney cartoon character. Mars in Virgo has the militant sense of order similar to the chronic nurse in *One Flew Over the Cuckoo's Nest*. And that's precisely how I'd rate this relationship: out of the "cuckoo's nest." Venus would be far too limited, constrained, confined by the somewhat neurotic needs and demands of Mars Virgo. Venus Sagittarius is a born artist (or free spirit) and Mars Virgo's precise ways of doing everything will quench her (Venus) spirit in a short time. Possibly these two can work on some artistic project that demands a careful respect for detail or restoration; but I cannot see where their artistic respect for one another could be grounds for a meeting of heart and soul, however. (There are always exceptions which, more than likely, mean the couple has other highly compatible connections *elsewhere*). The needs of each are very different and not in an easily complementary way.

In a single chart there are internal conflicts between being true to one's free spirit and bohemianism which is considered wrong and decadent by one's internal voice of precision. Mars Virgo believe that only certain ways and means are right and sacrifices happiness in pursuit of "rightness." This individual will need to work toward self-respect which will then become a kind of center, enabling him/her to choose various life options wisely.

Mars Virgo/Venus Capricorn

These two fastidious, ambitious, hard workers will likely meet at work or at work-related activities. They may be drawn to the sense of order, neatness, and propriety that each emanates. Venus Capricorn believes that love should help fulfill the career and Mars in Virgo is often married to their own particular career line of expression anyway. Both will be critics to the other, but in a loving way that helps each to refine his/her professional skills and move closer to their own brass-ring definition of "success."

On a level of romance, either is a particularly starry-eyed romanticist, in fact for both, "What have you done for me lately?" means a lot more. Each places stock in punctuality, commitment, and loyalty; and each is capable of living up to such needs in the other. This can be a workable relationship where each primarily support the others' career aims.

Neither position is entirely sexual, but when sex occurs, each will try hard, will work hard (and I mean it in those terms) to fulfill the other. Sex, like everything else to a workaholic earth sign, represents a skill to be mastered rather than an experience to be flowing at one with. But it will work for them at their level.

In a single chart the combination points to a craftsperson or one who can ascertain quality in objects: whether it be art, jewelry, food, or a fine wine. This person could become a specialist in antiques, a fine jewelry consultant or expert, a clockmaker, a big business accountant, or one in charge of product repairs and services. Patience runs quite high and so does skill and mastery of one's chosen professional line. There is tremendous perfectionism.

Mars Virgo/Venus Aquarius

If Mars Virgo presumes to love one with Venus Aquarius, then Mars will do his best to please this novel creature of imagination and wit. Venus Aquarius can be unconventional and outrageous regarding sex, love, and emotional demands. Mars in Virgo will aim to please. Both are very clean and fastidious about appearance and may enjoy sexual relations outside in the rain or in the shower at home. Mars Virgo has to be very open-minded (can Mars Virgo be?) to follow the spontaneous freedom and flights of fancy common to Venus Aquarius. If both feel completely free and open about their bodies and minds, these two can have a fantastic adventure in sharing. Venus Aquarius is seldom faithful and Mars Virgo believes in "what is right" (i.e., commitment) so there is bound to be tension over this issue. Venus Aquarius may not mention that he/she has other lovers and the purity of Mars Virgo might think never to ask. Thus Venus Aquarius doesn't feel that he or she is lying. There are tricky situations between them. This might not be an ideal coupling for a long-term marriage, but it will be fascinating for as long as both choose to sustain the rocky ride. Mars Virgo needs a bit of shaking up anyway, and who better than unconventional, law-unto-thy-self Aquarius can do it?

In a single chart the individual will be very well-groomed and might work with modeling or projects that demonstrate the cleaning of goods—cosmetics, beauty supplies, skin cleansers, etc. Inventive skills or mechanical genius might also be present. This individual might work with some state of the art technology of one kind or another. They will be very precise and yet unconventional in all things.

Mars Virgo/Venus Pisces

Venus and Mars, as naturally opposed planetary principals, always bear a magnetic tie, one to the other. In opposite signs, the magnetic principle is exaggerated and strongly felt. Does that make for compatibility? Hardly so. However, these two, if drawn together by fate, karma, or sheer libido, will learn some tough lessons from the interaction. Venus Pisces has an amazing ability to "become" the psyche of the loved one and is capable of amazing acts of devotion.

Mars Virgo can stop the flow by analyzing that which should be felt and trusted. Mars Virgo's analytical way may carve up Venus Pisces's mystical openness to life. Mars Virgo might teach Venus Pisces a few things about being punctual, separating white wash from colored laundry or paying bills on time, whereas Venus Pisces needs to open the heart on Mars Virgo and turn him/her on to life's inexplicable poetry. It's a very challenging combination in that Mars Virgo gets so stuck in precision and has difficulty letting go to the sheer magnificence. Mars Virgo may, at first, want to run the life of Venus Pisces and may be threatened by Pisces' lack of definition. Some Mars Virgo individuals know their limitations too well, and feel grateful that a more poetic creature has entered their life to get them to stop and not only smell the roses, but by meditation, become them! I recommend this tie for older, more mature, less rigid types.

In a single chart there is both the sheer inspiration necessary for artistic creation *and* the ability to capture the inspiration with old-fashioned hard work and attention to physical dexterity. This can, therefore, be the mark of an individual who can put their visions into practical use. The person might be interested in dance, fishing, hospital and social work, or gardening. This individual is apt to be sensitive and may be a bit up and down emotionally. Alternate periods of heavy work and doing nothing are possible. This person may have some healing aptitudes.

Mars Libra

Mars Libra/Venus Aries

Mars visits Venus' sign while Venus moves through Mars' sign. This cross-flow of energy can be very interesting and dynamic. Each is looking for a "lost part" of himself/herself through the other. This search can take a lifetime. Mars, normally assertive, seeks peace and equilibrium *through* relationships while in Libra. Venus, normally interested in balance and peace, seeks individual assertiveness while in Aries. Each represents what the other is not. This polarity could bring about intense passion or intense antipathy. Most likely if you're reading this, it's the first influence; although, a relationship could very likely show *both* trends. Both hold a common interest in the arts and beauty. Through cultivation of this interest the relationship could grow: Mars learns to concede to the interests of his partner; Venus learns to be less conciliating and more able to arrive at autonomy through this relationship's tie.

In a single chart there can be extraordinary grace in movement. Venus-Aries gives self-expressive energy and Mars Libra gives a sense of grace, beauty, and balance. This individual might be internally at war between creating close ties or being free. Relationships are subject to changes of mood or a relationship may need to reflect many moods. Artistic, self-expression seems the likely career choice.

Mars Libra/Venus Taurus

Both Taurus and Libra are ruled by the benefic planet, Venus, and in a sense are kinetic, cosmic cousins! This relatedness is both beguiling and intriguing. In Libra, Mars seeks to bring beauty, balance, and refinement to instinct. But Venus Taurus is pure comfort and sensuality. Mars is the one who has to concede to the needs of Venus and in her own sign, Venus can be very sexually and sensually demanding. Mars Libra is a social butterfly of sorts and Venus Taurus is happy at home with food and a warm partner. Can they reconcile their differences? Yes and no. There will be times when they flow well together, when Mars is in the mood for Venus alone. Venus Taurus is quite possessive. But at other times, both will wonder how they can stay together at all. Venus Taurus avoids changes in love for as long as possible and Mars in Libra feels a great need to avoid strife within relationships. Both may mask their differences and seek to create a relationship that makes the most of those positive interests they have in common: food, clothing, beauty, shelter, and the arts.

In a single chart the individual is very sensual and very relationship-oriented. This could fit the role of a model who uses her beauty to attract high-paying public relations jobs. Beauty may play a role in this individual's career. It could also symbolize someone involved in a legal field where property and finance is a major concern. This individual is very much motivated by fulfilling his/her overall sensual needs.

Mars Libra/Venus Gemini

Both planets occupy the air element and this brings a note of sharing and mutual understanding. Both get easily bored and both individuals seek a social whirl-wind within which to lose their inhibitions. Together they could be a couple more interested in going out than in probing one another through mystical intimacy. It is likely that they will meet through a social affair, party, or publicity event. Both love superficial conversations, light flirtations, and being around new people. It is their common interest in being free that allows them to socialize together. Unless other more binding aspects occur between them (check Sun-Moon, Venus-Saturn) they will not be the lovers of the century; but there's enough harmony to allow them to be deep friends. Friendship combined with spicy elements elsewhere can be the signatures of a long-lasting relation-ship.

In a single chart the person will be a glib conversationalist with a ready wit, sales skill, and diplomacy. They may be the proverbial "charmer" who can make everyone like him/her; but who may not really feel any special attraction for anyone. Communications skills, especially in sales and public relations run high and are professional assets.

Mars Libra/Venus Cancer

Sometimes Mars in Libra enjoys the social limelight but gets tired of it and wants a mate to really come home to. Venus Cancer usually works at home in one way or another and is often very content in having a home worth being in. These two can create a relationship based on complementary needs. Mars Libra can charm just about anyone and if he/she wants someone their love to be faithful, home loving, and somewhat traditional—Venus Cancer could fill the bill. The relationship of Mars and Venus in this combo is a square, which is very tense, but between a man and a woman, it makes for the tension associated with deep, sexual attraction. Mars Libra (if a man) has an interesting blend of masculine power and delicate grace; Venus Cancer is a very appealing woman *because* of her natural femininity. If the roles are reversed, the Venus Cancer man will feel something commanding about this woman, yet he finds her sexually appealing as well. The blend of forces makes this bond an interesting one.

In a single chart there is a very refined, cultural side of the personality that might incline one in the study of gourmet food and restauranteuring. This indicates a person who is genuinely sensitive about the needs of others. The problem then is how to be all things to everyone else (out of feeling those needs) without losing the sacred individualism of one's own core? This person will be vitally associated with home and family life.

Mars Libra/Venus Leo

This couple will be among the cream of society at their entertainment balls. Leo brings together pageantry and a position of honor with Mars. There may also be a connection between them made through art channels. Both have a natural regal bearing and appear (as if for eons) to have sailed through countless castle affairs throughout the Middle Ages as though its's still in their blood. Each believes in the nobility of the human soul and in living by high standards. They glamorize one another and may help each other to achieve the ideal of the helpmate. They may both be involved with law, politics, or matters of principle. This is a very uplifting coupling for both persons. They could form a mutual admiration society and neither will be quick to see the other's critical flaws, but all in all, each can give the other a great boost of love and spiritual growth for this life.

In a single chart there will be artistic talent, theatrical ability, and a taste for dynamic legal practice; or the product representation of fine artwork. This individual will probably associate with dignitaries, or people of power of one sort or another. There may be a bit of excessive vanity; a tendency to look down on others.

Mars Libra/Venus Virgo

Sometimes Mars Libra will want everything to be in perfect balance; this yearning for perfection is sometimes met by the constant attempts, on the part of Venus Virgo, to "make everything right for the other person." So for a while, Mars in Libra may be enamored with the illusion that Venus Virgo will right every element of his world for him/her. But Venus Virgo will get sick and tired of it, or hungry one day and then what? Mars in Libra usually likes to be out of the home, in the presence of the "beautiful people." Venus in Virgo likes to do useful work at home or in the office and doesn't have a need for the frivolous. They will not understand one another's differences well, although they can adapt to them. It's hard for me to perceive this as a passionate tie. Lovemaking would seem to have an element of duty, not necessarily splendor in it.

In a single chart the individual will have a very technical way of doing things. They may be inordinately proper, and may involve themselves in jobs such as mechanical drawing, architecture, accounting and budgeting. They can also be the ultimate bureaucrat: professionally friendly and uncommonly neurotic about details. If married, they will still remain cool and aloof in many ways.

Mars Libra/Venus Libra

Do you know those Olympian ice-skaters who balance on a razor's edge as they hold one another in a slow, flowing, arched grace? They probably share their Mars-Venus in Libra. Where else does that balance come from? In dance, they would be Fred Astaire and Ginger Rodgers. These two really move together and no one else has quite the same synergistic movements as these two together. It may be ice-skating, canoeing, skiing, or lovemaking. They are in sync! They will find the depth of their bond through music, movement, or other artistic forms of expression. They are both very interested in personal grooming, nice clothing, and physical appearance and might both be "peacocks" under the surface. Somewhat narcissistic, they feel the other is a good mirror image of themselves. It's actually self loving self through the other; but at least it is love or some similar, and can be a potentially binding allure. These two will turn heads when they dress up and go out . . . and out they go . . . hopefully with expense accounts or charge cards in hand.

In a single chart there is mastery of some chosen art form: it may be public relations, diplomacy, dance, writing, etc. This person will have many social graces, good manners, physical attractiveness, and great charm. It would seem Venus gave abundantly to this one; it was probably karmically earned!

Mars Libra/Venus Scorpio

Venus Scorpio can be a seductress in a woman and in a man, the type of individual who can use sex to obtain other favors. Mars in Libra likes life to move along in a peaceful way. Mars Libra enjoys having partnership in his/her life but really feels that he/she belongs to the world—especially a social world. Mars in Libra can enjoy deeply sensuous sex *on occasion*, but air signs by and large are not dominated by the body or its lusts. Venus Scorpio thrives on sexual relations and is very possessive of his/her mate. Therefore, there is some antipathy between the drives of each. In the beginning Mars Libra, the great diplomat, will make enormous compromises to suit the subtle and powerful demands of Venus Scorpio. For how long can compromise occur? The best relationships are those wherein each person is instinctively comfortable being him/herself in the companionship of the other. If there are other strong ties between these two, perhaps Venus Scorpio will spend more time hitting the social circle with Mars Libra and in turn, giving more intense (less frequent) sexual expressions between them.

In a single chart the individual will have an ability to please many people with sexual magnetism and charm. This person could be something of a social climber through their sexual prowess. They may also marry (in part), for position or financial comfort. They will know what to say and when to say it—a combination detective-human-psychologist. The question is, are they able to be totally true to themselves? Playing many parts, we lose identity.

Mars Libra/Venus Sagittarius

Both of these people know how to have a good time with friends or while traveling. Their hobbies and mutual interests will give them a relationship with a strong base on which to grow and endure. Mars in Libra loves to charm and be charmed by a wide variety of people, and Venus, in the sign of the "wild horse," likes to be free to roam somewhat romantically. These two can have a very romantic understanding of one another without cramping each others' style. They will have common interests in art, music, theater, beauty, and travel. Mars may be more the diplomat, between the two, but together, they exhibit a textured harmony that refines each of their natures just enough—without essentially changing either. They will have a very easy time of communicating their ideas, feelings, and thoughts. Each will feel they have found both a friend and a lover in the other. While this relationship does not suggest stormy passion; there is a healthy kind of love that frees each to do his/her thing and welcomes them back together into sensual oneness.

In a single chart the individual may well work with foreign commerce or become an international sales representative. There is skill in law, fine arts and architecture, and powers of diplomacy which render this individual at once likeable and trustworthy.

Mars Libra/Venus Capricorn

In a sense, each of these individuals is somewhat of a social climber. Venus Capricorn is shrewd and feels that love ought not be wasted on people or situations that ultimately will not fulfill career (or life-style) goals. Mars in Libra has learned from an early age (probable past life patterning, too) how to be charming and "win friends and influence people." Each of these individuals could be drawn together to seek status, publicity, or some external gratification. I feel that there would be something circumspect between them; neither would fully trust the other. Each would have a tendency to see through the other's more devious side of character and that would make the trust basic to love difficult. Now there are some highly honorable types with Mars in Libra who fight for "freedom and justice for all." And there are some noble Venus Capricorns who have just been very selective about not choosing "the wrong mate." There is some possibility that these two could get together and suit each other in a strange way. But that is the exception, not the rule. Besides, Venus Capricorn is something of a workaholic and Mars Libra will often earn income through social channels (the movies, entertainment fields, casinos, sales representatives with expense accounts—thus not giving each much room to tolerate the other.

In a single chart the individual will be quite cool and calculating. This might be seen in the chart of a lawyer who is the ultimate strategist, representing powerful firms. It can also be the signature of a cold-blooded social climber; sometimes one who champions the cause of underdogs within powerful companies or institutions. The person is searching for partnership, but has trouble relaxing his/her guard and trusting people!

Mars Libra/Venus Aquarius

This couple could be his and her MCs for a disco, restaurant, or even a political caucus; both are active and may be activists for various causes. Each is naturally chic and both project attractive qualities. They will be equally intrigued with each other, as with the world and its social groups.

Theirs will start out as both an attraction and a friendship; it may move through waves of love but will essentially remain as it began. That will give youth and freshness to this tie. Both will be involved in each other's social situations, both have a deep capacity to enjoy variety in life. This could even represent a nonpossessive marriage (right out of Emmanuel) where each is free to have other lovers! Modeling, politics, the arts are likely between them or in the initial association that brought them together.

In a single chart there is the making of an ambassador or other political figure who may not make powerful decisions, but has a place in rank and pageantry. If a lawyer, he/she will have an unusual turn of mind and be capable of unique interpretation and expression of law. To whatever this individual adapts him/herself, he/she will bring uncommon wisdom to the old truths. Possibly this person has a remarkable intellect and will require very "advanced" mates as lovers.

Mars Libra/Venus Pisces

Who will make the decisions between them? Both these individuals can forever waiver in their ability to "flow with life," moving with the various tides. If their inconsistencies are consistent with one another, they may engage in an unbalanced relationship that no one but themselves understands. Sometimes running hot and committed, other times cool and detached. They can all at once be lovers and strangers to each other—all over again. This kind of "love rhythm" has suited some, as in the poetry of unrequited lovers. Each may do a considerable amount of soul-searching, leading to a "fearless evaluation of one's moral inventory" as a result of being together. On a long-term basis, I can only say, "would you want to marry your therapist?" It would be challenging at best. Still, each has a very ancient idealism and romanticism deep within, and for exquisite moments each makes the myth live and seem real for the other. Fantasy is a hard thing to trade in for the dependable.

In a single chart this person ought to be a performer. They live in their own ideal world of both fantasy and idealism. Their beautiful fantasies are too pure for a denser world; yet they may be the ones who seed the imagination of these dense souls so that one day, enough people will agree with the Libra-Pisces vision to "make it so." Dance, music, writing, and teaching the arts are good professions. With earth for stability elsewhere, such a person would make an intelligent, empathetic therapist.

Mars Scorpio

Mars Scorpio/Venus Aries

Because at one time (prior to Pluto's discovery) Mars was said to have ruled over both Aries and Scorpios, ancient affinities remain between both signs. Like the Hindu gods Shiva and Vishnu, both are destroyer and creator forces! Mars in Scorpio can be fierce about pursuing desire for any given ends. In fact, this Mars position more than any other has an "ends justify the means" attitude. Venus Aries has a natural innocence, but in that innocence, will look out for number one—self! Both can be selfish in different ways and both expect to be the power within the relationship. Mars Scorpio is more a strategist than Venus Aries, yet Venus Aries is often "protected by his/her innocence." Mars Scorpio may take delight in initiating Venus Aries (an eager student) into some of the mysteries of sexuality, which Mars Scorpio knows well. But Mars in Scorpio is very possessive, and any major planets in Aries essentially suggest that the individual belongs to him/herself. This may be a very hot love affair in many ways; but will be difficult basis for a stable marriage.

In a single chart the person can pursue passion to an injurious degree. Venus Aries can be quite impulsive about love and once Mars in Scorpio gets "set" on something—anything—it can't find the brakes to stop the motion! Thus extremism sets in and the seasoning process of time can add wisdom to this somewhat reckless combination. There may be ability in body art, martial art, hair design, and sculpture (also a strong attraction to police and military work).

Mars Scorpio/Venus Taurus

This is a very hot and powerful combination. Two individuals will feel nearly irresistibly drawn together. Are they compatible? Not necessarily but trying to swim against the current which seems set on combining their magnetically attuned forces may be useless. Consider this a karmic link-up where libido overwhelms logic. It happens. It might be called love although in this combination between two sensual powerhouses; it's just as likely to be lust. Each will have a profound effect upon the other. The two are synergistic and will create a powerful entity—a relationship that goes above and beyond each as separate individuals. If these two can agree to apply willpower and energy to a common objective, they can make rapid and amazing progress toward its completion. They will be very possessive of each other, possibly to an unhealthy extreme: that's the negative connotation of Scorpio. But this polarity can also work as a healing force, bringing healing to one or both. They could be very successful in work that heals, rebuilds, regenerates, transforms, or repairs.

In a single chart this will be someone with vast magnetic powers and a near magic over the opposite sex. Inwardly, there may be some polarity that only seems to be quelled by sexual passion. This person will use sexual energy (if sublimated) in his/her work. It favors a body-builder, wrestler, aerobics teacher, martial arts teacher, model, topless dancer, etc. The person may have a strong mental association between sex and money.

Mars Scorpio/Venus Gemini

Mars Scorpio is a born sensualist who feels very comfortable with the unspoken language of flesh and its symbolic integration with the body of another. Sex becomes the language of love to one with Mars Scorpio; although they can be cold and detached as well. But Venus Gemini thrives on words, ideas, expressions of a verbal sort and is accustomed to experiencing love largely through the mind. Mars Scorpio wants to possess the lover through the especial sexual techniques he/she has learned for that purpose. But Venus Gemini wants to keep his/her romantic options open and be the perennial flirt. Do they have anything in common? Beauty is the great allure and it's possible that they too will find some superficial grounds on which to flirt with a relationship. The profound silence of Mars Scorpio will not be easily understood (if ever) by the analytical propensities of Venus Gemini. Each will invite the other into his/her world but neither will be able to speak the "language." This can be highly frustrating. Mars Scorpio is unkind if he/she feels betrayed. Venus Gemini is a creature of the wind and his/her loyalties are subject to change without notice. This can be dangerous for such a bond carries hard lessons.

In a single chart the individual will go to extremes in searching for psychological answers to his/her own deep motivations. This could be the chart of one who uses art to approach the unspoken language of the psyche; or a psychologist who relies on dreams and symbolism to unlock the "door to the unconscious." This person can be good at mimicking the ideas or beliefs of others.

Mars Scorpio/Venus Cancer

All streams eventually find the great river and their paths back to the sea. Water recognizes water and feels, spiritually, the soul recognition which ET aptly put as "go home." Mars Scorpio will feel an inner peace, a kind of spiritual "homecoming" with Venus Cancer. Both provide a nearly transcendental space for the other to let their guard down in. This relationship, if other factors concur, can be an alchemy of oneness right from the start. Each may feel instinctively "in love with the other" because water triggers the unconscious and brings up ancient bonds that we faintly remember deep within the psyche. Neither of these individuals will be able to hide anything from the other; they will "read" each other psychically. Both will be possessive of each other in the way a person might guard a precious jewel. Sexually, they are capable of a "melt-down," where egos dissolve and each experiences the equivalent of the cosmic consciousness through the sheer joy of merging with the other.

In a single chart there is much passion, sensitivity, psychic ability and compassion. This individual would be a very powerful maternal force who will sense the unspoken needs of the children. It favors day-care workers, teachers, camp counselors, youth psychologists, and people who work with nursing, midwifery, and family planning.

Mars Scorpio/Venus Leo

There is an interesting sexual tension here as each more or less taunts the other; each seeks a subtle conquest when up against the seemingly undaunted will of the other. Both are powerhouses and both place a great deal of importance on sex. It is, however, Venus Leo who is more apt to confuse powerful sex with ultimate love. Because these two bring out the "animal" in each other and move through inhibitions easily, the sexual bond is very strong. However, Venus Leo loves the stage, camera, lights, and action and has no inkling of privacy. To Venus Leo, life is love and love is life and he/she will ultimately broadcast grandiose tales of his/her love relationship. On the other hand, Mars Scorpio is shrewd, secretive, and wants to be a mysterious unknown. Venus Leo enjoys attention from many and tends to flirt; Mars Scorpio will brook no rival. There are personality clashes based on dissimilar life-style needs. But for as long as the glow of powerful sex occurs, each will make enormous compromises for the other. If rage, jealousy, and overemotionalism don't bring too many scars; the fire may be hot enough here to last a long time. But this won't be any smooth ride and is for roller-coaster lovers only!

In a single chart there is a tremendous Don Quixote type of love and passion. The person has a very strong libido which can dominate all life decisions. This individual will be ruled by a combination of love and lust. He/she may have enormous body magnetism and this may find him/her a career in dance, music, or in the other arts. There is a very insatiable sexual urge; although it can be siphoned into other things. This person feels anonymous at certain times, then craves the attention of others. It's a tough inner energy to balance.

Mars Scorpio/Venus Virgo

While Venus Virgo seeks to please and can be very devoted to a mate, he/she can not really meet the passion level of Mars Scorpio. This indicates the type of marriage in the Far East which occurs between people who can accommodate one another in the daily aspects of life. But the husband seeks a concubine elsewhere. The signs have mild compatibility, but Venus Virgo is usually too much the puritan to meet the uninhibited and tremendous sexual urges of Mars Scorpio. Interestingly enough, these two can have a good meeting of the minds and are both of a similar demeanor in terms of their willingness to work hard and ferret out details. They can do research projects together, tax accounting together, community planning, or health-related works together. But in terms of bedroom activities, this one is close to being doomed. If Mars Scorpio has much Taurus-Capricorn elsewhere and siphons that sexual energy into work-related projects, then the general compatibility may allow for this bond to function. But it brings a low reading to the von Richter scale of passion!

In a single chart we have the *detective extraordinaire*. This individual would be good at work where vast attention to detail is required: carving wood, making jewelry, doing intricate works with building and construction materials. This person will try to intellectualize away their strong sexual passions. In fact, the Virgo puritan ethic coupled with the unbridled passion potential of Scorpio could produce a televangelical minister with sinister leanings!

Mars Scorpio/Venus Libra

Venus in her own element (Libra) with Mars in his own element create a very alluring, although not intrinsically compatible (in the conventional sense) relationship. Venus Libra is the *coquette extraordinaire*, her demeanor may be that of Scarlet O'Hara in seeking the attentions of every potential male suitor. Mars Scorpio is possessive with an actual fierceness attached to it. Many with Mars Scorpio pursue martial arts as a hobby! Venus Libra adores being desired and desirable because of her beauty and charm. (This will affect males similarly.)

Mars Scorpio has such an intense desire that it can throw Venus Libra into an affair without giving her usual attention to the logic of it all. These two have the potential for having an interesting relationship. If Venus Libra can tone down her flirtatiousness and allow Mars Scorpio to go out and conquer the dragons (so to speak) it could be a very romantic and highly sexual entanglement. But Venus Libra is cooler, being an air sign, than Mars Scorpio and there will be times when Venus Libra hurts the ego of Mars Scorpio by simply stating (verbally or nonverbally) "not tonight, dear, it'll mess up my hair." That can drop the bottom out. Mars Scorpio has the Achilles heel of vanity attached to his/her sexual prowess.

In a single chart reckless self-abandonment and sexual adventures dominate this person. For this reason, you should certainly stay clear of any sexually conservative or hung up partner. Just as Mars rules Scorpio, you will you be the dominant force in any union. This high energy added to a desire for the beautiful in each and every lovemaking experience makes every affair, no matter how brief, an event! Though youth is often appealing to this native, maturity and experience are more likely to produce lasting enjoyment.

Mars Scorpio/Venus Scorpio

Two powerhouses of sensual magnetism meet in this dynamic duo. These two could meet at an X-rated video rental store! Both will have a great deal of intuitive experience about sex and together, they could write the equivalent of the "Masters and Johnson" manuals! Scorpio uses sex, unconsciously, as an energizer that literally renews the spirit. Persons with a lot of Scorpio placements don't want to intellectualize or explain what sexual force is about. It is nothing short of a prospector hitting gold for a Scorpio to find a mate of like spirit who understands the unspoken language of lovemaking. While neither may be very articulate about feelings, both will understand the power of each other's presence in the other's life. Together they could pursue yoga, metaphysics, meditation, or schools intended to transform human belief. Together they can also be excellent researchers, medical technicians, and detectives.

In a single chart the character is fed on sexual experience. If the individual is a mature Scorpio, their sexual power may be transferred to others as the equivalent of a "healing ray." In that case, the configuration favors massage therapists, healers, and faith healers. In the case of a lower spirit, the personality may constantly search for sexual exploits and fear intimacy; thus resulting in the syndrome known today as the "sexual addict."

Mars Scorpio/Venus Sagittarius

Venus Sagittarius may have the athletic suppleness that makes for ingenious (and difficult to achieve) positions in sexual relations. Mars Scorpio will love an adventurous, athletic mate primarily for that reason. What Mars Scorpio will not enjoy, is the general note of freedom and self-possession which belongs to the Venus Sagittarius native. Mars Scorpio wants to possess in the way an animal brings its prey to a cave and keeps it there! Remember: Pluto is god of the underworld, infamous for kidnapping a young goddess and finally agreeing to surrender her for six months each year. Pluto-Scorpio uses sexual power to abduct the reasoning powers of others! Because the nature of Sagittarius is that of the horse that loves to roam free, it will be a battle of basic intrinsic natures for these two to navigate a path of togetherness on a long-term basis. For the short term, the trade-off is exotic and interesting.

In a single chart there will be athletic prowess. Mars Scorpio hates to lose and is not a quitter; in difficult athletic feats, there is a stamina which can border on going beyond pain. This individual is suited to a sportsman's life, the military, espionage, political (secretive) maneuvers, martial arts, and body building. Through military or travel affairs, such a person would be likely to marry a foreigner.

Mars Scorpio/Venus Capricorn

If we "read" the Zodiac as a wheel of evolutionary karma, then Capricorn is later on the wheel of experience than is Scorpio. For this reason, these two shrewd characters meet and Venus Capricorn is able to work wonders of discipline on the beloved Mars Scorpio. Mars Scorpio is, as has been mentioned, an extremist and has difficulty applying the brakes to any human endeavor. Venus Capricorn will be the "loving brakes" to his/her mate! Capricorn is interested in protocol, reputation, practicality, and usefulness. They are not wasters; they live by the credo of quality before quantity. Mars Scorpio may have less sex (Venus Capricorn can also be married to his/her work) but when it occurs, there will be an exotic tension that leaves both quite fulfilled in its wake. Mars Scorpio is ambitious and Venus Capricorn will not rest until some pinnacle is attained. It can be for some with this combination that Mars Scorpio does borderline illegal activities which bring a certain (unearned) status to Venus Capricorn and the two live well together. Both expect to live well and both are capable of using sexuality to attain ambitious ends. A match of equals here.

In a single chart the person has a will of iron. This individual may set challenging goals for him/herself and will eventually reach them. An indomitable power and readiness to stand any test exists. Such a person, may unconsciously attract challenge to themselves. This would be the configuration, me thinks, of Indiana Jones, himself, in fact, it favors risky ventures, deep researches, and political intrigue.

Mars Scorpio/Venus Aquarius

Venus in the air signs (Gemini, Libra, Aquarius) gives charm and vast social appeal. The woman with this configuration is often surrounded by a bevy of courters. Mars Scorpio likes to win and enjoys conquest and Venus Aquarius fits the bill in his search for someone to "win." The problem here is that once won, Venus Aquarius may prove very responsive to Mars Scorpio's sexual advances and gourmet techniques . . . but (and it's a big BUT) that will not change Venus Aquarius' basic nature which is personal liberty. Venus Aquarius will absolutely drive Mars Scorpio mad with jealousy. He/she is not playing games or trying to arouse the wrath of Scorpio; it's just that Venus Aquarius has so many people he/she enjoys the company of that a sexual experience occasionally develops, and Venus Aquarius sees it as perfectly natural and within his/her right! Mars Scorpio still believes that to love is to possess and he/she will try many ploys and greater and greater sexual attempts to hold the unstable attentions of Venus Aquarius. This can even be dangerous. Venus Aquarius will probably not change—being a fixed sign itself. Either these two make the affair brief, or both take out life insurance policies.

In a single chart the person can be one who exploits the opposite sex. The lack of emotional commitment common to Venus Aquarius couples up uneasily with the strong sexual lusts of Mars Scorpio. This individual may have great difficulty really being vulnerable and surrendering to the love of another person. They may have a strong sway over people and this favors those in teaching, advertising, and sales work. But in themselves, there is much to be resolved . . . and it has to do with learning about love, commitment and perhaps even sacrifice of personal ego.

Mars Scorpio/Venus Pisces

This bonding is close to being heaven on earth if other factors concur. As mentioned earlier, water blending with water is without boundary. Each flows into the other and the two become one. Their identities will change, each becoming more like the other in love's most exquisite form of alchemy. Venus Pisces may have been a martyr in some way, before meeting Mars Scorpio. Mars Scorpio can be cruel, can be an opportunist and can feel that the "ends justify the means." But the soul beauty of Venus Pisces will melt some of the ice from the water sign Mars Scorpio and he/she will be capable of a more profound relationship with the infinite depths of understanding possessed by Venus Pisces. Venus Pisces usually loves without judgment and gives the loved one so much room to be him/herself. Mars Scorpio needs this "permission" to let down his/her guard. Both can change enormously, and for the better as a result of the union. However, Mars Scorpio can project a very self-destructive level of sensory satisfactions. If Mars Scorpio has any addictive habits, he/she can easily pass these on to the devoted, trusting Venus Pisces. Then neither will be of much use to the other and much harm could result.

In a single chart the individual is very intuitive and psychic. Possessing much empathy to human suffering, this person could work in psychology or some field where their ability to work through others' problems or handicaps is used. This individual has a strong stomach and a lot of compassion for retarded and autistic children, the criminally insane, and those with chronic health problems. I would expect to see such a person in a program combining medicine, healing, and New Age technology to help others. Sexually the intuitive level brings great rapport with other lovers.

Mars Sagittarius

Mars Sagittarius/Venus Aries

These two free spirits find both a friend and a lover in each other. Mars Sagittarius is a nearly insatiable explorer, a lover of nature, and a highly physical, athletic sort. Venus Aries also loves adventures that take him/her off the beaten track. Venus Aries resonates to the beauty and primitive harmony of the natural world and both really share many interests. They blend well together, and that's saying a lot since neither is particularly interested in blending at all—both being highly independent, freedom-loving individuals!

If both are in good physical condition, they might enjoy hiking, skiing, camping, or other forms of exploration including those into the mind whereby they may take courses together at the local university. They both sparkle into sexual peaks and it is likely those peaks will correspond, amazingly, with each other's natural physiology. But above and beyond that, these two genuinely like each other and easily share in mutual interests.

In a single chart the individual has a great thirst for beauty, truth, justice, and pure beingness. This person may live far from city noise and traffic, or pursue a life-style where there are periodic immersions in a Thoreau-like Walden Pond setting. There is also a healthy physical force that can allow the person an occupation involving movement, strength, and fitness. Professional athletes, train conductors, airline pilots, and wilderness park officials might have this signature.

Mars Sagittarius/Venus Taurus

Perhaps Mars in Sagittarius would like to go hunting and needs a chef who can really do something special with that venison! Venus Taurus was born with cooking hands. Will Venus Taurus take off on the hunt along with Mars Sagittarius? Not likely, unless Venus Taurus has a lot of Aries in his/her chart. But there is some complimentariness here. Mars Sagittarius can take his/her time away, traveling for work reasons or for pure pleasure. Venus Taurus is usually content to be home, in a comfortable setting. (Mars Sagittarius just better help with paying the bills.) Each will have a very separate life from the other; but that can be a workable arrangement. Besides, Venus Taurus has a big appetite for sex and Mars Sagittarius often provides the athletic rigor to fulfill Venus Taurus' very appetite. That, in itself, can be binding. So while each represents a highly different approach to life, they can negotiate an interesting relationship.

In a single chart Mars Sagittarius and Venus Taurus give a decidedly physical approach to life. This person could be a star athlete, possessing the sheer love of sensation and stamina of Venus Taurus along with the physical inclination of Mars Sagittarius. Artistic skill is probable and anything this person sets their Sagittarius arrow toward will eventually come to pass. Here is a fine blending of visionary insight, creative visualization, and the stamina to carry it through. He/she would probably have a big appetite for food, too!

Mars Sagittarius/Venus Gemini

These two will be like two kittens fooling around and turning even serious issues into humor and games! Each will taunt the other and possibly tease, too. Both are active sorts with a big appetite for life's curiosities. But Mars Sagittarius is far more athletic than Venus Gemini. Still, they will enjoy sharing philosophical (and other) conversations. Both need to be active since both hate and fear boredom of any kind. They may plan outings to nearby parks or campgrounds, or to museums and art shows. Each will have an internal itinerary that he/she wants to share with the other. As long as neither gets tired of being on the move, this tie can work rather well. Sexually there is a tremendous element of play and a willingness to try many things. Since curiosity runs high for both, some kinky sexual agendas may result. Venus Gemini will try just about anything at least once. There is also a complimentariness here. Mars Sagittarius believes that experience is the ultimate school while Venus Gemini loves the world of words, beliefs, ideas. Each will try to "convert" the other.

In a single chart the individual is a born explorer of ideas, places, people, and things. Not prone to marriage or committed to love, this free spirit has the makings of a writer-philosopher or commentator (even in sports) and will abhor anything that tries to tie him/her down.

Mars Sagittarius/Venus Cancer

I don't know what drew you two together in the first place. Venus Cancer wants home, family, babies, and security, while Mars Sagittarius wants to be out and off experiencing the great unexplored world!

I can see this being the bond of two kids in high school who can't control the libido's pull on them. He goes off to the military; she entertains ideas of a little house and 2.3 children. But will that work between them? Mars Sagittarius can enjoy aloneness and explore on his/her own. Venus Cancer seldom exhibits the "explorer" traits. Each will be profoundly lonely within this tie since each is expecting something entirely different (conscious or subconsciously) from a mate! If (as with Mars Sagittarius/Venus Taurus) the Mars is content to go off by himself, since upon return, a perfectly run home is waiting—the tie could work. This reminds me also of ancient societies where men went off to war and left the women to take care of their homes. Reincarnationally speaking, any two drawn together with this combination may have a past life pattern mirroring this. It seems to be a big compromise for both.

In a single chart a person will be eternally searching for the perfect home and feel like a twentieth-century nomad in the process. This individual may also be searching for an emotional common denominator among peoples; the ultimate religious or philosophical overview of "this thing called life." Not the most stable person, the thirst to understand psyche is strong and this individual will experience frequent, inexplicable mood changes. As the mood changes, he/she may take off for another adventure.

Mars Sagittarius/Venus Leo

Venus Leo would like to play "peacock" and have the lover fawn all over him/her. Yet Mars Sagittarius is a lovable, at times clumsy adventurer, naive as a child. Venus Leo could learn to love him/her and it won't be because they lay a lot of flattery on Venus Leo, either. Venus Leo may abdicate his/her royal throne to romp around with the spirit of childlike play that Mars Sagittarius emanates. They may travel together and experience sports events or fitness exploits together. Mars Sagittarius may even get Venus Leo to find the majesty of the natural world and leave his/her make-up and fur coat and Mercedes behind! There is a strong like-mindedness at the soul level, although both have pursued different values in terms of the outer world—at the personality level. This tie bares both their nakedness to each other and can be therapeutic, promoting greater self-respect (without camouflage) for each.

In a single chart the person is magnanimous, generous, and a lover of life. This individual would be a tremendous motivator to young adults and children and would be an ideal scout leader, or leader in a similar pursuit. They may also be a lover of literature, science, and education. A very inspiring teacher, molding the minds of the young is a probable result of such a tie.

Mars Sagittarius/Venus Virgo

Mars in Sagittarius is an inspired person who acts on urges that come in the way flights of fancy do. Venus Virgo is a born critic, even if the criticism is good and "for their own sake." But enough criticism will, in time, burst the fabulous bubble that inspired Mars Sagittarius chooses to live in. Venus in an earth sign may have enormous consistency and loyalty, but certainly lacks imagination and the Disney-type of fantasy which all fire signs, especially Sagittarians (Disney's own sign) are prone to. Now maybe Mars Sagittarius wants someone who does pay the bills before the first of every month, just to guarantee him/her the legal right to go off, unencumbered (by bills) on his/her adventures. But very little of those adventures can be shared between these two dissimilar elements. Sometimes if we had a very critical parent, we internalize the parent and marry someone similar. This could be the case with those souls who dare marriage, with these planetary ties!

In a single chart the person has interesting flights of fancy, but doubts them and fears acting upon them. They will seem to be at sixes and sevens with themselves, because they block themselves often enough from pursuing the adventures the soul seeks—due to illusions (or real pressures) of duty, responsibility, and commitment to others. An inner state of unrest results until the person learns to make priorities with time and allocate a percentage of time to lofty pursuits.

Mars Sagittarius/Venus Libra

Who would think that graceful and charming Venus Libra, with her perfect China and manicured nails would fall for the woodsman-handyman-carpenter-type . . . Mr. Mars Sagittarius? (It can work the other way around where the perfectly groomed executive falls for the woman who has a blackbelt in karate and a very physical job). Opposites do attract and each of these has appeal for the other in the way that persons from differing cultures are curious about one another's mores. This is more than curiosity, it is respect coupled with occasional awe. Each has something to gain from the other. Venus Libra may have to remind Mars Sagittarius to walk softly around the glass menagerie; and Mars Sagittarius may feel like a field guide when he/she acquaints Venus Libra with the great outdoors. Each can be taken by the beauty of spirit and natural beauty that each exposes the other to. They also notice the beauty in one another's bodies. Venus Libra is so often wonderfully groomed and Mars Sagittarius usually boasts the body of a well-toned athlete. Sexually they blend well together and are gently intoxicated with each other's differences, rather than afraid of them. This bond can be a long and strong one—to the surprise of friends and strangers alike. Mars Sagittarius is blunt and says what's on his/her mind while Venus Libra always tries to say "the right thing" to please others. These different approaches will teach them each more balance.

In a single chart the individual has a strong, supple body that can bring them into athletics, dance, modeling, or other physical pursuits such as figure skating and gymnastics. The individual will enjoy social activity, travel, and may be quite popular. There can also be an interest in law.

Mars Sagittarius/Venus Scorpio

Venus Scorpio can fall in love with sex, and Mars Sagittarius ought to be the lover destined for stamina and fitness. Therefore, theirs can be a sexually powerful bonding. Venus Scorpio will not easily trust the freedom-loving, high-spirited Mars Sagittarius and therein lies the rub, not a sexy one, either! Because Venus Scorpio so fully needs to "possess" the lover, he/she will not let Sagittarius Mars be free. If unfettered, probably Mars Sagittarius will express freedom through sports, not bed-hopping. But once suspicion and restriction surround the Mars Sagittarius, they may just break the rules since they resent their existence in the first place. Generally, besides sex, little areas of mutual interest exist. Venus Scorpio is not too interested in travel, except maybe to the Egyptian pyramids and their ancient underground tunnels. Mars Sagittarius wants to go to sporting events, camping events, and country picnics. I'd suggest that this be a love affair with a high libido threshold. It will be memorable; but to try to hold on to the comet, means you can get burned.

In a single chart there is a tendency to live very much from the body, flesh, and physical conquests. This person could be a professional wrestler, car racer, or a health-fitness teacher. The individual may pursue the perfect body to the point where mind and soul do not develop as they should. Sexually there is great prowess and a possible interest in trying aberrant sexual behavior as well. The individual could pursue anything he/she loved with powerful resolve. But the body seems the primary urge unless the individual is very intelligent.

Mars Sagittarius/Venus Sagittarius

Two free spirits collect their various, unconventional selves (both are dualistic, mutable signs) and venture together on the quest of life. Each knows that life changes; each can live fully in the moment; freely they move together, and move about they will. Each loves travel, sports, fitness, and an independent mind. As long as each remembers that freedom is what brought them together (not bondage), the tie will remain. These two can put a lot of mileage under their belts, even philosophically since neither really looks at society with a sense of conformity and each feels very relieved to be so fully themselves (social icono-clast, rebel that they may be) in the other's company.

Both may have artistic leanings or strive toward athletic excellence and as long as neither takes free time away from the other, both can aid the other in meeting his/her personal goals and choices.

This bond might not bring in children as each preciously guards freedom; neither requires marriage since once again, their goal is personal freedom. However, should there be marriage and children, I hope the kids will be fire or air signs to keep up with the parents!

In a single chart there will be a great love of liberty and such a person could be a Ralph Nader who stands up for consumer or other rights. This individual will likely be into fitness of mind, body, and spirit. It could indicate a college professor, sports educator, or publisher of a sports-related publication. There is a vast interest in travel and a love of art and art history. Marriage can only exist if the partner has a very independent life of his/her own.

Mars Sagittarius/Venus Capricorn

This is a tough combination. Mars Sagittarius with its striving for freedom meets up with the restrictive, guilt-oriented voice of Saturn through the Venus Capricorn lover. Guilt, according to Emmanuel, draws all things to a halt and the momentum and love of life, given to Sagittarius ought not be halted! Venus Capricorn, like all earth signs, needs practical reasons for why things ought to be done. Yet Mars Sagittarius, like all fire signs, must move with the sheer power of impulse to give the activity the momentum it requires for manifestation. Venus Capricorn quite plainly slows down that process for Mars Sagittarius and may render Mars Sagittarius impotent with his/her (Venus Capricorn) insistence on reason, logic, and practicality. It's not worth the compromise. Venus Capricorn would be happier with someone else and ought not waste his/her reservoirs of patience on changing someone who is fine the way they are.

In a single chart there will be visions of creativity that come from Mars Sagittarius; many will be patiently cultivated on a level of arts or crafts, through the patience of Venus Capricorn.

Mars Sagittarius/Venus Aquarius

Probably neither has found someone who makes them feel as free as this individual does. Venus Aquarius is a party person and loves people—all sorts, shapes, and sizes. Mars Sagittarius ranks freedom as an inalienable right. So both can enjoy one another's company, while neither holds the reins too tight on the other. Very pleasant and not the passion that painful love stories are built on, a good friendship exists between these two. If they were attracted to one another in the first place, it is likely that the friendship will have its sensual moments. But it remains in many ways a friendship. Friends tend to give each other more space for growth and personal expression than lovers traditionally do. These two individuals may be very active together. They may be involved in philosophy and metaphysics, politics, ecology, or some state of the art inventive technologies. Both are untraditional and somewhat visionary. Traveling together would bring exotic, out of the ordinary adventures to both, also.

In a single chart the individual loves personal freedom as well as "liberty and justice" for all. This person will have a broad spectrum of interests and may particularly enjoy music. There may also be great travel adventures, political interest, and an ability to work with sophisticated technology. This individual would be philosophical and might become a writer or professor.

Mars Sagittarius/Venus Pisces

A common interest to both is music. Before Neptune's discovery in the nineteenth century, it was thought that the planet Jupiter ruled both Pisces and Sagittarius. An ancient bond exists and both signs are drawn to travel, music, and religion on various levels. Mars Sagittarius loves to be free and Venus Pisces, if in love, is devoted to the beloved and able to adapt him/herself to that other individual. Venus Pisces is looking for someone to be devoted to or some cause to be devoted to. Mars Sagittarius can be very philosophical and help Venus Pisces to identify his/her cause and why it is important. Both Pisces and Sagittarius are, however, mutable signs, so that each is subject to changes of mood. Each will seem at times to be fickle and uncommitted to the other. I can only recommend this bond if both share in ideals, spiritual questing toward self-development or music. Otherwise, a lot of obscurity blocks each from being fully true to the other—all the time.

In a single chart there can be exceptional musical talent or dance ability. The individual might lack the perseverance (unless there is earth present in the entire chart) to work hard at developing the latent talent. This person may waiver a lot, even philosophically, and needs to learn to "build his house on solid rock." There can be an attraction to cults, drugs, and philosophy as an escape from daily responsibility. The path of discipline will curb this individual's life (if he/she lets it) to something of creative value. Discipline is the key and may be sorely lacking, unless other factors provide it.

Mars Capricorn

Mars Capricorn/Venus Aries

Different strokes for different folks is essentially the motive of this combo. Mars Capricorn is highly ambitious and quite able to put off immediate (sexual or otherwise) gratification until the goal sought is grasped. On the other hand, Venus Aries is a very "right now . . . I want it!" sort of person. So how do they reconcile differences? If Aries is intent upon staying an *enfant terrible* and the ever-patient Mars Capricorn is willing to indulge the tantrums, it could work. But Mars Capricorn is dedicated to work goals and Venus Aries wants plenty of attention; unless Mars Capricorn is subsidizing a boutique, art business, or make-up classes for Venus Aries. Generally, while Venus Aries carries an attractive blend of "youthful folly," Mars Capricorn represents vintaged maturity. Will the "age" difference of philosophy cause a father-daughter or mother-son relationship? Or any at all? For a while, it will be an interesting blend; each could learn to see him/herself more objectively through the mirror of so vastly different a companion. For life, it would be tough.

In a single chart the combination can be difficult. Mars Capricorn is intent on career goals and Venus Aries flights of passion keep getting in the way of the "big picture." This individual probably gets pent up with remarkable self-discipline but then can, at untimely moments, surrender to impulse in a way that upsets the goal sought after. Emotions and desire are not working in sync. It's a good combination for a mechanic, mathematician or engineer. This person has technical skill and patience, coupled with headstrong creativity.

Mars Capricorn/Venus Taurus

These two earthy animal signs meet and mate and mix well. It can mean a strong and long commitment when these two get going. The relationship will probably not be a fiery whirlwind of passion, but each may get a sense that "this is it" when they meet. Like the stories we hear of women in forty-two-year-long marriages suggesting that the first time they saw Herbert, they knew he was *the one*. I think only earth signs still believe in the traditional thought that there is some *one* out there; rather than "many."

Each is interested in material comfort and security, both highly respect accomplishment and financial achievement. Similar drives allow each to egg the other on to completion of tasks and eventual ambitions. Sexually they may have each held back more with others than they do with each other; they sense that this is "for keeps." Ironically both being somewhat old fashioned could make them a bit more reserved with each other . . . simply because it is for keeps, not a sexual lark!

In a single chart the individual has the makings of success in the business world. They ought to be practical and work well with concrete financial ideas and projects. Building, construction, real estate, and farming are also good areas for such a person. In terms of the sexual, they are extremely strong in stamina, though moral training (conservative values) may put a yoke on it.

Mars Capricorn/Venus Gemini

Mars Capricorn is seized by ambition for status and power and love is often secondary to that urge. Venus Gemini can speak on many subjects and give the impression of being all for Mars' Capricorn goals; but in reality, the other twin may have a completely different state of mind. Mars Capricorn will normally have a lot of patience, but will not apply it (or wish to) much with Gemini's fickle turns of mood and fancy. Mars Capricorn would rather have a solid mate he/she can count on than one who is often off pursuing whims. Even sexually Venus Gemini likes variety, experimentation, and even occasional "kind." Mars Capricorn expects his/her prowess and stamina to be "enough." It is "enough," it's just that Gemini is mentally insatiable for all kinds of experiments. The urges of these two individuals are vastly different. It would be a very awkward relationship unless other planets give different "testimony." Even so, their sexual natures will rarely ever blend into real oneness.

In a single chart the individual has many clever ideas and Mars Capricorn will have to exert the discipline to see some of them through. There may be skill with the hands, especially in construction or various kinds of building. The temperament is somewhat cold and ambitious and love can be a fickle adventure, more than a committed union. This individual doesn't know how to be close to another; and masks it by being a little bit close to many.

Mars Capricorn/Venus Cancer

Capricorn is the traditional archetype of father while Cancer is the traditional archetype of mother. Thus their roles are traditionally expressed through the polarity of Mars and Venus in this tie. If the woman has Mars Capricorn, she will likely be the worldly ambitious one in this union (or a "Lady Macbeth" for Mr. Venus Cancer's career) while he is the honorary "house husband." Venus Cancer is lord of the home and kitchen and Mars Capricorn wants to climb in the world of business and achievement. Mars Capricorn is the kind of individual who can take care of financial responsibilities well, freeing Venus Cancer to be the cook and housewife *extraordinaire*. Sexually their opposite elements bring them into a transcendental blending and very binding feelings of oneness prevail. Of course, opposites also have their conflicts, but the undeniable high of oneness usually overrides these in the long run and this can likely be a bond that endures.

In a single chart these are the workings of a successful family business; a business that caters to products for the home; a restaurant business or other occupations that combine property and homes with business acumen. The individual's life may be polarized in that work is work and family is family and never the twain shall meet. Generally, if this person seeks inner balance, they will enjoy both family and work spheres. Ambition, probably to maintain a family, is present.

Mars Capricorn/Venus Leo

The fiery, effervescent Venus Leo could be drawn to the quiet, powerful Mars Capricorn just because she (it'll probably be she) senses he can provide for her royal needs. Mars Capricorn usually is unable to settle for second best; in ladies, he will sense that she has class and expects the best. That's a good incentive for him to work toward that best. If roles are reversed, the successful Mars Capricorn woman may sense that Venus Leo is the male to let down her guard for and party with. While fire and earth are not easily blended elements, each admires the qualities of the other. Mars Capricorn has great sexual stamina and Venus Leo wants to feel that he/she is the "great lover" and will interpret the prowess of Mars Capricorn to be a credit toward that "title." Sexually they can bring out the best in one another; it will almost be a performance. Mars Capricorn is not likely to shower attention or affection over Venus Leo in public; Mars Capricorn has great (too much) respect for protocol and privacy. Venus Leo will demand gestures of love which will likely then be preserved for the bedroom, and likely, worth waiting for. This relationship can work with other compatible factors supporting it. She can be the queen who reigns over volunteer work, the community, the home as long as she allows his long periods away while he pursues grand and ambitious goals.

In a single chart the person's ambition knows no bounds. This individual could also (male or female) consciously cultivate marriage to someone who would improve his/her career and social status. There is a belief that he/she deserves the best in all things; this person probably still believes in a class society, where certain individuals, by birth, are entitled to more status and power than others. Politics will appeal to such a one; as would the in-company politics of big business. There may also be an attraction to theatre or hotel management.

Mars Capricorn/Venus Virgo

No one will run a home or business better than this team, if they team up together with goals in mind. Venus Virgo can fall in love with work and become devoted to his/her mate's lifework, since Virgo seeks to serve—in some manner—love. Mars Capricorn's quest for status is nearly legendary. Both really want success in the material world and because they are both earth signs, they blend and their lack of resistance to each other allows things to flow more or less smoothly. In a sense, sex could become another duty to this couple which would be harder on Mars Capricorn who really has strong and abundant animal instincts. But Mars Capricorn can easily put off current gratification—for a long-range goal and may, in fact, sublimate his/her sexual force into work-related goals and projects. Sometimes we don't know what we're missing if we haven't had it. This is not to say Venus Virgo wouldn't want to please his/her lover; it's just that Venus is not really sexy in Virgo and it takes some sexiness to stir the Mars Capricorn passions into their powerful pitch.

In a single chart the combination produces a person who is a perfectionist in his/her work. No one will doubt this individual's professional performance, since undoubtedly they will set high standards for themselves and be their own worst critic at times. Willing to learn from mistakes, they constantly seek to perfect their work. Their potential is as great as their ambition because they integrate constructive criticism, continue to grow and do a very fine job at whatever they are committed to. For this person, career is life and marriage is secondary—if it exists at all. Were it not for social mores and family expectations, this person would prefer solitude.

Mars Capricorn/Venus Libra

Even though a tense relationship exists between Mars and Venus, there *is* undeniable attraction between these two. It is likely they would meet at a business, political, art, or office function. Mars Capricorn would exude power and Venus Libra beauty. How often these two become a trade-off that even history has been affected! They may not agree about a lot of things, although Venus Libra can be very conciliatory and compromising if he/she wants to be. Mars Capricorn wants success and part of the American dream of success includes a beautiful, well-groomed mate. Many beautiful people expect power and riches due to their genetic "birth right." So these two will be drawn together. As long as Venus Libra has his/her parties, social occasions, credit cards, or expense allowance (probably all provided by workaholic Mars Capricorn) all goes well. Each is somewhat detached, and both can role-play. This is not unlike the arrangement between a politician and an expensive call-girl, except by name and legal status. Each ultimately wants space to do his/her own thing while each provides the picture of a successful life-style that the other wants.

In a single chart, the individual will be a shrewd diplomat. He will have the ability to influence others, be it in sales, politics, foreign affairs, or whatever. The ambitions are strong, and he enjoys being involved in the jet set or beautiful people class. This person is somewhat cold-blooded and will also use relationships to suit *other* needs—frequently of status. If a woman, will likely marry (at least in part) for status.

Mars Capricorn/Venus Scorpio

There'll be no secrets here, each a Columbo in his own right! Both have similar instincts and inclinations. Scorpio and Capricorn are both very private signs interested in status and winning. Together as allies they will be a very formidable team against life's various tests and quests. This would be a typical couple in high political circles. Each knows instinctively what face to put on to the crowd, and what to be "at home." They are both very sexual signs, yet each can sublimate the sexual force into other things. That force is essentially what *all* power is about; and these two may choose to sublimate the sexual force into power of other kinds. When sexual relations occur, the unspoken feelings between them become strengthened. Neither is an articulate Robert Browning, singing love songs to the other. The fact is, both are quite untrusting of others and yet each lets down his/her guard and trusts the other. The very fact that their secret society of self has multiplied by two is their highest expression of love—for one another. This bond can be long term; besides, neither wants the other to "escape" with his/her private life known!

In a single chart here is a mind that can produce war strategies, business strategies or FBI/CIA-type work. Secrecy, research, protocol, honor, duty, and authority are high on the list. Such an individual is suited to military life. There may also be skill in mechanics, martial arts, engineering, and the like. The person will have a strong sexual nature but will probably distance him- or herself from deep, committed ties. Some will marry for life and possibly conduct discreet sexual affairs on the side. They paradoxically carry guilt *and* sexual hunger. They may then marry a traditional person to suit their "guilt" side and conduct devious alliances to assuage their strongly sexual nature.

Mars Capricorn/Venus Sagittarius

Venus Sagittarius can always be happy to stay a perpetual student, enrolled in classes; or to travel continuously in an attempt to graft art (of all cultures) onto his/her soul. Mars Capricorn, a workaholic by nature, could provide the financial wherewithal to Venus Sagittarius' flights of fancy. But when will they be together, and how? Venus Sagittarius isn't interested much in housework or tradition which is strong on Mars Capricorn's list of essentials. If these two got together, it might be something akin to Donna Rice and Gary Hart. The workaholic takes a break to travel for a weekend reprieve from his usual high-pressure itinerary. This is a bond difficult for me to find strength in. There may be some sexual attraction, but Mars Capricorn is not apt to take Venus Sagittarius too seriously. Venus Sagittarius might pop up in the life of Mars Capricorn for that express purpose: to bring a reprieve and a chance to dance with life through travel. Mars Capricorn needs to be anonymous to let down his/her guard; Venus Sagittarius could prove to be the inspiration for such a getaway. But life, to be lived on a daily basis, is much more than sporadic getaways. This is not forever.

In a single chart one might have a ship captain or person endowed with authority and strong self-discipline in a travel-related field. The owner of a hotel, dog track, or horse track might bear this planetary signature. It could also represent someone working with the travel industry on a broad basis. The individual would see love as escapism and possibly marry a woman of a different culture who was more comfortable with male-breadwinner/woman-at-home type roles.

Mars Capricorn/Venus Capricorn

When people like the same things, it's easier to share in life's activities. Both under the same element Capricorn brings natural affinity. Venus Capricorn will be an inspiration and a push to Mars Capricorn's strong ambitions. They can work together as partners in pursuit of status and financial goals. Both are creatures of privacy with a high regard for tradition, reputation, and protocol. Therefore sex between them may not be often, each believing that less lofty aspects of life come first. But when they do engage in sex, especially over time, they will grow into a powerful explosion. Capricorn, as a rule, matures over time. Both are slow moving earth signs, who reach heat slowly . . . but it never dies. This will be a love that permeates all areas of life, letting the normal duties to one another become something more sacred. There is the kind of love and patience for one another, seen in those durable marriages which last many, many years.

In a single chart the person is by and large, a pragmatist. Possessing so much earth, he/she requires a more whimsical mate just to put the magic back in life. (That's why we have Spielberg and Disney, folks!) This individual will work long and hard for his/her chosen ambition. Business, politics, mechanics, and commerce are favored areas.

Mars Capricorn/Venus Aquarius

This will be a veritable "owl and the pussycat," for Mars Capricorn is so frequently repressed, straight-laced and "under control." Venus Aquarius can throw reputation to the wind, merely interested in living fully and completely in the moment and being accountable to a law-unto-self, alone! So what would attract them to each other? Sometimes opposites do attract and many negotiate some of the world's most unique relationships ever observed or documented! Mars Capricorn can spend a hard day at the office and come home to oriental foods and kimonos with the unconventional Venus Aquarius. Or Mars Capricorn might have a business trip to Japan, only to return to a surprise party in his living room MC'd by yours truly, Venus Aquarius. This is bound to be a very upsetting and also invigorating tie. Venus Aquarius will slip smoothly through all of Mars Capricorns buts and excuses and teach him/her to enjoy sex with unprecedented abandon. Mars Capricorn may decide he/she wants to "keep" (earth signs think in terms of ownership) Venus Aquarius; but this lofty creature belongs to the world and is capable of loving many—and intimately, too. They see the unique in people, not the failings. Enjoy it while it lasts.

In a single chart we might find the workaholic who plays just as hard in after-hours. This person could be the most popular executive in a large firm, who jumps over seniority conventions to make it to the top first. Hard working and exuding enormous charm, this individual will win friends and influence people. He/she would make a good lawyer, company executive, computer engineer, or complex hi-tech official.

Mars Capricorn/Venus Pisces

Venus Pisces, composed of water, wants a mate to provide the vessel-like closure that solid earth signs are known for. Mars Capricorn sometimes lacks imagination of which Venus Pisces has ample reserves. And Mars Capricorn is excellent at administering and managing the less pleasant aspects of life like paying bills, emptying the garbage, and making sure the car has oil. Those are things very easily forgotten (or never recognized at all) by Venus Pisces. So if Mars Capricorn wants his/her home life to be filled with imagination and escape from the pressures of work, it could be with the gentle Venus Pisces mate. Venus Pisces will encourage successful (or nearly so) Mars Capricorn to buy a boat or condo near water, and together they will spend time in the Venus Pisces dreamy world of peace, beauty, and tranquility. Sometimes if Mars Capricorn becomes too entrapped by his/her innate workaholic tendencies and overly neglects the impressionable (easily rejected) Venus Pisces, Venus Pisces can turn to drugs or alcohol for the illusion of comfort and companionship. To avoid this, both need to set aside time for togetherness. Potentially each provides the missing links which the other lacks and that could bring a really synergistic compatibility.

In a single chart the visionary, unlimited imagination of Venus Pisces couples with the practical, hard-working ambitions of Mars Capricorn and anything can transpire. This might be a person who creates scenery or special effects for the movie industry; or a landscape artist who turns a weeded mess into a palatial haven. Hard work and imaginative, creative ideas can yield many types of professional expression. This person truly has the best of both worlds. He/she can relax and enjoy the inner life and also put his/her best foot forward into the outer world.

NOTE: When our own Venus-Mars are compatible, we bring more balance into our associations and can handle relationships with more security. Those with inharmonious Venus-Mars aspects in their *own* charts, require mates who have earth-water combinations, earth-earth, or even fire-air combinations for balancing.

Mars Aquarius

Mars Aquarius/Venus Aries

Mars Aquarius is a gregarious, freedom-loving, true individualist. Venus Aries can be singularly creative, independent, and fond of others' ideas. The two match well. Mars Aquarius may have broader dreams than those of Venus Aries; but if Venus Aries is willing to learn from Mars Aquarius, the two can work toward common objectives. No one really possesses an individual with Mars Aquarius; they belong to life itself, and frequently to life's great causes (political, scientific, and social). Venus Aries likes to be "where the action is" and will, probably admire the social urges of Mars Aquarius. At times, Mars Aquarius may find Venus Aries to be naively self-centered; but, as in the film, *Educating Rita,* an attraction to Venus Aries' sheer delightfulness can develop. These two are both creatures of the wind and each is capable of losing inhibitions (or perhaps never harboring any from the start). They can flow into exquisite moments where anything, including fun-sex, can occur. These two will have fun together; each becoming suddenly youthful in the other's presence.

In a single chart this might be the expression of the crusader *extraordinaire*. Such a person will be a daring individualist who may be a fountain of creative, futuristic ideas. This person will have ideas ahead of his/her time and essentially be open to many unconventional (by others' standards) life experiences. It would be difficult to be the parent of such an iconoclast; this person could become a major rebel against the establishment.

Mars Aquarius/Venus Taurus

These two will be as different as night and day. We all carry the equivalent of Freudian complexes within; it is possible that the ultimate revolutionary has a mother complex and in spite of his/her iconoclastic beliefs, harbors the vision of the earth-mother mate. To this person, a bond of Mars Aquarius and Venus Taurus is possible. I didn't say harmonious, I said "possible." Mars Aquarius is a creature of impulse and lives from moment to moment which can mean that the rent money is spent for a "cause." Venus Taurus wants the home to be his/her castle and thinks in terms of personal comforts and possessions first and foremost. (Although both believe that the hungry ought to be fed and could team up for that cause!) Mars Aquarius has a large social whirlwind of friends (many are called friends five minutes after being introduced). Venus Taurus wants a mate who can be possessed like a favorite chair. No one ever really possesses someone with any major planet in Aquarius. Venus Taurus will not find this a steady secure bond and Venus Taurus is his/her most loving and sensual when security is part of the romantic equation. When both are naive or college-bound, they might be drawn to each other's bodies, but their spirits reign in different domains, making real communion virtually impossible.

In a single chart the individual has a deep inner conflict between marriage, security, and personal comfort; and has the desire to get involved with a "mission" greater than self and its personal needs. The individual could try to live both extremes and feel inwardly polarized. Such a person could also have a very active life—politically and a very conservative mate to provide a kind of "anchoring" to his/her life. Sexual fidelity will be difficult; an inner moral struggle can occur about just that.

Mars Aquarius/Venus Gemini

If the Venus Gemini twins themselves don't penetrate some level of understanding the iconoclast Mars Aquarius, few will be able to! Gemini loves curiosities and Mars Aquarius will be at least that. Venus Gemini can't stomach boredom of any kind. Mars Aquarius is so subject to change without notice that the mutable Venus has the requirements to love, in spite of it. "I can't make dinner," and Venus Gemini thinks of a contingency plan that works so that his/her evening isn't ruined and no resentment builds up. Mars Aquarius may try to keep commitments but feeling often as all things to all others, many commitments seem to overshadow each other. You'll just have to be willing to share someone with Mars Aquarius. Venus Gemini loves parties, flirtations, meeting new people, and generally being busy with his/her own interests anyway. Each has a high tolerance level for the others faux pas for they intuitively read each other fairly well. While neither is the picture of passion, they both enjoy the game of love and both are fairly uninhibited. Joy more than communion will characterize their sexual interplay. This partnership has good potential for endurance.

In a single chart we have an actor, communicator, MC, or a fabulous salesperson. Anything this individual is convinced of (and I mean anything) they can influence others about. There is ability with radio announcing, newspaper reporting, general teaching, writing, and research. Love is more on the mental than physical level for them.

Mars Aquarius/Venus Cancer

Although Mars Aquarius is committed to causes that frequently take him out of and away from the home, he/she could be drawn to the home-loving tendencies of Venus Cancer as a safe harbor to rest at! But Venus Cancer, borrowing from its crab symbol, has long, tenacious claws and doesn't always let go easily. Would a Venus Cancer individual be able to trust a Mars Aquarius to near constant outside adventuring? If the two have other powerfully crossed aspects, they may want this relationship and work to negotiate mutual trust and consideration. Old role patterns will not easily work. Each has to give the other a lot of freedom. Mars Aquarius can enjoy, deeply, some moments "at home" with Venus Cancer; but Venus Cancer either learns to travel with Mars Aquarius, or be content with his/her own hobbies and life-style at home.

In a single chart we might have a revolutionary who prints materials at his/her home. This would also favor an interior designer who used eclectic styling in his/her work. A chef who majored in health food could have this configuration, as could a homemaker with strong political inclinations. There is an interest in improving the outer world from one's own home.

Mars Aquarius/Venus Leo

Opposites come together and can either find a rare and unusual relationship based on their very acute differences, or part ways and miss out on one of life's unique adventures. Mars Aquarius champions causes and Venus Leo is looking for flattery and a single fan. Now if Mars Aquarius wants a love entanglement with Venus Leo, he/she knows how to court. It's just that Mars Aquarius is, at least in part, committed to saving the world. Venus Leo has to share the spotlight of his/her heart with other causes. Opposites are a part of the divine plan in that they represent the magnetism that animates all life. When opposite sexual planets (Venus/Mars) meet, they sense this primordial link—although it may be more intuitive than conscious. Blending brings such a high (probably unknown to either before this "alchemy") that each may be willing to hang in there and handle the lapses of attention from the other. Venus Leo will even abdicate her throne to march among the multitudes, experiencing Mars Aquarius' cause with him/her.

In a single chart there is an inner split on the soul level involving whether to follow humane interests and dedicate one's life to humanity; or whether to pursue self-interest and passion. The individual may intersperse love affairs with his/her spiritual mission, which can confuse issues. This sign has much love but has to learn how and where to channel that powerful love force. Leadership, the arts, social work, welfare counseling, and educating the young are typical "callings."

Mars Aquarius/Venus Virgo

Both individuals are impressed with cleanliness and good grooming and may be drawn to each other, in part, for this "purity" of appearance. Mars Aquarius is able to channel sexual energy into spiritual and professional pursuits. Venus Virgo usually does not possess a particularly strong sex drive and like Mars Aquarius, channels much of his/her basic energy into work. Both have an abstract inner dedication to helping people in some way. While this may then not result in the most passionate of couplings, both can be helpmates to one another in other ways. Venus Virgo can commit to Mars Aquarius' ideals and the projects which these generate. However, Mars Aquarius will brook no resistance from anyone, and anything in Virgo is the born critic who notices which details of *any* project need amending. Venus Virgo's tendency to criticize in the name of "helping" will get on Mars Aquarius' nerves. So at times it will be best that they give each other space. The bond has good and difficult aspects to it; it works best when both have ideals to serve outside of their relationship.

In a single chart the person will be ultrafastidious and possibly too critical of self (and others) for their own good. There may be medical and scientific, as well as technological visions presently encouraging a career in one of these pursuits. This individual is very much a perfectionist and could easily be the politician preaching for human rights but being very intolerant of those close at hand. We "teach best what we most need to learn."

Mars Aquarius/Venus Libra

Mars Aquarius can be the shining star of politics, the legal profession, or in technological wizardry. Venus Libra, usually (consciously or not) uses his/her good looks as a trade-off for status and financial comforts in a relationship. Even if neither of these two is rich or famous, they will take a genuine liking to each other. Air signs understand each other and just as air moves around freely, air signs seldom enforce rigid codes of behavior on each other. If either has had a problem past (many of us have), then this partner will be understanding, rather than judgmental about it. It will be understanding that gives this relationship a kind of "glue" that holds it together. Libra placements prefer order and harmony but are surprisingly tolerant in the face of unconventional, disruptive, or irrational behavior on the part of their mate. This union can work. Both enjoy friends and social outings and both are air signs, which suggests a similarity of biological rhythm—right down to the sexual urge. Neither is addicted to sex; both can feel communion on a mental level often enough to forget about the body. But even in one another's bodies, there will be a pleasing kind of harmony and comfort.

In a single chart we have the makings of a great lawyer, a human-rights or environmental activist. This individual will probably stand up and "count for something." There is an abundance of charm, a desire to be fair to others, and live the positive law of karma. This person will probably be attractive to others on many levels and can bring peace and harmony to situations where there was little or none.

Mars Aquarius/Venus Scorpio

That passion flower of Venus Scorpio will be seductive to Mars Aquarius; she might even be the Mata Hari that betrays his plans! Very few persons with Venus Scorpio are willing (or able) to share their lover. Mars Aquarius may have several alliances at once, which can bubble into sexual relations; however, more significant than this to his/her make-up is the devotion to a cause. Venus Scorpio will feel rejected when Mars Aquarius takes up his/her arms and marches for one cause or another. Venus Scorpio will use sex as a manipulation if need be to hold the attentions (or try to) of this wanderer. Since Venus Scorpio is primarily moved by sex, he/she will not understand why or how Mars Aquarius can shift from being a responsive lover to simply detaching and going off (anyway!) to do his/her own thing. This may convince Venus Scorpio that foul play is going on even when it isn't. The sting of the Scorpio is legendary (note its symbol: scorpion). There can be battles over jealousy here which will be far from pleasant; violence is even possible if the Venus Scorpio is not highly "evolved." This combination is going to leave someone broken-hearted, or at least, injured in the pride department.

In a single chart the individual will have strong political beliefs and be quite a strategist who moves toward these beliefs. It may be said that this individual will follow an "ends justify the means" attitude in pursuit of his/her ideals. The ideals may be quite good; the means, questionable. It is likely a part of this individual's soul purpose to sort out pure idealistic strivings from desires of the ego. It will be challenging and may be a "karmic replay" from another life.

Mars Aquarius/Venus Sagittarius

These two free spirits will feel joyous deliverance about finding one another. Each is outgoing, each has an idealistic vision about human nature and the probable direction of humankind; each expects and enjoys personal liberties. They are well suited to a friendship which evolves into love. In fact, there are so many compatible points, that the explosive factors, sometimes taken to mean sexual passion, may not be present. These two would grow into love as they become familiar with one another. They will give each other as much room as either needs and not get in the way of each other's personal quests and dreams; in fact, each is prophetic and visionary in his/her own way and each will give the other unique insights that aid in his/her work. Sports, travel, political events, archaeology, and the study of metaphysics would give these two even more common ground to connect. It is a highly favorable combination.

In a single chart there exists the world traveler who really has chosen to travel in this lifetime and come to know intimately the thousands of variations on the theme of being human. The position would most favor a teacher, writer, archaeologist, or a New Age healer-psychologist. This individual will never accept anything at face value; the pursuit of truth is the center of his/her life. All values emanate from being free and true to self. Marriage may prove too restrictive, but love affairs will follow him/her about. This individual radiates a high-spiritedness.

Mars Aquarius/Venus Capricorn

Perhaps I am prejudiced, but if volatile, free-spirited Mars Aquarius couples up with an earth sign Venus (and other major planets) there is going to be trouble; *unless* Mars wants the traditional home as an escape from the fight and struggle he/she exerts on the outer world in his/her crusading efforts to speed up human evolution and its various appendages. Venus Capricorn can be a pragmatist and manage to run a household in the absence of Mars Aquarius (which could be frequent); he/she can also pay bills on time . . . that's one of the assets of most earth signs! Venus Capricorn will need extraordinary patience to maintain balance with Mars Aquarius since this Mars position is so subject to change of plan. The whole world is his/her friend and as friends cross his/her path, spontaneous social occasions instantly develop, throwing off the plans already agreed upon with Venus Capricorn. ("No, I won't be home late for dinner, tonight, dear . . ."). If two people love each other enough, then with megadoses of patience and tolerance, this relationship can continue. Mars Aquarius can use a little stability and Venus Capricorn can let in a little spontaneity (I said "a little"). Neither will change the other; try as they might.

In a single chart there are ahead-of-their-time urges and ideals which can be slowly worked on with Venus Capricorn. This could also represent "the inventor" who marries socially "up" and has a wife who can support him. Usually the individual is impractical and ingenious, but strives for practical application of his/her works. It is a somewhat frustrating combination to the bearer.

Mars Aquarius/Venus Aquarius

There's no telling what these two extreme iconoclasts will be up to together. They might sell everything and live in a geodesic dome in the deserts of New

Mexico. Whatever they finally do, it will be crazy, kinky, and outrageous and people will inwardly think, "I wish I had the guts to do that!" Both of these individuals are creatures of spontaneity and serendipity, and have a very good dose of trust in the Creator. They live for the moment and frequently close to the edge as well. Who but another bearing the rays of Uranus could live with Mars Aquarius? Venus and Mars march to the beat of the same drummer here; and as mentioned, it is a unique one! They will compete with each other in the way couples jog together to keep fit. This tie will keep each on his/her toes. It may even involve faithfulness; though neither would probably be spontaneously faithful to anyone else; they both satisfy so many urges of one another on so many levels! Sex will be fun, uninhibited, and sometimes outrageous.

In a single chart life will be visionary and in direct rebellion to many existing social standards. This person could be an astronaut, rock star, or a super genius with math or computers. This person's perceptions outreach those of most of his/her peers which could make him/her feel like an outcast or as a leader or both! There will be multiple ties since this individual will have difficulty finding others at his/her level and will therefore seek "nourishment" in pieces from many. An unusual life has been chosen and will be had.

Mars Aquarius/Venus Pisces

Venus Pisces can read into the soul of just about anyone, due to his/her enormous level of sympathy and sensitivity. But, trying to read into Mars Aquarius' soul is like trying to analyze complicated trigonometric formulas. This complex individual is often in a state of flux and quite difficult for others to find a rationale trajectory to explain the direction of his/her actions! The key is to observe and seek to flow together, when moments together exist at all. If Venus Pisces doesn't get caught up in feeling too martyred about it, it could work. But should Venus Pisces listen to all the threats leveled at him/her by family who still want to see the American dream portrayed by this couple, many tears will flow. Pisces rules the sea. If other *very* strong factors have brought these two together, they might exchange lessons. Venus Pisces could remind Mars Aquarius about the human element of peoples' feelings, which sometimes get lost in his/her abstract theories. In turn, Mars Aquarius can help Venus Pisces to become more objective about things that require objective review, not just compassion. It will, however, be a tough trade-off.

In a single chart there is a visionary who has a seer quality that may involve insight into higher math, music, physics, and chemistry—in a word, how our world works. The individual will be able to use higher science, math, art, or writing as a vessel for sharing knowledge coming from a higher plane for which this soul is a conduit. In terms of personal life, this person will need much time for his/her philosophical musings; but is capable of liquid blending when sexual relations occur with an understanding (of his/her arhythmic needs) mate.

Mars Pisces

Mars Pisces/Venus Aries

Mars in Pisces is frequently a dreamer and without earth in his/her own chart is going to have difficulty making major life commitments. Venus Aries really wants someone who is a leader and Mars Pisces frequently is not. Mars Pisces is water and a creature of strong mood swings and Venus Aries is not the most easy person to live with. Each of these individuals needs a mate who is well grounded and patient enough to love them through thick and thin. It is very doubtful whether either of these persons can project the kind of love that makes for lasting partnership. Venus Aries is delightful, but quite self-centered and Mars Pisces can be dedicated to something outside of the self, because there is a very deep quality of devotion present. I just don't think these two will get far being dedicated to each other. Dishonesty and escapist behaviors would more than likely prevail.

In a single chart the person probably entertains naive assumptions about love and relationships. If his/her pride is injured, this individual could resort to very self-destructive or other unwise behavior. This individual could work vehemently on behalf of others, especially abandoned children or the like. But they need to experience self-love and positive self-esteem (and therapy might be needed).

Mars Pisces/Venus Taurus

Here is an interesting relationship tie. The dreamy, sensitive Mars Pisces finds a Rock of Gibraltar to anchor him/herself to in Venus Taurus. Venus is very strong in her own sign and being earthy, provides structure, security, warmth and the capacity for a lasting relationship. Mars Pisces is a voyager of life and has experienced the full spectrum of emotions, sometimes with too much an emphasis on self-pity. But if Venus Taurus loves Mars Pisces, he/she can ground him/her and enable his/her tremendous creativity to surge freely. Mars Pisces can be an artist, musician, boat builder, dancer, and in general, a highly imaginative person. Venus Taurus knows how to help Mars Pisces make his/her dreams and other endeavors practical and saleable. These two can team up well. Venus Taurus is a very sensual person and his/her touch can be healing. Mars

Pisces seems to absorb the slings and arrows of everyone else's outrageous fortune, yet Venus Taurus can soothe Mars Pisces and help him/her to release those empathetic absorptions. Each can be a poet to the other and sexuality knows no bounds. Although here Venus contains Mars, and here Mars needs it.

In a single chart the great craftsperson, musician, songwriter, sculptor, or gymnast would have this signature of planetary interplay. This individual is moved by something nonmaterial and often inspired. Venus Taurus helps the individual to grasp the vision and bring it down to earth, frequently through a creative outlet. This individual has the best of both worlds in a harmonious joining between earthy hard work and mystical inspiration. In love they will be capable of profound sacrifice for the beloved, and there will be much stability in their relationship.

Mars Pisces/Venus Gemini

These two could, quite literally, drive each other crazy! Mars Pisces is so sensitive to sadness, pain, and human injustice and Venus Gemini moves so quickly, he/she hardly notices when his/her witty comments cause hurt to another. Gemini is, after all, a prankster. But his/her pranks are far too heartless for the impressionable Mars Pisces. Besides, each is a double sign and neither will show the same side twice in a row. This makes for a rather complex pattern of relating; both are so busy hiding and shading themselves that the authenticity needed for real love and intimacy never seems to really crystallize. These two might be good partners in improvisational theatre or a photography class. But for life, it would be asking for "the nut house." They might even work together where one brainstorms fantastic ideas and the other writes these down. But when it comes to understanding one another, these two couldn't be further removed from truth. Too many mirrors within them reflect simply out-of-context fragments of each other.

In a single chart the individual will have a tough time grasping for willpower to put his/her unique (and they will be unique) ideas into practice. The person may be overly sensitive and then overly analyze their own sensitivities to the point where feelings and intellect are in a veritable battle. Helping others would be the wisest professional choice, for in getting our minds off ourselves, answers to our own life longings magically manifest.

Mars Pisces/Venus Cancer

While these two will dreamily recognize one another through the water element, they may sweep each other out to sea. Their bond can be so complete that the rest of the world is shut out. Hopefully, the kind of love and beauty they bring to each other will come to bear on each of their life works and prove to be a support to (rather than conflict with) that work.

These two will "read" each other telepathically and hardly need to rely on the ambiguity of speech at all. They will be highly compassionate toward one another and may indulge each other with pampering, attention, and love. Each could even unwittingly suffocate the other with "too much" love!

They ought to take up boating or live near water. Each has a very romantic nature and seems to fit many of the internal images that the other feels their relationship is "supposed to be."

In a single chart there are very strong domestic urges. In fact, such a person could live on a houseboat or become first mate of some water vehicle. The Coast Guard or Navy would also appeal if elsewhere in the chart there are placements in Capricorn or Scorpio. This individual is prone to deep emotional involvements and if these should not work out, escapist behavior aimed at drowning out the pain would be manifest. There is much compassion, and in women a very maternal instinct that favors teaching.

Mars Pisces/Venus Leo

Although both are artists, (frustrated or accomplished, and art or music could likely draw them together) their natures are very different. Each is prone to fall in love with love, and if the illusion of love germinates between them, it may be a while before they realize they're each in love with an image of love (which the other mirrors, or seems to fulfill) not with each other! While the illusion lasts, Mars Pisces can teach Venus Leo about flowing with life, imagination, and movement which Venus Leo will later weave into his/her own creations. Venus Leo just loves to love and can be supportive of the ego (and obliterate various insecurities present in Mars Pisces) to Mars Pisces. But Mars Pisces is far from a pragmatist and may live financially from day to day (unless there is strong earth elsewhere). Venus Leo really wants to live like a queen or nearly so. This mate will not provide for that in the long run. And Venus Leo wants much flattery and tends to be haughty; if Pisces is treated in too servile a manner, he/she will simply swim off and look for new mates to flow into life with.

In a single chart there is a highly quixotic dreamer with abilities in acting, theatre, music, and especially in dance. This person may "see" images or be gifted with a kind of inspired channel that sends creative ideas—by direct line—into this individual's range of actualization. Inspired art is the key here. In love, there is much loving but there may not be a wise choice of partners. Not as possessive as Othello, but apt to love unwisely, and too well. There is also much compassion and love for children and an ability to work with the handicapped ones.

Mars Pisces/Venus Virgo

There's usually a lot to be said about opposites, but when the opposites are in double-signs of a mutable nature, it's more like a minimum of four people (not two) relating at any given interval, and that's when they're both centered! Crowd scenes can develop! Planets in Pisces frequently make the individual susceptible to a kind of "bleed through" between (or among) layers of consciousness, rendering the person subject to strange moods which can represent past lives. The opposite sign will trigger this effect even more. It will be very tough for these two to trust each other; they are so vastly different and to each other appear inconsistent. (Unless other miraculous aspects enable them to get used to each other's seeming inconsistency). Pisces is ruled by Neptune, mythological god of the sea. Since the sea currents frequently change, Mars Pisces simply "goes with the flow." But no sign more than Virgo wants precision, order, and organization, and tries to impose that order over the tides is well—a disorderly presumption! Venus Virgo loves order and precision, or the illusion of it. How can these two fulfill each other's different needs? If Virgo understood he/she needs Pisces for flights of fancy and if Mars Pisces were willing to discipline him/herself enough to allow in just a teeny bit of order, they might find enough poetry in each other's to stick around for the hard karmic work promised to such a union.

In a single chart it will be a tough but fascinating combination. This individual will be so rigid about some things and so flexible about others. They could possibly take the visionary insights from Mars Pisces and conduct them into tangible work with Venus Virgo. There is also the escape hatch of working with the disabled, the blind, or the mentally ill. This is the best way for this combination to find their own sanity, otherwise self-willed perfectionism can lead to alcoholism!

Mars Pisces/Venus Libra

The attraction to beauty, the arts, and lofty ideals brings these two together. Venus Libra might be the patron of the arts and Mars Pisces, the *enfant terrible*—a genius (like Mozart) who wants a patron especially a sexually intimate one. They will be quite tolerant of each other having some (but not all) insight into each other. Both their ruling planets (Neptune and Venus) are feminine in nature so the relationship will veer to matters of art, music, home activities, cooking, and literature. They could inspire each other's artworks or inner development and they will, by and large, create their own romantic cocoon. This will work best if one or both has a wealthy spouse or expense account. Neither is ambitious for "hard work"; both are lazy, can be self-indulgent (especially when together), and love the good things in life, perhaps too much so.

In a single chart there is not a lot of backbone or discipline. If the person was blessed with good looks (and it could turn out to be quite the reverse of a blessing if no inward development follows), they will likely marry into financial security and live out their days dabbling in art and taking up self-indulgence as a way of life. Weight problems, shopping or other addictions may ensue. Everyone needs a *raison d'être*.

Mars Pisces/Venus Scorpio

Venus Scorpio loves by instinct and should he/she choose one with Mars Pisces, I doubt if Mars Pisces would be strong enough to swim against this magnetic current. Mars Pisces, like a fish, will get snagged. The relationship will work as long as Venus Scorpio has the power or control and as long as Mars Pisces fits the mystiqué of lover, projected at him/her from Venus Scorpio. Pisces is highly adaptable, and being ruled by Neptune, the planet of illusions, this position can make one an actor. In other words, Mars Pisces can live up to the projection, coming from another person. This is similar to the concept of number fifty-four, "The Marrying Maiden," in the I Ching. There is, of course, magnetism here in that each is a water sign; and has been repeatedly mentioned, elements of the same sign have a natural affinity. This affinity is doubly strong among water signs, water being such a definitive element to the very nature of human love and feeling (not to mention intuitive links from other lives as soul memory). Neither really trusts the other once the early infatuation of love wears off. They could even stay together long after love's illusion has passed, just because they get addicted to living each other's projections. It's a form of psychic ping-pong!

In a single chart the person will have a lot of sexual magnetism and if they are lazy, they will use it to secure financial security (one way or another) from a more down to earth type! There is ability with dance, aerobics, t'ai chi, martial arts generally, and yoga. Some self-aggrandizing gurus might fall into this astrological bracket, as well. Willpower is conspicuous by its utter absence here. There is a lust for sensation—possibly including drugs, alcohol, etc.

Mars Pisces/Venus Sagittarius

Both of these individuals would probably sail the world and experience every culture if they had their wish. Together, they would be much oriented toward travel too. Neither is particularly "down to earth," and therein lies the rub! Both being dreamers, who will pay the bills? If their charts show heavy earth emphasis elsewhere, this influence may win them both a reprieve from the heavy demands of material living. They will both be drawn to music and art. Together their imaginations can invent toys, childrens' books, vacation plans, etc. It probably would be joint creative interests or travel that drew them together in the first place. Both of these positions are in double signs of the mutable element which in a word means extreme changeability. Neither will bore the other, that is for sure. Each will have to take a philosophical detached view of the other from time to time, and that is a very hard thing to do with someone you love! Each will remain, on a personal level, a mystery to the other but both can have the kind of tolerance to let that be a given within the relationship. They must learn to be practical together and not encourage pie in the sky daydreams where solid work is necessary instead.

In a single chart we have a twentieth-century nomad. This person would be ideal for the military, except for the fact that both his/her Venus and Mars are gentle signs! Music would come naturally to this person as might a life at sea or secluded in nature, such as a national park employee. The person will always belong to him/herself; although he/she will be subject to very loving and romantic adventures. For this soul, life is predominantly an adventure—nothing solid, stable, or routine.

Mars Pisces/Venus Capricorn

This could be a very interesting bond. Mars Pisces provides the romantic escapism and Venus Capricorn provides the grounding for a viable (that means taxes paid) life in the physical world. The trade-off requires that each be tolerant of the vast differences between them. The Creator designed it to be that way; earth and water having a tremendous and natural appeal for each other, much like the tide (water) pulled to shore (earth). Mars Pisces can be an unwise, impulsive spender and Venus Capricorn saves and recycles everything, preferring things of lasting value from the start. Who will be in charge of credit cards? Venus Capricorn can also be somewhat cold about sex; Venus is looking for status and achievement in Capricorn (or a mate who reflects those), not passion. But Mars Pisces, being water, is like rain on the desert from Venus Capricorn's point of view. Mars Pisces can open up someone with Venus Capricorn and get them to directly experience their feelings, and few break through *any*thing in Capricorn better than planets in Pisces. So this can be a very creative interplay of human character traits. Honesty and open communication is essential here, as it may also be in most unions.

In a single chart there is a wonderful coupling of creative vision (Mars Pisces) with physical handiwork and handicraft. Thus, this individual can take his/her dreams and visions and be productive through them. They will also be balanced in giving time to work and time to leisure and being rather thorough with each. This favors relating potentials with others, because the person is probably a very tolerant, old soul who has found some kind of inner balance and brings that quality into partnership.

Mars Pisces/Venus Aquarius

In this union, there will be a trade-off of neurosis as each plays "shrink" to the other. Both are unconventional and perhaps unusual in many ways and each notices these idiosyncrasies from the start and subconsciously thinks: "Wow, I can be my own crazy self with *this* one." This could be a wild partnership for several weeks or months. Each may experiment with the limits to and limitations of human consciousness through this bonding. Eventually, Mars Pisces will get teary and Venus Aquarius will get detached and separate they probably will. Venus Aquarius stays friends with any lover, past, present, or future; so they may continue an unusual bond over the years. Again, each playing therapist to the other. They may coach each other in dance, yoga, or in metaphysics. They may experience their first astral-projections together. These kinds of "firsts" hold them spiritually together. In a way, each grows in self-respect from letting down their guard in this unique tie.

In a single chart the individual may have some confusion about their limitations or "place" in the world. They can either be overly confident or very insecure. There is a need for spiritual development and training. This person would never be satisfied with material-world achievements alone.

Personally, I feel that such a person will feel marked early in life as being "different" from his/her peers. There is a more spiritual calling that initiates (or will) various "quests" across lifetime. The position favors massage therapists, health-food workers, spiritual writers, spiritual painters, and musicians who seek to interpret moral law through music.

Mars Pisces/Venus Pisces

Two fish come home and meet at the core and understand the Force all at once. It can sometimes feel like perfection; sometimes perfection makes ordinary reality that much harder to cope with. Each of these "fish" will have to work hard to accept their material world obligations as this tie can also encourage powerful escapism behaviors such as living in an ashram, using drugs, using alcohol, or living on a houseboat, reclusively. There is an enormous capacity for each to lose ego, with or without sex, and experience a transcendental tantric kind of joining. The higher souls with this contact will perceive the relationship as a definite aid to their spiritual search for God within. Other persons may have such a strong effect on one another as to render them completely dependent on the other. Their identities can literally fuse together; so let's hope that in such an impressionable and connective bonding, the best two individuals are placed together. Music, art, yoga, meditation, prayer, t'ai chi are just some of the ways these two mystics can grow into oneness together and simultaneously evolve from within.

In a single chart it is the signature of a natural mystic who can connect with a higher consciousness and perhaps draw insights which will help others. This person may experience precognitive dreams also. Highly sensitive, the life work can revolve around helping others or using the channel of sensitivity in art, music, dance, or other creative works. This individual is highly empathetic and must guard his/her environments as well. This person should stay away from bars and dangerous drugs.

FINAL NOTE

So now you have it—all 144 combinations. Much of the general relationship potential shown is relevant to other planetary combinations, especially Sun-

Moon. You may wish to reread the Venus-Mars guide substituting your own Sun position to your mate's Moon and vice versa to see other dimensions of compatibility.

You may also want to study the Moon's nodes for possible karmic ties, suggestive of past-life associations, with those whom you have very close relationships.

—III—

YOUR ASTRO-
NUMEROLOGICAL
GUIDE TO SEX

People, let's face the truth! Despite what church and state has tried to do with sex, the fact remains that every healthy male and female wants, needs, requires, yearns, and thirsts for sex. Sex can't be put down because of fear or insecurity, because when handled properly it takes away fear and makes one more secure.

Astrology, which predates all religions and all cultures, has long taught that civilizations err in putting too much or too little emphasis on sex. Today, Americans also put too much emphasis on eating and dieting, on sleeping and insomnia, and on other matters that scream for normalcy instead of all this to-do.

Sex is a fact of life. Without sex, there can not be life; and how often does enduring, intensely rewarding love begin with good healthy, fat, thick, long sex?

Every man and woman is intensely aware of their sexual organs. How wise of the Divine Master to have made it so. Without enjoyment of sex, there wouldn't be sex, and therefore there wouldn't be procreation and life itself. *Increase and multiply* was the simple command that Adam and Eve received when they were banished from Eden. All real attempts to play down sex ended in the Garden of Eden.

The day you were born, you were aware of your sexual apparatus and had a pretty good instinctive idea about how to use it. Infants make what the military calls "that nasty movement." They seem to be telling us they are ready.

Dr. Freud, whose teachings have inspired many lives, taught that a person is sexually aware at age five. Then, society insists the child bury that awareness to as great an extent as possible.

People do things for sex that were once rather revolutionary. Boys and girls leave home and get their own pads to have sex. Boys drop out of school and join the Navy to have an abundance of sex. People marry for sex and they divorce for sex. They go to school to find sexual partners. They dress up, use cosmetics, perfumes, and scents beyond belief in order to attract sex, much as all animals do these same things in a completely instinctive manner.

Men and women die having sexual intercourse. Deprived of mates in single-sex boarding schools, the military services, and jails, they still engage in sex. Once masturbation was considered a crime, a sin, unhealthy, and a cause for blindness and madness. Today, the libraries are full of books on the joys of masturbation.

When you were born with the great gift from God, certain sexual trends were set in motion because of the heavenly spectacle under which you were born. Where the Sun was and what it was doing is of prime importance in your sexual horoscope. The following messages will give you a bird's-eye view into important sexual trends set in motion on the day you and your friends were born.

January

1 You are quick, sudden, forceful, cheerful and generous in sexual encounters. You love new sexual experiences. You are supercharged sexually over
the middle of July and the middle of August, but generally your high-
frequency sexual months are January, April, and November. Saturdays are
special in your sexual autobiography. Your best hours are right after lunch,
and restaurants carry a big sexual punch in your story. Where you are
helpful, you often end up in bed.

2 You are always pleased with a sexual partner, never fussy or critical. You
can not put down anybody who has made love to you and with you. You are
nice, sweet, and endearing in sexual encounters and people may forget your
name or your face but never that epilogue conversation. Generally, your
high-frequency sexual months are late January, early March, late June, and
early August. Add to this May 16–31; September 18–26; and December
27–31. Tuesdays and Thursdays are high-frequency, supercharged days for
you. Oh, what that period just before sleep can do for you sexually.

3 You respond strongly to the Venus-Neptune arrangement in your sexual
experiences—translation: You like it and lean toward the exotic, glamorous, and unique. Still, you will not tolerate being considered a plaything
or taken less than seriously. Your more rewarding sexual encounters take
place during March and October, on Wednesdays, right after noon or just
before midnight. February 20–26 and August 17–31 are the most sensitized toward passion and the possibility of sudden passion.

4 You are not easily satisfied sexually. You demand the best, the most, and
like big people who can overwhelm you. You have a strong feeling for the
secretive, for the unusual, and different. Still, you can not bear to be
dominated in any way that is too obvious. Your most rewarding sexual
encounters take place during May and November; Thursdays between 2:15
P.M. and 5:00 P.M. are unbelievably satisfying. January 14–26 and September 2–18 are ultrasensitized in potential for overwhelming sexual
passion.

5 You love the compelling demands of the exceptionally bright and energetic
lover. People in military uniform literally cream you. Also, people from
your parents' generation have a way of affecting your libido. July and

August are the months when your most memorable sexual encounters take place. Thursdays are the big sex days in your life. April 2–14 and December 11–19 periods are ultrasensitized in passionate responses.

6   Born on Little Christmas, Twelfth Night, you love the humor that lurks between the sheets, the funny side of sexual encounters, lovers' spats, and grand reunions. Sexual intercourse also brings out much more energy than you realized you have in reserve. January and August are the months when your libido literally itches for action. Fridays are big sex days in your experience. The midnight to dawn period are your witching hours, accent on March 20–31 and November 10–24.

7   You love to know all about the adored one. You are inquisitive in any prologue and epilogue to sex. You may be considered a little brusque by lovers. Your high-frequency sexual months are February and July. Saturdays are big days in your sexual experiences. June 14–30, August 17–31, and November 4–11 are other periods for rewarding copulation beyond the norm. Notice people whose first name begins with A.

8   You are tops at relaxing with and in sex and somehow work this miraculous method and attitude on lovers. Sex need not raise your blood pressure. You can take a lot of lovemaking in stride. Memory plays a large role in your sexual joy. The months of January, April, and July are permeated with the type of sexual drive that makes sense to you. Sundays are your sexual joy days. Pay plenty of attention to people whose first name begins with V or Y. The May 16–31 and December 26–31 intervals are loaded.

9   You have been known to keep sex rather impersonal on occasion. Mediterranean types can excite you in a strange way. You experience strange surges of energy once you are halfway into a sexual prologue and this can mystify you as much as others. Lovers speak to you from their hearts and sexual apparatus rather than in the normal, acceptable way. May, October, and Mondays play important roles in your sexual memories.

10   You view sex as curative, healing, and medicinal. Sometimes you are the doctor; often you are the patient. The months of June and November, every other Tuesday, people with Sun in Gemini and Libra, and the midnight to dawn cycle are all strongly marked in your sex chart. Take special note of people whose first name begins with D, F, or I. Also be alert to sexual opportunities between January 1–9; February 14–22; August 20–31 and December 4–11.

11   You demand free reign in sexual matters. You want a lover who accepts all the duties of sexual commitment and then you will return more than your share. You are a loyal, devoted, and faithful lover. The months of February, June, and September are high-frequency months, all three sexually supercharged. Wednesdays have a leading role in your sexual experience. Note people whose first names begin with C, J, or Z. Be alert to sexual opportunities between March 10–19; April 16–30; and October 20–31.

12 You are strongly aware of the business, employment, career, professional, and status potential related to sexual matters either closely or in some unacknowledged way. You know the cost of operating or living in a love nest, on some back street, and can make definite decisions against sexual hanky-panky. Thursdays and Sundays play roles in your sexual experience. Note people whose first names begin with P or B. Be alert to the sexual opportunities that come to the fore between March 2–11 and June 22–30. Generally, July is it.

13 You dislike confusion and confrontation in sexual matters. You like everything spelled out. You are inordinately honest but often find this hard to find in lovers. You dislike promiscuity. February, July, and November are your high-frequency months. You are supercharged on Fridays and between March 19–26, April 13–27, and December 23–31. Pay strong attention to anybody you meet whose first name begins with Q, Z, or E.

14 You dislike carelessness, overcautiousness, anger, shame, and dishonesty, especially when these touch that sexual experience you want to be completely rewarding. You are quick to sense the shadow side of a lover's personality. You are quick to know the faults of the opposite sex. Your high-frequency sexual months are late January, early February, late June, and early July. Mondays and Tuesdays play leading roles in your sexual experiences. Be alert to those whose first name begins with O.

15 You do not like business, family matters, or anything else to interfere with your sexual hour. The months of April and August are your high-frequency sexual months. Sundays have a big role in your sexual experiences. It would be wise to pay strict attention to people you meet at parties without partners. Also be wide awake between January 1 and 5; May 12–31; September 1–9 and 22–30; and the days right after Christmas. Try 2:45 P.M. to 6:15 P.M.

16 You experience enormous luck in your sexual experiences. You are good at immediately recognizing a future lover, fine at gauging the stranger's sexual potential. Your high-frequency sexual months are July and October. Mondays are your ultrasexual days; your most rewarding sexual hours are 9:00 A.M. to 10:15 A.M. and 11:00 P.M. to midnight. Pay strict attention to newcomers whose first name begins with F and G. Also to April 4–11 and November 10–19.

17 You can not abide thoughtlessness in sex. You don't even like frivolity. Sex is hard work and all business in many ways with you and nobody can give more to the act than you. Your high-frequency months are January, February, and November. Tuesdays are your most memorable days. Try the periods between noon and 12:59 P.M. and 8:00 P.M. to 9:15 P.M. The old motels on the old, half-forgotten highways of life are the right places. People whose first name begins with M are the ones and give due attention to June 20–30.

18   You often worry about the end of love, the defection of the treasured lover and such trends can defeat joy. Try to know that life does not intend to cheat you over any long period of time. Oh, what Friday and Saturday evenings can do for you! Your high-frequency months are January, March, July, and December. Give special notice to people you meet on bus, airplane, train, or highway, at service stations and motels. The June 4–30 period is sensitized.

19   You never seem to really organize a sexual encounter. Things just happen and rarely are you ready for them. Disorganized sex for you can be something akin to rape. You never seem to catch up with the demands, potential, and action of your lover. Your high-frequency months are May and July. Sunday afternoons and Wednesday mornings (early) could really put you together. Give due attention to people with whom you work. The daring period is around Thanksgiving.

20   You are adept at articulating your sexual needs, desires, whims, and fetishes. You inveigle the perfect lover into love. You have little difficulty getting on the other person's sexual wavelength. Your high-frequency months are April and June, and you also have high-frequency periods between February 12–18, July 18–24, and November 16–26. Don't ignore a potential lover whose first name begins with N or R.

21   You are strongly intuitive in sexual matters. Rarely do you make a mistake in gauging what the sexual partner is all about. You know how to take and give the lead. Your high-frequency sexual months are March, August, and December. Oh, what a Wednesday dawn will do for you after a good night's sleep or prologue. You can jump aboard a sex train after it's left the station. A partner whose first name begins with T or B and the Ides of March are superright.

22   You are dreamy and creamy in sex. You bestow memorable occasions on others and they never forget having been your partner. Your high-frequency day is Saturday, high-frequency time is 9:30 P.M. to midnight; and high-frequency months are February, August, and September. It would also be wise to give a tumble to the January 9–13, February 22–24, and November 12–27 periods. Pay close attention to people you meet at parties without partners.

23   You have few peers in the realm of sexual satisfaction. You confer, you bestow, you administer, you heal, you cure; your sexual adeptness is miraculous. Passion always pays off for you. High-frequency sexual day is Friday; high-frequency sexual months are late April and early May, late November and early December. Pay strict attention to people you meet at PTA, YMCA (YWCA), libraries, and stores—more so when their first name begins with A.

24   You have no trouble getting your sexual points across. You are one of those lovers who learns more each time you participate in the sacred act of sex.

You are at your best early in the mornings and late in the evenings. Try the lunch hour and pay strict attention to people whose first name contains five or six letters. Generally, your high-frequency months are June and July, along with January 29–31, March 17, June 20–24, and Christmas.

25 You have great powers of versatility in sex. There is not much you don't want to experience. Sometimes you might surprise yourself; more often, you surprise others. It would be wise to pay strict attention to people you meet whose first name begins with K. Generally, your high-frequency months are August and September, and the periods of February 19–23, April 16–30, and December 25–31. Thursday is your day. The best hours are 4:30 to 6:00 P.M. and from midnight to 2:30 A.M.

26 You have great powers of giving pleasure, especially with young foreigners. You like to romp about naked and have your body admired, so keep in good physical shape. Choose underwear with care and without any thought of expense. Best days for sex are Mondays, Thursdays, and Saturdays. Best months generally are March, April, July, October, and December. Give due attention to any new immigrant you meet with a dark eye on your glory.

27 You may be a little slow to take positive steps in a sexual encounter. This hesitation endears you to the partner and contributes to the flow of joy that results. Sunday afternoons and evenings are perfect for you. Your high-frequency sexual months are the hot summer months. Add to this the periods January 1–4, April 6–20, November 20–30. Perfect timing is a must now and then and you can't beat the hour just before supper and the hour just before midnight.

28 You are always in the lead, always in command of any sexual encounter. You do well wandering about Europe and sampling the wares of other countries. You have a way of attracting favorable looks in restaurants and on trains. Generally, your high-frequency months are May, July, and late December, as well as February 19–24, March 6–13, and November 19–30 intervals. Thursdays and Fridays are high-frequency days for you. You are especially supercharged in the clinches with people who don't speak English well.

29 You tend to break too many hearts because you tire now and then of anything that smacks of promiscuity and you tire of the outside paramour. Of course, all is fair in love and war. Your high-frequency sexual periods are the Ides of March, the last four months of the year, while Wednesdays and Saturdays are supercharged for you in sexual matters. It would be wise to pay quick and strong attention to any newcomer whose first name begins with C, P, or T.

30 You are the born diplomat who charms and captivates. You play it down, softly, and then suddenly when least expected, you increase the tempo and the pace until the golden blending of two souls takes place. Generally, your

high-frequency day is Monday and your high-frequency months are April, August, and late September. You're also in the pink between February 9–19, June 13–26, and October 20–29. Somebody whose first name begins with L may have it for you.

31   Your sexual relationships tend to run smoothly. You are a good actor in all sexual matters, very dramatic, and this seems to add to the pleasure in the happy aftermath. Generally, your high-frequency months are late January, late May, July, and late November. Saturdays are special in your sexual history. It would be wise to take special note of people you run into after not having seen them in a long time. Also, just before and immediately after Christmas carries a high sexual potential for you.

February

1   You respond strongly to the Neptune-Venus-Mercury arrangement in your sexual experiences. You have a great deal of sex appeal and yet people may not be able to explain just what it is about you that turns them on at odd times and in odd ways. You can be a disturbing influence in any office or plant, depending on the way you walk, enter, and leave rooms, and how you sit in a chair—all of these movements tend to be very sexually stimulating to others, including members of your own gender. You achieve many rewards and much sexual satisfaction over the February-March, July-September, and November periods of every year ahead of you.

2   You respond strongly to the Neptune-North node arrangement in your sexual experiences. Dragon's Head gives you some illusions about sex that make you an interesting sexual partner and yet others may not be able to figure out just what it is about you that makes you so great in bed. A rare type of beauty adorns you once you have undressed. Yearly, there will be good connections between your developing sex life and people who drive very large expensive vehicles. Sexual satisfaction each year is marked over April-May and October-November cycles.

3   You respond strongly to the Neptune-South node arrangement in your sexual experiences. Dragon's Tail can give you a special feeling for very permissive types and yet you may fear marriage to these people and draw wide boundaries between those you love in a highly physical sense and those you love in a more spiritual and sacred way. People born on February

3 do not make good celibates. Sex becomes increasingly important to you. Your most memorable sexual encounters during any year will occur over the May-June and late-November–early-December intervals.

4 You tend to encounter your perfect sexual partner mysteriously, so often while least expecting the encounter to take place. There are exotic as well as erotic foundations in your sexual history. Ultimates in ecstasy await you at beach resorts, more importantly the less popular resorts. Rains in off-seasons bring unforgettable love to you. The color "old rose" is aphrodisiacal, as are campsites, port cities, places where large ships come in.

5 Men and women, who fly, who sail, and who are in a sense foot fetishists reign in your sexual horoscope. The totally liberated man and woman, the unconventional types, those with compelling smiles are surging forward in your sex chart in the years ahead. California, North and South Carolina, southern Oregon, and the Florida and Texas gulf coasts are places beckoning you for unforgettable sexual encounters, with the accent on the months of early June, late July, September, and early October of any year.

6 Always, your sex chart is stimulated by Jupiter-Mars aspects and where the atmosphere is gay, carefree, optimistic, enthusiastic, affirmative and positive, you will experience sexual ultimates that will remain with you all your days. In sex, as in most things, people born on February 6 of any year seek liberation and emancipation from the routines and schedules of life. You are always willing to take another bold step into the area of unexplored feelings.

7 Responding strongly to the Uranus-Pluto-Jupiter-Mars arrangement in your horoscope and sexual experiences, you tend to be rather daring and to enjoy an unusual awareness about what your partner wants and doesn't want from you even before you become very close to this partner. You are experimental, zealous for learning and teaching, and you may feel that you are communicating more and better during sexual encounters than at any other time. Your most satisfying intervals for sex are February 19–27, late March, April 19–27, May 20–29, June 5–18, July 4–14, late August, early September, mid-October, November 7–17, December 10–20.

8 You respond strongly to the Uranus-Mercury-Mars arrangement in your sexual experiences. You tend to be somewhat sure in sexual matters, very up-to-date, a little permissive at times, and you want to be very much a part of your own generation on the go as distinguished from your parents' generation. You are modish, peculiar in sexual matters and a great pleaser of the *hoi-polloi*. In the future there will be good connections between your sex life and people you haven't seen in a long time, people you went to school with years ago.

9 You respond strongly to the Uranus-Mercury-Moon arrangement in your sexual experiences. You are experimental, inventive, innovative in sex, and love to be first with the most on any dramatic sex scene. Yearly, you will

enjoy a good connection between your expanding sex life and people who grew up in far-away places and who tend to be more permissive than you and others in your immediate environment. Each year, your rewarding sexual encounters will take place between January 1–14, February 22–28, March 19–30, April 1–14, May 20–31, June 6–16, July 3–16, August 2–20, September 9–21, October 14–24, November 3–15, and December 10–16.

10   You respond strongly to the Saturn-Venus arrangement in your sexual experiences. This makes for extreme harmony since in astrology Saturn always has been considered the friend of Venus. There is unbeatable endurance to your sex appeal and it functions well into the senior years. Annually, your most promising cycles for sexual joys are January 4–14, February 8–28, March 6–15, April 10–21, May 2–13, June 13–23, July 4–12 and 22–27, August 18–29, September 3–11, October 3–23, November 6–14, and December 22–31.

11   In the future, you can count on good connections between your enduring sexual encounters and younger people, newcomers in your area, foot-loose types, people whose age is hard to judge, and those involved with insurance, tax, and savings matters. Your most promising sexual cycles are January 1–12, February 20–26, March 4–13, April 16–27, May 3–22, June 4–13 and 24–30, July 6–14, August 18–28, September 19–30, October 4–13, November 12–25, and December 7–15.

12   You can count on good connections between your sexual encounters and people who have recently liberated themselves from old ideas about sex and gender. With a strong Jupiter response in your sex life, you tend to profit from the mental reverberations that others experience and it is often said that you are there when you are wanted sexually. Your most promising yearly sexual cycles are January 13–24, February 2–12, March 14–27, April 2–17, May 16–29, June 12–22, July 4–18, August 20–30, September 4–20, October 7–15, November 20–29, and December 2–9.

13   Don't speed sex up as you may want to do during various periods of each year when Mercury-Pluto and Mercury-Neptune pressures build up in your chart. Take things easy where sex is concerned, let things build up to their crescendo in a nice, easygoing, relaxed way. You can have your most memorable sexual experiences over the April, late June, late-July, and entire August-September periods. Combine sex with travel during early November. Organize your life better so that there is more time for imaginative and romantic living.

14   Your sex life is going to be more dramatic in the future. There are indications of some big surprises in love and sex over the closing days of January and again over the late-October and early-November periods of each year. Give your love life a big break by meeting your perfect sex partner more than half way. You have some good things going for you

sexually during the May–June and early September periods also. There are good connections between your sexual experiences and travel during the peak of high summer.

15   The future brings considerable emancipation and liberation in the matter of sexual experiences. You are going to be more casual in your sexual encounters now and there is a big chunk of Asia represented in your sexscope—Vietnam, Cambodia, Laos, Korea, Japan, Taiwan, to say nothing about Tahiti and the other islands in the South Pacific. You will love the Asian way now; you will learn much about the sexual lore of the South Pacific. You will feel more free, more personally independent through your sex life.

16   You respond strongly to the Mercury-Venus arrangement in your sexual experiences. You are extremely loving, considerate, well disposed toward others and, naturally, it follows that you are easy to love. To your lover you deny nothing. You realize instinctively that to give all is the real secret of loving and of being loved. In the future your most promising periods for sexual encounters are January 1–15, February 2–22, March 15–26, April 18–29, May 3–13, June 2–17, July 21–31, August 14–25, September 9–15, October 20–31, November 10–20, and December 7–14.

17   You respond strongly to the Venus-Moon arrangement in your sexual experiences. You are willing to meet your lover more than halfway but you can only give love in abundance when you are secure in the love of your partner. Over the years ahead, your most satisfying periods for sexual encounters are January 19–26, February 2–16, March 8–13 and 20–28, April 16–29, May 3–14, June 13–27, July 2–10 and 20–28, August 4–14 and 24–31, September 7–16, October 7–20, November 20–30, and December 26–31.

18   You respond strongly to the Jupiter-Saturn arrangement in your sexual experiences. You look for luck and greater self-confidence through sexual activity and generally you find it. Your most promising intervals for sexual encounters are January 12–23, February 4–17, March 3–17, April 15–27, May 1–14 and 26–31, June 3–13 and 24–30, July 3–14, August 23–30, September 3–19, October 9–20, November 21–30, and December 3–11. In the future there is a connection between your sex life and people who invent things.

19   You respond strongly to the Venus-Neptune-Pluto arrangement in your sexual experiences. You like to be courted, invited, attracted, tempted into sexual encounters. Nobody enjoys the prologues and epilogues to sex more than you. Over the years, your most promising periods for thrilling sexual encounters are January 11–25, February 8–20, March 2–13, April 16–27, May 3–11 and May 23–31, June 13–26, July 20–31, August 3–13 and 24–31, September 4–17, October 18–28, November 2–15, and December 18–28.

20   You respond strongly to the Mars-Moon-Pluto arrangement in your sexual experiences. You are strongly egotistical, full of pride and self-confidence in sexual matters; you are sure to lend your partners. You have what has often been called a secret weapon and this is in your touch and kisses. Your most promising periods for sexual encounters are January 1–15, February 1–20, March 16–26, April 3–13, May 2–12 and 22–31, June 4–15 and 25–30, July 6–17, August 21–31, September 3–14, October 12–20, November 2–7 and 17–27, and December 18–28.

21   You respond strongly to the Sun-Moon-Jupiter arrangement in your sexual experiences. You are lucky, jovial, optimistic, enthusiastic, positive, and affirmative about sex. You are a kind of sexual gambler and win often. You see the humor in sex, love, romance and this makes you rather unusual. Your most thrilling sexual encounters will fall during the following cycles: January 3–18, February 13–22, March 6–14, April 20–30, May 1–17, June 15–30, July 2–12 and 23–31, August 14–25, September 17–27, October 2–15 and 28–31, November 1–20, and December 17–29.

22   You are particularly virile, strongly involved in sexual desires, compulsions, and impulses and have sexual longings that know no boundary. This date produces particularly strong successful people who enjoy doing what they shouldn't do and when they shouldn't be doing it. There is some threat of scandal in your life connected with sex. Your most promising sexual encounters will occur between January 3–14, February 20–26, March 1–15 and 24–31, April 3–17, May 20–31, June 3–14 and 24–30, July 19–29, August 1–14, September 21–30, October 17–27, November 3–20, and December 2–11.

23   You respond strongly to the Mars-Moon-Dragon's Head arrangement in your sexual experiences. You are somewhat peculiar in that you can absorb a great deal of sexual pressure and you can maintain the lead and interest in fierce repetitive sexual intercourse longer than most people. All the mysteries and intrigues of thrilling sex really appeal to you. You understand the differences between the genders more than most people. Sexual encounters are limitless and rarely will there be schedules; all is spontaneous with you.

24   You respond strongly to the Sun-Moon-Neptune arrangement in your sexual experiences. You understand what is and isn't sexy more than most people. Your eyes are inclined to be the X-ray type more so than those born on other days during any year. You have great sexual awareness, sexual ingenuity, you're inventive, and nobody can be more romantic in sexual prologues and epilogues to sex than you. In the future there will be interesting connections between your developing sex life (accent on April-June and October-December) and people who are about to move from your environment.

25   You respond strongly to the Saturn-Vulcan-Venus arrangement in your sexual experiences. You are self-protective, you demonstrate a fine en-

durance and your sex interests never flag. You are not above making a study of sex and you tend to learn from many of your prime sexual encounters. In the future your most rewarding sexual encounters undoubtedly will take place during the following sex-powered intervals: January 7–18, February 3–13, March 18–28, April 16–30, May 2–14 and 24–29, June 3–15, July 8–18, August 14–28, September 3–10 and 24–29, October 4–18, November 22–30 and December 14–22.

26 You respond strongly to the Saturn-Lilith-Pluto arrangement in your sexual experiences. You are restrained during sexual prologues and epilogues. You are something of a prime tempter of the innocent and uninitiated once you let yourself go, however. You are without a doubt one of the best teachers of sexual techniques in the Zodiac. Your most rewarding sexual encounters occur during the following intervals: January 21–31, February 16–25, March 15–31, April 4–17, May 2–16, June 15–30, July 3–13, August 21–31, September 4–19, October 2–20, November 7–16, and December 21–31.

27 You respond strongly to the Neptune-Lilith-Venus arrangement in your sexual experiences. You also make an ideal teacher of sexual techniques. It is your destiny to never be really forgotten by those you have loved. Your most rewarding sexual acts take place during the following sex-powered intervals: January 1–14, February 20–28, March 3–13, April 15–24, May 2–14, June 13–25, July 21–31, August 4–14, September 19–29, October 16 27, November 4 9 and 22 29, and December 1 8 and 27–31.

28 You will receive a great deal of sex appeal from your ruling planet Neptune. Actually, there is a surfeit of magical witchery in your chart. The Sun, which rules your solar 6th House, has made sexual encounters practically medicinal in your life. Venus has authority over your zone of sex and makes you a particularly loving person who finds giving love very easy. You can count on good connections between your developing sex drive and people whose personality rather than their physical appearance open doors for them.

29 Born during the mystical and mysterious Leap Years, you not only have a great deal of Neptune-related sex allure, but you respond strongly to the Lilith-Mercury arrangement in your sexual experiences. There is a lot of the tempter in you and it is your fate to come up against a great deal of forbidden fruit during your lifetime. While you have no propensity for kinky sex, you certainly are open to the many varieties of orthodox lovemaking. Over and over, there are good connections between your sex life and people who are rather close-mouthed or silent.

March

1   You can count on greater stability in your love life through the years. The power for working out any possible impasse between you and your beloved is particularly strong during the months of February, late May, June, and early November. There are love gains emanating from the forgive-and-forget motive to the fore during the first week of January and the second half of December. Love's bounty is strongly represented where there is greater spirituality, increased kindness to in-laws and others.

2   Sexual threads in your horoscope accent the illusion and evasion of Neptune, with increased sex appeal represented during the second half of February, and over the months of June, August, and December. The potential for rewarding brief encounters is there during the mid-June and late July intervals. Sex appeal can be increased where new attention is given to hair style and perhaps more should be spent on footwear, with the accent on brighter colors and higher heels. Phone people you met casually at the homes of friends.

3   Sexual accord is a fact of life in your horoscope over the second week of March, and more assuredly during early July, early September, and throughout the month of November. There are interesting sexual threads touching people of similar political and philosophical persuasion. Exceptionally strong fascination is related to people you met at rallies, and somebody you met during a trip beyond the 300-mile radius of your home. Spur of the moment socializing has a sexual undertone.

4   You can turn on people who rarely respond to sexual stimulation. Your touch is more electric and electrifying than that of most people. Also, your voice has a boudoir tone to it that works well in the clinches. You can count on unusual connections between your expanding sex life and people who want marriage, security, or something rather valuable out of you. Loving without giving everything else may be difficult but not impossible. Peak sexual periods are March, late April, early June, July 4–August 19, and late November.

5   You respond strongly to the Neptune-Sun-Moon arrangement in your sexual experiences. It's difficult to pinpoint your exciting and thrilling sex appeal. It is, however, capable of driving stolid, generally immune types into compulsive and impulsive frenzies. Experienced master spies who

recruit others always look for men and women with your type of sex appeal to compromise the morals and secrets of enemies in high places. Peak sexual periods for you are February-March, late May, early June, early July, and October 8 to December 6.

6 Your sex life tends to have a certain evenness and serenity that most people lack. You invite, court, and encourage faithful and devoted types of lovers. There will always be a good connection between your sex life and people who have an affinity for water, sailing, surfing, swimming, etc. Your intervals of greatest sexual potential are January 12–20, February 1–16, March 21–31, April 17–27, May 6–19, June 4–16, July 2–14, August 23–31, September 1–15, October 9–19, November 7–21, and December 18–27.

7 You are rather idealistic about love and sex and try to keep them walking hand in hand. You respond strongly to the Neptune-Mercury arrangement in your sexual experience. In sex, you are sharp, impressionable, rather easily tempted, and you can fall madly in love with the perfect physical lover. There will be good connections between your sex life and people who believe strongly in themselves and in the good images they project, people who are ambitious, and even with some who can be classified as workaholics. High water periods for sexual encounters are January 20 to February 6, March 20 to April 13, May 5–18, June 14 to July 7, August 19–29, September 16–28, October 4–15, and December 1–20.

8 There will always be a good connection between your sex life and newcomers in your community, divorced and separated people, members of military families, people who like to dance and who possibly have won prizes for their dancing. You respond strongly to the Neptune-Venus-Lilith arrangement in your sexual experiences. You are a born tempter and charmer of those who would like to remain immune. Your peak sexual intervals are January 1–17, February 3–13, March 23–31, April 4–20, May 23–31, June 1–14, July 25–31, August 6–20, September 14–24, October 18–27, November 3–13, and December 8–18.

9 There will be a good connection between your sex life and people who have served time in one way or another, people who have known great disillusionment and disenchantment in life, people who were once religious but who have lost their faith temporarily. Your sex power is restorative, medicinal. Your peak sexual intervals are January 22–30, February 2–13, March 4–16, April 9–21, May 10–20, June 6–15, July 21–31, August 7–17, September 3–13, October 2–12, November 13–22, and December 1–14.

10 You respond strongly to the Saturn Mars arrangement in your sexual experiences. There can be some unevenness in your sex life, with peaks often separated by six or seven years only to occur again. There are good connections between your most joyful sexual experiences and travel, ban-

quets, musicals, special nights out, and the opera. Your most promising sexual cycles are January 14–24, February 4–13, March 16–26, April 4–13, May 17–27, June 12–24, July 3–14, August 19–28, September 14–23, October 19–28, November 16–30, and December 8–17.

11   You have a lot going for you in sexual power because your urges are full of Mars-ruled compulsiveness. There is a good connection between your sexual happiness and people temporarily living in your area, people who are less critical than those with whom you are more familiar, people who tend to live and let live. Your most promising sexual cycles are January 1–12, February 21–27, March 13–23, April 4–15, May 19–30, June 14–23, July 2–14 and 22–26, August 6–15, September 23–30, October 19–29, November 12–22, and December 16–22.

12   You tend to desire more in unorthodox sex than you ever care to let on. Many of those subterranean urges that have known no tongue will break forth into the open and you may know some spurious guilt, embarrassment about what you are really like in the over-sexed clinches. Your most promising sexual cycles are January 2–11, February 20–26, March 12–22, April 3–14, May 18–29, June 13–22, July 1–13 and 21–25, August 5–14, September 22–29, October 18–28, November 11–21, and December 15–21.

13   Saturn often has a way of toning down your sexual desires and actions, but this won't be true over the May-July and October-December intervals when you tend to break free, and come up against what appears to be a shocking gender confrontation but what in effect turns out to be raw, naked, unadulterated sex; and you may never quite be the same again. This series of sexual joys can be associated with paying a bill, dealing with a new type of machine, driving in the wrong neighborhood, or admitting finally that you want the spouse of a friend.

14   The cycle ahead can make for peculiar sexual patterns in the lives of people born this day. There are meetings and then there are encounters and little time is wasted under existing aspects. You may feel that your potential lover is jumping the gun, and wanting dessert before the main entrée but it's that kind of love. Your best sexual intervals are late March, late April, July, September, and late November. In travel, go where you have never been before. Meet the kind of people you have more or less avoided up until now.

15   You tend to respond strongly to Sun and Moon patterns in your chart where sexual experiences are concerned. You like a bit of mystery and even intrigue in your sex life. You like unexpected sex, unplanned sex, and this is the kind of cycle you can have, perhaps with another Pisces who knows all about you in ways that other solar groups never can know. There is an unveiling motive ahead, a veritable striptease motive, something a little shocking.

16   You respond strongly to the Neptune-Mars-Vulcan arrangement in your
      sexual experiences. You are really much more aggressive in getting what
      you want sexually than would ever meet the eye. You have exceptionally
      strong sexual desires and are far more compulsive and sure of your sexual
      power than you may give off at times. Ahead, there will be a good
      connection between your sex life and people who have just arrived in your
      community, people younger and less sophisticated than you. You will excel
      as a sex professor.

17   You respond strongly to the Neptune-Mars-Moon arrangement in your
      sexual experiences. You have well-rounded ideas of what you want sexually,
      which is generally more than the average person wants to give; but you get
      all this when you engender lover in your sex partner. There is a good
      correspondence between your sex life and people who wear a lot of jewelry,
      rather dramatic people, who are more formal than informal. There is a
      strongly aristocratic trend in your sex life.

18   You respond strongly to the Neptune-Saturn-Moon arrangement in your
      sexual experiences. Sex is very medicinal for you. It heals and cures and
      gives you a strong desire to get on with the job of living grandly and well.
      There is a good connection between your sex life and people who have had
      nervous breakdowns or something similar, people who need your attention
      and love very much, people who have been sorely used and hurt during
      past years, and people who have come to your area to be healed.

19   The Pluto-Venus-North node arrangement in your sexual experiences
      makes you an exciting, dynamic, and yet, at times, a cautious lover. You
      have a kind of radar system that tells you when another person would be or
      wouldn't be interested in having a sexual encounter with you; so very little
      time is wasted in your pursuit of love. There will be a good correspondence
      between your sex life and people who are rather shy, embarrassed easily,
      and yet hungry to be loved completely. Your most promising periods for
      sexual encounters are late February, March 13–24, early April, late May,
      June 14–22, July 19 to August 8, September 14 to October 4, late
      November, and December 1–9.

20   You respond strongly to the Mars-South-Vulcan node arrangement in your
      sexual experiences. Nobody is more sure than you are in your attitudes and
      approaches to sex. You are sensitive to the special needs of others and will
      adjust your sexual preferences to suit a partner now and then. Over the
      years, there will be a good connection between your sex life and people who
      are rather formal, very stylish, even elegant in their clothes. Also, you can
      experience the most satisfying love with people who on the surface don't
      seem to be very sexy.

21   You respond strongly to the Mars-Neptune-Mercury arrangement in your
      sexual experience. You are subtle, shrewd, sublime, somewhat mysterious,
      and certainly exotic in your approach and attitudes to sex. As time goes on,

there will be a good correspondence between your most satisfying sexual experiences and people who were born in Spanish-speaking countries. Your most promising sexual encounters can take place between January 4–13, February 14–23, March 6–15, April 22–30, May 1–17, June 15–30, July 4–14, August 1–19, September 3–17, October 2–12, November 15–30, and December 26–31.

22   You respond strongly to the Mars-Pluto-Moon arrangement in your sexual experiences. You are strongly self-confident in sex, can use sexual encounters for ego purposes, and you tend to engender long periods of fidelity in those you love. There will be good correspondence between your sex life and people who are less self-confident in sex, people who may have experienced rejection by their former lovers over the past two years or less. Your most satisfying periods for sexual encounters are the third week of January, the last six days of February, the opening days of March, April 21–30, May 16–27, June 14 to July 8, August 24 to September 11, October 21 to November 7, and in late December.

23   You are strongly involved in special, unusual, and unorthodox sexual desires, and these should be discussed with your lover rather than pushed aside. Always you will enjoy a good connection between your sex life and people who are very financially but not emotionally secure, people who give the impression that they have something unusual to tell you but just can't bring themselves to speak. Your most satisfying periods for sexual encounters are January 10–22, February 2–19, March 12–27, April 16–29, May 5–15, June 9–18, July 6–17, August 2–17, September 9–20, October 23 to November 10, and December 6–17.

24   You respond strongly to the Mars-Venus-Moon arrangement of your sexual experiences. You are apt to demand and command in sexual desires only and those who share your bed may find you very different from their expectations. You can enjoy good connections between your developing sex life and people who wear military uniforms, people who are temporarily visiting in your community. Best periods for getting the most satisfaction out of sex are the March-April, late-June early-July periods, August 23 to September 9, October 19 to November 7, and late December.

25   You respond strongly to the Venus-Sun-Mars arrangement in your sexual experiences. You have little difficulty shifting from the aggressive lover to the passive loved one. Some of your most rewarding sexual experiences tend to defy gender and the ways of gender. Your most satisfying sexual encounters take place during these sex-powered intervals: January 23–31, February 1–16, March 3–13, April 17–27, May 9–24, June 11–22, July 3–14 and 23–31, August 14–24, September 2–12, October 3–13, November 6–20, and December 23–31.

26   You respond strongly to the Mercury-Moon-Mars arrangement in your sexual experiences. You are intellectual rather than emotional in many

approaches to sex. You enjoy having sex with brilliant people and feel that such conquests stimulate repeat performances for you. There is a good connection between your sex life and people who are retired from the military services. Your most rewarding sexual encounters take place during the following intervals: January 2–12, February 13–24, March 1–17, April 20–29, May 6–16, June 13–23, July 2–15, August 3–13 and 23–31, September 8–19, October 4–26, November 7–11, and December 12–19.

27   You respond strongly to the Pluto-Jupiter-Moon arrangement in your sexual experiences. Your inner awareness of how to seduce, convince, attract, court, and invite is second to none. Your sexual countdowns are rather short and others seem to know this about you and cooperate fully. Your most rewarding sexual meetings are January 1–9 and 24–31, February 14–23, March 8–18, April 3–13, May 6–16, June 13–23, July 2–11 and 24–31, August 16–27, September 2–13, October 5–15, November 12–27, and December 3–11.

28   Grandeur and accord are the code words that come to mind when one examines the sexual potential in your sex horoscope. Dignity, formal occasions, expanding appetite are other expressions that come to mind. Your peak pleasure periods are usually in mid-March, late April, early May, the July-August and late-October, early-November intervals. Sex is helped along by travel, visits to places of historic interest, and with a willingness to cross generational lines.

29   You can count on greater sexual drive in the future. Sexual joys are associated with forbidden fruit, the giving of overwhelming, almost cureless ecstasy to a stranger who turns you on by his/her entry in a room. The more you are intent on giving the best and the most sexual credit to this stranger the more you are going to reap in unforgettable living joy that will remain with you forever. Pleasure periods are the July-August, late-October, early-November periods.

30   Your greatest sexual potential is related to loving an arrogant, self-indulgent, almost insanely jealous person more in love with self than with anybody else. In loving this person and upping his/her self-esteem, you literally turn him/her into a payer on demand, into a lover without peer. This sex partner works to honor your faith in his/her ability to deliver the goods, sexually speaking. Late afternoons over the June-July and October-November periods carry the greatest wallop for you in sex.

31   Seek love and sex encounters in areas you are visiting for the first time, in western states such as Utah, Wyoming, Colorado, Oregon, and Washington. Friends of your friends have much going for you. Your sex life will be more active in the future. Potent sexual periods exist between April 18–30, May 6–14, June 30 to August 20, October 14–27, November 7–19, and the last ten days of December.

April

1   Dramatic love encounters are strongly represented in your chart. This trend is especially evident during early January, throughout the April-May interim and again around Thanksgiving Day. An old flame can suddenly reappear in your life and where fear was a strong inhibition formerly, there is greater personal bravery in love this time around. You can come up against some potent need for decisiveness in love during the years ahead. There is love potential where the mountains fall into the water.

2   Love and sex matters are undergoing a sorting-and-sifting operation. Conscience is strongly represented and also the determination not to repeat an old mistake. Correction and improvement is the greater cosmic undertone of the sexual trends in your chart during April, late July, and over the entire October-November interval. Sexual threads are related to places where you have been happy in the past, trips to water, and situations where one wears gloves. The week including July 24–29 carries a wallop.

3   Some veils are being lifted in your sexual experiences by the potent Pluto-Neptune trends in your chart. Knowledge you feared, turned from, or weren't really exposed to in the past can suddenly stand there raw and naked. There are sexual threads in your chart related to air travel, special stopovers, and job-related conventions and seminars. Summers can bring your highest peak of sexual rewards, but the post-Christmas period also can be a heady one when new love blossoms.

4   The most salubrious days turn rather salacious over the months of June, July, and August. The Sun, Mars, and Venus trends in your horoscope peak about high summer and expose you to situations in which you can find a perfect sex partner. You are more routine in your sex life over the January-February period, while very late March exposes you to naughty situations involving newcomers to your community. Mid-November has trends that accent a grand release of sexual tensions.

5   You will find an urgency for unusual sexual release strong over the early March, late June, entire July, and late October periods. There is grand exposure to the perfect sex partner at all of these times and trends by which you are inviting new attention from enchanting strangers when you cavort where there is group singing, ballroom dancing, where precious stones

are mined, placed into designer jewelry, and marketed in some *sub-rosa* fashion.

6   You find your sexual high tides over the late spring, throughout the summer months, and again as October's bright blue weather is peaking. Bold sexual trends in your chart are linked to both church and club membership, publishing houses, libraries, newsstands, and bookstores. Your reading and learning processes have a strong sexual connotation. The things your parents never told you are moving to vital areas of your mind and heart now.

7   You will always have some memorable sexual encounters with people you have been carrying torches for a long time. There is a good sexual summing up going on in your life now, a reevaluation of sexual hits and misses. You respond in sex matters throughout your life to the Venus-Jupiter-Neptune arrangement in your horoscope, which means strong ego involvement, good health involvement, and a high sense of social as well as sexual adventure. There is sexual accent on late March, late April, May, July-August, November, and early December intervals. You will enjoy a good connection between your sex life and people who are in service to many other people.

8   You respond strongly to the Venus-Jupiter-North node arrangement in your sexual experiences. There is love, of course, but there is also enthusiasm and joviality that warms the cockles of your sex partner's heart. There are good connections between your sex life and people who fight drugs. Your most promising sexual encounters will take place between January 4–24, February 16–25, March 9–14, April 3–30, May 19–29, June 4–14, July 20–31, August 16–29, September 3–15 and 28–30, October 4–17, November 3–13 and 26–30, and December 8–18.

9   You respond strongly to the Venus-Jupiter-Lilith arrangement in your sexual experiences. If you are going to consider your sexual allure, your magical witchery, first throw out all ideas about sexiness that come from disturbed Hollywood or even the ideas that are encouraged by do-gooders. You are sexy and this has nothing to do with the clothes you wear or don't wear. Let Europeans, South Americans, Africans, Asiatics see you at your best and they will tell you how sexy you really are. Best periods for sexual encounters are January 18–29, March 4–16, April 3–13, May 2–20, June 5–25, July 4–18, August 20–31, and November 16–30.

10   You respond strongly to the Jupiter-Venus arrangement in your sexual experiences. There can be more turning on of you than you in turn excite others and this is particularly true during the years ahead. Some of those secret loves of yours can disrobe so to speak and present you with golden opportunities and fiercely hot moments of truth. Your most promising sexual cycles are January 3–9, February 21–26, March 4–19, April 12–27, May 4–13 and 24–29, June 3–16, July 2–17, August 9–18, Sep-

tember 2–12, October 16–25, November 1–12, and December 21–30.

11   You respond strongly to the Uranus-Mercury arrangement in your sexual experiences. Tomorrow's sex is always going to be more rewarding and, ironically enough, this has proved to be true again and again. Your sexual happiness enjoys good connections with books, libraries, book stores, publishing, and printing. From now on, you will be particularly imaginative and romantic about sex between January 22–30, February 1–17, March 2–14 and 25–31, April 6–15, May 22–31, June 12–20, July 1–8 and 23–28, August 14–24, September 9–21, October 4–13, November 7–19, and December 19–24.

12   You enjoy good connections between sexual encounters and dressing up formally, looking rich and royal, being present at the big dramatic political affairs, following the Sun and becoming more active around clubs. There is increased supersensory perception about the secret sexual drives and motivation of others. You are particularly imaginative and romantic about sex between January 2–19, February 14–23, March 9–19, April 4–24, May 20–27, June 11–21, July 16–29, August 4–16, September 9–20, October 1–14 and 27–31, November 6–18, and December 2–13.

13   Challenging and dramatic sexual encounters are strongly represented in your chart. This trend is especially evident during the last of March and most of April, and again over the peak of high summer and the autumn days of early October and early November. There are connections now between your enjoyable love life and a spouse or former spouse with whom you haven't been getting along of late. There is a new deal for you in marriage and also in live-in arrangements in the future.

14   You have a lot going for you in sexual encounters provided you guard against being overly possessive, overly insistent about having things your own way, and being overly suspicious of your sex partner. Live and let live should be your motto if you would bring out the passion, concern, kindness, and capacity for turning you on that your favorite sex partner has there in abundance. Don't give this person anything to be jealous about over the tense, but wonderful days of high summer.

15   Where you shift from one plan to another you are apt to annoy your partner and this annoyance tends to detract from the higher level of sexual performance that means so much to you. Sex has a good connection with swimming pools, skiing parties, camping, and visiting former neighbors. You can write new tickets for yourself and your sex partner in late April, early May, mid-June, and the entire July-September intervals. Also sex and travel do well together every November and the closing days of the year.

16   You respond strongly to the Mars-Jupiter-North node arrangement in your sexual experiences. You generally are sympathetic to people who are strongly attracted to you and it isn't difficult for you to engender love within you for those who so assuredly are in love with you. But there is

always some smidgin of suspicion that you are to have an ultimate sexual experience one day and this can drive you on to more and more adventures. Over the years, there will be a good connection between your impulsive sex life and people recently arrived in this country.

17 You respond strongly to the Mars-Saturn-South node arrangement in your sexual experiences. You want a great deal of privacy surrounding your sex life. You avoid gossips and lovers who kiss and tell. Over the years ahead, you will enjoy good connections between your developing sex life and people who are very ambitious for career and financial success. Your most rewarding sexual encounters occur during the following periods: January 4–13, February 20–27, March 6–17, April 9–22, May 3–16, June 14–27, July 3–10 and 22–31, August 14–24, September 8–19, October 3–14, November 20–30, and December 12–23.

18 You respond strongly to the Mars-Pluto-Mercury arrangement in your sexual experiences. Sex gives you a strong sense of ego and of personal worth. Your awareness of drive and motivation in sex is sound and you might surprise others by telling them all about themselves. There are good connections in your horoscope between your sex life and people who drop their shoes in and out of doors for any reason and even without reason. Your best sexual encounters take place during late March, early April, May 16–30, June 5–18, July 20–31, August 17 to September 9, October 4–14, November 6–16 and December 8–22.

19 You respond strongly to the Sun-Venus-Mars arrangement in your sexual experiences. You tend to be extreme in matters of gender (all man or all woman) and you like partners who are this way, too. As time goes by, there are good connections in your horoscope between your developing sex life and people who tend to be a little prudish. Your most satisfying sexual encounters take place during the following periods: January 6–19, February 12–23, March 3–13, April 15–30, May 6–18, June 11–24, July 9–23, August 14 to September 7, October 20–31, November 3–14, and December 26–31.

20 You respond strongly to the Sun-Mars-Mercury arrangement in your sexual experiences. You like to keep sexual matters light and cheerful, full of joviality, somewhat intellectualized at times. Loving you can be good fun. There are some good connections between your developing sex life and people with sloping shoulders. Your most promising sexual encounters take place between January 1–16, February 2–22, March 6–26, April 4–14, May 9–19, June 4–13, July 16–31, August 14–30, September 4–10, October 17–27, November 3–13, and December 19–31.

21 You respond strongly to the Sun-Mars-Saturn arrangement in your sexual experiences. You are self-protective, somewhat conservative and traditional and you have enormous endurance in sex and great promises of sexual longevity. You enjoy good connections between your sex life and very large

people. Your most promising sexual encounters take place between January 19–29, February 13–26, March 15–31, April 10–24, May 19–29, June 14–30, July 4–15, August 2–15, September 20–30, October 4–17, November 13–20, and December 12–22.

22   You respond strongly to the Venus-Jupiter arrangement in your sexual experiences. You have no trouble giving love to the person who makes you sexually happy, even if this person is very different from you in all other ways. You entertain the notion that sex is lucky for you—that it makes you lucky. There is good correspondence in your horoscope between your sex life and people who love and ride horses. Best sexual encounters are: January 13–26, February 9 to March 3, March 14 to April 10, May 20 to June 7, all of July and August, September 3–13, October 15–30, November 22–30, and December 16–31.

23   There is good correspondence in your horoscope between your expanding sex life and people who are rather miserly, cautious with money, hesitant about taking a chance on love and sex. Born with the Sun in Taurus, you respond strongly to the lunar nodes and what they compel in your sexual experiences—peace of mind, a desire to please your lover, and a capacity for giving everything. Your best periods for sexual encounters are January 1–20, February 22–27, March 17–27, April 5–15, May 6–26, June 4–14, July 20–31, August 9–17 and 24–28, September 5–16, October 3–13, November 26–30, and December 1–10.

24   You respond strongly to the Venus-Sun-Neptune arrangement in your sexual experiences. Your desire to give love knows no bounds and fortunate are those who come within the vortex of your love. There is a good connection between your sex life and people who are associated with the law in some way. Your most promising periods for sexual encounters are January 19–29, February 4–13, March 22–31, April 1–12, May 23–31, June 4–15, July 1–12 and 21–31, August 14–24, September 24–30, October 2–9 and 18–26, November 20–30, and December 3–11.

25   You respond strongly to the Uranus-Pluto-Saturn arrangement in your sexual experiences. These empower you to always remain the individualist in sex, to keep completely abreast of the times in your lovemaking techniques and to know the limitations of what can be done and shouldn't be attempted. Your most rewarding and satisfying sexual ventures take place between January 13–24, February 6–13, March 4–20, April 17–24, May 3–7 and 17–27, June 9–17, July 5–17, August 14–24, September 22–30, October 3–13, November 23–29, and December 10–17.

26   You respond strongly to the Pluto-Saturn-Mercury arrangement in your sexual experiences. Therefore, you are alert to sexual opportunities and apply the standards of the geographic area where you happen to be rather than those you may have been taught at another time and in some other place. In sex, you are at home every place. Shyness falls once you are

sexually stimulated. Your most rewarding and satisfying sexual encounters take place between January 1–11, February 14–21, March 2–13 and 25–31, April 4–14, May 6–17, June 13–25, July 4–14, August 22–31, September 13–26, October 5–15, November 14–23, and December 23–31.

27 You respond strongly to the Saturn-Mercury-Vulcan arrangement in your sexual experiences. Therefore, you are self-protective and rather conventional in lovemaking. You become something of a real sexual worker in the vineyard around the time you are twenty-four and this can last up until age thirty-seven or thirty-nine when you tend to be more the sexual dilettante, certainly more discriminating. Push for sexual opportunities over the second half of February, the last five days of March, April 2–12, May 6–16, June 13–24, July 3–13, August 4–19, September 20–28, October 14–28, November 2–8 and 22–28, and December 16–20 and 29–31.

28 Your most rewarding love and sexual experiences are those where you are able to attribute to the adored one all manner of perfection that in truth he/she doesn't possess. You are playing a game in a sense, and there is nothing wrong with this, for in the clinches and clutches, the supposedly perfect one becomes close to perfect. This is your secret power that is strongly brought into focus over the late-March/early-April period and again during late August, and over most of September and October.

29 You are destined to be loved by many people, including some who are not free to marry you. Beauty may be in the eye of the beholder, but suffice to say that you seem to attract many with eyes only for you. Your preferred love and sexual periods are the last week of January, the second half of April, the entire July-September period and the time just before Christmas. The longer your hair, the more you invite sexual desire.

30 You are destined to know secret loves, forbidden loves, and members of your own gender will be disquieted about their ultimate feelings for you. Your best and most potential sexual periods are the first week of March, the second half of May, June 9–13, and July 18–24. Also, the last week of September and the third week of November. Very large cities, special parties, family get-togethers, and annual meetings are all related to the advancement of sexual experiences in your horoscope.

May

1   A grand return home, or to some place where you experienced peculiar sensations in the past can be related to increased love and sexual opportunities. Each year, late March, early April, the months of June, September, and December are rich with promise where you want to mature into the genuine rewards that sexual refurbishment can bring. Members of the opposite sex introduced to you by aunts, uncles, and older friends of your parents are represented in your sex chart.

2   You can be sure that your sex life will know a fast pace and tempo under Uranus trends in your horoscope. There are sexual joy threads related to people in uniform, people you met for the first time at fairs, fetes, and carnivals, and the summer months are rich with potential at beach resorts and where small boats are moored. Washington, D.C. and state capitals are part of the picture in your love and sex charts.

3   The spiritual and physical love trends in your chart have a serenity thread permeating them. Never was love more medicinal for you. You rise to greater heights of giving in love and learn that these are far more potent sexually than are the receiving peaks. There can be a throwing away of inhibitions, of vanity, and a greater acceptance of the core of gender truth. Love becomes a strongly liberating force in your life over the summer and autumn months. In genuine love, you see the face of a deity.

4   There are hard facts of life represented in your sex chart. There is a new awakening to your own sexual potential indicated for late January, early February, the third week of June, the last ten days of July, and the months of August and December. There is a facing up to truths about your own sexual longings that know no barrier. Your perfect sex partner is a kind of Pied Piper, whose melodious voice disturbs your peace of mind and you begin marching to the piper's lovely tune.

5   You will reach your sexual heights about late August and early September. Other propitious times for meeting your perfect sex partner, perhaps on horseback, are the last five days of March, mid-April, the first two weeks of June, mid-July, and the entire month of November. Where large animals cavort, in open fields, at animal shows, where construction projects are going on, and in the living room of your own home you can meet this enchanting stranger.

6 Each year you peak sexually during the third week of August and the first sixteen days of September. Other auspicious sexual times are the first week of January, the last four days of March, the middle of April, all of July, and the entire month of November. Sexual trends in your chart are linked to music stores, musical events, clever interpretations, and utilization of your astrological powers and prayer. The perfect lover becomes an exact fixture in your chart.

7 You respond strongly to the Mercury-Saturn-Mars arrangement in your sexual experiences. In matters of sex, you are intellectual, idealistic, conservative, well-meaning, and self-protective. You can take steps when an affair should be broken up. You won't stand for any selfish nonsense. You will also enjoy a good connection between your expanding sex life and people who are on diets and who are overly conscious of their figures. The most rewarding intervals for sexual encounters are January 15–25, February 9–18, March 1–20, April 6–15, May 20–31, June 4–17, July 20–29, August 3–13 and 23–31, September 4–13, October 17–27, November 2–15, and December 19–28.

8 You respond strongly to the Mercury-Pluto-Mars arrangement in your sexual experiences. You are quick in spotting sexual targets of opportunity. You do not like to disappoint beautiful people with a firm "No." You will enjoy good connections between your unique sex life and people who are disgusted with marriage and traditional love affairs. Your most rewarding intervals for sexual encounters are January 1–13, February 19–26, March 3–16, April 14–30, May 17–31, June 14 to July 7, July 20 to August 13, September 9–22, October 14–23, November 7–15, and December 20–31.

9 You have a sound respect for the person who loves you effectively and often will make all manner of excuses for this person who falls short in other ways. You will enjoy a good connection in your horoscope between your sex life and people who talk too much even when they have something to say. The chatterboxes, gossips, and rumor-mongers may have their faults but they can require your sexual attention just the same. Your best intervals for rewarding sexual encounters are late February, early April, the May-June-August-September intervals, and in late December.

10 You respond strongly to the Jupiter-Mercury arrangement in your sexual experiences. You tend to build up some memorable sexual experiences that are the result of the unexpected, of the spur-of-the-moment decisions and situations. Your most promising sexual encounters can happen somewhat unexpectedly and certainly in an unplanned way between January 2–7 and 21–29, February 4–11 and 22–25, March 9–17, April 17–24, May 16–30, June 13–23, July 1–14 and 21–29, August 4–14, September 21–30, October 2–12 and 23–29, November 4–19 and December 8–29.

11 You will enjoy good connections between sexual satisfaction and short-

distance travel, improved communications, a fall of shyness, dance halls, bridge games, club membership and participation matters, and self-employment interests. Now and then you will be particularly daring and perhaps somewhat disorganized in sexual encounters between January 22–31, February 2–12, March 16–26, April 4–20, May 2–13, June 14–25, July 1–9 and 19–28, August 4–14, September 16–27, October 22–27, November 3–18, and December 5–17.

12   You will be shrewd, wise, strong, and self-confident in all matters connected with your sex life. You are going to want more immediate and lasting satisfaction and can make new love and friendship arrangements. Your most promising sexual encounters can take place over the second and third weeks of January, February 18–27, March 3–13 and 23–31, April 6–14, May 19–29, June 8–21, July 4–10 and 22–27, August 9–19, September 6–18, October 4–14 and 24–29, November 3–13, and December 26–31.

13   Romance has more say than raw, naked, unadulterated sex over the peak of high summer, while you tend to attract more imaginative sexual partners during the late winter and late autumn. There are good connections between your sexual joys and unexpected travel, spontaneous parties, special once-a-year entertainments, and visits to people you haven't seen in a long time. Usually your sexual encounters are at their best during the late September and early October intervals.

14   Your best periods for getting the most out of sex are the second week of February, the last ten days of March, the middle of April, the entire May-July and November-December intervals. Thursday is your best sex day, Friday and Saturday evenings are excellent, but Sunday mornings bring on frustrations. Be more specific with your lover, speak frankly, don't leave things unsaid and up in the air, so to speak. Be youthful in all approaches to sex no matter what your age.

15   Erotic action is best when it takes place in bed and the very idea of such travel has a strong link with the Ides of May, the time of the year you happened to be born. Sex will be more romantic, more imaginative, more daring in your chart. Your best periods for enjoying sex at its best will be the last six days of January, the March-April and July-August periods, the last ten days of September, and the period right after Christmas. It is you, not your partner, who tends to interfere with sexual patterns when they are at their best—so watch it!

16   You respond strongly to the Mercury-Jupiter-Lilith arrangement in your sexual experiences. You are idealistic, full of good intentions, and a square shooter in your attitudes and approaches to sex. You are more the tempter and charmer than you realize, however. Your most rewarding sexual encounters take place between January 1–19, February 4–14, March 21–31, April 6–17, May 10–23, June 14–24, July 3–13 and 21–28, August

14–25, September 17–29, October 4–15, November 2–12 and 22–30, and December 1–9.

17 You respond strongly to the Mercury-Jupiter-South node arrangement in your sexual experiences. You want to avoid troubles and problems as a result of indiscriminate sexual activity and because of this you often say, "No." There are good connections between your unique sex life and people who wear wigs and hair pieces. Your most rewarding sexual encounters take place between January 23–31, February 8–15, March 21–31, April 6–13 and 23–30, May 1–11, June 11–24, July 3–18, August 10–24, September 3–12, October 9–19, November 3–17, and December 12–19.

18 You respond strongly to the Mercury-Jupiter-Uranus arrangement in your sexual experiences. You are fast, sudden, aware, lucky in sex, and you are anxious to do everything in life at least twice. There are good connections between your sex life and small people. Your most rewarding sexual encounters take place between January 3–15, February 3–13, March 8–19, April 20–30, May 22–31, June 3–13 and 23–30, July 4–9 and 19–25, August 8–19, September 24–30, October 4–18, November 7–17, and December 24–31.

19 You respond strongly to the Mercury-Uranus-Pluto arrangements in your sexual experiences. You are sensitive, intellectual, zealous for acceptance, and strongly aware of what your sexual partner is thinking, wanting, and hoping. There are good connections between your developing sex life and people connected with law enforcement. Your most rewarding sexual encounters take place between January 10–21, February 11–24, March 1–9 and 22–29, April 4–15, May 10–25, June 14–26, July 3–16, August 14–28, September 19–30, October 1–8 and November 14–24.

20 You respond strongly to the Mercury-Uranus-Jupiter arrangement in your sexual experiences. You are swift in mind and loving action, anxious to please, very entertaining in the boudoir, and you can be jovial and enthusiastic about ultimate joys. There are good connections between your developing sex life and people who are connected with the arts, music, writing, dance, painting, and sculpture. Your most rewarding sexual encounters take place between January 3–14, February 2–12, March 20–31, April 1–10, May 6–16 and 24–31, June 3–13 and 26–30, July 19 to August 8, September 24 to October 10, November 8–18, and December 1–9.

21 You respond strongly to the Mercury-Uranus-Ceres arrangement in your sexual experiences. You are swift to see the humor in what others may be taking too seriously. You make sex a lot of good wholesome fun and others will always give you credit for this. You can enjoy good connections between your sexual experiences and people connected with education. Your most rewarding sexual encounters should be between January 1–8 and 24–31, February 14–17, March 3–15, April 18–30, May 6–10 and

25–31, June 9–19, July 3–7 and 27–31, August 8–18, September 10–20, October 22–31, November 9–19, and December 3–10.

22   You respond strongly to the Mercury-Neptune-Mars arrangement in your sexual experiences. You are entertaining, witty, light-hearted in love and sex, but beneath the surface there can be some longings that can know no tongue and now and then a bit of brutality in staking claims on the "perfect" lovers. You are imaginative, romantic, and highly desirable. You will enjoy good connections between your sex life and people who seem to make a career out of being glamorous, sexy, alluring, and especially promiscuous and permissive.

23   You respond strongly to the Mercury-Pluto-Mars arrangement in your sexual experiences. You are going to get what you want (sexually speaking), although others wouldn't believe this about you. You are far stronger and far more demanding in sex than is expected. Once somebody sleeps with you, they want to have your love again and again. You carry not only a big wallop sexually but a lot of surprises. Your most promising periods for sexual encounters are January 24 to February 9, March 16–31, April 4–17, May 9–29, June 4–23, July 21 to August 11, September 23 to October 4, October 20 to November 10, December 22–31.

24   You respond strongly to the Mercury-Saturn-Mars arrangement in your sexual experiences. You are blessed with marvelous sexual endurance or as the Chinese say—you maintain long time. Your allure goes before you, so to speak, and carries a lot of weight with those who recognize it for what it is: You exude sex which is another way of saying this. You will always enjoy a good correspondence in your horoscope between your developing sex life and people who like to wear hats and keep their heads covered.

25   In your sexual experiences, you respond strongly to the Jupiter-Mars-Lilith arrangement in your horoscope. You are affirmative, positive, enthusiastic, and jovial in your approaches and attitudes to sex. You are turned on by those who are built sexy and often may see temptation where others don't realize that it is lurking. Your most satisfying sexual encounters take place between January 1–15, February 3–20, March 9–19, April 14–24, May 6–11 and 18–24, June 10–16 and 25–30, July 4–14, August 3–14, September 16–29, October 8–18, November 23–30, and December 7–12 and 27–31.

26   You respond strongly to the Saturn-Mercury-Vulcan arrangement in your sexual experiences. You save yourself in a sense so that you can give the most and the best to sex; you never stint self or partner on the reward potential. You are rather daring in going after the unorthodox of sexual quarries. Your most satisfying sexual encounters occur between January 23–31, February 4–15, March 2–17, April 22–30, May 3–12 and 24–31, June 16–29, July 1–13 and 28–31, August 8–18, September 2–20, October 2–16, November 3–20, and December 14–21.

27 You respond strongly to the Sun-Moon arrangement in your sexual experiences. you have your own rules about sex, your own standards and your own methods of evaluation. Sex without concern, kindness, something that smacks of love doesn't make much sense in your book of life. You retain your sexual power into old age. Best periods for rewarding sexual encounters are January 12–20, February 14–22, March 1–9, April 12–23, May 2–14, June 13–21, July 14–26, August 1–13 and 28–31, September 16–26, October 19–29, November 2–11, and December 14–30.

28 Impassioned is the code word coming to mind upon due examination of your sex chart. Sexual encounters evoke feelings you never realized you had in your body and mind and especially during the months of April, May, June, and July 18–25, August 4–22, and the last two weeks of November. Travel, legal settlements, new contracts and agreements are all related to your sexual encounters and joys. Vermont, Delaware, North Carolina, and the port cities of Texas are special meccas for you.

29 There is a grand providing of love indicated in your sex scope. You give without obvious interest in receiving and therein find the solution to life and love's greatest riddles. There is a point over which the true giver of love passes and it is ecstasy never to be known by the takers of love. Your most promising sexual periods are the last days of January, the months of May, June, July, and late October and early November. Sexual meccas for you are Niagara Falls, South Carolina, rural Georgia, and the gulf coasts of Alabama and Florida.

30 Atmosphere plays an unusual role in the sexual ecstasy that you find. Monaco, Sardinia, Corsica, Malta, Gibraltar, Costa Rica, Bermuda, Barbados, Southern California can deliver the goods as few other places can. Your peak sexual periods are the third week of January, the closing days of February, the months of May, June, August, and November. You provoke love, you stimulate love under Neptunian and Venusian aspects in your chart.

31 Seek love and sex where conventions are being held, where annual meetings are prospering, en route to and from lovely settings. Maine, New Hampshire, South Carolina, Key West, New Orleans, and Galveston-Corpus Christi are your preferred love settings. Your sex life is activated over the last six days of February, the middle of March, the period between May 4–21, the period between October 9–24, November 4–18, and the last six days of December.

June

1 There are indications in your sexual trends that old frontiers of love are disappearing and that there will be a more progressive and up-to-date approach to these matters in your life. Sexual threads touch desert areas, barren wastelands, where people of tougher fiber drink deep from the cup of life. The defiance motive comes and goes over the months of March, July, August, and October. There can be a breaking of some ties so that new ones can be formed.

2 Along the compellingly inviting road of sex, there are longer stopovers during May-June and late November each year. There are old doors being closed so that new doors can be opened. There is unraveling, much rewinding, and out of the milstrom of living comes greater ambition and higher career motivation. Happiness from your love department spills over into other departments of life. The sexual trend is investigative, inventive, creative, full of archly romantic imagination.

3 New love experiences will most assuredly follow anything that smacks of disaffection or rejection. From the withered flowers of an earlier love, new blossoms spring forth. New love is always an offspring of old love in your chart. Sexual threads in your chart touch relatives and friends of former lover-ins. Encounters are headier during the last week of June, over the months of July and August. There are indications of greater self-confidence born of greater love for another.

4 There is linkage between your perfect sex partner and the signs Scorpio and Aquarius. There is linkage with depressed cities, exclusive summer resorts, and your ability to transform the dream into a reality. You will attain your highest level of sexual happiness over the months of June, August, and September. Other propitious sexual cycles for you are the first week of February, the third week of March, the last ten days of October, and the opening days of December.

5 Meeting your perfect sexual partner has linkage with the friends of your siblings, parties that office friends give during the summer months, places where your peers gather for conversation. You will attain your highest level of sexual release during the months of February, June, July, August, the last week of October, and first week of December. There are indications that the lover you meet will remain strongly fixed in your life for a long time to come.

6   You will meet your perfect sex partner in places you have never visited before: Mexico, Puerto Rico, Barbados, and the mountains of Canada are strongly represented. Your strongest sexual cycles are the third week of January, the closing week of April, the months of June, August, and October. Travel to meet love, which tends to be a series of brief encounters rather than anything permanent in your life at this time.

7   You respond strongly to the Mercury-Jupiter-Lilith arrangement in your sexual experiences. There is an intellectual attitude and approach toward sex which seems to be right for you but now and then you may be chastened by the fact that some see you as an enchanter, a tempter, and a seducer. You will enjoy good connections between your developing sex life and people who go in for trivia, who pride themselves on having the answers. Your most rewarding intervals for sexual encounters this year are the May-June, very late July, mid-August, and the late October periods.

8   You respond strongly to the Mercury-Jupiter-South node arrangement in your sexual experiences. You are clever, shrewd, fast in sexual matters, quick to spot targets of opportunity, and quick to gain from cruising about where interesting types are likely to gather. You can count on good connections between your expanding sex life and people who spend more money on shoes than on any other wardrobe items. Your most rewarding intervals for sexual encounters are the April, June-July, late August, and early November periods.

9   You respond strongly to the Mercury-Jupiter-Neptune arrangement in your sexual experiences. You are idealistic about sex and love and want these two to become congruently one. There is a great deal of glamour working in your behalf after your thirty-third year. Your endurance in sex is phenomenal. You can count on good connections between your sex life and people associated with banks, brokerage firms, with handling money in either a custodial or administrative way. Your most rewarding sexual encounter periods fall during March, July-August, very early September, and very late November.

10 You respond strongly to the Saturn-Mercury arrangement in your sexual experiences. You are restrained at times, but there is a very youthful compulsiveness that at other times can't be denied or really controlled. There will be good connections between your sex life and unemployed people, those who are looking for work in your area. Your most promising sexual encounters take place between January 3–15, February 19–27, March 4–17, April 14–28, May 2–12 and 22–31, June 14–25, July 20–31, August 6–18, September 15–30, October 4–11, November 7–23, and December 2–20.

11 You respond strongly to the Uranus-Mercury-Venus arrangement in your sexual experiences. You have a kind of innocent faith that sex is something that improves each time it is experienced and in many ways sexual

intercourse remains medicinal for you. There are good connections between your sex life and people who tend to be rather world weary. Your most promising sexual encounters can take place between January 24–31, February 6–19, March 3–10 and 23–30, April 9–29, May 8–19, June 10–22, July 4–18, August 20–30, September 14–28, October 3–13 and 26–30, November 2–17, and December 8–16.

12   You enjoy good connections between sexual encounters and the art of friendship, interesting conversation, visits to former neighbors, career advancement; improved relationships with people in positions of authority, and changes in command. During the years, you will be particularly creative in your sex life between January 1–19, February 16–26, March 8–18, April 4–25, May 18–27, June 10–23, July 14–27, August 4–15, September 19–30, October 2–17, November 5–13, and December 1–15.

13   There is some promise where you travel alone, where you stop at motels, where lectures are being given, and where you resurrect some high-school relationships that still mean much to you even though they never really got off the ground in the old days. Your wish to get more out of your romantic and sexual experiences will be honored by the Neptunian and Venusian trends in your sex scope over the last six days of February, the third week of March, the second half of April, the months of May, July, very late September, and the period just before Christmas.

14   Promising Jupiter-Uranus trends in your horoscope suggest a deepening of your sexual experiences. Your interest in getting more out of sex runs hand in hand with the greater sense of material and personal security that you are enjoying. You want more than money, more than gold and diamonds; you want emotional fulfillment. The periods when this power is paramount are the late-March to late-May interval, the June 7–19, July 3–22, August 9–24, and very late September cycle.

15   It's vital to you that your sex life be equally romantic, imaginative, and creative. The accent is less on the physical than on the emotional in your horoscope. Royal, regal, expensive, knightly, historic atmospheres give you a helping hand in the realization of your highest level of sexual experience. Particularly promising for sexual ecstasy are the closing days of April, the months of May, June, July, very late August, and November.

16   You respond strongly to the Mercury-Jupiter-Pluto-Mars arrangement in your sexual experiences. You are versatile, flexible, very much at home in sexual matters. Nothing in the way of sexual proclivities will ever throw you. There is a good connection between your sex life and people who love to play, to engage in sports, who want fun out of life rather than success and money. Your most promising periods for rewarding sexual encounters are late January, late March, the June-August, late September, and early October periods.

17 You respond strongly to the Mercury-Jupiter-Uranus-Venus arrangement in your sexual experiences. You are adept in all sexual matters and you adapt and adjust quickly to the wishes and desires of your sexual partner. There's a good connection between your expanding sexual drive and people who are new to sex, still learning so to speak. Your most rewarding sexual encounters will take place between January 1–14, February 21 to March 14, April 6–19, May 5–20, June 18–30, July 4–15, August 8–12 and 20–31, September 3–14, October 1–19, and November 24 to December 10.

18 You respond strongly to the Mercury-Jupiter-Venus-Moon arrangement in your sexual experiences. Sexual intercourse is medicinal for you and its success tends to spill over into other areas of your life. There's a good connection between your sex drive and people who own a considerable amount of real estate and other types of property. Your most rewarding sexual encounters take place between January 2–21, February 4–15, March 16–31, April 9–19, May 6–23, June 14–30, July 8–19, August 2–20, September 4–13, October 1–9, November 22–30, and December 1–12.

19 You respond strongly to the Moon-Jupiter-Mars arrangement in your sexual experiences. You are certain, assured, confident, and reliant in sexual matters and you tend to attain peaks of good humor, affirmation, and enthusiasm through rewarding sex. You can count on a good connection between your sex drive and people who like to sing in public. Your most rewarding intervals for sexual encounters are late January, late February, March 6–17, April 3–18, May 9–19, June 20–30, July 2–15, August 7–15, September 19–29, October 14–24, November 3–15, and December 1–10.

20 You respond strongly to the Moon-Jupiter-Mercury arrangement in your sexual experiences. You are constant, loyal, devoted in your attitudes and approaches to sex. You believe in doing right by your sex partner. You can count on good connections between your developing sex drive and people in the entertainment field. Good wit, plenty of laughter are going to characterize your sex life this year. Late January, early February, the May-June and August-September intervals bring your most rewarding sexual encounters.

21 You respond strongly to the Moon-Jupiter-Mars arrangement in your sexual experiences. You are not one to forget any sex partner. Also for you, each sexual experience has something uniquely its own about it. You will enjoy good connections between your sex drive and people who are homebodies above all else. You move close to happy parents and their children. Your most rewarding sexual encounters take place during early March, early April, the second half of May, the June-July, late August, and late November periods.

22   You respond strongly to the Moon-Neptune-Mars arrangement in your sexual experiences. You are sensitive, overly kind, anxious to overindulge those with whom you have sex. You feel you are indebted to the person who gives you great unadulterated sexual joys. You will enjoy a good connection between your sex life and people who grew up in very cold climates, people from New England and the upper Middle Atlantic states, Canada, and Northern Europe. The best periods for sexual encounters are May-July, and early September to late October.

23   You respond strongly to the Moon-Pluto-Venus arrangement in your sexual experiences. You are always prepared for spontaneous sex, for target-of-opportunity sex. You particularly enjoy these spur of the moment encounters. You are going to enjoy a good connection between your developing sex life and people who only recently were liberated from nineteenth-century views of sex and morality. The best periods for sexual encounters are April-May, August-September, and the last ten days of November.

24   You respond strongly to the Moon-Saturn-Mercury arrangement in your sexual experiences. You recognize the limitations of sex and prefer love affairs in which there are good communications to those that leave so much unsaid. You don't like mysteries and certainly spurn anything that smacks of intrigue in your sexual encounters. You will enjoy good connections between your expanding sex life and people from deprived backgrounds, particularly during May, July, August and November.

25   You respond strongly to the Sun-Uranus-Neptune arrangement in your horoscope. You are self-contained in many ways but in all attitudes and approaches to sex, you manage to subdue self so that your giving of pleasure makes you one of the really great lovers in the Zodiac. You have a great deal of allure in the boudoir that doesn't signify much in the kitchen, parlor, or the office. Your most rewarding sexual encounters take place between January 23–31, February 1–12, March 6–14, April 12–23, May 16–27, June 3–13 and 25–30, July 18–31, August 6–11 and 20–31, September 4–15, October 9–20, November 1–23, and December 10–16.

26   You respond strongly to the Moon-Uranus-Saturn arrangement in your horoscope in all matters pertaining to sex and tend to be easily turned on by people who have love as well as sexual pleasure to offer. You may expect sex to answer rather than create problems. You will do well in all relationships with corporate executives. Your most satisfying sexual encounters transpire between January 1–13 and 23–31, February 13–23, March 4–14, April 16–28, May 3–20, June 13–21, July 3–17, August 19–29, September 14–25, October 8–19, November 22–30, and December 14–20.

27   You respond strongly to the Uranus-Aldebaran arrangement in your sexual experiences. You want to be known as a great lover. You want to intrigue,

to mystify others in the boudoir, and the royal stars of Persia permit you to wear this crown. Your most satisfying sexual encounters take place during the second half of January, February 3–12, March 3–15, April 21–30, May 2–8 and 18–23, June 4–17, July 3–13 and 23–31, August 4–14, September 3–18, October 18–27, November 19–29, and December 1–9 and 27–30.

28 Be decorative in dramatic settings to get the most and the best out of sexual encounters. You can not overdress under cosmic aspects, wear too much jewelry, or dramatize your hairdo too much. Indications are for dramatic atmospheres and surroundings. People with Sun, Moon, or several orbs in Gemini, Aquarius and Libra will be interested in you. Your most promising sexual periods are the late March, May-July, late September, and late October periods.

29 Your sexual meccas are the West Coast, Luxembourg, West Germany, London, and Plymouth in England, and the oil boom areas of Scotland and Norway. Sex is all the greater for you when you feel in the know, in an economically burgeoning area of the world, and when you feel the great vitality of others surrounding you. Your sex scope is particularly inviting during the months of late February, early April, May, July, August, and late December.

30 Sexual joy is related to spur-of-the-moment travel, blond people, people who sing or who fancy themselves singers and ethnics who feel that they are unhappily exiled in the United States. Love from a strongly ethnic type is certainly indicated in your sex scope. Make the most of your sexual strengths over the months of April, June, July, August, and late November and aim for greater magical witchery in your appearance and more sensuous actions.

July

1 There is an ebb and flow to your sexual drive. Sexual threads are related to new travel experiences, to the intangibles of your job, the social side of your career aspirations, to chance meetings with former neighbors and co-workers, and to places where fragrant flowers grow in great abundance. The high watermarks come during the middle of April, over the months of

July, November, and December. There are love failures and disappointments possible during February and June.

2   The increase in inner awareness that you are experiencing can most assuredly touch your sex life and romantic successes. Courtship is particularly enjoyable over the spring. Your unusual perception can impress somebody and be at the root of this person's evident desire to know you more intimately. Joint endeavors, joint investments, special weekend travel are all part of this developing scene. Greater creativity and imagination in sexual encounters are real threads in your life.

3   A simpler life-style makes for greater joy from love and sex. Get far from the maddening crowds with your beloved so that there can be more general sharing and less interference. Harmony, symmetry, and greater balance and moderation dot your sexual landscape over the first six months. After July, there is always greater accent on escape into love, into sex, away from pressing but perhaps unnecessary problems. Love and sex have an emancipating thread over the last three months of the year.

4   Your sex life may require some reorganization. Where plans are well established and protected, your best and most intense potential for meeting this fabulous personality peaks during the October-November period. You have good sexual trends operating to your advantage as each year begins and ends and again during very late February, the month of July, and the last ten days of August. Your sexual intuition and awareness are unbeatable.

5   Neptune is lifting veils in your horoscope so that what you want and require in the perfect sex partner finally are revealed to you. Your sexual allure usually peaks over the fall months. But you have good sexual trends operating to your advantage over the second week of January, the last six days of February, the middle of April, the last four days of May, and the entire July period. Pluto's rays induce unbeatable awareness and transformation power in your sex chart.

6   You can count on enormous Neptune-Pluto power in finding and holding on to your perfect sex partner. Your sexual power peaks during the middle of March, the last six days of April, and holds pretty steadily over the three months of summer, only to wane as November says adieu. Your perfect sex partner is strong on joviality, persistence, endurance, optimism, and self-confidence. Never overlook the advantages of loving a strongly Scorpio person.

7   You respond strongly to the Moon-Saturn-Mars arrangement in your sexual experiences. This means you are sensitive, quiet, dignified, conservative, and traditional in sex, and yet never with any fall of self-confidence or self-reliance. Your most rewarding sexual encounters will take place with people new to your environment. Your most rewarding intervals for sexual encounters are January 1–11 and 24–31, February 9–20, March 3–

16, April 17–27, May 2–15, June 13–26, July 4 to August 1, September 19–30, October 14–24, November 3–13, and December 1–15.

8   You respond strongly to the Moon-Saturn-Venus arrangement in your sexual experiences. This means you are restrained, careful, cautious in sexual matters, but beneath the surface you can be aggressive when you are sure. You most likely can be called compulsive in sex matters between your twenty-sixth and thirty-eighth and fiftieth years. There is a good connection between your sex drive and people in the field of education. Your most rewarding intervals for sexual encounters are January 13–26, February 3–14, March 17–27, April 3–15, May 19–31, June 2–10 and June 25 to July 16, August 22 to September 9, September 25 to October 14, November 3–14, and December 12–20.

9   You respond strongly to the Moon-Saturn-North node arrangement in your sexual experiences. This means that you are soft-hearted, so to speak, and that you forgive lovers quickly. You look to the future in the arms of your lover. You seek forms of perfection in sex. Good connections with people who farm. Your most rewarding intervals for sexual encounters are January 1–10 and 25–31, February 5–15, March 12–20, April 14–24, May 17–27, June 3–15, July 20–31, August 9–18, September 3–15, October 24–31, November 7–15, and December 17–28.

10 You respond strongly to the Pluto-Mercury arrangement in your sexual experiences. You are adept at understanding the innermost feelings, aspirations, fears, and uncertainties of your sex partner and you can help your beloved put these hopes into words. Your most promising sexual encounters take place between January 11–22, February 3–10, March 4–17 and 27–31, April 18–29, May 16–30, June 2–18, July 6–14 and 24–27, August 2–15, September 8–20, October 1–12 and 23–30, November 4–17, and December 8–30.

11 You enjoy good connections between your expanding sex life and improved communications with friends and neighbors, greater ease in getting around and seeing people you don't ordinarily see. There are good connections between sexual encounters and law enforcement people. Your most promising sexual encounters take place during January 18–27, February 3–15, March 6–17, April 2–29, May 2–7 and 18–28, June 14–24, July 16–27, August 4–16, September 20–30, October 4–19, November 6–21, and December 14–22.

12 There are good connections between your expanding sex life and people who are involved with the printed word, people involved with the news, people in publicity, advertising, and public relations. Your most promising sexual encounters take place between January 26–31, February 1–13 and 22–27, March 3–13, Apri 16–30, May 2–12 and 24–31, June 19–29, July 2–21, August 14–25, September 6–22, October 3–23, November 1–13 and 22–29, and December 26–31.

13   Tenting, camping, mountains are among the code words that can be associated with the planetary trends in your sex scope. With Mars a strong sexual significator in your birth chart, you have an unusual knack of covering up what might seem aggressive in another person; this trend is particularly strong and nets you sexual victories. Your more promising intervals for upping your sexual power and satisfaction are January 9–14, February 21–27, March 4–18, April 17–25, May 2–30, June 13–19, July 18–24, August 7–19, very late November, and the period right after Christmas.

14   Where the Sun is setting, your sexual power always seems to be accented. There are pioneering trends in your sex scope, indicating that you blaze sexual trails, that you often are first with the most and that you set good paces in romantic affairs which have a memorable trend to them. Your most promising sexual periods are January 14–24, March 4–18, April 19–28, May 9–27, June 4–17, July 19–24, August 2–14, September 4–20, October 16–27, November 4–10, and right before Christmas.

15   You have a strong sexual response under favorable aspects involving transiting Jupiter and Uranus with your Sun in Cancer. Surprise, short-distance travel, improved communications, school reunions are suggested by the sexual trends in your horoscope. Your peak sexual promises fall between March 7–22, April 4–23, May 6–26, June 3–18, July 3–24, August 18–29, September 4–11, October 17–27, November 6–11, December 27–29.

16   You respond strongly to the Moon-Jupiter-Mars arrangement in your sexual experiences. You are well disposed toward people you share any type of living arrangements with and will go all out to prove loyalty and devotion to these persons. There are good connections between your sex drive and people who are exceptionally patriotic and perhaps even a bit jingoistic and warlike. Your most rewarding sexual encounters take place between January 1–16, February 13–23, March 21–31, April 2–14, May 4–20, June 6–19, July 6–26, August 10–23, September 1–9 and 23–30, October 11–30, November 2–14, and December 3–11.

17   You respond strongly to the Moon-Uranus-Mercury arrangement in your sexual experiences. You very much cry out to live fully and to be part and parcel of your own times. You link sexual activity in the back of your mind to remaining young. There are good connections between your sex drive and people who tend to be fearful, uncertain, and unsure of themselves, and who need all that you can give them in the way of love and confidence. Your most rewarding sexual encounters take place during late March, late May, over the June-August and November periods.

18   You respond strongly to the Moon-Neptune-Venus arrangement in your sexual experiences. You want to dig more deeply into your sex potential and certainly into the sex potential of your partners. Your sex appeal is partic-

ularly high. You can count on good connections between your expanding sex life and people who have a strong affinity for good food, for cooking, baking, and entertaining. Best periods for rewarding sexual encounters are late January, late February, late April, early May, June 4–20, July 6–24, August 8–28, and the late October and early November periods.

19   You respond strongly to the Sun-Jupiter-Mars arrangement in your sexual experiences. You are imbued with the idea of giving to a partner, of contributing good feelings, inspiration, a real purpose to your togetherness. You want to leave your partner happier than he/she was before you arrived on the scene. You will enjoy a good connection between your increasing sex drive and people who are in the creative arts. Best periods for sexual encounters are late February, early March, April 9–20, May 6–23, June 14–30, July 3–10 and 22–31, August 13–26, September 19 to October 11, and December 4–16.

20   You respond strongly to the Sun-Jupiter-Venus arrangement in your sexual experiences. Lovemaking is a lot of fun for you and you convey these feelings well to your partner. Good humor, a jovial disposition, a sense of partying before and after love are all part of the picture you bring to lovemaking. You will enjoy good connections between your multiplying sex drive and people connected with libraries, books, publishing, and printing. Best periods for rewarding sexual encounters this year are early February, early March, late April, the entire May-June period, the last six days of July, the first eleven days of August, September 19–28, October 4–15, and November 22–30.

21   You respond strongly to the Sun-Jupiter-Mercury arrangement in your sexual experiences. You inveigle, you persuade, and make love to many people who had no intention of making love when they first ran into you. You are an adept lover, warm, demonstrative, very passionate. You will enjoy good connections between your sex drive and people from Hispanic countries. Best periods for rewarding sexual encounters are January 14–28, February 9–17, March 3–15, April 6–22, May 23 to June 14, July 25 to August 12, September 20 to October 8, and December 5–20.

22   You respond strongly to the Sun-Neptune-Mars arrangement in your sexual experiences. You are strongly imbued with ideas as to your own vital importance. You have a great deal of vitality to put into your sexual encounters and inject something of mystery and of the exotic now and then as well. You will enjoy a good connection between your developing sex life and people who have grown up in rather glamorous atmospheres. You will be exposed to many permissive types each year and may indulge yourself sexually more than you did in the past.

23   You respond strongly to the Sun-Pluto-Venus arrangement in your sexual experiences. You tend to be very correct in your sexual encounters, very well balanced, careful to give as much as you receive. You would never

want a sex partner to feel that you have taken advantage of him/her in any way. Especially in February, late April, May, late June and the August-September periods, you will enjoy a good connection between your expanding sex life and people with very thin or thinning hair. Also with people who have done a lot of field work in their time.

24   You respond strongly to the Sun-Saturn-Venus arrangement in your sexual experiences. You aim for good balance and a strong sense of personal control in your sex life. Your date of birth is the best day in any year for completing some course or courses of study. During late January, late February, the April-June and September-October periods, you will enjoy a good connection between your broadening sex life and people from very warm places—the Sunbelt, Southern Europe, Latin America.

25   You respond strongly to the Moon-Uranus-Venus arrangement in your sexual experiences. You are sensitive to what passes and what doesn't pass with your generation of lovers and you like to see yourself as very much a part of the times in which you live. There will be good satisfying connections between your sex life and people on the go, fast moving, achieving people who have to squeeze in their sex encounters. The more flexible you are about time, the better your lover will like it and appreciate you. January, March, June-July and October-November are your sexual high water marks.

26   You respond strongly to the Pluto-Neptune-Lilith arrangement in your sexual experiences. You are sexier than the average person, capable of tempting others to try some of your forbidden fruit. Nobody knows his/her way to the apple tree as well as you. You will enjoy good connections between your sex life and people who immigrated to this country over the past decade. February, the May-June, and the late July and early August periods are your most rewarding intervals for sexual encounters.

27   You will undoubtedly enjoy your expanding sex life in the company of spouse, in-laws, and old friends. New trails can be blazed in sexual experiences mostly because you and your beloved can discuss sex more openly and fully now. You find your most rewarding and satisfying sexual encounters between January 13–27, February 9–13 and 21–25, March 14–23 and 29–31, April 4–18, May 6–26, June 14–23, July 16–25, August 2–12 and 18–28, September 13–17, October 9–14 and 23–27, November 7–18, and December 19–27.

28   Sexual happiness has a close association with getting away from the maddening crowds, visiting fishing villages, spending time where life is simple, quiet, and where one's personal freedom is honored and respected. Greeks come bearing gifts for you. What you say, what you represent seems greener grass to strangers than what they are accustomed to. Your peak periods for unadulterated sexual joy are the first half of April, the last ten days of May, the entire months of June, July, August, and October.

29 Your sexual code words are bountiful, abundance, and giving. To those who would love you completely and beckon you into unexcelled joy, nothing is more appealing than that sense of doing good and spreading goodwill which are such important parts of your basic personality. Your desire to give joy is unmatched during the first half of April, the last ten days of May, all of June-July, the last two weeks of August, late September, and early November and brings forth extra effort from those who want to impress you, match your kindness and goodness, and be your partner for a long time.

30 There is strong sexual awareness represented in your chart over the late spring and throughout the summer; it's like you can read the minds and hearts of others. Your magical wizardry is unmatched from time to time and captures the attention of very important people. Love—sex if you will—can lead to marriage during the next few years. Your sexual happiness is closely associated with people you have known a long time, with New England, Canada, friends of former spouses, acquaintances of your parents.

31 Seek love and sex encounters where new building is going on, where the emphasis is on tomorrow rather than yesterday, where people gather in large fields for special outdoor sporting events, and let the accent fall on California, Florida, Colorado, Arizona, Nevada, Western New York, Nova Scotia, and Newfoundland. Your sex life is activated most strongly on Saturday evenings and particularly during late January, very late March, the period between April 19–30, May 2–14, throughout the October and November periods, and just before Christmas.

August

1 The tempo can reveal the foolishness of trying to plan your love and sex life. Spontaneity is evident during most of the months and it is the spur, the path, the manner in your most unforgettable love experiences. Be on guard against deception over the January-February period and be willing to make compromises for in depth love experiences over spring and very late autumn. Love is fragile, love is brutal, love can't be denied.

2 Your love chart reveals Spanish music and dancing. The sexual thread in

your life can be related to theater, a music hall, and summer musicals, also to concerts, and special musical festivals in historic and traditional settings. Silence is certainly the better part of valor in some strange and mysterious encounters. Words and letter-writing tend to trap emotions which can't prosper in such entrapment. You go forth to meet love rather than letting love find you.

3   Let conscience be your guide when threads of confusion enter your sex life. There are lines in lust and in love over which no angel should stride. March, late May, the July-September intervals are rich in marital happiness and in adjustment potential that make marital love more rewarding. It may be difficult during any April or December to turn your back on somebody who is dynamically attracted to you. There are facts of life that can't be given or even described; they must be experienced.

4   You respond strongly to the Sun-Jupiter-Mars arrangement in your sexual experiences. This means that you are somewhat self-centered, that you expect the best and the most from sex, and that you are capable of pushing your own sexual interests, drive, and motivation for all they are worth. You will enjoy a good connection between your dynamic sex drive and people who are dramatic, pretentious, and who make noticeable entrances and exits. Your most rewarding periods for sexual encounters are late March, May-June, July 17–27, August 4–14, early October, and late November.

5   You respond strongly to the Sun-Saturn-Mars arrangement in your sexual experiences. This means that you are careful, cautious, quick to evaluate people and that you are rather adept at telling a saint from a sinner. You are strongly self-protective in all matters of sex. You can count on good connections between your developing sex drive and people who are somewhat fearful or uncertain about marriage. Your most rewarding periods for sexual encounters are late January, early March, April 6–16, May 9–29, June 14 to July 10, August 19–29, September 14–24, October 3–13, November 20–30, and December 4–14.

6   You respond strongly to the Sun-Pluto-Mercury arrangement in your sexual experiences. This means that you have a good workable understanding of the other gender and that you can intellectualize some of your sexual desires. You can count on a good connection between your electrifying sex drive and people who have been slow to become involved in sex. Your most rewarding periods for sexual encounters are early January, early April, late May, June 13 to July 5, August 20–30, September 3–15, October 5–17, November 22–30, and December 4–15.

7   You respond strongly to the Sun-Moon-Mercury arrangement in your sexual experiences. You are good-tempered, well mannered, a leader, and a professor of sex. You are turned on sexually by the sun, by warm days and lazy afternoons. You will enjoy good connections between your sex life and people who like boats, and who are connected with them and beaches in

some way. Your most promising periods for sexual encounters are January 7–20, February 3–18, March 4–24, April 10–18, May 17–27, June 11–15 and 26–30, July 4–20, August 23 to September 10, October 14–24, November 22–30, and December 1–15.

8   You respond strongly to the Sun-Mars-Mercury arrangement in your sexual experiences. You are sure of yourself, anxious to convey your assurance to uncertain partners and in many ways a real delightful lover. Your kindness in the clinches is phenomenal. There are good connections between your sex drive and people from the West Coast. Your most promising intervals for sexual encounters are January 1–10, February 22–27, March 3–13, April 11–19, May 20–31, June 4–13, July 23–31, August 14 to September 7, October 20–31, November 2–10 and 23–30, and December 9–16.

9   You respond strongly to the lunar nodes and your Jupiter-Mercury arrangement in your sexual experiences. You are capable of taking greater pleasure from sex than many of your partners and at times you may meet some resentment here. You will enjoy good connections between your sex life and people who are rather majestic and elegant in their personal appearance. Your most rewarding intervals for sexual encounters are January 14–23, February 3–17, March 12–20, April 18–28, May 3–15, June 15–30, July 4–19, August 21–31, September 14 to October 10 and November 23–30.

10   You respond strongly to the Neptune-Mercury-Mars arrangement in your sexual experiences. You enjoy privacy and know how to create and cash in on it. You exhibit a marvelous self-confidence in sexual encounters that impresses your partners. Your most promising sexual days are between January 1–19, February 14–23, March 3–20, April 14–29, May 16–26, June 2–13 and 25–30, July 6–21, August 8–17, September 12–20, October 4–26, November 7–15, and December 3–13.

11   You respond strongly to the Saturn-Venus-Mars arrangement in your sexual experiences. You give the impression to others that you are more self-disciplined, less compulsive, and less impulsive than you actually are in sexual countdowns. You represent a high, extreme gender measurement. Your most promising sexual days are between January 20–30, February 1–12, March 17–31, April 1–11 and 22–30, May 3–23, June 4–18, July 22–31, August 4–17, September 12–23, October 14–27, November 6–14 and 28–30, and December 2–12 and 27–30.

12   You respond strongly to the Uranus-Venus-Moon arrangement in your sexual experiences. You are investigative, experimental in sex and want to experience every thrill ever discovered by past masters. You enjoy good connections between your sex life and people in the medical professions. Your most promising days for sex are between January 11–24, February 19–27, March 2–13 and 28–31, April 6–22, May 5–20, June 13–24,

July 2–15, August 9–21, September 3–14, October 5–16, November 12–20, and December 25–31.

13   Your sex life enjoys good connections with club membership, annual picnics, holiday parties, long-distance travel, very large cities, places where music is low, quiet, and moody. Emotional currents are more electrifying as time goes by. Your most promising sexual ecstasy intervals are January 1–11, February 20–26, March 16–28, April 17–25, May 6–14, June 13–23, July 2–30, August 10–31, September 22–27, October 24–30, November 10–22, and December 4–11.

14   Your sex life enjoys good connections with gardening, spending time in stores that specialize in feed and seed; riding horseback; cavorting in large open fields where larger animals frolic; places where gambling takes place, including Monaco, Baden-Baden, Nevada, Miami, and Mexico City. Your most promising sexual ecstasy intervals are January 4–23, February 1–12, March 16–24, April 20–30, May 4–10 and 23–29, June 14–24, July 2–23, August 13–22, September 16–26, October 26–30 and November 24–30.

15   Your sex life enjoys good connections with animal shows, aquariums, very high buildings, unusual bars and pubs with antique furnishings, and certainly with members of the Pisces solar group. Sexual joys await you in medium-size towns. Your most promising sexual ecstasy intervals are January 1–9, February 4–21, March 13–24, April 17–25, the entire month of May, June 14–24, July 22–30, August 11–21, September, October 13–23, November 7–12, and December 3–10.

16   You respond strongly in your sexual encounters to the Sun-Jupiter-Mars arrangement and tend to increase your sense of ego through sexual activity. You are inclined to take the lead in sex and in initiating it. In March, June-July, late September, and during the October-November period. You enjoy good connections between your sex drive and people who are new to your area. Your most rewarding sexual encounters take place between January 1–16, February 20–25, March 10–21, April 6–17, May 21–31, June 4–18, July 2–19, August 6–26, September 5–23, October 23–31, November 16–30, and December 4–14.

17   You respond strongly to the Sun-Jupiter-Venus arrangement in your sexual experiences. You are very much in control during sex, very much on top of things, full of self-confidence, and of that hail-fellow-well-met spirit. You will enjoy good connections between your sex drive and people who tend to be rather secretive. Your most promising periods for sexual encounters are January 16–31, February 10–21, March 1–11 and 25–31, April 4–19, May 16–30, June 2–15, July 17–31, August 1–14, September 19–30, October 2–13, November 7–20, and December 17–28.

18   You respond strongly to the Sun-Jupiter-Lilith arrangement in your sexual experiences. You are amiable in love, serious but light-hearted, and you

have a special knack of turning others on more than they are prepared to be turned on. You will enjoy good connections between your sex drive and people who are particularly independent, free, gifted with a rare appreciation of independence. Your most rewarding sexual encounters take place between February 4–24, March 6–17, April 19–29, May 22–30, June 4–15, July 7–19, August 3–15, September 21 to October 8, November 3–18, and December 19–29.

19 You can count on good connections between your increasing sex drive and people who have recently changed their life-style and tend to be loners at this time. You respond strongly to the Sun-Mercury-Venus arrangement in your sexual experiences. You like to be in the crowd to a certain extent, not to stand out, and you don't want to be considered different. Your most rewarding sexual encounters occur between January 1–13, February 15–27, March 3–11, April 21–30, May 4–16, June 12–24, July 2–19 and August 6–23, September 13–29, October 3–16, November 23–30, and December 3–13.

20 You can count on good connections between your increasing sex drive and people who have good credentials in the garment and/or food industries. You respond strongly to the Sun-Mercury-Vulcan arrangement in your sexual experiences. You have a very strong physique and an equally strong and forceful drive to get what you want in life. Your most rewarding sexual encounters take place between January 3–13, February 9–20, March 11–24, April 1–14, May 6–22, June 3–18, July 16–31, August 14–24, September 3–15, October 9–24, November 23–30, and December 8–15.

21 You respond strongly to the Sun-Moon-Mars arrangement in your sexual experiences. You have a good sense of balance between the emotional and the physical. You don't push too hard to get what you want but at the same time others may have the feeling that you are in control. There's a good connection between your sex drive and people who are connected with real estate, land, and other property. Late March, early April, the May-June and September-October periods are your best for rewarding sexual encounters.

22 You respond strongly to the Mercury-Moon-Venus arrangement in your sexual experiences. You are inclined to favor traditions, routines, schedules in your sex life, and there's nothing wrong about this inasmuch as you have a greater sexual output than most people. Earthy, you can become a rather different person in the sexual clinches, rather raw, demanding, impulsive, and overly passionate; your partners do not forget you. During the March, June-July, and October-November periods, you enjoy good connections between your developing sex life and people who live on farms and in small rural areas.

23 You respond strongly to the Mercury-Ceres-Dragon's Tail arrangement in your sexual experiences. You build up a great deal of sexual tension now

YOUR ASTRO-NUMEROLOGICAL GUIDE TO SEX

and then and like to take the problem rather far from home, certainly over the 300-mile radius. You are not one to complain to a sex partner about what you aren't getting in the way of relief. There will be a good connection between your sex life and people who speak Spanish, Italian, or Greek. The Mediterranean Sea and its many islands beckon you in all sexual matters.

24   You respond strongly to the Mercury-Pluto-Mars arrangement in your sexual experiences. You are fast on the sexual uptake, quick to identify a promising target of opportunity, and you are capable of remembering when Earth had only one gender during moments of peak enjoyment of sex. There is a good connection between your developing sex life and people much younger or much older than you during the late January, early March, the May-June, late July, late August, and late November periods.

25   You respond strongly to the Pluto-Jupiter-Mercury arrangement in your sexual experiences. You are unduly aware of the needs of silent and shy ones in the matter of sexual stimulation and can be the life of the party and community providing this. There are good connections between your sex life and people, who love to swim, surf, spend time in the sun. Naturally, the beaches of the world can become your favorite mecca. High water sexual intervals are between January 20–31, February 1–14, March 17–29, April 4–17, May 22–29, June 1–12 and 17–27, July 1–13, August 5–15, September 19–27, October 4–18, November 2–17, and December 1–9.

26   You respond strongly to the Pluto-Saturn-Mars arrangement in your sexual experiences. You are able to lure the reluctant ones into doing themselves a lot of good—sexually speaking. You are a fine catalytic agent in all sexual matters and can defend the unorthodox ways of loving better than most. There are good connections in January, late March, April 16–30, May 4–14, June 19–29, over most of July, very late August, September 9–19, October 22–28, early November, and very late December between your sex life and those in the medical professions.

27   You respond strongly to the Jupiter-Saturn-Venus arrangement in your sexual experiences. For you, the sexual act always gets better and better, and as a result you are reluctant to really end any affair or sexual encounter. There will be a satisfying connection between your developing sex life and people who have not for one reason or another made love for a long time or have not had much sex in their lives. You will excel in awakening these sleeping tigers to the joys of sex. May-June, October-November are your best periods for sex.

28   You can count on good connections between your developing sex life and people who speak your language with slight accents. Mars, which rules your sex department, gives you considerable self-confidence in lovemaking. Your most rewarding sexual encounters take place between January 1–14, February 17–27, March 3–18, April 21–30, May 1–14 and 24–31,

June 12–29, July 2–20, August 4–14, September 23–30, October 14–27, November 3–13, and December 20–31.

29 You can count on good connections in your horoscope between your expanding sexual interests and people who favor very light-colored accessories, pastels, and even psychedelics. You respond strongly to the Mars-Lilith-Jupiter arrangement in your sexual experiences. Your most rewarding sexual encounters will take place between January 23–31, February 2–16, March 14–24, April 9–21, May 15–31, June 11–27, July 3–19, August 14–27, September 23–30, October 4–16, November 1–16, and December 4–11.

30 You can count on good connections in your life chart between your expanding sexual drive and people who have been married many times in the past. You respond strongly to the Venus-Lilith-Jupiter arrangement in your sexual experiences. Your most rewarding sexual encounters take place between January 1–15, February 16–27, March 1–13, April 10–21, May 5–17, June 1–11 and 21–30, July 13–24, August 4–15, September 3–16, October 24–31, November 16–30, and December 11–22.

31 You will be more meaningful in a sexual sense. Love and sexual matters favor Mondays, with the Neptunian trend making for special magical witchery in your horoscope. There is greater sexual potency available to you over the October-November period and over the last week of February, the third week of April, and the period between May 10 and June 23.

September

1 There may be a greater need for responsibilities and accountability in love and sex. Much is rumbling in the dungeon of your chart that should not get out. Gossip follows unconventional behavior from time to time and the threat of this is strong over the middle of June and again during the month of December. A lover can be chided once too often during the May-August period. During February and November sexual desires should be played by ear.

2 Love brings solace as well as excitement and major thrills. Shared unhappiness can be one strange path to sexual splendor. Your sex garden contains much forbidden fruit and things you may not wish to acknowledge can literally plague you delightfully from time to time. You can love the

stranger any year but may have more difficulty loving the overly familiar one. Many questions are represented in your love and sex charts for the cycles to come.

3   There are love secrets, mysteries, desires that may be called benign. Recognition that they are there over each March-April period can make for a kind of tantalization. There is a greater tendency to cast away some restrictions and inhibitions in love once you are deep into summer. The sexual graph is a constantly rising one. The lines of demarcation between friendship love and sexual love are not so clear or recognizable over the last three months of the year.

4   The positive affirmative jovial and enthusiastic spirit of Jupiter accents all of your feelings during sexual action. You can count on good connections between your strong sex drive and people who are in the insurance and tax businesses. Also with people who are buying or selling vehicles. Your most rewarding intervals for sexual encounters are January 9–14 and 24–31, February 4–13, March 6–18, April 22–30, May 6–18, June 15–26, July 3–15 and 25–31, August 7–17, September 19–27, October 1–11, November 23–30, and December 4–14.

5   You respond strongly to the Mercury-Jupiter-Venus triad and are given to good spiritual-material balance in sex matters. You not only enjoy sex but want to know all about it. You study sex and learn from each experience. You will enjoy good connections between your sex life and people who have been married many times. Your most rewarding intervals for sexual encounters are January 1–11, February 21–27, March 4–15, April 19–29, May 2–13, June 13–27, July 2–14 and 26–31, August 20–31, September 14–24, October 18–25, November 3–13, and December 16–26.

6   You respond strongly to the Mercury-Jupiter-Mars triad and relate and communicate better than most. You make one of the best sex partners possible because of your ability to be close to another person. You will enjoy good connections with people who need inspiration and guidance. Your most rewarding intervals for sexual encounters are January 20–31, February 3–14, March 1–17, April 22–30, May 4–14, June 12–29, July 4–15, August 5–20, September 19–29, October 3–13, November 6–17, and December 26–31.

7   You respond strongly to the Mercury-Sun-Moon-Saturn arrangement in your sexual experiences. You are very much the total person, personable, stalwart, flexible, versatile, anxious to maintain control during lovemaking and still make certain that your partner is never shortchanged. You can count on good connections between your sex drive and people who have turned their backs on large cities. Your most rewarding sexual intervals for encounters are late January, late February, March 9 to April 7, April 27 to May 14, June 15–28, July 1–20, August 6–30, September 17–25, October 6–16, and November 13–25.

8   You respond strongly to the Mercury-Sun-Saturn-Ceres arrangement in your sexual experiences. You believe in building up a good sexual relationship and in this trust time as you trust it in just about every facet of life. You can count on good connections between your sex life and people from deprived backgrounds. Your most promising intervals for sexual encounters are January 1–13, February 20–26, March 3–16, April 14–24, May 18–29, June 10–30, July 2–14, August 21 to September 13, October 14 to November 3 and December 5–16.

9   You respond strongly to the Mercury-Moon-Pluto arrangement in your sexual experiences. You are intellectual in your approach to sex, strongly physical and biological. You also are experimental and believe that sex is the one human experience that permits humans to become gods for a time. You can count on good connections between your increasing sex drive and people who have come to you from over the water during March, July-August, late September, late October, and early December.

10   You respond strongly to the Sun-Neptune-Mars arrangement in your sexual experiences. Mystery, intrigue, drama, privacy, and strange revelations are part of this picture. Sex illuminates life for you and in many ways it is medicinal. Your most promising sexual encounters take place between January 4–21, February 12–23, March 13–27, April 2–20, May 14–21, June 13–19, July 2–13 and 22–29, August 4–20, September 5–16, October 20–31, November 4–8 and 22–30, and December 8–19.

11   You respond strongly to the Moon-Jupiter-Venus arrangement in your sexual experiences. Good fortune, fabulous rewards, happy memories, and the spilling over of achievements from the private to the public departments of your life are all part of this positive sexual trend. You enjoy sexual encounters between January 1–11, February 19–26, March 2–20, April 17–27, May 2–14 and 23–29, June 1–13 and 23–29, July 14–24, August 11–23, September 9–20, October 4–13, November 22–30, and December 2–14.

12   You respond strongly to the Saturn-Mars arrangement in your sexual experiences. You exhibit an endurance in physical matters that can surprise others. You are very earthy in love, romance, and sex. You demonstrate the highest self-confidence and this endears you especially to shy types. Your most promising sexual encounters are between January 12–20, February 9–19, March 2–20, April 20–30, May 3–15, June 6–13 and 23–28, July 18–29, August 6–23, September 10–19, October 2–13, November 19–27, and December 3–11.

13   Your sex life enjoys good connections with local festivals, lawn fetes, fairs; with teachers, lawyers, and the siblings of people you loved many years ago. Your sexual force field upsets the emotional apple carts of many older people. Your most promising sexual ecstasy intervals are February 1–12 and 21–24, March 9–14, April 16–24, May 6–24, June 4–24, July 3–

13, August 17–20 and 24–29, September 14–22, October 3–13 and 27–31, November 20–30, and December 10–15 and 27–31.

14   Your sex life enjoys good connections with bakeries, places where unusual foods are served; places where examinations are going to be held; places where people in uniform carry sidearms. You could marry for sex rather than for any other reason. Your most promising sexual ecstasy intervals are January 20–30, February 4–13 and 22–27, March 13–25, April 21–30, May 3–29, June 2–24, July 4–10 and 24–29, August 16–27, September 3–20, October 25–31, November 6–18, and December 8–14.

15   Your sex life enjoys good connections with in-laws, the younger siblings of your first love; with places where people tend to find themselves; with places where older people vacation. The more organized your life is, the more time you are going to have to contemplate your navel excitingly and rewardingly. Your most promising sexual ecstasy intervals are January 2–22, February 20–26, March 4–23, April 13–24, May 4–20, June 21–30, July 1–11 and 24–28, August 17–27, September 4–14, October 22–27, and November 22–29.

16   You respond strongly to the Mercury-Neptune-Mars arrangement in your sexual experiences. You tend to innovate, invent, experiment, and create in sexual adventures. There are good connections between your sex drive and people who live in mobile homes, in shacks, tents, and other interesting nonhouse places. Your most rewarding sexual encounters take place between January 3–20, February 5–16, March 8–19, April 2–20, May 6–17, June 14–27, July 2–20, August 18–29, September 21–30, October 14–24, November 11–25, and December 3–14.

17   You respond strongly to the Mercury-Neptune-Vulcan arrangement in your sexual experiences. There is something machine-like in your endurance and maintenance, sexually speaking. You will enjoy good connections between your sex drive and people who like to garden and cross-pollinate. Be sure to make those flower shows. Your most rewarding sexual encounters take place between January 10–30, February 1–18, March 4–13, April 9–21, May 4–24, June 12–20, July 2–16, August 3–16, September 13–26, October 12–20, November 9–17, and December 26–31.

18   You respond strongly to the Mercury-Neptune-Saturn arrangement in your sexual experiences. Your sexual allure comes on strong but still you give your partner the feeling that you are more spiritual and more strongly in control of self. You enjoy good connections between your sex drive and people who love to drive vehicles and who are forever taking off on trips. Your most rewarding sexual encounters take place between January 1–9 and 26–31, February 3–14, March 20–31, April 2–19, May 3–14, June 16–30, July 10–22, August 4–23, September 19–29, October 21–31, November 16–30, and December 9–26.

19 You respond strongly to the Neptune-Mars-Mercury arrangement in your sexual experiences. You are creative and original and a little mysterious in your attitudes and approaches to sex. You have a great deal of allure or old-fashioned sex appeal. You can count on good connections between your developing sex life and people who read a great deal and who well may have literary ambitions. Your most rewarding periods for memorable sexual encounters are January 19–29, February 18 to March 9, April 12 to May 3, May 17 to June 12, June 22–30, July 17–27, August 19–25, September 3–16, October 5–15, November 23–30, and December 15–27.

20 You respond strongly to the Uranus-Mars-Mercury arrangement in your sexual experiences. You can count on good connections between your sex impulses and compulsions and people who drive small cars and who have the knack of looking smaller than they really are. Your most promising periods for rewarding sexual encounters are January 1–17, February 2–14, March 4–20, April 24–30, May 16–26, June 10–21, July 5–17, August 23–31, September 1–14, October 23–29, November 7–19, and December 4–11.

21 You respond strongly to the Uranus-Mars-Venus arrangement in your sexual experiences. You can count on good connections between your sex life and people who curse too much and who tend to tell too many off-color jokes. Your most promising periods for rewarding sexual encounters are January 23–31, February 14–24, March 2–20, April 17–27, May 3–15 and 22–31, June 18–30, July 1–9 and 23–31, August 14–25, September 13–26, October 9–15, November 21–30, and December 26–31.

22 You respond strongly to the Venus-Saturn-Pluto arrangement in your sexual experiences. You are loving and you want to literally adore and worship your lover. You are apt to see your lover in much better light than the world sees him/her. You are strongly imbued with the idea that if your sex life is happy, everything else in life will move along fine. You may be right. In early February, early April, late May, the June-July and very late October and November intervals there is a good connection between your sex life and people of exceptionally high vitality.

23 You respond strongly to the Venus-Jupiter-Pluto arrangement in your sexual experiences. You are strongly positive and affirmative, and nobody is more enthusiastic about spur-of-the-moment sex than you. Sex gives you the feeling that you are well loved, strongly appreciated, and that you are in the best of health. In late March, early April, early May, the July-August and late December periods, you will enjoy a good connection between your sex life and friends of a former spouse or lover.

24 You respond strongly to the Venus-Jupiter-Saturn arrangement in your sexual experiences. You are concerned, considerate, easily pleased, strongly positive, and agreeable in sex and love matters, and you seek to keep a good thing going by demonstrating loyalty and devotion. There will be a good

connection between your broadening sex activity and people from the southwestern states. Your most promising periods for sexual encounters are January 1–11, February 14–23, March 8–19, April 9–29, May 6–14, June 13–29, July 16–26, August 3–15, September 7–17, October 17–27, November 9–19, and December 7–14.

25 You respond strongly to the Jupiter-Neptune-Lilith arrangement in your sexual experiences. You are a born charmer and sexually something of a gad-about in search of love. There will be marvelous connections between your sex life and people on the go—types who fly here and there getting big things done on time, and you may have to schedule your lovemaking at odd times to suit these titans of action. Appreciate all you have going for yourself in sex between January 13 to February 8, March 25 to April 16, May 5–15, June 25–30, July 4–12, August 19 to September 6, October 14–29, November 16–29, and December 2–14.

26 You respond strongly to the Mercury-Moon arrangement in your sexual experiences. You never get bogged down in sex and you certainly know when to end an affair that is headed nowhere. Nobody believes in marriage more than you and in a sense all sex that you experience tends to make you a better and more appreciative spouse. There will be good connections between your sex life and people in the building trades and in construction. Best sexual intervals are early January, late March, April 9–19, May 6–17, June 14–28, July 9–20, August 1–13, September 20–25, October 4–20, November 17–27, and December 10–20.

27 You respond strongly to the Venus-Moon arrangement in your sexual experiences. You never get false messages concerning sex. Your feelings about those who are interested in you are right on the button. You will enjoy good connections between your sex life and people who sell things for a living. Your most rewarding sexual periods are January 1–19, February 14–24, March 1–19, April 6–15, May 20–31, June 11–24, July 2–15 and 22–31, August 9–19, September 4–14, October 2–20, November 7–17, and December 26–31.

28 You respond strongly to the Venus-Uranus-Neptune arrangement in your sexual experiences. Love is a strong force in your life and tends to keep you young and healthy. You are very up-to-date in your view of sex and come through the frame of reference of other people as rather experienced and full of mystery and magical witchery. You can count on good connections between your developing sex life and people who love winter sports. January, late March, the May, July, late August, and early November periods are your most promising for sexual encounters.

29 You respond strongly to the Venus-Uranus-Pluto arrangement in your sexual experiences. You have learned early on that love is more rewarding when you are giving rather than receiving it. It is your destiny to teach others how to love. You can count on good connections between your

developing sex drive and people you went to grade school with but lost touch with over the past decade. Make love during late March, early April, over the May-June, late-August and early-November periods.

30 You respond strongly to the Venus-Uranus-Saturn arrangement in your sexual experiences. The local view of sex and of mores holds you strongly and you are apt to be critical of the morals of people who live far away from you. In sex you are very discriminating and know how to say "No." You can count on good connections between your fervent sexual desires and urges and people who have just moved into your neighborhood.

October

1 Your sex appeal is rising under renewed Neptune-Venus stimulation. Where orders are being given, where ships come into port, where the tang of the sea fills the air—your sexual attraction can be at peak power. The generation gap is not recognized by lovers. There are implications in your horoscope that what you could not do via the love path earlier in life, you very well can do during the years ahead. There can be a need to guard a reputation at times.

2 You are entitled to love and sex but not to the orgies that can be more evident in your environment during strange years. Unconventional behavior can make the headlines. Keep threats of scandal at arm's length. Possessiveness is an enemy to your love experiences during the late spring and early summer. Chance encounters are represented in your chart during the first half of September and the last week of November. Love threads hook onto the shopping ventures.

3 Dynamic as sexual experiences can prevail but there is a need for accord between lovers. Knowing what is in your lover's mind can be pretty hard to come by now. Love is not necessarily a sexual ingredient to some people although it is very much one to you. Marital bliss is more dependent on your ability to get away from the small fry and other loving interference. You may not be married to your in-laws but they are very much a part of your loved one's care and concern. Love and sex improve as each yearly cycle passes.

4 You are ultrakind, considerate, and strongly concerned in all sexual matters. Your partner in sex immediately becomes important to you, a kind of

relative. You respond strongly to the Venus-Neptune-Mars arrangement in your sexual experiences. You will enjoy good connections with people who are taller than average, including the possibility of a real handsome beanpole. Best intervals for sexual encounters are late March, April 9–19, May 16–31, June 14–24, July 4–18, August 9–29, September 4–15, October 3–13, November 21–30, and December 15–24.

5   You are extremely proud. You respond strongly to the Sun-Jupiter-Mercury arrangement in your sexual experiences. You may choose some sexual partners because you sense some status in knowing and loving them, you, in turn, can be chosen for the same reason. There is an elegance connected with your sexual experiences. There is a connection between your developing sexual drive and people just back from overseas. Your most rewarding intervals for sexual encounters are mid-January, late March, early April, May 22 to June 14, July 6–23, August 1–14, September 9–29, October 4–14, November 2–20, and December 1–10.

6   You are exceptionally kind, considerate, concerned, loyal, and affectionate and this wins the devotion of your sex partner. You give the impression that you exist to please others and you are capable of really adoring the partner who gives you a series of memorable sexual thrills. You yearn for constant ecstasy and respond strongly to the Sun-Jupiter-Moon-Mercury arrangement in your sexual experiences. There is a good connection with people who are forceful, sure of themselves—corporate executives.

7   You respond strongly to Venus-Saturn-Mercury arrangement in your sexual experiences. You are restrained, quiet, serious, somewhat spiritual and certainly idealistic in your approach and attitudes toward sex. You aren't at all boastful. You can count on good connections between your expanding sex interests and people who are members of your church or club, people you share other interests with. Your most promising periods for sexual encounters each year are late January, early March, early April, May 10–21, June 12–25, July 16–31, August 1–17, September 23–30, October 3–19, November 3–23, and December 14–24.

8   You respond strongly to the Venus-Uranus-Mercury arrangement in your sexual experiences. You are forward-looking, you believe that everything will be better tomorrow, including the rewards from sex. There are good connections between your sex drive and people who can be classified as gourmets. Your most promising intervals for sexual encounters are January 4–14, February 3–21, March 6–17, April 20–30, May 21–29, June 15–27, July 3–14 and 25–31, August 16–31, September 1–9, October 10–22, November 13–26, and December 3–11.

9   You respond strongly to the Venus-Uranus-Mars arrangement in your sexual experiences. You are forgiving, self-sacrificing and yet there are times when you are too turned on to escape extreme selfishness. You have high-blown ideas of what you should get from sex. There are good

connections between your sex drive and people who own a great deal of property. Your most promising intervals for sexual encounters are January 20–31, February 1–13, March 4–15, April 6–19, May 3–15, June 11–21, July 24 to August 11, September 23–30, October 14 to November 3, and November 23–30.

10 You respond strongly to the Mercury-Venus arrangement in your sexual experiences. You are particularly loving and understanding when you are sure you are loved. To your proved lover, you deny nothing. There will be good correspondence between your sex life and persons who are unsure of themselves and seek to find reassurance through sex. Your most promising periods for sexual encounters are January 1–16, February 2–22, March 16–26, April 19–29, May 4–13, June 1–17, July 22–30, August 14–23, September 9–15, October 20–31, November 10–19, and December 8–14.

11 You respond strongly to the Venus-Sun arrangement in your sexual experiences. You are particularly loving but demand a similar measure from the person to whom you would deny nothing. Older people tend to turn you on in a strange, desirable, compulsive, and thrilling way. Your most promising periods for sexual encounters are January 20–26, February 2–16, March 8–28, April 17–29, May 4–14, June 15–25, July 2–10 and 21–27, August 14–23, September 7–17, October 8–20, November 20–29, and December 25–31.

12 You respond strongly to the Jupiter-Saturn arrangement in your sexual experiences. You look for luck and greater inner confidence through sex, and generally find it. You are not above using sex for ego purposes and do well in the clinches with those who also are out for ego food. Your most promising periods for sexual encounters are January 1–12, February 14–22, March 8–18, April 16–27, May 4–14, June 8–18, July 4–15, August 23–31, September 3–19, October 10–20, November 22–30, and December 1–12.

13 You tend to be fair, honorable, and just in your sexual experiences; anxious to please, eager to get the last smidgin of ecstasy, and to give just as much as you receive. This makes you an ideal sexual partner. But love often can get in the way of sex since you are so strongly Venus-ruled. There are Neptunian arrangements in your sex scope that promise intense sexual participation over the June-July and September-November periods. April is always a rather romantic month in which sex bows to love.

14 You would rather please in sex than be pleased during the years between your nineteenth and fortieth birthdays. The desire for sexual joys can reach a new intensity after age forty, however, during which you demand to be satisfied beyond the norms of satisfaction. You can hit some of these impossible highs during the second half of June and at various times during the long month of October. These splendid sexual encounters are

related to the work you do, to visiting lecturers, people from large southern cities such as Atlanta, Birmingham, Miami, Norfolk.

15 There is something very legal about your approach toward sex. You can have secret hang-ups that are hardly more than fears of being caught doing something that is sexually forbidden. And so, you tend to go in the opposite direction and can build up inhibitions. You will be pleased to know, then, that years ahead is the kind of cycle when you can drop these inhibitions and realize sexual joys denied to you generally. There can be a connection between these and unexpected travel, small towns, motels, unusual restaurants.

16 You respond strongly to the Venus-Sun-Neptune arrangement in your sexual encounters. You are loving, amiable, well disposed toward partners, but your sexual needs are deeply rooted and may know no tingue. You want what you want when you want it. You can count on good connections (accent on late March, early April, May, June, late August and late October) between your sex drive and people who were born abroad and who still speak broken English. You will make love to people you disagree with very much politically.

17 You respond strongly to the Venus-Sun-Uranus arrangement in your sexual experiences. You are full of love but others never really move fast enough for you. You have dreams of the perfect sex partner and wish he/she would come along. Who knows—for the cycle ahead shows good connections between your growing sex drive and very impulsive types of people in military uniform. Your most rewarding periods for sexual encounters are late January, late May, early April, most of May, late June, late July, August 4–17, September 19–29, October 3–17, November 9–23, and December 28–31.

18 You respond strongly to the Venus-Sun-Saturn arrangement in your sexual experiences. You are easy to love and you tend to give your all to your partner, but in the epilogues to sex, there may be a more discriminating you—full of criticism. You know what you want and will admit that in this day and age this person isn't easy to find. Keep the faith for there is a good connection between your sex drive and newcomers in your community. Best periods for sexual encounters are late January, early March, April 9–28, May 6–22, June 14–23, July 4–20, late August, late September, October 9–24, and November 11–21.

19 You respond strongly to the Pluto-Lilith-Vulcan arrangement in your sexual experiences. You are strongly aware of what you want from people and of how to go about getting it. You have the ways of the enchanted Prince/Princess at times. Once you set your mind on something, a team of wild horses couldn't sway you from your quarry. You can count on good connections between your developing sex life and people who tend to be ultrafastidious. Best periods for rewarding sexual encounters are late Janu-

ary, late March, early April, the entire May-July interval, late August, late September, and early November.

20 You respond strongly to the Pluto-Uranus-Saturn arrangement in your sexual experiences. Sex is never going to control you or throw you for a loss. You have everything well under control in your life. You are up-to-date in all of your views on sex and gender but no trend in your horoscope is any stronger than the one that screams self-protection. You can count on good connections between your developing sex life and people who are perhaps much older than they own up to. Your most promising periods for sex are January 24–31, February 2–15, March 17–27, April 23 to May 11, June 20 to July 5, July 24 to August 14, September 21–30, October 14–23, and November 22 to December 4.

21 You respond strongly to the Venus-Uranus-Saturn arrangement in your sexual experiences. You have a built-in guarantee that you will never be bored by either sex or the opposite gender. You can count on good connections between your sex drive and people who see conspiracies where they don't really exist. Enjoy these rare types but be careful just the same. Sex can be at its best over the March-April, July-August, and October-November intervals.

22 You respond strongly to the Mars-Pluto-Saturn arrangement in your sexual experiences. You are assured, reassuring, and extremely capable in sexual attitudes and approaches. You have good insight into what makes your lover tick or fail to tick. Never let it be said that you left any lover without a new tick that sounded good. You will enjoy a good connection between your sex life and people in the medical professions, healers, and protectors with the accent on the April, June, late July, August, and October intervals.

23 You respond strongly to the Mars-Saturn-North node arrangement in your sexual experiences. You are brave, protective of your lover, a person who will kiss but never tell. You enjoy the secret side of sex and of living generally. Nobody is more adept at keeping a hot and heavy romance under wraps. In late March, early May, late June, the July-August, and October-November intervals you will enjoy a good connection between your sex life and people who have been very unhappily married.

24 You respond strongly to the Mars-Pluto-South node arrangement in your sexual experiences. You are sure of yourself in love and can do much for the partner who is not really sure. You are the born professor of sexual techniques. You can maintain wonderful relationships with people who practically make a career out of sexual joy. Your most promising intervals for sexual encounters each year are January 2–17, February 4–24, March 9–14, April 17–28, May 2–22, June 7–15, July 23–31, August 1–19, September 14–24, October 13–25, November 6–15, and December 12–20.

25   You respond strongly to the Jupiter-Vulcan arrangement in your sexual experiences. These empower you to get your way in sex more often than not. You were endowed at birth with a particularly strong body and know how to put it to first-rate utilization in sexual communications. Over the years, your sex life will enjoy good connections with people who have been unhappily married, and with people who need in-depth sexual satisfaction after many years of such denial. Your more dynamic periods for sexual encounters are late January, mid-February, the last ten days of March, April 5–17, May 7–19, June 20–30, July 4–16, August 1–13, September 14–23, October 19–29, November 2–7, and December 8–13.

26   You respond strongly to the Saturn-Jupiter-Venus arrangement in your sexual experiences. These empower you to find the perfect sex partner and to really let yourself go in what might be called a sexually inventive and creative way. There are good connections between your sex life and people in uniform. Best intervals for sexual encounters are January 2–13, February 14–24, March 8–18, April 9–22, May 5–15, June 13–28, July 1–20, August 24–31, September 4–19, October 19–29, November 3–14 and 20–26, and December 3–15.

27   You respond strongly to the Neptune-Jupiter-Mars arrangement in your sexual experiences. Your sex appeal is always functioning and it tends to invite, attract, and court for you. Position in life can be greater because of your sexual allure. You will find sexual encounters at their best during January 1–13, February 23–27, March 4–9 and 19–28, April 1–12 and 23–29, May 6–15, June 12–22, July 8–20, August 14–28, September 1–14, October 20–31, November 3–14, and December 27–31.

28   You respond strongly to the Pluto-Mars-North node arrangement in your sexual experiences. Sex is a very necessary part of each day for you. Your potent physical appetite can show up in your face, particularly about your mouth. You can count on good connections between your developing sex life and people who grew up in very warm climates. Your more satisfying sexual encounters take place between January 22 to February 14, March 17 to April 11, May 16 to June 23, July 2–22, August 18–31, September 18 to October 13, and November 22 to December 14.

29   You respond strongly to the Pluto-Moon-South node arrangement in your sexual experiences. You have unusual insight, perception, and intuition in sexual matters and sense what the peculiar needs of your sexual partner might be. You can count on good connections between your developing sexual appetites and people who work in heavy industry. Your more satisfying annual sexual encounters take place between January 1–20, February 3–14, March 16–31, April 3–11 and 19–29, May 6–15, June 14–26, July 7–18, August 11–21, September 3–16, October 1–19, November 14–29, and December 3–13.

30   You respond strongly to the Pluto-Moon-Lilith arrangement in your sexual

experiences. Others see you as an enchanting tempter with secrets that you want to share. You can count on good connections between your sex life and people who grew up in very cold climates. Your more satisfying sexual encounters take place between January 11–21, February 1–12, March 4–17, April 6–26, May 3–13 and 27–31, June 4–13 and 27–30, July 7–15 and 26–31, August 14–25, September 22 to October 11, November 24 to December 10.

31 Love and sexual encounters are wreathed in hallowed memories of faraway places, with some special accent on Pennsylvania, New Jersey, Bermuda, and the Bahamas. Grand returns to places where you have been happy in the past renew sexual creativity. Your peak sexual periods are the June-July interval, the second week of January, the final week of March, opening days of May, the last week of October, and the last ten days of December.

November

1 Bodily synchronization is one of the most definite figures in your sex chart. Your sexual thread is related to air travel, isolated motels, forgotten restaurants, and broken dates. There is an increase in sexual perception and awareness registering in your chart over the opening months of the year: January has its love pitfalls, while the March-April period accents the new, the different, and the unfamiliar in love-sex. Paths must be beaten through the dross to the true gold of love.

2 The lonely, displaced person can make an appearance in your love-sex life. Push for greater rewards in romance and marriage over the months of February, May, and October. Watch pride when it shows signs of becoming an enemy of love. This will prove to be the time when you are very certain that you love and are loved. This frees the mind for greater career achievement in which the loved one is very much the inspiration. Read romantic novels. Escape into the eighteenth century.

3 Somebody you noticed mentally quite a while ago can reappear in your life now and make a big difference. Love becomes more creative under present Neptune-Uranus stimulation. There is a special cleanliness of heart evident in your love chart over the summer months. Spruce up your personal appearance in order to be ready for overwhelming love as summer ends and

autumn gives greater promise to love's endurance. A former critic can become a friend.

4   You respond strongly to the Pluto-Mars-Lilith arrangement in your sexual experiences. You are very much at home in close sexual relationships. Permeating your mind, soul, and body is the feeling that man and woman must blend and become one. As a result, there is an almost sacred approach toward ultrarewarding sex. Still, the forbidden fruit is there and the Snake of Eden can spur you on into areas of sex you may in retrospect wish you had left untouched. You enjoy good connections between your sex drive and military people.

5   You respond strongly to the Pluto-Mars-North node arrangements in your sexual experiences. You have a built-in radar system that gives you sexual signals denied to many people. You were born with a remarkable understanding of the opposite gender. You will enjoy good connections between your electrifying sex drive and people connected with real estate, the building trades, with property transactions. Your most rewarding intervals for sexual encounters are late January, late March, early April, the May-June periods, also July 9–16, August 17–27, very late September, and early November.

6   You respond strongly to the Pluto-Mars-south node arrangement in your sexual experiences. You may feel at times that you know things about sex that others are loathe to admit. You may feel victimized at times by people who refuse to own up to their compelling interest in sex. Frigid types are not for you. You will enjoy good connections between your expanding sex drive and people just back from jobs or long-time travel overseas. Best periods for sexual encounters are January 1–9 and 24–31, February 4–14, March 10–20, April 16–26, late May, very early June, July 12–23, August 19 to September 12, October 14–24, November 12–20, and December 24–31.

7   You respond strongly to the Pluto-Mars-Sun arrangement in your sexual experiences. You have good foresight, insight, a high level of awareness, self-assurance, and an amiable personality that goes before you in all close relationships. You can count on good connections between your developing sexual power and people who have been born or lived long periods of time on islands. Your most promising sexual encounters take place between January 1–7 and 27–31, February 3–13 and 24–27, March 8–18, April 7–19, May 20–31, June 14–25, July 20–29, August 1–12, September 19 to October 8, November 13–23, and December 2–11.

8   You respond strongly to the Pluto-Mars-Moon arrangement in your sexual experiences. You relate well to others and come to a quick understanding of another's special hang-ups. You are ultrasensitive to what others expect and need from you. You can count on good connections between your sex drive and people who are inclined to be very saving, perhaps even miserly at

times. Your most promising annual intervals for sexual encounters are January 20–31, February 1–17, March 10–20, April 6–16, May 10–22, June 4–14, July 24–31, August 9–19, September 23 to October 14, November 24 to December 9.

9   You respond strongly to the Pluto-Mars-Mercury arrangement in your sexual experiences. You are strongly supersensory in your sexual perceptions. You have good connections between your sex life and people who live on your street and in your community. Also with people who have just moved into your neighborhood. Your most promising intervals for sexual encounters are January 14–24, February 3–19, March 20–31, April 15–30, May 5–11 and 23–29, June 5–17, July 3–23, August 17–31, September 16 to October 8, and November 22 to December 6.

10 You respond strongly to the Venus-Pluto arrangement in your sexual experiences. You like to be led on, so to speak, understood completely by your lover and rather talked into letting down your hair even more. Your most promising periods for thrilling sexual encounters are January 12–25, February 9–20, March 1–13, April 17–27, May 1–10 and 23–31, June 14–24, July 19–27, August 4–13 and 23–31, September 4–17, October 18–28, November 3–15, and December 17–27.

11 You respond strongly to the Mars-Moon arrangement in your sexual experiences. You are strongly self-confident in the clinches and able to lend some of this feeling to your zealous partners. You have what might be called a secret special sensation about sex and you prefer to keep it to yourself. Your most promising periods for thrilling sexual encounters are the second week of February, the last ten days of March, April 4–14, May 1–13 and 23–30, June 13–21, July 4–22, August 4–12, September 21–28, October 14–24, November 9–21, and December 4–14.

12 You respond strongly to the Sun-Jupiter arrangement in your sexual experiences. You are happy-go-lucky and anxious to please your lovers. You laugh a lot, see the humor in everything including love and sex. You want to be friends with all of your ex-lovers but this doesn't always work out well. Your most thrilling sexual encounters are apt to fall in the following cycles: the last six days of January, the middle of February, March 9–19, April 4–13, May 20–31, June 6–20, July 2–12, August 14–24, September 9–19, October 2–13, November 15–30, and December 27–31.

13 There is a great evenness and balance to your sex life between the twenty-fourth and forty-sixth years. Your sex scope shows greater awareness of what it is you really want from your sex life and knowing your quarry is part of the job of really soaping up ego and ID. Sexual ecstasy is strongly represented in your chart over the late April, early May, entire June, late July, entire August, and late September periods. Travel meets sex more than halfway just before Thanksgiving Day.

14 Your magical witchery works wonders for your sex life over the last week of

January provided you are following the sun and in the right places, preferably on or near water. Other favorable periods for sexual encounters are the middle of May (romantic, light-hearted), the last days of June (bold, a little vulgar perhaps but rewarding), the entire July-September period and again as each year ends (mysterious, ultraromantic and while not incestuous, it can give you the feeling of something akin to incest).

15   Forbidden fruit is strongly represented in your sex scope. There is some knocking down of usual limitations and guidelines, matters of race, color, religion, and even gender possible under these pithy and potent Neptune-Venus-Pluto trends. You may become involved in the type of compulsive sexual affair that you once thought impossible for you. There is a certain "I don't care" trend working in your chart and perhaps it should be watched over the summer and early fall.

16   You respond strongly to the Pluto-Vulcan-Moon arrangement in your sexual experiences. You give complete, undivided attention to sex. You will enjoy good connections between your sex drive and people from Latin America, and the islands of the Caribbean. Your most rewarding sexual encounters take place between January 2–20, February 16–26, March 3–13 and 23–31, April 14–30, May 6–17, June 14–24, July 1–20, August 2–15, September 23–30, October 4–15, November 3–14, and December 1–9.

17   You respond strongly to the Pluto-Moon-Mercury arrangement in your sexual experiences. You learn all that there is to know about your sex partner before giving and taking love. You can count on good connections between your sex drive and particularly tall people. Your most rewarding sexual encounters take place between January 1–11 and 24–31, February 3–13 and 18–27, March 4–14, April 18–29, May 1–13, June 15–30, July 16–31, August 4–9 and 24–31, September 6–17, October 4–14 and 24–31, November 8–15, and December 17–27.

18   You respond strongly to the Pluto-Moon-Venus arrangement in your sexual experiences. You have good insight, foresight, and are rather perceptive about your sexual partners. You enjoy all the epilogues to sexual activity. There will be good connections between your developing sex drive and people connected with schools and gymnasiums. Your more rewarding sexual encounters take place between January 24 to February 9, March 3–13, April 22–May 14, June 17–27, July 4–24, August 9–20, September 24–30, October 1–9 and 23–31, November 14–23, and December 9–17.

19   You respond strongly to the Jupiter-Lilith-Moon arrangement in your sexual experiences. While making love, nobody is more beautiful than you. You can count on good connections between your increasing sex drive and people who are exceptionally fond of animals. Your most rewarding sexual encounters should be scheduled between January 4–16, February 6–20, March 3–23, April 17–27, May 19–29, June 15–25, July 6–17, August 21–31, September 24–30, and November 24 to December 10.

20 You can count on good connections between your phenomenal sex drive and people who are particularly conscious of the impressions they make in large groups. You respond strongly to the Jupiter-Moon-Saturn arrangement in your sexual experiences. Your most rewarding sexual encounters are between January 1–10 and 24–31, February 5–15, March 1–20, April 14–24, May 9–20, June 13–24, July 3–18, August 20–31, September 4–13, October 18 to November 7, and December 12–20.

21 You respond strongly to the Jupiter-Sun-Neptune arrangement in your sexual experiences. You tend to have a high level of ecstasy in your sex life and much good fortune in realizing peaks of satisfaction. You can count on good connections between your developing sex life and people who aren't particularly interested in sex and who have to be coaxed into participation up to that magical point when things begin working for them. Your most promising annual periods for sexual encounters are April-May, July-August, and November.

22 You respond strongly to the Jupiter-Mars-Venus arrangement in your sexual experiences. You are very lucky in the way you choose your sex partners or are chosen by them. You tend to gain from all lovemaking in one way or another. You will enjoy a good connection between your expanding sex life and people who love to gamble. Your most promising intervals for sexual encounters are January 19–29, February 2–13, March 6–26, April 1–15, May 19–29, June 11–27, July 1–9 and 29–31, August 14–23, September 16–28, October 3–12 and 26–31, November 9–19, and December 3–10.

23 You always do well sexually with people who teach. This is one of the trends really in force along with a good connection between your developing sex life and people who work in heavy industries and in the automotive industries. You could move from sexual joy to marriage and you really make a go of this enduring relationship. Your best periods for happy sexual encounters are January 1–10, February 2–13, March 10–21, April 12–25, May 1–19, June 23–30, July 19–31, August 4–15, September 13–27, October 4–15, November 1–13 and December 2–12.

24 You respond strongly to the Jupiter-Neptune-Mercury arrangement in your sexual experiences. This means luck, good feelings about your lover, glamour, high sex appeal and an almost galloping allure that really turns you and your partner on. There's a good connection between your sex life and people who are about to leave your environment. Your most promising intervals for sexual encounters are January 13–23, February 14–26, March 3–19, April 16–27, May 10–22, June 15–28, July 1–27, August 19–29, September 10–21, October 12–20, November 1–7 and 26–30, and December 14–24.

25 You respond strongly to the Jupiter-Sun-Ceres arrangement in your sexual experiences. As a result, you tend to be rather lucky in winning the

devotion of others. Your carefree and casual ways enjoy good protection also from your Sun-Ceres. There are some crude temptations put in your way when you are very young, however, and these can mark certain attitudes toward sex throughout life. You enjoy good sexual encounters between January 9–16, February 2–12, March 1–18, April 9–20, May 6–14, June 15–28, July 2–12 and 23–31, August 4–19, September 2–15, October 8–18, November 3–13, and December 17–27.

26   You respond strongly to the Jupiter-Moon-Lilith arrangement in your sexual experiences. As a result, you are full of magical witchery, full of the power to tease and tempt others. Once somebody has been in your arms they can't really forget it. Old flames are always ready to be ignited again. You enjoy thrilling sex between January 2–20, February 14–23, March 18–29, April 16–27, May 4–15, June 17–27, July 13–23, August 19–31, September 3–14, October 29–31, November 22–29, and December 14–24.

27   You respond strongly to the Pluto-Sun-Lilith arrangement in your sexual experiences. It is difficult for you to stop once sex has been initiated. Prologues to sex have to be taken very seriously because you are quick to reach that point of no return. Your most rewarding intervals for sexual enjoyment are January 14–20, February 9–22, March 4–15, April 16–30, May 2–18, June 4–11 and 22–30, July 1–11 and 25–31, August 3–13, September 2–12, October 14–26, November 12–23, and December 3–15.

28   You respond strongly to the Jupiter-Moon-Mars arrangement in your sexual experiences. You can count on good connections between your developing sexual appetites and people who tend to be fashionable, elegant, majestic, and formal; and who are given to high dignified thoughts and have roles of community leadership. Your more satisfying sexual encounters take place between January 1–24, February 3–19, March 21–31, April 6–14, May 16 to June 8, June 22 to July 11, August 19 to September 4, September 24 to October 9, October 23 to November 8, and November 23 to December 11.

29   You respond strongly to the Jupiter-Saturn-Pluto arrangement in your sexual experiences. Sexually, you have eyes in the back of your head and can pretty much judge what another person really is like in a physical sense. While you tend to be rather conventional yourself, you have great sympathy and understanding of the unconventional bohemians. You can count on good connections between your increasing sex life and people who ask questions much more than they volunteer information about themselves.

30   You respond strongly to the Jupiter-Uranus-Pluto arrangement in your sexual experiences. You are capable of making many sacrifices for love. Sex is important to you but many people who share your birthday have given up sex because that seemed to be the better way of wisdom. You can count on good connections between your exploding sex life and people who have

wanted children very much but haven't been able to have them. Your most rewarding sexual encounters will take place between March 14 to June 23, and between July 31 and September 7.

December

1   The years ahead bring new experiences but what is of greater importance it gives you the power for improving and correcting old experiences. Love is a cornucopia of mixed joys and pleasures, with special accent on early February, late June, and all of July and September. You can now know that greater maturity in which a former lover can become a treasured friend. There are questions that only your beloved can answer for you during the last three months of any year.

2   When it comes to love and sex, you are both enthusiastic and inspirational. Although your actions are often impractical, due to your highly impulsive and headstrong nature, your will is cast-iron when it comes to getting and keeping "who" you want! The January-February period finds you coasting. Expect a dramatic rise in your encounters in mid-May with a crescendo reached during high summer. In October, expect a slight dip with a rise again in the November-December period. Shining jewels, fragrant flowers, spontaneous travel on and near water, and a surprise encounter with a foreign-born stranger fulfills your natural zeal.

3   Your sympathy and adaptability lead you to a wealth of sexual experiences not often equalled. Unfortunately your high intellect and capacity for work combined with some arbitrary decisions you make often cool some flaming ardor or prevents a genuine sense of unity with a dear and beloved friend. Hobbies, research, long summer evenings touch the sexual thread permeating your chart. You are inviting love when you fix yourself up with wardrobe and hairstyle as you aim for the rich and royal look.

4   You respond strongly to the Jupiter-Sun-Mars arrangement in your sexual experiences and are good-natured in love, strongly positive, full of self-confidence. You enjoy good connections between your dynamic sex drive and people who work for the government or for very large businesses with nationwide offices. Your most rewarding intervals for encounters are January 12–20, February 14–24, March 19–29, April 5–15, May 10–24, June 13–25, July 6–18, August 21–31, September 17–27, October 13–26, November 1–9 and 16–26, and December 4–12.

5   You respond strongly to your Jupiter-Moon-Venus arrangement in your sexual experiences. You believe that sex is good for you and also good for your partner and often preach this doctrine everywhere to the annoyance of others. You will enjoy good connections between your sex drive and people who complain a great deal about economic matters. Do what you can to get them to keep these grievances away from sex. Best intervals for sexual encounters are early January, early March, April 9–14 and 22–27, May 4–17, June 15–30, July 1–16, August 23–31, September 4–15, late October, and early November.

6   You respond strongly to the Jupiter-Moon-Mercury arrangement in your sexual experiences. You are positive in your attitudes and approaches toward sex and have a good impact and influence on others in these matters. You court, attract, and invite in an admirable way. You will enjoy good connections between your sex life and people who are rather religious. Your most rewarding periods for encounters are late January, late February, March 12–20, April 23–30, May 17–31, June 3–15, July 8–18, August 20–31, September 9–14 and 24–30, late October, and late November.

7   You respond strongly to the Jupiter-Sun-Moon arrangement in your sexual experiences. You are very well balanced, even-tempered, highly desirable, and full of goodwill in your sexual relationships. There is a good connection between your sex drive and people who are forever bettering themselves and their own chances of achievement. Your most promising annual periods for sexual encounters are January 6–15, February 9–18, March 3–13, April 20–30, May 1–13, June 12–26, July 14–28, August 3–17, September 9–29 and October 23 to November 12.

8   You respond strongly to the Jupiter-Sun-Uranus arrangement in your sexual experiences. You are full of goodwill, inspiration, faith in self and a sense of good luck that you want to share with sex partners. You can count on a good connection between your developing sex drive and people who are very skilled with their hands. Your most promising periods for sexual encounters are January 1–13, February 14–22, March 17–27, April 9–29, May 1–14, June 5–17, July 1–13, August 3–13 and 23–31, September 4–16, October 21–31, November 2–12, and December 1–11.

9   You respond strongly to the Jupiter-Sun-South node arrangement in your sexual experiences. You are well disposed toward your sex partners, are full of concern when things don't go well in their lives and will go out of your way for them and their loved ones. You can count on good connections between your dynamic sex drive and people who have a great deal of trouble in their lives, people who are bowled over by problems. Sexual encounters are accented in your life over late February, early March, April 10–22, May 4–15, June 19–29, July 2–17, August 3–17, late September, and early November.

10   You respond strongly to the Moon-Jupiter arrangement in your sexual

experiences. You tend to be positive, affirmative, enthusiastic about sex at all times, and you are sensitized to the special needs of quiet, shy, hesitant people. Your most rewarding sexual encounters are apt to take place between January 1–19, February 3–13, March 4–19, April 17–27, May 2–13, June 12–23, July 9–20, August 4–15, September 21–29, October 1–18, November 2–20, and December 1–13.

11 You respond strongly to the Jupiter-Venus arrangement in your sexual experiences. You want to please your lover and will bend over backwards in order to do so. Second-time-around sex can have special meaning to you. Doing what you don't want to do at times also can create special joys. Your most rewarding sexual encounters are apt to take place between January 23–31, February 1–16, March 4–15, April 9–23, May 16–27, June 4–13 and 23–30, July 14–24, August 3–19, September 20–30, October 4–14, November 21–30, and December 4–13.

12 You respond strongly to the Uranus-Venus arrangement in your sexual experiences. The thought that love and sex might become jaded, boring, overly routine is something you can't abide. Changing sexual environments always work wonders for you. Your most promising sexual encounters are apt to fall between January 5–15, February 22–28, March 1–21, April 22–29, May 6–17, June 14–24, July 2–17, August 9–23, September 4–14, October 8–21, November 2–22, and December 16–27.

13 Personal joys tend to be in proportion to what you are willing to put into them. There is a trend in your horoscope that suggests the more you build up the ego of your lover, the more you are going to fall out of love. Your best sexual intervals are the last six days of January, the mid-March, late-May, the entire June-July, and late-August to early-September period and the last ten days of December. Go all out in loving and you will be loved.

14 You have a strong ability to reap and give pleasure during prologues and epilogues. This trend never was stronger than it shall be during the next few years and it makes the cycles rather unusual. There are good sexual connections with people of deep religious faith. Your most promising sexual interludes are late February, early April, the last three weeks of May, the middle of June, the entire July-August and late-November periods. Travel and sex can be combined over the third and fourth weeks of July of each year.

15 Adore, worship your beloved for best results. There are times when love may not be enough and the more you adore the more love is going to lift you up to the pinnacles of ecstasy. Your most promising interludes take place during March, late April, mid-May, the entire June-July and November-December periods. There are good sexual connections with travel in the Sun Belt region of this country. Organize your life better so that there is more time for love, relaxation, and romance.

16 You respond strongly to the Jupiter-Moon-Vulcan arrangement in your sexual experiences. You have graduate degrees in sex because you have

enjoyed it so much and gone after complete knowledge in the field with all the tools of the trade. You can count on wonderful connections between your abiding sex drive and people who love sexual activity more than you. Your most rewarding sexual encounters take place between January 1–19, February 18–28, March 1–13 and 23–31, April 13–30, May 4–16, June 15–30, July 1–15, August 10–25, September 22–30, October 5–16, November 2–15, and December 3–9.

17 You respond strongly to the Jupiter-Moon-Lilith arrangement in your sexual experiences. You are fortunate in your love life and money can come to you through a successful love-marriage. You will enjoy good connections between your sex drive and people who are quite well off. Your most rewarding sexual encounters take place between January 19–31, February 2–14, March 6–22, April 10–24, May 5–17, June 1–17, July 1–14, August 11–26, September 20–30, October 7–17, November 1–13, and December 5–12.

18 You respond strongly to the Jupiter-Sun-Mars arrangement in your sexual experiences. You are lucky in that love loiters, so to speak, and that marriage is the real epilogue of any rewarding love affair. You will enjoy good connections between your sex drive and people born not very far from where you were born. Your most rewarding sexual encounters occur between January 4–15, February 4–21, March 7–17, April 12–25, May 7–17, June 11–21, July 3–16, August 1–20, September 22–30, October 21–30, November 2–15, and December 20–31.

19 You respond strongly to the Saturn-Jupiter-Mars arrangement in your sexual experiences. You never take a good thing for granted but will continue to administer to what you have going for yourself as though you could lose it tomorrow. Nobody takes sexual activity more seriously than you. During late March, early April, May 4–16, June 20–30, the first half of July, August 9–19, late September, late October, and early November you can count on good connections between your diligent sex drive and people who tend to lecture, teach, speak constantly off the top of their heads.

20 You respond strongly to the Saturn-Jupiter-Venus arrangement in your sexual experiences. You are protective of the good working, rewarding sexual situation but there is some distrust of sexual epilogues. You prefer to *do* rather than to say or talk about it. There are good connections between your sexual drive and people with many nieces and nephews. Your most rewarding sexual encounters will take place between January 23 to February 9, March 6–17, April 22 to May 13, June 4–24, July 6–20, August 21–31, September 3–15, October 5–15, November 20–30, and December 10–20.

21 You respond strongly to the Saturn-Jupiter-Mercury arrangement in your sexual experiences. There is gratitude, appreciation, a desire to be ultra-helpful to the one who gives you sexual joy. You are more than ordinarily

aware of the fact that love needs another person. There are good connections between your growing sex drive and people born in New Mexico, old Mexico, Arizona, Texas, and Oklahoma. Your most rewarding sexual encounters take place between January 1–18, February 2–15, March 3–18, April 25–30, May 1–13, June 5–17, July 18–29, August 4–17, September 3–13, October 21–31, and November 7–17.

22   You respond strongly to the Saturn-Jupiter-Mercury arrangement in your sexual experiences. You are restrained, conservative, zealously anxious to please, and you love to warm over old sexual memories. You will enjoy a good developing connection between your sex life and desires on one hand and very thin people on the other. Your most promising intervals for sexual encounters are January 13–25, February 2–16, March 13–24, April 15–30, May 2–16 and 27–31, June 11–25, July 17–27, August 3–20, September 2–12, October 8–20, November 6–15, and December 18–27.

23   You respond strongly to the Saturn-Jupiter-Lilith arrangement in your sexual experiences. Sex tends to make you a titan and often after sex, you achieve something very worthwhile in a material or career sense. You will enjoy a good connection between your sex life and people engaged in charitable and humanitarian interests. Your most promising sexual intervals are January 3–14, February 17–27, March 11–20, April 10–22, May 12–26, June 1–8 and 23–30, July 14–27, August 13–25, September 12–22, October 5–16, November 7–16, and December 20–31.

24   You respond strongly to the Saturn-Jupiter-South node arrangement in your sexual experiences. Sex has a strong impact on you in that it's difficult for you to run down emotionally afterward. Sex keeps you walking on air and the myriad feelings of sex can be recaptured when you are alone. Your most promising intervals for sexual encounters are January 1–10 and 25–31, February 16–26, March 2–17, April 20–30, May 16–26, June 15–30, July 3–15, August 19–29, September 20–29, October 4–15, November 16–28, and December 17–28.

25   You will always be noticed and treated in special ways. In sex, you respond strongly to the Sun-Saturn arrangement, which empowers you to win love and to retain it throughout life. It is certainly true in your case that love grows, gets better, and that the best years are always those immediately before you. An encounter is certainly the instrument by which you express your undying love. Your best periods for this special closeness are January 6–13, February 14–22, March 20–27, April 4–15, May 14–24, June 12–22, July 8–20, August 14–24, September 1–10, October 20–31, November 4–14, and December 14–27.

26   You respond strongly to the Moon-Saturn arrangement in your sexual experiences. These empower you to outlast all opposition and make you a great survivor in love as well as in life. You are utterly sensitive, easily hurt by those you love most, and can be somewhat embarrassed with certain

types of sex partners. You question some unorthodox ways of lovemaking. Your most rewarding sexual encounters take place between January 1–11, February 20–28, March 6–16, April 4–17, May 20–31; June 3–15, July 2–10 and 22–31, August 4–14, September 5–25, October 18–27, November 2–11, and December 23–31.

27   You respond strongly to the Mars-Jupiter arrangement in your sexual experiences. You will enjoy good connections between your developing sex life and people who like to wear hats and gloves; also with newcomers in your community. Your most rewarding sexual encounters take place between January 20–31, February 1–9, March 2–12, April 14–24, May 19–29, June 2–13, July 4–15, August 20–31, September 12–22, October 14–24, November 18–23, and December 4–9 and 26–31.

28   You respond strongly to the Saturn-Jupiter-Moon arrangement in your sexual experiences. You can count on good connections between your developing sexual appetites and people who tend to be excitable, not easily appeased, ambitious people who somehow just can't get along with others. Your more satisfying sexual encounters take place between January 1–14, February 3–18, March 24–31 and April 10–21, May 6–16, June 8 to July 4, July 15–31, August 19–29, September 10–23, October 4–16, November 20–29, and December 17–28.

29   You can count on good connections between your expanding sexual appetites and people connected with computers, with database management, and other scientific projects. You respond strongly to the Saturn-Jupiter-Mars arrangement in your sexual experiences. You are very sure of yourself sexually. Your more satisfying sexual encounters take place between January 10–25, February 7–19, March 3–19, April 21–30, May 6–20, June 9–24, July 3–15, August 6–26, September 19–29, October 4–15, November 10–30, and December 4–15.

30   You can count on good connections between your developing sexual appetites and people who work in the most modern jobs, such as anti-pollution industries and services. You respond strongly to the Saturn-Jupiter-Mercury arrangement in your sexual experiences. Your more satisfying sexual encounters take place between January 1–14, February 1–17, March 3–21, April 13–23, May 4–19, June 10–22, July 4–16, August 7–27, September 9–22, October 3–19, November 10–28, and December 26–31.

31   Love and sexual encounters have a grand-return motive, a sense of repetition, of paradise reexperienced. Your sexual awareness is more potent now than ever before and special closeness to the adored one is possible in ways that make the years ahead unique. Your peak periods are April-May, the last week of June, the second week of August, and October 14 to November 24.

—IV—

CONFESSIONS OF
A PRACTICING
ASTROLOGER

In the next few chapters, for the first time, I will share with you some of Zolar's more unusual cases. They should lead you to a better understanding of the ancient art and science of astrology. I know you will enjoy reading about other's love problems and how they were solved. Know well that this can also be done for you and by you.

While kings and queens throughout the ages have often had their court astrologers, you do not have to be a member of a royal family to use astrology in your life. Just as you can venture outdoors on a clear night and look to the stars, so can you, too, benefit from the knowledge of your very own stellar script.

So, turn the page and prophet!

I'm Fat Because
I'm Sexually Frustrated

Most of us have a tendency to simplify our personal problems when we mull them over. Many people, for example, get fat because they are frustrated and eat compulsively, then they become even more frustrated because they are fat. They may begin to think the cause of their misery is overweight, and lose sight of the real situation which brought on their overeating. Their corpulence becomes their obsession, and they tack all their woes onto this one cause. Of those who realize their predicament is not solely physical, there are many who will blame their plight on one apparent reason, such as sexual frustration.

Our complex lives, however, are intertwined with other complex lives. In order to rid ourselves of an unhappiness we must first see clearly all the reasons for it, not just the one or two most obvious ones. Edith, who first got in touch with me in 1961, is an example of someone who was so steeped in her own misery she had lost sight of its true and very complicated origins.

"I wish I could do something about my weight," she wrote, "but none of the so-called diets really help. I used to be a knock-out and had to beat the boys off with a club. Now they look at me and just smile. I was born October 14, 1939, and I know I'm Libra and I've read some place Librans like to eat. I don't think astrology is right about that. I eat only because my husband neglects me. It's a vicious circle, in that the more he neglects me, the more I eat, the fatter I get, and the funnier I look. I'm so sexually frustrated that there's nothing left for me to do but eat."

Edith included two snapshots with her first letter. It was hard to believe both were pictures of the same person. The first one showed a beautiful girl, eighteen years old, 5'4" tall, weighing 101 pounds. The second was of an obese woman weighing 184 pounds. She was twenty-two years old, had been married four years and was the mother of two children.

Although obesity usually results from overeating, it can be caused by an organic disease or by a glandular disturbance. Edith had gained weight so rapidly and so unnaturally I feared some illness lay at the root of her trouble. So in my reply, in addition to sending her horoscope, I urged her to see a doctor. Her response was immediate and typical: "Naturally, I've consulted doctors. My first two diets were regulated by doctors. There's nothing wrong with my glands. I'm fat because I can't stop eating, and I can't stop eating because I'm sexually frustrated. Just stick to my horoscope, please!"

Edith's horoscope showed her Sun and Venus in Libra, which rules justice and equality. Librans can be self-indulgent, it is true, and that is why Edith read that overindulgence in food and liquid has been attributed to members of her solar group. Libra, in the Cosmic Figure, rules the intestines and the stomach generally. Since Venus in Edith's horoscope is in the last degree of Libra, about to cross into Scorpio within hours after her birth, her Venus-Scorpio relationship is important. Scorpio, in the Cosmic Figure, rules the sex organs, while Venus is the symbol of love, romance, and sexual fulfillment. Edith, in short, can be called a strongly geared and passionate person.

Edith's womanly Moon, moreover, is also in Scorpio, giving her a preference for a bold, dynamic, aggressive, and passionate man. I asked her to supply the date of her husband's birth.

In her initial letter she had written:

Frank seemed ideal for me. We are of the same religion and from the same income group. He lived in my neighborhood and we kept company about six months before our marriage. This was no shotgun marriage either. We kept our heads right up until our wedding night. My family was as happy as his family and they gave us a very nice wedding.

Our honeymoon was everything a honeymoon should be, with Frank the kind, tender, happy man I knew him to be. Our first child, Darrin, was born exactly nine months and two days after our marriage. I weighed 101 pounds when I married, went up to 116 during my pregnancy, then down to 110 right afterward. I wanted to level off about there because I've always liked a nice figure; and Frank was always crazy about my curves.

Our first crisis came two months after the baby's birth. Frank's father died, and since Frank had fewer responsibilities, his family figured we should take care of his widowed mother. Well, I always thought she was pretty nice, as mothers go, but she was disappointed that one of her sons didn't become a priest, or at least one of her daughters a nun. She's very devout, coming from a little village in Italy. Frank and I are only moderately religious. My people were born in this country and my Italian grandparents were from Milan and not overly devout. You know, there's religion and there's religion.

When I say we took care of my mother-in-law, I mean just that. None of the others have ever helped. It wasn't easy for me to see another woman come into my small apartment and just take over. We only had two bedrooms and I planned on one being a nursery. In the beginning we had to walk on eggshells to keep from waking her up and sending her into mourning. She'd just sit around all day complaining about how she had lost everything, husband, home, and children. It really got on my nerves. She tried to tell me how to wash the baby, when to feed him, and sometimes I wanted to scream.

Worst of all, right after she came to live with us, Frank began staying out at night. On the way home from his job at the chemical plant, where he's a pipefitter, he and the boys would stop for a few hours. Then, there were nights when he had to attend union meetings and after those, he'd stop for a lot of beers and he'd come home in no condition for anything but sleeping it off.

I kept telling him that we needed a house, not an apartment. His mother and I were getting in each other's way. 'What do you want me to do?' he would shout, 'put my own mother out?' He began to say I was selfish, not being kind to an old woman of sixty-seven who had raised nine children. Just hearing about the other eight always made my blood boil—I mean I would like to see a little money from them once in a while, a few bucks for her keep. After all, why should Frank and I be forced to assume all the responsibilities?

Arguments and name calling are bad for lovemaking. I'd always try to make it up with Frank before we'd go to bed, but he seemed to have lost all his desire for me. This worried me! At the same time, I kept putting on weight, reaching 138 pounds by the time I realized I was pregnant again. Frank was glad. We moved into a suburb, renting a nice little house with three bedrooms. But this meant he was much further from work and it took him longer to get home. When he began to say he wasn't hungry because he had a sandwich with those few beers, I really blew my top.

His mother always took Frank's side in everything. She would remind me that he was working, as though it was some disgrace I wasn't out working. She never worked outside her home one day in her life, but some of her married daughters had jobs. "Two women to run this little house you don't need," she would say. She felt she should run the house, rear the children, and I should work in some factory, and save my money so we could afford to buy a big house. This wasn't the way I planned it, when I promised to love, honor, and obey.

It was a difficult pregnancy for me. The doctor was worried about the weight I was putting on. I went up to 151 by the time I gave birth to my second son, which we had to name Anthony to suit the old lady. It was her husband's name. I wanted to call the baby Kevin, because it's always been one of my favorites.

Frank and I argued a lot in those days. He said he didn't want any more children. We had enough! I didn't want to practice birth control. His mother's solution for that was a hot one—you just kept away from each other. Of course, she had nine children in thirteen years.

The doctor had told Frank not to love me for at least a month after Tony was born. Frank stretched this out into forty-seven days by my exact count. Instead of a husband, I had a bowl of spaghetti and some of Mama's good baking. I missed ice cream if I didn't have it at least once a day.

Frank, meanwhile, had begun playing on a baseball team that summer—
as though his work, union meetings, visits to the bars with the boys, and so
on, weren't keeping him away from home enough. But I never thought he was
a chaser until I found something in his wallet once which wasn't meant for
lovemaking with me.

I blew my top. I didn't care if his mother was listening. I let her know what
her precious son was. I told my family. I told his brothers and sisters. I
demanded that he come home directly from work. He said he had some rights
to independence, this was a free country and so on. We really had some good
fights in those days. I bounced cups and saucers off his head, because he
wouldn't admit what he had in his pocket was used for sex. It was just
supposed to be some joke.

I wouldn't buy it. I even asked the priest to talk to Frank, but then Frank
didn't go to Mass any more.

I learned this: It's hard to make love when you've been fighting like that. I
accused Frank of sleeping with other women—that had to be the explanation
for why he didn't want me. First, he said he didn't want me to be pregnant.
We argued some more, and it really hurt when he shouted, "Because you've
become a fat pig, that's why I don't want any part of you!"

Nice talk from the man you love, from your husband, especially the pig
bit. Sure, I was fat. He was right. I weighed 174 pounds the day he said I was
too fat. I tried diets. I'd lose only to gain it right back again.

When I was unhappy one night, I left the house and looked for Frank in the
bar where he and his friends used to hang out. He wasn't there. And why did
he always shower and change his clothes at work? Because he was chasing
women. Frank wasn't the kind of man to go without his sex. I had really been
a fool. He was getting it every night, but not with me.

But he had his come-uppance and not through me. I was almost glad when
it happened, because it showed him up in the newspapers for what he was.
There was a party out in a bad part of town. The police raided it. They found
women stripping. They were from the burlesque show in town. They found
about twenty-five men and six women there in the orgy. When they opened
the door, they found Frank in bed with one of the women. Both Frank and the
old bag were arrested, but not for anything normal. This, I would have to live
with the rest of my life. I couldn't stand the sight of him. And that crack
about my being fat. You should see what she looked like! She must have been
forty years old, at least.

In the end, I forgave him. I wanted a husband. I wanted the real kind of
love, and children. . . .

Edith's next letter supplied Frank's date of birth, July 31, 1935. In his chart
both Sun and Moon were in Leo, the sign of male splendor. The Sun, symbol of
the male, is at home in Leo, which is ruled by the center of the solar system. The
Moon, which rules his link with women, is also in his Sun sign, and this Sun-

Moon duo in Leo, the Gate of his chart, without modification by other planetary presence accents ego and strengthens the impact of his personality on both males and females. Frank is not only attractive to women, he is also a man's man. His hail-fellow-well-met personality makes him popular among men.

Frank's Sun in Leo is in unfavorable square aspect to Edith's Moon in Scorpio. Their philosophy of life is not in tune. This does not necessarily mean their marriage could not be a success, but it does mean that both parties would have to work a little harder than usual for their mutual ultimate happiness.

Frank's Mars is in Scorpio, revealing he is the bold, aggressive, hearty and lusty male of Edith's desire. But Frank's Mercury is in Cancer, which rules mothers and motherly women. In this home torn between being husband and father on the one hand, and son on the other, the rays of Mercury support the role of son. Any identification between his mother and wife is unfavorable for arousing his passionate instincts.

This was the crux of Edith's problem. If she were to protest having his mother in their home, Frank would see her as selfish and unfeeling. But Frank himself secretly does not like having his mother with them. She represents the past—his youth, his premarriage life, his boyish goodness, and the guilt he feels for having failed her in not becoming a priest. Sex did not exist for Frank in his mother's home. He is not stimulated much in his home, because it has become his mother's home. He probably feels as frustrated as Edith, and this would, in part, account for getting in trouble.

His mother-wife conflict is revealed also in the manner in which secretive, nefarious, transiting Neptune, symbol of sexual uncertainties, has been hovering over his natal male Mars during the past few years.

Mars at the fourth house angle of his horoscope means Frank must rule his home, possibly as his father once did. He must be top man, not somebody's little boy. In order to prove to himself that the combination of totally dependent mother and clinging wife have not emasculated him, it is not unusual that Frank would seek the companionship of other men, and join them in their orgies. In the perversion he was caught practicing, Frank well may have been subjecting a woman symbol of his domineering mother-wife to some imaginary slavedom. Men who seek such relationships are often punishing either wife or mother. There is some need to degrade, to enjoy a sensation without sharing it in the approved conventional manner with the women involved.

Remembering that Frank's male Mars is in Scorpio and Edith's female Venus is completing its transit of Libra and entering Scorpio, we find that there is in their charts one of the classic bases for a highly successful marriage: an especially satisfying physical relationship. It is no wonder they were so physically attracted to each other and that all went well until the arrival of Frank's mother.

Edith had more or less correctly related her obesity to her sexual frustration. But there were obviously many more frustrations gnawing at her. She felt she was without her own home and Frank was his mother's son rather than her husband. The lack of money was a problem, and Edith felt guilty because she, unlike Frank's sisters and the wives of his co-workers, was not working in order to carry her share of the burden. Frank saw Edith as a parasite, and a complaining one. She sat around all day, eating him out of house and home, and then pounced on him by night like a duck on a June bug.

Edith had two small children, which ordinarily is ample reason for a young wife to remain at home. But when her mother-in-law moved in her constant presence was no longer necessary. It is easy to see Edith grow up believing that marriage would solve all her problems. It would give her security: a home, children and sexual fulfillment. She was more than willing to meet all her husband's needs and was hurt and angry to find these could be met by other women for a fee, or by his own mother at the stove and wash tub. In another letter she wrote: "I have a hard time fighting with my mother-in-law for the chance to use the vacuum cleaner, prepare a meal, dust, keep my own room and even care for my children."

Our exchange of letters continued for over a year. Edith was often humorous, more often argumentative. Her weight reached 204 pounds. I asked Edith about her education and learned she was a high-school graduate and she knew how to type. Since money was a problem in her home, and she and her mother-in-law were getting in each other's way, I suggested she should consider taking a job. She was annoyed at the idea, even insulted, and vehemently advanced several weak reasons for not going to work. But a month later, she did pull herself together and found an office job—temporary, she emphasized.

Away from the continual conflicts in her home and surrounded by girls of her own age, she became more cheerful. She didn't lose weight at first, but continued to indulge herself in huge meals and snacks. There were, however, changes taking place in her attitude: "I came home from work the other night dead tired, and my mother-in-law decided to be generous to me."

Then Edith joined some of the other girls at work in a diet contest. She lost ten pounds the first week through what she referred to as "starvation pure and simple" and gained six pounds back the third week. She wanted to buy herself some dresses for the office that summer and tried to diet even harder.

I didn't hear from her during the next six months and often wondered what happened. Then, I received a brief note with a snapshot. She was down to a handsome 145 pounds. She had just put a down payment on a house with four bedrooms, a family room and a den in the basement. She and Frank had argued over the kind of house they wanted, but it was "Nothing serious."

"My mother-in-law began to wonder if we weren't moving too far out," she wrote. "She said we were getting high-toned and maybe she should go and live with her daughter Lucy. From Lucy, with six children, I knew just how popular Mama would be, like the whooping cough again. 'No, Mama,' I said, 'You can't pull anything like that on Frank and me. We need you now that I'm working.' That persuaded her and all of us are now comfortable in our house—four levels, basement, ground, second and attic. Frank always picks me up at the office. He has a lot of respect for me as his good working wife. But when and if I have another baby. . . ."

In her last letter to me, Edith wrote: "I still say women eat and eat because they are frustrated. Any fat woman is an unloved woman. The skin-and-bone type is really getting her love kicks from some man. I didn't really depend on that diet. It was standing up, earning Frank's respect, being kind to his mother and helping him grow up and become a man. It was doing something about my everlasting nagging and about having so much time on my hands. My mother-in-law is a good grandmother to my little boys. I think the children profit from having her in the house. And I think you were right about Frank's needing to be away from Mama before he could really function as my husband. I tested that by getting him to stop at a motel on my second payday. That's why I really bought the house, to get Mama upstairs with the kids. From the beginning I had my eyes on that bedroom off the living room, and that big den in the basement. Frank is more attentive to me in the den than any place in the house. I think he needs two floors between us and his mother. Anyway, you've just got to stop, start and begin all over again, if you want to avoid real trouble like a divorce."

It had not been easy, but Edith had finally understood the source of her unhappiness and made a successful effort to cope with it. As is so often the case, she held the solution to her problem within herself—it had only been necessary for her to find it.

Am I a Nymphomaniac?

One of the most misused terms in sexual psychology is "nymphomania." Rarely is it used in the correct clinical sense, but is often applied, for example, by an incensed husband to a wayward wife, to any woman who is indiscreet in the bestowal of her favors, to prostitutes, and even to married women whose sexual drives seems to exceed the "norm." The term satyriasis, the corresponding state of the male, is seldom encountered in clinical literature and even more rarely in common usage. This is one more manifestation of the double standard: a strong sexual drive in a man causes little consternation; in a woman, it is considered pathological.

As in most manifestations of the double standard, there is a long historical basis for such an attitude. For centuries, it was believed women lacked sexual desire. The Greek sage, Solon, lectured that ten days should elapse between sexual acts, Mohammed recommended an eight-day interval, and Martin Luther advocated the norm to be twice weekly.

Only in recent times has it been recognized and accepted that women also have sexual desires which demand gratification. In the Kinsey report, it was revealed the average young couple indulged in sex about four times a week; and even more important, the frequency is governed very often as much by the tastes and desires of the woman as the man. Another important aspect of our sexual lives was revealed in this report: there is no real rule which can be applied to frequency of sexplay. There are many who have intercourse daily, and also many who never exceed a limit of twice a month.

When a woman's desire for intercourse becomes an insatiable urge—an urge which destroys other important parts of her life and her relationships with others—then there is a strong possibility the condition is pathological, and the term "nymphomania" is applicable.

When any one drive of man takes over control to the point of destroying adequate functioning, it must be considered a problem. Even within the wide latitude of varying acceptable sexual tastes and drives, there is a common rhythm: desire, movement toward gratification or action, climax and repose. Many different clinicians have a different definition of this state, but there is one

344

point of almost complete agreement. When this cycle is incomplete, when there is never quiescence, but rather a constant state of tumescence, this state is considered nymphomania or satyriasis.

The following letter came to me from a young woman who had good reason to wonder whether the term could be applied to her.

I was born the day Pearl Harbor was bombed, December 7, 1941, Beatrice wrote. My family included a divorced mother and two older sisters. My only brother, who was a year older than me, was killed by an automobile when he was seven years old. It may be important that my parents divorced in 1945 and I have no memories of my father. He was in the war when I was a baby and, after the divorce, he lived out of the country a great deal. He remarried, had a second family, and was killed in an air disaster when I was fifteen years old. My mother never remarried. She always had many men friends, some of them business acquaintances she met in her advertising job, but whether she ever took a lover during those years, I don't know. My sisters married when they were young and appeared to be happy with their husbands and children.

I always liked my mother's male friends. Though I was without a father and brothers during my formative years, men never seemed mysterious to me, as some of my lovers have suggested. I just liked them and got along with them.

I had my first sexual experience when I was thirteen, with a handsome, blue-eyed blond boy. He lived next door to my grandmother, who I often visited. He was fifteen. We used to play together—scrabble on rainy days, or canasta when it was too late to be out riding our bicycles. One evening while grandmother was dozing upstairs, he and I danced together. We kissed, discussed sex, and then decided to undress and dance together. It was all meant to be bold and funny, that's all. We became frightened after we were fully naked, and nervous, perhaps, for fear that grandmother might come downstairs, so we quickly dressed. He was a big boy for fifteen, sophomore in high school, on the football team. For days, I wondered if he thought about me as much as I remembered how he looked, standing there so tan and naked. I found excuses for visiting grandmother again and again, always hoping he would show himself to me again. One night I was staying at grandmother's house, and I could see him doing his homework at the kitchen table across the yard.

After grandmother was sleeping, I went out on the back porch and began throwing small pebbles at his kitchen window. I believe he had been thinking about me as much as I had been thinking about him. We kissed very passionately and then stole into the garage, where my grandmother's car was parked. We engaged in sexplay and then achieved full, successful coitus. After that, we indulged ourselves frequently. Nobody ever learned our secret—he always made sure that I wouldn't become pregnant.

I enjoyed not only intercourse, but all the preliminaries and post-climax sexplay. I enjoyed the curiosity and adventure of the game so much that I made advances toward other boys, especially the older ones. Before I was fourteen, I was having intercourse every day with two or three boys at school. The tragedy was they talked behind my back, and soon many boys were trying to date me with one thing in mind.

Almost every male I saw interested me in a sexual way. I would wonder what they would be like nude, how they would make love. My most thrilling experiences took place the summer I was fifteen, when I was picked up by a man from out of town. He was at least forty, balding, but with a wonderful sense of humor. Not only did he give me great pleasure, but I knew that he was enjoying himself as never before. I was miserable when he would leave town, but because of me, he always came back.

I lived near a marine base, and there were always lots of young, handsome marines about. Several of them fell in love with me, but they never considered marrying me. "I don't understand you, Bea," a marine said to me one evening when I was seventeen. "You're the most beautiful girl I know. How can you be such a nasty little tramp?" I cried more over his using the word nasty than over the word tramp. He admitted that I had never been nasty or mean in any way. What bothered him, he said, was that he was in love with me and hated to think I was also sleeping with other marines. By then, I had learned men have double standards. While they want to sleep with girls like me, they want to marry the other kind. I was somewhat worried about my family learning about my life. Fortunately, my mother was always on the run in her career, and my sisters were considerably older and went their own ways.

People used the word *nymphomaniac* with me before I was quite sure of what it meant. All I knew was that I loved to have sexual intercourse. I loved making love to men, giving them pleasure and obtaining pleasure myself. There was no difficulty finding men every night, but secretly I would miss having men about early in the morning as well. I don't think there were many times during the day that I didn't think about men. Even after having had intercourse with hundreds of them, I was still curious and adventuresome. It was exciting to know that I would still be meeting new ones. I loved variety, especially older, married men, who might not realize they were handsome, or who might be surprised that a pretty young girl desired them. I loved to see the marines remove their uniforms and it was exciting to tease and flirt with casual passers-by I might see on the bus to and from school.

One of the bus drivers on the line had quite a yen for me. But he was afraid to put it into words. He would just grin when I caught him looking at me. I enjoyed playing up to him, to the point where he couldn't bear it any longer. I think he hated himself when he asked me to meet him on a street corner one night. He drove me to a lover's lane and was slow getting started. So I made advances to him that all but threw him for a loop. When it was all over, he acted like he was a giant.

One boy who fell in love with me learned of my reputation, and decided he had to beat me up. In his frustration over loving a nymphomaniac he burst into tears. Men are such hypocrites. They say they want free and easy women, but sometimes I wonder.

I decided that if I were ever going to marry, I would have to find somebody who didn't know anything about me. I went off to junior college, two hundred miles away, and I behaved myself for the first month. I was attracted to one of the teachers, but he was married. Just about then, I met my husband, Lee. He was a salesman, twenty-five years old. He made passes at me, but I pretended I didn't understand them. We became engaged and he felt we should give ourselves the privilege of going the whole way before marriage. I agreed. We were married four months later, because I became pregnant. I wanted to be pregnant. And it was during this time I decided to turn over a new leaf. I was a good wife to Lee for that year or so. Even Lee said I was a good wife.

I was unfaithful to Lee for the first time fourteen months after we were married. My baby was walking by then and a man came to sell a set of encyclopedias. He was very handsome and I saw at once I bothered him. I noticed that he was "wool-gathering" a couple of times when I asked questions about the books. We were sitting on the davenport, looking at the pictures illustrating an article on California, when I saw that look of hunger about his mouth and in his eyes. He had difficulty swallowing, and I think the presence of the baby annoyed him. I leaned still closer to him, getting the good smell of him, and he had to light a cigarette for protection. He was twenty-seven years old, recently married. We talked about that after he had made love to me. He returned several times a week after that for over a period of four months, but once when he arrived, I was making love to the superintendent of the apartment house. My salesman for the book company was shocked. I used to wonder if my husband ever met customers like me. Lee sold electronic equipment, however.

Lee was a good husband, and we had sexual intercourse almost every night. But when morning came, he had to go off to work. Then, there were many times during the day when something would suggest sex to me. There are always men around—the cop on the beat, salesmen, magazine subscription boys, superintendents, meter readers and so on and so on.

One of my brothers-in-law had come to our town on business. I had always liked him and used to wonder what he would be like as a lover. He was very handsome, athletic, and masculine. My sister always said he was quite a man. It was natural for him to call while he was in town and I asked him to come out for coffee, at least. He was giving me that little-sister-in-law kiss when I let my lips linger a little longer, with my body close up. It doesn't take much to give a man the idea. Why are they so shocked and guilt-ridden later?

When Lee found out what I was like, he felt he had to divorce me. I took it as a great compliment when he said, 'And the worst thing, Bea, is that I still love you.' But since I had refused to be treated by a psychiatrist, he felt there was nothing else to do. What hurt me most was he began wondering if our child was really his.

Because he loved me, or felt sorry for me, Lee let me get the divorce for incompatibility. He still pays me alimony and sometimes when he and his second wife aren't hitting it off, he drops by and makes love to me. In many ways, I still feel I'm married to Lee, and I do love him very much.

I'm twenty-three now and I see no relief in sight. What is there in my horoscope that makes me love men and sex so much? Will any one man ever come along who will be able to satisfy all my needs?

There was nothing in Beatrice's chart to indicate she was a victim of malific influences, but there was a basis in her horoscope for the behavior she described. Her Sun was at the mid-point of Sagittarius. Her womanly Moon was in Cancer, the sign of the matriarch. In a certain way Beatrice did mother all her men. In the affairs she described, she was as desirous of giving pleasure as receiving it. Her descriptions of her encounters give the impression that a great deal of her gratification was derived from the enjoyment and pleasure the men received from her attentions.

Her Venus was just entering Aquarius, her third solar house, which rules mental and manual skills, and brothers and sisters. Her words give the impression she would have worshipped her brother, and his untimely death left its mark upon her. Having never known her father and losing her brother, it is not improbable that Beatrice is unconsciously searching for both of them, or at least some substitute. It is interesting to note she divides her attention between fatherly and brotherly types of men.

Her Mars is in Aries, the sign of boldness, quick wit, and aggressiveness, and it appears it is this type of man which appeals to her most. Yet, her letter reflects no scorn for less dashing males. True to her Moon in Cancer, she tries to answer the sexual needs of all men, never portraying a man as weak.

Beatrice's Jupiter is regressed in Gemini, the portion of her horoscope which rules change. It is, moreover, in exact zodiacal opposition to her Sun-Mercury configuration in Sagittarius. This pictures the conflict between Beatrice the individual, and Beatrice the partner in marriage.

Her solar 12th House of the secret sensations of the soul is weak. All efforts to hide her problems are weak or to no avail. Rather than being secretive, she will frankly talk or write about her problem, sometimes to the point of bluntness. Her Uranus is regressed in Taurus, in the sixth zone of her horoscope, which rules physical health. Regressed with Uranus is Saturn, the symbol of self-discipline. This conjunction between two regressed planets in an unfavorable square aspect to her Venus in Capricorn, indicates there is a void of positive interplay between insight into her problems and the ability to sublimate or postpone gratification of the moment's sensations.

Mars in her 5th House in Aries would give her the ability to follow paths where "angels fear to tread," impetus for her sensuous Mars to be independent, ardent, daring, with nothing halfway. This also is the increase in her impulsiveness. Further, it gives her a tendency to feel sex is a game—a competitive venture.

Her physical attractiveness is heightened by Venus in her 3rd House of Aquarius. This heightens her demeanor, dress and looks, which attract the opposite sex. Venus here causes Beatrice to reach out for love expressed as sex because of a deep basic loneliness, and the wish to express herself as an individual—in the one way she knows—through sex.

Beatrice's Sun in Sagittarius, also her ascendent, gives her the opportunity to be either portion of the Sagittarius symbol—the beast or the man. One type is fond of a "good time," with the demand their desires be met, even though their needs could be in conflict with other's standards. The opposite Sagittarian is as different as day is to night, being idealistic, altruistic, and enthusiastic in their efforts to help others. Beatrice, through her use of sex (which she called love) is in a negative manner blending these two aspects of Sagittarius.

Beatrice had no desire to seek psychiatric assistance. A basic premise of such treatment is that a person be in sufficient "pain" to be motivated to try to alter behavior. Her words did not convey a deep desire for change, but minor frustration over not yet finding a man who could match and meet her own needs. She received some minor pain from her promiscuity, but there always was some new "love" to soften the temporary frustration. Any behavior pattern so ego-satisfying, without penalties significant to the individual, is not likely to be changed, except slowly by growing to maturity, or by benevolent transits. These transits could bring influence to bear which would give play to strengths inherent in her chart, which would provide the opportunity to sublimate in a very positive manner her strong basic drives. I mentioned this to her in my letter.

At the time I wrote to Beatrice, in early 1964, her transiting Neptune was strong in her 12th House of secrets. She was fast reaching the point at which she could no longer indulge in self-deception. Transiting Jupiter, moreover, had recently moved into Aries, near her Mars in favorable trine aspect to her Sun. There was strong indication she would receive many benefits from the Jupiter transit through Aries. She would receive deeper insights into her own nature, for her Mars in Aries would be buttressed by Jupiterian wisdom. Jupiter is important in her chart because it is the natal ruler. Though beginning life with Jupiter regressed in Gemini, opposite her solar conjunction with Mercury, she was soon to receive all the advantages which transiting Jupiter can bring, as it trines her solar conjunction, and still forms a favorable sextile with her natal Jupiter.

Beatrice's horoscope showed possible motives for her strong sexual drive, but it could not explain all of her actions. Her chart would give her a springboard to deep self-knowledge, but knowledge is power only when it is used. When habits become as thoroughly established as hers, it takes real effort to change their impetus. I strongly recommended she consult a psychiatrist. I believed she would learn she was not truly a nymphomaniac, but that her problem stemmed from deep psychological needs, rather than a pathological condition. Psychiatric treatment would help her find and cope with the true motivations underlying her behavior.

I could only surmise the early tragedies affected Beatrice more than she consciously recognized. The loss of her father and brother in two unconnected disasters could have caused emotions in her which manifested themselves as the desire to please men sexually—or to mother them, because of an indelible impression of the fragility of men's lives. There is also the possibility she felt guilty about some real or imagined responsibility in her parents' divorce. To speculate without more significant facts than Beatrice volunteered not only can be foolish, but dangerous to the individual, so I kept these thoughts to myself. I recommended that she should seek clinical assistance, and explained her horoscope would prompt her to help herself with the dark byways of her personality.

I did not hear from Beatrice again, so I can not report on the result of my astrological advice. I can only hope it provided the first step in the amelioration of her problems.

Sex as Adventure

Currently there is conflict over the argument as to whether sexual immorality is greater in our age than it ever has been in other periods of history. The main point in this whole discussion is the word "immorality." There is no doubt this generation is more involved in sexual expression than many other past generations. Sexual fulfillment as a subject dominates a vast portion of our books, articles, television, movies, and advertisements, which emphasize how a particular product can be a vehicle to a more satisfactory romance or to more intense sexual happiness.

There is little doubt that the development of almost foolproof methods of contraception has increased sexual expression. But is sexual expression "immorality?" Aid to dependent children not supported by their fathers has skyrocketed in the past few years. Illegitimate births are increasing completely out of proportion to the population growth. If the definition of immorality is "that which is not proper behavior," just what is the concept people have of proper behavior? The examples set by the actions of many people who influence the general population—and after all, "right" is what the largest number of people in a setting agree to abide by—is such that many sexual conventions have turned topsy turvy.

An eminent sociologist has called sex modern man's "last frontier" because, he maintains, it is one of our few modes of personal expression left for the individual in our conformist society.

No nation—no individual—is potentially more insane than one who is rigidly, completely sane all the time. Just as an inflexible steel building or bridge will not withstand a storm, so will the individual who rigidly orders his life break under the stress. Sex has become the outlet for this frustration. Interestingly, when Eastern mystics begin to speak of and describe an ecstatic state, their description parallels various phases of sexual fulfillment. This is not to say the ecstasy of our great mystics, who have given us profound insights into religious philosophy, is sexually oriented. But the feeling of oneness through esoteric discipline is available only to a few, while the excitement, fulfillment and identification available through sexual expression is available to all.

351

Another similar expression is intoxication. William James called liquor "the poor man's mysticism," because under the influence of liquor the eternal "no" becomes an eternal "yes." Anything becomes possible for a few moments at least. There is a feeling of oneness with all life. This same feeling is often present in sexual expression.

Whether or not these theories are valid, my experience as an astrologer has been that most of the sexual affairs which people write to me about are for the most part not colored by lust or undue sentiment. Extramarital and premarital affairs seem to give some people a sense of excitement—derived from the need for secrecy, the flouting of taboos, and the risk of pregnancy or discovery. The following case of a man I shall call Jack illustrates this observation more vividly than any other which has come to my attention.

I was born October 3, 1932, early in the morning. My mother died a few weeks later as a result of my birth, so there was just Dad and me in the house. Dad had some woman look after me until I was old enough to go to school, then I just stayed in school all day and ran wild until he finished his job at the plant about five each evening. I enjoyed the independence the other kids didn't have.

Dad and I got along fine. We played golf and saw all the best football and baseball games together. Sometimes he would have one of his lady friends along. He encouraged me to go out for all the sports and I did pretty well in high school.

My aunts and uncles used to wonder why Dad didn't marry and give me a stepmother. The truth was that neither he nor I wanted a woman in the house. Dad was handsome and hard-living, and he had all the women he could handle. As soon as I was able to surmise the changes a woman might make in our house I let him know I liked the way things were going—without a stepmother. Maybe, looking back on it now, I was a little selfish, but Dad never seemed to think so.

I was always a good son, and never got into trouble except once—and that happened not because of anything I did, but because I had a few wrong-guy friends. I heard some of them planning to break into a barber shop for kicks and I wanted out. The rest of them went ahead, and they got caught. The police knew I was in the gang and figured maybe I had slipped out some back window. They questioned me for two days—even Dad thought I was lying. It all straightened out when I proved I had been with a girl friend that evening.

I became interested in sex personally when I was fourteen. I say "personally" because I had always been aware of its existence. Dad used to bring women back with him from bars, and I would hear them in the parlor and later in his bedroom. Sometimes, the woman would be there for breakfast the next morning. I learned early in life to ignore those women if I saw them walking with their husbands or children.

There was one girl I always liked, Linda. She said she loved me. We used to neck in the drive-in movies when one of my friends could get his old man's car. Everything was fine between us until Linda became jealous of the way some of the older girls in school were friendly toward me. I was well-built and people usually thought me older than I was. One night at the drive-in Linda claimed I was trying to take liberties beyond mere necking, and when we argued, she went home and told her mother some of the things we had been doing and other things I suggested we do.

Linda's mother called Dad. He awakened me the next morning and demanded to know how far I had gone with Linda. I told him the truth. Dad said that Linda was a "good girl" and I should not get involved with girls like her. If I was feeling my oats, he said, he could arrange to have me taken care of, but he didn't want me to run the risk of getting a good girl in trouble.

That night he drove me across the city. He rang the bell of a house, and a bleached blonde called Aunt Brenda opened the door. She was a lot older than Dad and seemed to know him quite well. He asked if Helen or Ivy were about. She said Helen had married a cop and Ivy had gone home to her father. He asked about Maisie, but she was "busy upstairs." Just about then, two girls in their late twenties came into the parlor where we were sitting. He introduced me to Rita and Rose and told them I was fifteen years old and raring to go. I went upstairs with one of them. This was the beginning, in August 1948.

Dad said I was to drop in on Aunt Brenda and her girls anytime I felt like it. I didn't need money. He would take care of my bill. Looking back on it all, I guess it was not a very good way for a fifteen year old boy to learn about life and sex. But it was Dad's way. He said it would keep me out of "woman trouble." Anyway, I became a frequent visitor to Aunt Brenda's place.

I was a pretty good student in high school and Dad wanted me to go to college. He said he wanted me to have the breaks he never had. From the stories he told, he had been mistreated pretty badly by his drunken father. He had to run away from home, and had never had anything to do with his folks since.

Maybe I would have gone to college, but the summer I graduated from high school the Korean War broke out and I enlisted in the Air Force. I had a pretty good time in the service, bumming around the country, with plenty of women in my life. I usually cared quite a bit for a girl until I got what I wanted from her, then I seemed to tire of her.

I left the Air Force in 1955 when I was twenty-three years old. Dad was glad to have me back. The mechanics course I had in the Air Force taught me a lot, and Dad took me on as a partner in a service station he bought.

Dad was slowing down a little as a woman chaser at fifty-four. He wanted to marry a woman named Viviane, but she was having a rough time getting her husband to let her have a divorce. She was thirty years old and had two little girls.

I enjoyed my work at the service station and had the feeling I was really helping Dad out, because a lot of the younger people began bringing their cars in. Some of the girls would give me a come-on, and I never let a pass go by. I had all the girls I wanted, including Linda who had married while I was in the Air Force. Getting a girl to come across, whether she was married or not, was child's play. But I was bored and dissatisfied. I decided maybe I needed my own home.

I thought I'd have a better chance in marriage if I chose a young and inexperienced girl. I began dating a few I knew in the neighborhood. I was always actually disappointed when they let me get to first base. Finally I dated Jean, a new schoolteacher in town, from out West. She was engaged to a medical student. She didn't consider dates with me wrong; and she always limited me to a goodnight kiss. I fell in love with her, annoyed at times because she wouldn't come across, jealous of the medical student, embarrassed and angry when she would play the snob with me and correct my grammar. But I had to have her.

But after two months of dates, I was still only getting goodnight kisses. Finally, I told her that I couldn't stand seeing her any more, I was crazy about her and wanted to marry her, but she wouldn't show me she loved me, too. She started reassuring me, and we began kissing and feeling each other, until she had gone too far to back out. And she knew it. When it was over I told her I still wanted to marry her, but she said she didn't want to see me again. I was persistent and she was lonely in a strange town. We saw each other again and made love again. Then she became pregnant and we were married in June 1956. Our baby was born seven months later.

No marriage could have been any happier during the first two years. I was unfaithful to her only once, with Linda who wasn't getting along with her husband.

Then, in 1958, I felt the need to break out. I needed some kind of challenge. Jean's older sister, a happily married woman, came to visit us. She was even prettier than Jean and I wanted her. She forgot herself one night in the car when we were supposed to be going to the laundermat. Instead of being afraid Jean might find out, I had a strange sense of enjoying the dare, the challenge of being discovered.

When Jean's sister went home, all I could think about was how much I had really enjoyed the risk. My father had just married Viviane, who finally got her divorce, and for some reason I became very excited at the idea of making love to her. I made the necessary approaches, and after a while she wanted me to take her to a motel. But I wanted to make love to her in the bedroom she shared with Dad. I think I was always conscious of the risk of Dad's coming home unexpectedly. He never did, any of the times I was with Viviane and soon I became bored with her.

I started seeing Linda again, and one night her husband caught us. He threatened to shoot me and told Jean about me. Jean said if I ever got off the beam again, she'd divorce me and take the baby away. I didn't want that, but it seemed I couldn't help myself. I began going after any woman I thought I had a chance to get.

Viv, my Dad's wife, wanted a child by him. She didn't want one by me. But because I knew this, I enjoyed forcing her to risk pregnancy with me. When she became pregnant, I was sure the baby was mine. She thought so, too. It was exciting to think that I had put this over on Dad, although I was sure I loved him as a father.

Jean divorced me in 1959. She had the goods on me with several women; and I got a big bang out of admitting to her she was right. I even told her about Viv and she was disgusted. She said I was "sick, sick, sick."

That's the pattern in my life. I learned from Viviane that my father had to marry my mother. She was just about to have me when they were actually married. I guess that was why he steered clear of marriage through all these years. But he hadn't wanted me to know he didn't love my mother.

Does astrology have anything to say about the kind of sex drive I have? I mean where there had to be a risk of getting caught with the wrong woman? I wish I understood it. I just can't enjoy an easy love affair. I want something which seems impossible, like some of the wealthy women in town, women who think they're above a grease monkey like me. I enjoy being with them those few moments when the affair is over and they realize what they have done.

Is all this in my horoscope? What does the future hold for me? Will I ever have a happy marriage in which all my urges are answered?

I drew up Jack's chart, and found the scaffolding for the behavior he described. Jack's Mars, the symbol of his sex drive, is in Leo, the sign of the aggressor. It is near his Venus, symbolic of inner needs, and of the desire for sexual fulfillment. There is a configuration in Leo, which implies aggressive leadership. Jack's Moon, which rules women, is at the second angle of his chart, the angle of possessiveness. The portrait we obtain is one of the aggressive male, enjoying domination over women. Jack's horoscope reveals a man who must conquer, and who enjoys his conquests. His is not an ill-favored personality, nor is it one which would make a happy marriage impossible; but played upon by the influences of his home life, it did become a dangerous game for Jack.

Some other strong factors in his horoscope are his Moon in Scorpio giving him an intensity of purpose, and the inclination to resist anyone who attempted to interfere in his affairs. This intensity is magnified by his Venus in Leo, increasing his passionate nature, but still allowing him to turn his emotions on and off at will. His Mars in Leo enhanced his personal charm and magnetism—in fact, giving him the type of personality which people quickly forgive when he errs.

His Sun and Mercury, which are near each other in the positive degrees of Libra, indicated a light approach toward life. This is evidenced even more strongly because his Sun and Mercury are opposed by a regressed Uranus in Aries. This regressed Uranus dominates his seventh angle, which rules marriage. His Saturn, the symbol of restrictions, is in the fourth house of his chart, the zone of home and family. Throughout his life he has sought to retain a link with the only family he knew as a child—his father.

Because Jack's introduction to sex in a brothel seemed to have had serious consequences for him, I did a chart for August 1948. In it, Jack's Mars is near deceptive Neptune in Libra. This is an unfavorable configuration for any Libra chart. Mars, in fact, was just passing over his natal Sun when the experience in the brothel occurred. The Sun and Saturn are in Leo, spotlighting the angle which contained his sexual Mars at the time of his birth. It was to be expected he would face harrowing experiences at this time in his life, but a wiser father or a better informed Jack could have lessened the effects of the crisis.

At the time I wrote Jack, in the mid 1960s, I told him that his Pluto, an inducer of awareness and improvement, was transitting his solar 12th House at the angle of truth and revelation. The period between July 20 and June 21, was going to be a very good one for him. During this time Venus would conjoin with Pluto at 8 degrees, and Virgo would be in his 12th House angle of self-completion and self-realization. Mars would conjoin Pluto in the same propitious zone of destiny. I urged Jack to use this period to make progress out of the maze in which he found himself.

Over the next decade, Neptune will be establishing itself more firmly in Scorpio, giving Jack additional planetary support at the second angle of his chart, an angle of earning power Uranus, the alerter and provider will be establishing itself in the 12th House. His chart shows he will be concerned with improving his material situation in life. Chances are he will want more than the mechanics job with his father. He will probably want his own shop. Because his capacity for leadership appears great, it is probable he will be successful in his business.

Jack has a native intelligence and character which will enable him to cope successfully with the complex array of emotional disturbances which have enveloped him, providing he will make an effort to do so. He had asked in his letter whether there was anything in his horoscope which would indicate the reasons for his sex drive. As we have seen, there are danger areas, but nothing which could not have been countered by a little thought and preparation. I pointed this out when I sent my analysis. I urged him to look more closely at his background and his environment than at his chart. I even suggested that he see a psychiatrist—realizing full well the chances of his doing so were slight.

I suggested, though he had written about it light-heartedly, his father's promiscuity could not have been very pleasant for him. It was obviously a disturbing factor for a little boy to see a succession of strange women at the breakfast table.

His first attempt to fulfill his sexual drive with Linda was not only thwarted, but was also severely censured by Linda, her mother, and his father. Then, in a well-meaning though ill-advised gesture, his father sought to help Jack by buying sex for him, not taking into account the sexual act is more than a biological urge; it is also an expression of an emotional need.

Jack did not send me his father's date of birth, so I was unable to construct his horoscope. But it seems apparent from Jack's letter that his father had a contempt for women which stemmed, perhaps, from his forced marriage to Jack's mother. It seems obvious the father, like Jack, was substituting sex for some badly defined need within himself.

Sexual fulfillment which can be basic to a man's happiness, even to his success, can operate negatively when it is lost in the miasma of mental disturbance. It is a form of mental disturbance to substitute the essence of the male-female relationship, a total emotional and physical involvement, for some other personality needs they may have.

For Jack, sexual conquest became an easy way for him to prove his superiority. When he met Jean he had already developed something similar to his father's contempt for women. So she, a schoolteacher who was engaged to a medical student, was a bigger challenge than he had ever met. She corrected his grammar, she came from a different social environment than he had ever known. She considered herself his superior.

She submitted to him, and he was faithful to her for two years. Though Jack did not describe his married life, I surmised that he had met a constant challenge during that period with her. One does not conquer a whole environment and personality easily. There is reason to suppose he was never satisfied that he had conquered Jean, and possibly this is why he turned to her sister.

The element of risk he mentions was certainly there, as it is in so many extramarital affairs. Many men who have passing affairs with their bosses' wives often confide they enjoyed the risk much more than the actual affair. What isn't often mentioned is that jealousy of the boss may drive them to take something from him which he values—to cuckold him. It seemed to me there was an element of this jealousy in Jack's make-up, and for that reason he chose his wife's sister.

For the same reason, I believe, he seduced his father's wife. Though I believe Jack sincerely loved his father, at the same time I am sure he harbored resentment against him which he expressed in the most effective way he knew. All the undefined rancor which had accumulated because of the parade of strange women during his childhood, the trip to the brothel, the lack of intelligent guidance—all this was probably the impetus for his affair with his stepmother.

I urged Jack to look closely at his past, and to try to interpret it. I believed he was ready to change his life, because he was dissatisfied enough with it to ask for help. I advised him to try to get his wife back, pointing out there is sufficient challenge in marriage—that is, the challenge of keeping the daily and growing affection of one person—to satisfy even the strongest male vanity. I also suggested he turn his energies to his business for which the signs were so propitious.

Jack is an intense person, one who, in terms of personal motives, finds it difficult to ignore pain or pleasure. The placements of his planets give him a great deal of magnetism and charm. Without even really being aware of it, he began to transfer his drive for achievement and power to the sexual sphere. It was here he received personal feelings of challenge with accomplishment, power, success, and achievement. This continual proof of success and status was necessary to his emotional health because of the early environmental factors. With a satisfactory return of focus of this drive to his occupation, Jack would concentrate and work with the same intensity toward success.

Pregnant by Her Ex-Husband

Few people are shocked by our high divorce rate these days, and the taint which used to be associated with "divorcee" has now faded to obscurity. Yet, I am surprised at the great numbers of letters I receive from divorced people, and even more so at the circumstances surrounding some of these divorces. I have received letters from people who have dissolved marriage after one year, and from people who have decided they could not make a go of it after thirty years of living together.

Far too many people in the world today are preoccupied with "instant and immediate" gratification. The moment a frustration appears it is not accepted as a challenge or an opportunity for growth, but simply something to be avoided at all costs. In far too many situations the person simply runs away from the problem in obtaining a divorce.

I have never considered divorce an evil. When love and respect are truly gone, and a home is continuously filled with anger and discord, with no hope for reconciliation, it is only humane to avoid ruining two or more lives. What often happens, however, with a frequency which constantly amazes me, is that two people will obtain a divorce and then find in spite of everything, they still love each other. Sometimes a mistake like this can be rectified by remarriage; but more often, one or both of the parties have married someone else by this time. Following is the case of a young woman named Virginia, who suffered through such a situation. Virginia wrote me in May 1960.

What does astrology have to say about the mess I have made of my life? I was born May 22, 1928. When the war ended in 1945, I was only seventeen, but I think my generation grew up rather quickly and I married a returning soldier, Mike. I stole his name and military address from a girlfriend when I saw a snapshot of him with her brother, and had written long, daily letters to him all of 1945. I sent him my picture, as many young girls did during the war, and told him I was nineteen years old.

I don't know whether you remember or not, but we did a lot of silly things during the war. I guess I thought I was doing my part when my letters became genuine love letters, written as I mooned over his handsome features in the photograph. He was lonely in the South Pacific and poured all of his loneliness into his letters. Soon, we were telling each other we were in love.

When he came home and learned that I was only seventeen, he was annoyed because he wanted to marry me at once. He was twenty-three years old then, having been born November 1, 1923. Since I was still in high school my parents wanted me to wait. They didn't like the idea of my being in love with a stranger from another state. Mike stayed with us a week; and during that week I was everything to him. It just happened while we were out on New Year's Eve. He went on to visit his married brother, and I began counting the days and months until school ended and I would be eighteen. I got quite a jolt early in March when I realized that there wasn't any doubt: I was pregnant.

Mike and I were married April 11, 1946, and I set up housekeeping in part of a quonset hut on the campus where he was studying for an engineering degree. We were ideally happy and although we were constantly facing money problems, we had great faith in ourselves. Our first child, Michael, was born the following October and by Christmas of 1946 I was pregnant again. Our second child, Linda, was born in late 1947.

While I was carrying our third child, Rachel, in 1948 I learned quite accidentally that Mike was unfaithful to me. He attended a stag party with some buddies from his old unit and they ran into some girls. One called him at home the next day; she genuinely did not realize he was married. I didn't understand or know which way to turn. After all, we were in love! I was pregnant with his third child, yet he could go off with some girl he ran into at a party. Mike and I quarrelled during the remainder of the time I carried Rachel. He promised that he would never be unfaithful again. I dried my eyes, but I never really felt secure again.

In June 1950, Mike received his degree and got a job with an aircraft plant. By then, I was pregnant with my fourth child, Tommy, who was born early in 1951 close to my own twenty-third birthday. We bought a house on a GI loan, and I thought I was one of the happiest women in the world.

We had a good circle of friends, mostly young engineers from the plant and their wives. It was at one of our parties that I heard some of the fellows kid Mike about his new secretary, Joyce. I gathered she was very attractive.

I didn't think much about it when Mike started working a lot of overtime during 1952. After all, there was the Korean War. I had become familiar with the soft, liquid, and even provocative tones of Joyce's voice on the phone whenever I called my husband, but I had never met her nor really thought much about her.

One weekend he told me he had to go to another state for the company; they were testing some equipment he had worked on. It was during that weekend that little Rachel became very ill with pneumonia. I was terribly concerned as her fever soared and I thought I should let my husband know. I called the company to find out where I could locate him. It became clear at once that Mike was not away on company business. I called Joyce's apartment and received no answer. The more Rachel's fever raged, the more my own anger built up.

By Sunday evening when he returned looking as though he had been on drugs or something, Rachel was over the crisis. At once, he was genuinely concerned, for he had always loved his children very much. When he came to me in our bedroom, I told him that I had been calling the company all Saturday, and his sheepish look changed to one of fear. He didn't quite know what I had learned.

I told him that I was sure that he had spent the weekend out of town with Joyce. At first he denied it, but I didn't believe him. I became almost hysterical with anger. Finally he admitted he had been with Joyce, and he said it wasn't the first time he had ever been unfaithful and it probably wouldn't be the last. He said something to the effect that was the way he was built, and I should just accept it.

What did the future hold for me? The following week I packed up my children, went home to my parents and sued for divorce. I was granted custody of the four children and alimony.

But even before my divorce was final, I realized I was still very much in love with Mike. He wrote me on several occasions, begging me to call it off, but I was too proud to do so. I began accepting dates, but none of the men looked as good to me as Mike. None of them entertained me, amused me, interested me or fascinated me the way he did. Divorce disillusioned me more than his infidelities.

When the summer of 1955 rolled around, Mike came in July, hungry to see his four children, but with Edith on his arm. He told me she was his wife, and the daughter of one of the vice presidents of Mike's company. She was a lovely girl, about my age. Her birth date is February 14, 1928. She told me that she wanted to know me because Mike had always spoken well of me, and she hoped they could have the children for a vacation now and then.

The night before he and Edith were to leave for the West, he came by our place alone, bringing the children more gifts, thanking my parents for being good grandparents to his kids, making small conversation with me, even telling me that he hoped I would marry again and be happy. Long after my parents and the children were asleep we sat talking about the way our lives had gone. He was still Mike—self-sufficient, male, with a big grin, and a sense of humor. When I was bidding him goodnight on the front porch I broke down. He took me in his arms and told me that everything would be all right. But I couldn't stop shaking and crying and I told him I still loved him.

He made love to me then. I half-hated his attitude, but I was starved for fulfillment with him. I didn't count on the fact that he would wangle several business trips east during the year that followed, and on each trip, he would go out of his way to see me, date me, take me to a motel. I was ashamed and felt like a tramp who was taking Edith's husband away from her, just as Joyce had taken mine from me.

When Edith had her first child, I told myself my relationship with my ex-husband had to end. On the rebound, I married Harry when he proposed. He was considerably older than I, and I think he wanted my children as much as he wanted me. Harry was born September 15, 1918. He had never married because he had taken care of an invalid mother. Right after she died in 1955, one of my sisters introduced me to him and on our fifth date, he brought along a gorgeous engagement ring. We married in late 1955.

No woman could have asked for a more devoted husband than Harry, nor for a better father for her children. When Mike and Edith came east with their two children, they got along famously with Harry. We were all being very modern and very reasonable. For the sake of the children, we told ourselves. But every time I saw Mike, I wanted him. Harry couldn't awaken my desire nor pacify it once Mike had awakened it.

Harry wanted children of his own. But two years passed and I didn't become pregnant. I consulted the doctor and was told that there was no reason why I couldn't have additional children. Harry shied away from going to the doctor. He had his masculine pride. But I think he suspected it was he who was unable to have children, and he became nervous, self-despising and even lost confidence in his job. My heart went out to him. I wanted so much to have his child.

In late 1959, Mike made one of his trips east to see the children and transact business for his company. One day as I was walking with him and our four children, I noticed him looking at me with his old look. He told me I was more beautiful than ever. The next afternoon, while Harry was at work and the four children were in school, Mike dropped in unexpectedly. It happened! Two months later, I was sure I was pregnant, and Harry was overcome with joy. Never did it dawn on my husband that I was carrying another child by Mike.

The baby, a boy, was born last week. He is the replica of Mike, but no one seems to notice. Harry is delighted! What am I to do? Can I keep this secret? Should I tell Harry the truth? Should I tell Mike that the child is his? And when I don't become pregnant again, will Harry begin to wonder about this baby?

Because of the complexity of this situation, I cast horoscopes for all four of the people who were most affected—Virginia, Mike, Harry, and Edith.

I explained to Virginia that her Moon, the prime significator in her chart as a married woman, is at 12 degrees Cancer in a favorable aspect to Mike's powerful Sun-Jupiter-Venus alliance in a vigorous Scorpio. Mike's trine aspect is one of the strongest there is for providing a basis for marriage. His Sun in Scorpio is potent, and his Venus in Scorpio gives him strong sexual appetites. Virginia's Moon in Cancer rules fertility, femininity, and motherhood.

"Yours is a dynamic sexual attraction," I pointed out. "It is like the meeting of two opposite magnetic poles when you are together. Even though your philosophy and personalities may clash, there will always be a strong attraction when you are close to one another."

I described how the effect of Mike's Uranus retrograding in Pisces was important. "Mike will always be alert to a passing romance. His Neptune and Moon are in Leo, signifying success in his work, enjoyment in his job, and devotion to his career. "He may often have a wandering eye," I added, "but no other woman but his wife will ever have a strong attraction for him.

"It is doubtful if Mike would have been faithful to you sexually, or presently to Edith," I wrote. "Nevertheless, regardless of his pecadillos, Mike would have desired to continue the marriage," I advised her. "He may have wandered in the past—and may in the future—but it is doubtful if he would take action to sue for divorce."

When Virginia did divorce him, he immediately found another wife—Edith, who was a little like Virginia. Edith's Moon is in Sagittarius, not too far away from Mike's Sun. Her Saturn is in Sagittarius also, protective of her position as a wife. Edith, more than likely, will make the necessary allowances for Mike: her protective Saturn will conserve her marriage. It will urge her to reconsider should she learn of Mike's infidelities, and give pause before contemplating divorce. Her Sun in Aquarius indicates she will become interested in a great round of social and humanitarian activities—this might even compensate her should she find out about her husband's indiscretions.

I described the implications of Harry's chart. "His Sun is in Virgo in favorable aspect to your Moon," I told Virginia. "Harry's Venus is restrained somewhat in Virgo and his Mercury is retrograding near his Sun and in conjunction with his Venus. Love came to him late in life as a result of that ominous conjunction of Venus with retrograde Mercury near his Sun."

"Remember he had been the son of an invalid mother for a long time," I continued, "and with his Moon in the house of romance, it is possible and very likely he loved his mother intensely, perhaps even too much. When he lost her, he lost a great deal of the underlying purpose in his life. He desires an intensely feminine woman, like his mother, and part of this desire is to work for and protect that woman who is important to his life. Your four children also have a strong positive significance in his life."

To summarize three of the four charts, here are some of the dynamic factors which were involved, in addition to the comments I have already made.

Virginia's Moon in Cancer makes her a complicated individual, though she may often voice that all she really wants is to be loved and understood. Her Saturn in Libra strongly indicated more than one marriage. Jupiter in Aries gives her a strong overoptimism—even to the point of wishful thinking. Mars and Uranus conjunct in Aries promoted a restlessness, with a tendency to be quite independent in her philosophy. Her Mercury-Sun conjunct in Gemini created the potential to be able to rationalize her involvement with one man, while married to another—yet also gave her the ability to happily and constructively adapt to her new marriage.

Her Venus in Taurus emphasized her strong emotions, and physical needs and responses. This also heightened her possessiveness and reluctance to give up Mike, even though the marriage was officially ended.

Mike's Sun, Venus and Jupiter in Scorpio gave him very deep emotional drive, a virile pride, and an intense possessiveness, with the need for exact fulfillment of his desires as he defined them. His Moon in Leo in square to the triad in Scorpio gave energy and action to his efforts to feel and be "someone special."

Saturn in Sagittarius gave him the tenacity to cling to his ideas—and to his feelings that Virginia still loved him, and belonged to him. His Mars in Libra strengthened his need to give and receive love, but with a certain lack of self-control. His Uranus in Pisces, besides what I have already mentioned, would make him a "law unto himself," where he would only find himself through himself.

Harry's Saturn in Leo would have the effect of restricting the expression of personal emotions, and particularly those relating to sex and romance, though his drives and needs were as great as Virginia's. This is further accentuated by his Jupiter in Cancer, giving almost fierce loyalties and the willingness to sacrifice self rather than hurt a loved one. His Mars and Venus in Capricorn gives him patience and control, with a strong sense of duty and discipline, and would explain his long silence until Virginia opened the door for honest discussion and evaluation. Mercury in Virgo further increased his reluctance to create an emotional scene between himself and Virginia.

I sent these four charts to Virginia. There was the crucial problem of whether or not to tell Harry about the true parentage of her fifth child. After careful evaluation of their charts, I gave her my answer. "I would advise you not to tell Harry at this time. His horoscope shows the warmth, understanding, and devotion to forgive you for the mistake, yet he too, has an ego and the shattering of his elation over fatherhood could result in grave repercussions. And neither should you tell Mike," I added, though I realized what an emotional burden I had placed on this woman. But there were so many lives involved. Although she did not completely approve of the advice, Virginia answered that she would keep the secret.

The following September Mike re-entered her life, ostensibly to see his children. Again, he tried to make love to her, but this time she resisted. He told her he knew he was the father of her last child. She tried to deny this, but at length broke down and admitted this was so. After Mike departed Virginia felt more guilty than ever; she had told Mike the truth, but continued to withhold it from Harry. She was eager to unburden herself to Harry, and again wrote for advice.

I repeated some of the same counsel of the previous letter and added, "Perhaps when your marriage is more secure with Harry—when an opportune time arrives you can tell him." Often people are eager to confess in order to absolve their guilt, or to punish the other person, failing to realize that confession is only the first step in reconciling an error. Without a positive plan to rectify the error, hasty confession only causes more anger or frustration.

On Thanksgiving day in 1960, Virginia learned she was finally carrying a child by Harry. She was overjoyed. When the baby was born, she told Harry the whole story. "The guilt which had been eating me away, just vanished," her happy letter reported. Harry told her he had suspected as much from time to time, and the suspicion had torn at his soul as much as Virginia's guilt had corroded her every minute. He had secretly been seeing a doctor. When he first began treatment, shortly before Virginia's fifth child was born, he learned that he was partially infertile—so much so it was apparent the child Virginia had been carrying could hardly be his. This was emphasized by the fact that the doctor took it for granted he had fathered no children. Though the thought plagued his mind, he tried to carry on and drive it from his thoughts. Now, however, having actually fathered a child, he could accept Virginia's infidelity and forgive her. His own pride had been restored.

In Virginia's last letter she said that she was very happy with Harry and he with her. "I hardly ever think of Mike any more," she wrote. "When I discovered that I had the strength to resist him for the first time I really felt mature and strong."

This case history had a relatively happy ending as far as Virginia's life was concerned. I doubt if she will ever be able to forget Mike completely, because he is father of five of her children, and she naturally would be wise not to tempt herself with any close proximity to Mike. Her horoscope shows the tendency and ability to replace Mike with the love of her children and the devotion of Harry. She is more fortunate than most divorced people who learn too late a divorce decree is only a piece of paper and not necessarily the end of sexual desire and love.

I'm in Love with My Boss

There are few eyebrows raised about adultery anymore, at least when it is treated in a general manner. Our age has become very sophisticated on the subject. But what is too often forgotten is that though it may be material for wit and comedy on the stage and in literature, it rarely ever amuses the people who are actually involved in it. There is inevitable furtiveness, lack of dignity, and conflict of emotions involved in adultery. There is almost always pain. The following case of a young girl I shall call Nancy is, I'm afraid, all too typical.

Jack is my boss in an electronics plant. I began as his secretary four years ago and now he's made me his administrative assistant, which is a fancy title he got for me in order to give several raises, since I've been his mistress for three years.

I want to be fair to Jack. He never promised to marry me. How could he? He's been married for twenty-one years and has four children. His wife's religion forbids divorce. Not that he wants a divorce. I think he loves his wife. I do know I'm beginning to hate myself!

If my parents knew anything about this I think it would kill them. Never did I think I could become involved in anything so cheap. Yet it's not really cheap, because I'm sure that Jack, in his own way, loves me. And I love him. He's the first and only man in my life. Oh, I've dated other men, but I've never let anyone else go as far with me as he does.

I was just out of business school, eighteen years old, and very green, when I went north to work. Right away I liked and respected Jack. He is a marvelous administrator, and he is kind and humorous.

Even though I liked him I never dreamed I would become his mistress. If for no other reason than the fact that he is only one year younger than my father. I don't think he had intentions at first. He always complimented me on my appearance, and I caught him appraising my figure several times, but that was only natural in a man like him.

I had good reason to believe he was unfaithful to his wife, because he was always getting calls from different women at the office. But he never made any advances toward me.

All that changed at the Christmas party. It was a typical office party with too much to drink, mistletoe and some of the people making complete asses of themselves. Jack had given me two raises during the year and a very nice present, so I was grateful to him. It was only natural that he kiss me under the mistletoe. When he kissed me he let his lips linger longer than was supposed to be right at such a time. I felt myself responding to his kiss pretty strongly; people were laughing when we finally broke. I walked across the office and began talking to one of the girls. When I looked back at Jack, he was talking to his boss, but his eyes were on me. He smiled, not a grin this time, but a rather forced, serious smile. I blushed!

Shortly after, he asked me if he could take me home. As soon as we were in the car, he turned the heater on and seemed solicitous of me. Then, even though some attendants were watching, he took me in his arms and kissed me again, longer and more meaningfully than the first time. I controlled myself as he drove through the heavy traffic, and asked him to let me off in front of a department store nearby.

He said it would be silly to end the evening so abruptly and drove to a motel near the air terminal. I know it sounds stupid, but I didn't protest because I didn't really foresee what would happen. I think I can explain this because I was so green, and besides Jack was the best friend I had in town. I just couldn't imagine his doing anything to compromise me.

I simply took it for granted when he said he brought me to the motel so we could have dinner in a place that wasn't crowded, he meant it. It was inconceivable to me that anything else would be involved. Looking back, though, I am sure I was lying to myself. I believe I was as willing as he was!

He ordered drinks, and told the attendant we'd order dinner later. Then he put his arms around me and kissed me again. I surprised myself with the passion of my response, for I had never felt that way before. It was as though I were in a trance when we made love.

That was three years ago. Now I live in an apartment that Jack pays for and we take all our vacations together. When he has to go out of town on a business trip, I nearly always go along. I know there is a great deal of gossip at the office. I can't say I don't care, because I do. But not enough to give Jack up.

I love him and he loves me. There is never any talk of divorce, though, and I never try to force him into something more permanent. But I know this can't last. I am giving him my youth and have lost my reputation. I want to give him up, but I can't bring myself to do without him. Is there anything in my horoscope that will help me?

Nancy had been born on April 19, 1939, when the Sun, Saturn, and Mercury and Moon were in Aries. It was no surprise she was an excellent administrative assistant. She was perfectly adapted by temperament and personality to meeting the public and attracting favorable attention for an idea or product. With so much power in Aries, it was natural that Nancy should leave home and make her way in a strange city. She not only had the daring of her pioneering Aries Sun, but also the stability of Saturn, the charm of the Moon and the strength of Mercury in Aries.

Her Moon in Aries would make her quite impulsive, though this would be stabilized by Saturn. She believed in her feeling for Jack, and her Moon here would allow her to be unconventional, and to keep it a secret. Her Venus in the waning degrees of Pisces, her 12th House of secrets, would increase her tendency to make secret alliances and to gain satisfaction even from a secret affair.

Nancy's Moon in Aries indicated that though she might fail, she would try again and again. Saturn here also indicated a strong promise of real happiness and security in middle or later life, but that it would only come through extended effort.

Nancy and Jack both had Mars in Capricorn, indicating strong ambition and the willingness to shoulder responsibilities, even those not rightfully theirs. Marriage is very important to their careers and their happiness. Both had a strong sense of duty with strong self-control.

Nancy's Venus Pisces gave her the impetus, in a way, to feel she was Jack's wife. She was with him eight hours a day, and at night she became his buffer against the world.

Her Jupiter near her Venus enhanced her abundant love and beauty. It increased her idealism, with a tendency to overlook her own misfortunes. At the same time, she would easily neglect her own deep needs, goals and desires in favor of altruistic actions for someone she loved.

Nancy had sent me Jack's birth date and I made a chart for him. His male Mars in Capricorn had moved into this sign of big business just before his birth. This intensity and dynamic creativity would be expressed in business and in romance. His Moon and Mercury in Capricorn made it an absolute necessity that he not lose face. It could also give him the tendency to forget the needs of others if they conflicted with his own.

The conjunct of his Sun and Venus in Sagittarius provided some of the ability to rationalize betraying his wife by having Nancy as his mistress, no matter how much he told himself he was going to be loyal.

Jack's Sun is in Sagittarius and it forms a favorable trine aspect to Nancy's Moon in Aries; this is perhaps the paramount classical aspect signaling a happy marriage. No wonder these two had little difficulty falling in love and maintaining a happy relationship. This is also a favorable aspect between his male Mars and her female Venus. Jack's Jupiter is regressing in Aries, where Nancy has her powerful stellium; and his Saturn taskmaster is weak, regressing in Leo (which in Nancy's chart is linked to romance, but not to marriage). It was this weak Saturn that made it possible for Jack to ignore the consequences of their relationship for Nancy.

I warned Nancy there was little hope for her in this affair. I suggested she make every effort to find another job and above all, to stop seeing Jack after business hours. They were, it is true, enormously compatible. But society has something to say about these things, and Jack had made a choice some years back. I could foresee only ruination for Nancy if the affair continued.

There were many problems to be solved in this affair. Where could Nancy earn an income as her present one? Where could she find a niche for which she was as well suited? Furthermore, Jack's wife had learned of her husband's infidelity, and was deeply wounded by it. Jack truly loved his wife and was afraid of losing her and his children. Finally, after much discussion and pain, Jack agreed to find another job for Nancy, and they both agreed to stop seeing each other.

I heard from Nancy about six months later. Her job had not worked out because the scandal of her liaison with Jack followed her, and her new boss took it for granted that part of her duties would be to sleep with him. Nancy was humiliated and hurt. She wrote that it was as though all her efficiency and business experience were nothing more than an excuse to be a mistress. She tried another job with the same results.

Then about a year later Nancy wrote that she had married. She had not been able to stay in the city, and had gone to the Midwest to work as a secretary in a university town. Her husband was a professor of social science.

She did not mention Jack. I can only speculate the outcome. I feel sure that he saved his marriage. He was a forceful man and if he wanted something badly enough, he was sure to get it.

This had been an almost classic case of adultery, since it wounded three fine people. All three have, I am sure, recovered. I am equally sure they have not done so without deep scars.

As I mentioned in the beginning of the chapter, the modern tendency is to treat adultery lightly, refusing to accept that something as important as an illicit romance is inevitably going to have a dramatic effect upon the psyche of the individual. The gravity of the affair may be suppressed, repressed, or rationalized; yet there are very often far reaching effects of guilt, hostility, or self-pity. Even in the case of so-called casual adultery, there are significant psychological ramifications. The participant may shrug off the implications, but the very fact that a barrier has been erected to block off the conscience simply means the conscience, like compressed steam, will find some other outlet, though it's path may seemingly have no connection to the sexual indiscretion. A constant companion of such an alliance is the spector of exposure and the often incendiary results.

The Unmarried Father

A person all but forgotten in the voluminous discussion of individual and society's problems: the unmarried father.

A great many of the letters I receive—more than I like—are from girls who have gotten into "trouble," who are going to have babies out of wedlock. Most of the girls write, I feel, not so much to learn from their horoscopes how to make the best of the situation, but simply in order to unburden themselves. Nobody ever thinks much about the father in these affairs, probably because one assumes he has little to suffer. In many instances this is probably true, but there are exceptions as the following letter shows.

Why does everybody sympathize almost exclusively with the girl in trouble, wrote Tim, and ignore the emotional impact of the trouble on the unmarried father? Do they really believe that the father feels nothing?

I had fallen in love with Edna the summer after leaving high school. We meant everything to each other. We were planning on getting married as soon as I finished college. We had made love, but it seemed all right since we were going to get married eventually.

Then one night Edna acted strangely. She refused to let me touch her, and she was silent all evening, as though she were angry about something. This wasn't like her. I drove out to the country and tried to take her in my arms so she would explain what was bothering her. She pulled away so sharply I was stunned. I begged her to tell me what was troubling her. She told me finally, and very coldly, that she was pregnant.

I was very upset, of course. Who wouldn't be? But I immediately said we'd be married. Edna, however, acted as though she took it for granted that I would leave her in the lurch. I tried to reassure her. At one point when she said she wished she could do something to get rid of the baby. I said it might be possible and she slapped me. She insisted I take her home immediately and told me she never wanted to see me again. She got out of the car without even looking back at me.

When I got home I tried to decide what to do. I was eighteen years old, having been born July 12, 1943. Edna was eighteen also; she was born

August 29, 1943. We had known each other for a long time, but had only fallen in love that summer. I didn't have any money to speak of, but I felt sure my parents would help.

Only I didn't know what to tell them. I couldn't even imagine what my mother's reaction would be. It was almost as hard trying to picture what Dad would say. We had discussed sex only once, when I was fourteen, and he tried to explain the facts of life to me about two years after I had learned them on a street corner. He was terribly embarrassed about it all.

Both Mother and Dad sensed something was wrong, though they didn't say anything about it at first. My mother heard me trying to get Edna on the phone several times without any luck. Finally she asked me if there had been a quarrel. She asked it kiddingly, as though it were some sort of joke. She had never cared too much for Edna's family because she felt that they were socially beneath us. My father's a lawyer; her father is a salesman and doesn't have a college degree.

She told me not to worry; that there would be plenty of girls for me to meet at college, and that I'd forget all about my puppy love. That was when I told her Edna was pregnant.

I knew her reaction wouldn't be pleasant, but I certainly didn't expect how hysterical she would get. She almost fainted, and screamed something like, "It's not true," several times. Then she ran to call my father at the office.

Dad came right home, but he was far from helpful. If anything he was worse than mother. He kept giving way to emotions, shouting, threatening, grabbing me by the shoulders. He kept begging me to admit that I hadn't been the only boy who had slept with Edna. This hurt more than anything else.

Dad took me to a room where we could be alone and began to tell me how he knew all about girls like Edna. He used vile language in front of me for the first time in my life. I was sickened; he was, after all, speaking about the girl I still intended to marry.

It ended with Mother and Dad figuring out a very nice way to save me. They said they would pay for Edna's confinement and take care of her until the baby was adopted. We all three set off for Edna's home.

Thank God she wasn't there when we arrived. She hadn't told her parents yet, and it was my father who broke the news to her mother. She just went white, and I thought she was going to faint. She didn't say a thing. Her husband accused me of lying, but I could tell he was shattered and wasn't even listening to the words he was speaking.

Then Edna came in. At that moment there was such a look of hatred for me on her face that I was speechless. Her parents asked her if it were true. She said yes. I said I wanted to marry her, but no one even paid any attention to me. My mother kept saying that my family would pay for the confinement. Finally Edna broke and screamed at us to get out. She said she had made arrangements and that the whole affair was nobody's business but hers.

My family was all too happy to lead me away. I kept trying to get in touch with Edna, but with no success. Her parents hated me. They wouldn't call her to the phone or let me in the house. Then I heard that she had left town, but nobody would tell me where she had gone.

I still wanted to marry her. I was sure that I could work and be a student at the same time. Other people did. I thought that after she had the baby she would reconsider. I left for college, and pretty soon I was all wrapped up in my studies and in the social life of the campus. I dated other girls, but they mostly reminded me of Edna. During the Easter vacation I learned where she had gone—to a large city about 200 miles from our town. I went there immediately!

I found her without too much difficulty. She actually seemed happy to see me. The baby had been born a month earlier, and had been adopted by people Edna had never even seen.

She spoke off-handedly about the baby, as though it were something which was completely indifferent to her. When I reminded her that it was my child as well as hers and that I wanted it, Edna told me not to be sentimental.

I'm back in college now and I'm studying hard, but there's a terrible feeling of guilt I can't get rid of. I still want my baby. I had nothing to say about its future and I don't think it's right.

Tim's Sun is in the strong family-ties sign of Cancer, and his Moon, symbolizing sensitivity is in compassionate Pisces. This could increase the potential for disagreement with others because of his lofty notions, and the inability of others to recognize them. Strongly aspected, this gives happiness through fulfillment of his ideals. Weakly or adversely aspected, it can create indecision and self-pity rather than positive actions.

Tim's vital and self-confident Mars is in Aries. Mars is not only the natural ruler of Aries, but is also 'rather aggressive in this part of the Zodiac. Tim will have his way with women. The physical is very important to him. It increases his self-interest and assertion, with strong impatience with anything which gets in the way of his plans.

His Venus in Virgo relates to his need for his feeling to be deemed very important, as was shown by his inability to understand Edna's needs or his parent's motivation.

Edna's Sun and Venus are in practical, logical Virgo and her Moon is in practical Leo, with a strong degree of self-reliance. Her Mars in Gemini further influences to direct action in order to change things to her own desires, even if the action is sometimes hasty.

There is a good angle of 60 degrees between Tim's male Sun and Edna's female Moon, a classical significator of a happy emotional relationship; this is one of the attributes we expect to find in marriage comparison charts of successfully married people. Even so, Tim's sexual Mars in Aries is not particularly well disposed to Edna's sexual Venus in Virgo.

Edna's behavior was remarkably practical. This could be predicted from her chart with her Sun and Venus in Virgo to her Jupiter and Neptune strong in Leo. Her Mercury in Libra gave her a better sense of balance than Tim and a more generous nature.

There is something grudging in Tim's view, although he raises a good point. But Tim dreams of ends without means; he sees effects, but doesn't always rightly determine the causes. The home in which Edna had her child would have given recognition to Tim's claims if he had made it. He should have made a greater effort to find the home and assert himself. This weakness is part of his astrological tendencies, and it can plague him again during life.

I sympathized with Tim, but I could not help feeling the best possible thing was done for the baby. I admired Edna's level-headed behavior. Obviously the child had been placed carefully in a good home with parents who can provide for it and give it the love which I felt neither Edna nor Tim could give at that particular time. They both had a lot of growing up to do!

I advised Tim to work hard and to try to put the matter out of his mind. He had made a mistake and he had paid for it. He should look toward the future. I also warned him against trying to see Edna so soon. She had been through a terribly difficult thing, but, from what I could gather from Tim's letter, she was working her way out of it with admirable control. Possibly, I wrote, Tim would like to see her later on, and could do so in a calmer more objective way.

I particularly warned Tim against the feeling of guilt he mentioned toward the end of his letter. I pointed out that everyone involved had forgiven him, and repeated that what had happened to the baby had happened for the best.

Only recently have the ramifications of divorce, or a problem such as this, upon a man's psychological well-being been given any significant attention. Heretofore, whenever the word "stigma" was mentioned, it was presumed to refer only to the woman. It was blithely assumed that there were no psychic implications or ramifications on the man worth mentioning. In the past decade, this area has attracted attention and research, resulting in an increased awareness of how psychologically important these are to the male psyche. This last story about Tim is just one of millions of possible ones, but it does illustrate that the unmarried father also has a major psychological adjustment to make in order to achieve peace of mind.

Of paramount import to the psychological well-being of our future citizens is the proper care of children who have been deserted by their fathers—deserted financially and emotionally. There is no general astrological picture that can indicate or predict this weakness in the father. Rather it relates to the general breakdown of the family so prevalent today and to individual charts. This is further increased by the attitude of the youngster who, as he or she grows and matures, can be inclined to mimic the very negative attitudes which resulted in their own separation from their father.

Incestuous Relationships

Recently I received this startling letter, which required an immediate reply. The serious problem it described could destroy the happiness of five living people. Dorothy's letter stated:

My husband, Darrell, threw me into shocking disbelief and into a kind of panic, by admitting to me the night after my mother's funeral that they had been intimate on three occasions, ten years ago. At first, I could hardly believe the story, but when I remembered how emotionally upset he was with guilt and remorse, I had no choice but to believe him, even though I wished to disbelieve.

Of course, this has made our marriage an impossible nightmare. I just can't stand for him to touch me and I know this isn't right.

Even though I've searched my heart, I don't know which one of them is to blame. It's heartbreaking to have recriminations against my dead mother, but I am human—and I am deeply hurt. After all, Becky was my mother, and I knew her only as a highly moral and responsible person. To even make this unbelievable incident worse, their affair occurred right after my father's death ten years ago, in 1960. We had only been married two years and I was carrying our first child.

He tried to justify his actions by saying she needed comforting, that it just happened, that it wasn't his fault. What kind of a society do we live in? Can I believe him and place all the blame on my dead mother, who isn't even here to defend herself? I just don't know what to do. We have three children, and I'm not really certain a divorce would solve anything.

I was born June 19, 1935. My husband's birthday is March 24, 1934. How could he involve himself in an affair with my mother, who was born October 30, 1909 and twenty-five years older?

We were staying in the family home when this took place. I had always been certain my mother loved my father—and she loved and respected me far too much to do what she did. I cannot help but wonder if this affair would have continued if we had continued to live in the same city as my mother. I am desperate for some type of understanding.

374

I explained to Dorothy that when she was born the Sun was in Gemini, the sign of adaptability, but in her case the Sun was standing alone in one of the weaker degrees of the third vernal equinox angle of the Zodiac. I explained that her Moon, which rules married women, was in Capricorn. Capricorn, at the zenith of the Universal Horoscope, rules big business, government, prestige, status, affluence and perfection, responsive as it is to Saturn, the planet of conservative ideas, righteous thinking and condemnation. She is inclined to demand the same perfection from others that she attempts to establish in her own life. Her ruling planet, Mercury, moreover, is regressing in Cancer, which is the sign of the matriarch and defends the next generation even at the price of this one.

Cancer also rules the retentive memory, so she is quick to criticize the male and is slow to forgive him his masculinity. Her Venus, which tells us much about the love trend in a female, is in Leo, qualifying as the third vernal equinox angle of her horoscope, and associated with relationships between brother and sister. In some ways, her attitude toward her husband is that of sister to brother and it may be that Dorothy was grasping at the straw of condemnation all these years later in order to relegate him to the position of a providing brother. Sexual expression is far less important to a Gemini woman, with such a scattering of planetary force, than it is to the two solar groups to which Dorothy's husband and mother belong.

Dorothy did not mention any brothers or sisters. We can assume from her letter that she assigned her husband many brotherly chores at the time of her father's death. Did she in some way assign him the task of comforting her widowed mother, of remaining with her?

We can assume from Dorothy's chart also that she was much closer to her father, possibly taking his death very hard, and she was also pregnant at the time. Was she so distraught that she turned inward in her grief, unable to abide the sight of both husband and mother in the days of her tragedy?

While slow to forgive and forget, her Mars is strong in Libra, the sign of tolerance, justice and forgiveness, so we can conclude that in time she will be able to forgive this indiscretion. Think of the remorse and guilt that he has known for ten years, and how he felt compelled to tell about this affair.

I wrote:

Your husband, Darrell, was still young when this affair with your mother took place, and your mother was fifty-one. Such sexual relationships are not as rare as you might think. Rather, a man at twenty-six is as highly sexually oriented as a woman might still be at fifty-six, something primitive races have long known about and accepted.

In your husband's chart, we find his Sun strong in Aries, the sign of courage, pioneering, and aggression. He was aware of sex at an early age, and male Mars is regressing in Libra, in near conjunction with your Mars. Libra rules marriage and with his Venus in Taurus, the sign of possession, we can assume he accepted your family and responsibility to your family from the day of his marriage. Chances are that your husband felt very much involved with your parents, the dead father and the unhappy mother. He would seek to comfort her; and while nobody can condone such an affair, with all its illegal complications and immoral incestuous undertones, it would seem to me that there is need for Christian charity also.

You ask which one of them is to be blamed. Your husband's Moon, which has much to do with his approach toward women, is in the highly geared, dynamic sign of Scorpio, which rules sex and the regenerative organs. At twenty-six, he well may seek to comfort a woman in the only way he knew how; and it is necessary at this point to study your mother's chart.

Your mother's Sun is in Scorpio, conjoined with your husband's Moon, implying that she was the type of woman he was most attracted to physically, while your husband certainly fulfilled your mother's ideas of what a man should be. Is it possible your husband fell in love with you because he was so attracted to your mother and hoped that one day you would show greater awareness of your heritage? Your Mother's Moon is in Taurus, again the sign of possession, and Becky considered your husband near and dear to her from the moment you decided to marry him.

There is potent physical attraction indicated between your husband and mother and at some precise moment, when both of them were emotionally distraught, you may have shown signs of rejecting both of them. You were unable to comfort either of them. They well could have gone one step too far in their need of each other, a touch of the hand, an inner awareness of mutual suffering, mutual aloneness.

That the affair took place in Becky's home, where you were also staying, presumably in some other part of the house, shows how unpremeditated it was. This is not the time for wondering about what might have happened if they were thrown together after those three occasions when they fell from grace.

Your mother is dead, she can't defend herself, and even if she were here, she might not be able to explain to you how such a shocking thing took place. Becky couldn't have explained it. Your husband can't explain it. But you feel some need for an explanation.

The problem is not what happened tragically ten years ago, but what is happening to your marriage right now.

Your Sun in Gemini is in favorable sextile relationship to Darrell's Sun in Aries. Your Mars is conjoined to his Mars in the sign of marriage and justice. You must forgive Darrell, especially now that your Pluto-induced awareness is moving ever closer to your natal Sun. And certainly, you must forgive your dead mother. Becky and Darrell fell from grace at a difficult moment, but remember, many mothers-in-law are secretly in love with their daughter's husband and vice-versa. The relationship is not only a meaningful one, but an impossible, highly emotionally charged and difficult one.

Deep analysis of your horoscopes, measuring Darrell's Sun distance from Becky's Moon, his male Mars from her female Venus, and his Ascendent from Becky's Descendent, makes it obvious that actual coitus was unpremeditated. She cried in his arms because she had just lost her husband, her lover. He attempted to comfort her, and he a young man bubbling with life to give, and your mother a highly geared woman sexually, stepped over the line where for them there was no turning back.

While both of them may have long been attracted to each other, their charts reveal that they didn't actually intend to have sexual intercourse, nor did Becky ever believe that her physical attraction for Darrell or her loss of a love could lead her into such a sin.

Feelings change automatically, instantly, and part of her feeling at that sad moment was to provide an outlet for his need to communicate love. That they indulged again and still a third time proved that there was love there as well as attraction. And God help them! They must have suffered a terrible remorse, apparently denying themselves during the ten years that followed. Since it was obvious that they loved each other and they sacrificed that love because both of them loved Dorothy more, I advised her to forgive and to forget.

Within Dorothy's story lie lessons applicable to many people—to adults in general and to parents with adolescent children. In my files are literally hundreds of letters which state, "If only I had known." It is startling how many otherwise alert people allow those they love to be placed in sexually stimulating atmosphere and blithely assume that nothing will happen. In my files are many cases of true incest which could easily have been avoided by even momentary alertness, and the awareness that a combination of certain factors can so easily lead to momentary indiscretion.

Alcohol, drugs, highly charged emotional situations—any of these can lead to momentary sexual actions which can destroy years of well-laid plans and happiness. One of the pervading reasons is that no parent or spouse wants to recognize or accept that their loved one could stray from the straight and narrow sexual path. It is the case of the three monkeys: hear, see and speak no evil—that is, until it is too late.

No intelligent person would consciously place temptation in the path of their loved ones—yet so many are guilty of the crime of blindness, of ignoring the explosion latent in certain situations or environments. Astrology does not dwell on sex because sex is simply one of the drives in human beings, and is merely a reflection of the total psyche. An intense, dynamic person—male or female—with certain planetary aspects is certain to have a lower temptation threshold to certain stimuli than another. This is not shocking. Almost every person knows someone they hold dear who has a biting temper. Being aware of this, you manipulate the situation or environment whenever possible to avoid the manifestation of this scalding anger. You do not really think any less of this person, you simply recognize he or she has a basic lack of self-control in this particular area. You don't offer a drink to an alcoholic or cream pies to a diabetic. You accept their weaknesses, and in most cases act in a protective manner.

In fact, a person—or the public—is reluctant to really accept someone who doesn't manifest at least one minor weakness. The person who appears perfect is immediately suspect. We feel they're covering up something. Certainly not every person has potential sexual problems in their chart, but every person has some significant problems. If it relates to sex, it should be faced as realistically as if it related to some other temperamental or personality trait.

I'm in Love with
My Best Friend's Husband

Anyone whose business is giving advice, as mine is, is often caught in the middle of conflicting standards. What is the moral thing to do? What is socially acceptable? What course of action will help the most number of people, or, more often, will harm the least number? What will give the most comfort to the often tormented person who asks for the advice? How can the individual be helped?

Ideally, of course, all these questions should have exactly the same response. What is socially desirable should be the best course of action for the individual, and this should also bring the greatest happiness for all concerned. But this is not always the case. It is unfortunate that what society ordains is often what the individual is least willing to comply with. When I receive a letter such as the following, I often feel that for me to give advice is a situation as fraught with difficulty, and even danger, as walking a tightrope over Niagara Falls. I can cast horoscopes, give advice, and sympathize, but I know there is no real solution which will dispose of all the aspects of the problem posed.

A woman I shall call Adele wrote to me:

I was born November 5, 1930, I was one of four children. I had a happy childhood and became an attractive girl. I thought I was in love a few times, refused two proposals, and at the age of twenty-two I took a Civil Service job in Washington, D.C.

One of the people I looked up when I got to Washington was my best friend, Leona. Leona, who was born May 30, 1929, had grown up with me in the West. We were inseparable schoolmates. We trusted each other and had the same tastes. She married Jim after her arrival in Washington, and had given up her job. Jim's birthday is March 27, 1920, making him nine years older than his wife and ten years older than me. He was a Major in the Army, and had just returned from Korea in 1952 when I first met him. I learned also he had been divorced before he met Leona.

I first met Jim when he picked me up at my apartment to take me to his

379

and Leona's home in Virginia for the weekend. At thirty-two, he had that boyish look so many American military men seem to retain into middle age. His sandy blond hair was crew cut, and he had a flat stomach and developed muscles. I thought he was terribly good looking, and I also found him charming. By the time we got to their place, I felt much at ease in Jim's company, as though we had known each other for a long time.

A little later, when Leona showed me to my room, I said how much I approved of her choice. A kind of sadness registered itself about her mouth. She replied that marriage is not all it's cracked up to be, or words to that effect. I didn't like to think Leona was disappointed in marriage, nor did I want to butt into her business. I pretended that this was a normal remark, and said nothing more about it.

We went downstairs to the patio where Jim had made drinks for us. As the evening wore on, I could sense a tension between Jim and Leona, which made me uncomfortable. By midnight, after we had exhausted all our reminiscences, the roots of this tension became apparent. I don't remember just how it started, but they raised their voices when they began discussing whether the children of Jim's first marriage could come to visit them for the month of August. Indirectly, they were putting the question to me. After spending an evening with them, I liked Jim very much; I sympathized with his desire to entertain his children. I was rather shocked at the vehemence with which Leona refused to have them in the house. I tried to persuade her to give them a chance; I told her that she would probably love the kids.

Her reaction was startling. She launched into a recital of grievances, saying that when she married Jim he had promised to turn over a new leaf, and that included ignoring the existence of his first family. Then she told me, in front of Jim, that his first wife had divorced him for adultery, and that, furthermore, he had been unfaithful to her, and that she would not put up with it. She seemed, in some way, to confuse the fact that he had had children by his first wife with adultery.

Later, Leona came to say goodnight and to apologize. She told me then she was pregnant, and she didn't want the child, particularly after she had learned that Jim had been unfaithful. After she left I couldn't sleep. I turned out my light and watched Jim on the patio, pacing up and down, smoking one cigarette after another and mixing himself drinks. All my sympathy went to him. I even excused his infidelities to Leona by blaming her for a lack of sympathy and understanding.

After that weekend I wanted to help them. Instead, I just became more involved. I couldn't get Jim out of my mind. Both of us worked at the Pentagon, so it was easy for us to meet. After refusing several of his offers to take me to coffee, I finally gave in. Even on coffee dates he was more exciting to me than any of the other men I was seeing at the time. I started having dinner with him from time to time. I loved him! He said he loved me.

Leona kept begging me to spend weekends with them. Nothing I could say shook her belief that Jim must not bring his children into her house. They continued to have terrible arguments in front of me. It seemed to me that there was no hope for their marriage, but Leona was pregnant and very ill, so I said nothing.

When August came, Jim couldn't let his boys down, so he rented a beach house in the tidewater part of Virginia. He intended to keep his sons for two weeks. A day after he got there he called me to say that one of his boys was ill, and could I come and stay with them? He said a woman's presence would help the child. I didn't really care, by that time, whether he was telling the truth or not; I wanted to be with him. I took a week's vacation and went to a hotel near his cottage. He hadn't lied; the youngest child had a mild summer complaint which he snapped out of soon enough. I liked the children very much and they seemed to like me.

It was that week Jim and I made love for the first time. We were on the beach, late at night, and from the moment he kissed me I gave in.

Back in Washington, I vowed that I must break with him. But Leona was ill and would continue to urge me to spend weekends with them. I would try to refuse myself to Jim, but could not. I even tried going with other men, but they bored me. This situation lasted through the fall of 1952 and into the winter when Leona was delivered of a baby girl. It was a difficult birth, and it was months before she recovered.

I wanted to get away. I felt guilty about Leona and even about Jim, because I knew he could not ask for a divorce without losing the child he had had with Leona. I begged my office to send me overseas. After a while I was assigned to Germany. In many ways it was a cowardly thing to do, but I thought it was the only way I could get over Jim. But I couldn't forget him. Nor did he forget me. He wrote me letter after letter telling me that he still loved me.

I also received letters from Leona. Judging by what they both wrote, I could tell that they were not getting along at all. Then, in late 1953, Jim was stationed in Germany. Leona refused to accompany him. She was pregnant again, and this pregnancy was, if anything, more difficult than her first.

Seeing Jim again swept away all my resolutions. I told him he must get a divorce as soon as the baby was born, that even if all his salary went to paying alimony, I would work and support us both. He agreed. Then Leona's baby was born and it was retarded. I couldn't help wondering if this were a punishment. Jim took a leave to be with Leona. Asking for a divorce was out of the question.

After Jim returned to Washington in 1954, I decided once more that we must finish the affair—it was impossible to continue together. I started dating other men. One of these men fell in love with me and asked me to marry him. I told him about my past with Jim. He asked me whether it was all over, and all I could reply was, yes, that I thought so. My response was so half-hearted that he stopped seeing me. I had wanted to get married, but now I think only because I thought I could discipline myself about seeing Jim if I had a husband.

At any rate it was time to return to Washington. I swore I would not see

Jim, but I knew I was lying to myself. I was scarcely settled into my apartment in Washington before the affair began where it left off.

People talked, and naturally there came a time when even Leona had to face up to what was going on. Her attitude shocked me. She very cooly said she would never give him a divorce; she also said he was sick and could never be faithful to one woman, so she felt sorry for me. I shocked myself when I began to defend him. I insisted again and again that she give him a divorce.

It was useless. Jim received an assignment in Japan and I told Leona that I intended to follow him. She told me to go ahead and throw away my life if I wanted to. She said she had two children to consider.

The years passed quickly. Everybody in Japan knew that I was Jim's mistress, but we never lacked friends. We were invited everywhere as though we were man and wife. I've always thought of myself as his wife.

We're going home next month. Neither of us wants to return to the States, but we have to go. His tour of duty is up. Besides, our living abroad had meant that we haven't really faced the facts—it's given us the feeling that we can go on this way forever.

Jim needs me; I have given him the only semblance of home life, of marriage, that he's ever had. We never quarrel anymore. We're still in love, and are always happy with each other. He's never unfaithful to me. When he was sent on detached service to a city containing many easy glamorous women, he begged me to come along because he would miss me so. In many ways our relationship is far happier than that of most married people.

But I feel guilty. My family back home knows now and they're unhappy and ashamed of me. I'm not getting any younger. I was thirty-one last birthday. Jim is forty-one. Where is it all going to end? I need help! Is there anything in my horoscope that shows what the outcome of this will be? Will Jim and I ever be married? Should I marry another man? Could I find happiness with another person?

Born November 15, 1930, Adele's Sun is in Scorpio, the sign of a dynamic passionate woman. Her Moon is located in Virgo, the practical self-effacer, and it is in harmonious sextile aspect to her Sun. In addition, her Venus is regressed in Sagittarius, her second house financial angle. She is an extraordinarily unselfish woman.

Adele's personality is warm and vibrant. With her Sun in Scorpio, sextile Moon in Virgo, she is a one-man woman. It was unfortunate that a woman who has so much to give to marriage, home, and family should have found herself tied almost indissolvably to a man who could offer her only an illicit relationship.

Because of the complexity of the situation, it was necessary to make horoscopes for all the people involved, Jim and Leona as well as Adele.

Jim's Sun is in Aries, the sign of the bold pioneer, the traveler, the warrior. It is the sign ruled by a masculine, military, ultrasexual Mars. Jim's male Sun is directly opposed to Leona's female Moon, which is found in Libra; this is one of the classical oppositions that can make a marriage difficult. Jim's Sun is far more compatible with Adele's Moon in Virgo. Actually, neither his second wife nor his mistress can expect to really plumb the depths of Jim's strange personality, certainly not to the extent a woman with her Moon in Aquarius or Gemini might be able to do.

Jim's Mars, symbol of his sex drive, is retrogressing in Scorpio, close to Adele's Sun in Scorpio. Both are strongly passionate people. Society had always demanded some rein on the female's polyerotic nature, but it has made few such demands on the male. Jim enjoyed relationships with many women. He seems to find it hard to be faithful to any wife, and he admitted infidelities even to Adele. At the time she wrote, Adele was proud that he had become faithful to her, pointing it out as though it were a sign of love. This fidelity probably speaks more loudly for her own lusty nature, and for the fact that she gives Jim a constant, successful and happy sexual outlet which he cannot find elsewhere. With strongly sexually oriented people like Jim and Adele such an attraction can go a long way to make a good marriage; but more is needed.

Adele wrote that though Jim is ten years her senior, he is boyish and youthful. Adele's strongly sympathetic nature (the Moon in Virgo configuration, in unfavorable aspect to her Venus in Sagittarius), has looked upon Jim in a protective, motherly way. In any crisis she comes to his defense, even when he has done something reprehensible. It seemed likely to me that Adele had fallen in love with the man who needed her most, the man with a problem. Because she is a passionate Sun-in-Scorpio woman, Jim has been able to satisfy all his sexual needs without diminishing the boyish impression he has given. I told Adele that it would be difficult for her to fall as deeply in love with a man who did not need her in other ways than just sexually.

A certain perverseness is implied in Jim's chart, because his disciplinary Saturn is weak and regressed in Virgo. His Venus and regressed Mercury are both in mysterious, or hard to define, Pisces, his Twelfth House of the secret sensations of the soul. There are aspects which indicate sexual problems, questionable drives, even deviation. An analysis of their charts showed that sexual passion notionally brought them together; their secret sex drives had cemented the relationship.

Leona was going to be of no help in breaking up the affair. Even though her Moon is in Pisces, near Jim's strange Venus-Mercury relationship, it was obvious that she could not meet all of his sex needs. Her Venus is in Aries, near his Sun, which gives her a respectable, even a cold and austere aura. Jim sees her on a pedestal, and the chances are that she will remain there, in strong possession of him when he is older. Her Mercury is in Gemini, close to her solar personality symbol, and in unfavorable aspect to her Moon in Pisces. She is a rather prudish woman who has a low regard for men in general. She is also very possessive. Even if it had not been for their retarded child, it is likely she would have found some other means of holding onto Jim.

Adele had asked about the future. At the time I wrote her I told her that her Moon in Virgo would shortly be buttressed by Uranus and Pluto, which would, respectively, alert her to new opportunities for happiness, and induce awareness of what was truly involved in her relationship with Jim.

In early 1963, Jim's Jupiter would be in Aries, giving him fortitude to recognize his part in her deteriorating personal situation. At the same time, Adele's Jupiter would be in favorable aspect to her Venus. With Venus trine Jupiter, she would have new support in whatever resolve she took about the affair.

I urged Adele to give Jim up; their situation could only end badly for her. It was apparent that Leona would never let Jim go, and once his sexual urge became more restrained he would be devoted to her. This would leave Adele to face her middle years and old age alone—something for which she was temperamentally unsuited. I suggested that if she took advantage of the favorable aspects of her and Jim's horoscope which were due, she would be able to break off completely. I realized that initially, at least, this would be neither easy nor agreeable. It was, however, the only practical solution.

Adele and Jim returned to the United States in late 1962. They continued their affair, but they found it more difficult with Leona and the children nearby. Then Leona did an about face and let Jim's nineteen-year-old son by his first marriage come to live with them. Jim was very fond of the boy, and spent a great deal of time with him. Several times he broke dates with Adele, using his son as an excuse.

In her effort to break off with Jim, Adele started dating other men. Before long she met a widower with two children whose wife had died tragically the year before. They became very fond of each other, and he asked her to marry him. Adele wrote to ask that I cast his chart. Analysis of his horoscope showed his Sun in very favorable aspect to her Moon, and his Mars in favorable aspect to her Venus. These were very auspicious signs for a happy marriage. They were married in July 1963.

In her last letter to me, Adele told me that she was very happy. She no longer sees either Jim or Leona unless her husband is with her. Jim had not made any new advances toward her. I suspect that Adele still harbors a strong attraction for Jim, which she is keeping in check through willpower. A man and woman as compatible as they, do not simply separate without leaving some scars. In my last letter to Adele I warned her to continue her self-control and to avoid Jim.

I think that, all things considered, this case can be said to have ended for the good of everyone.

One of the very important dynamic factors in compatibility charts is that rarely do all of the basic drives for sex, power, status, and money, plus needs for security, romance and adventure, balance in the horoscope of a man and woman.

Implicit within the statement or question: "Will this be a happy marriage?" are some very basic philosophical questions. Is this a marriage where both people will have an opportunity to grow, to expand existing strengths, and develop latent talents? Will they be able to provide an environment for the rearing of well-adjusted children and to develop a cooperative relationship rather than a dominate-submissive one? Is this marriage simply a focus for legalizing easily available sex?

Your horoscope will picture your strong motivations, and the environment will provide the instrument for the execution of these drives. Included in the environment are the transits of the luminaries.

Only deep within your own heart can the foregoing questions be answered, and then evaluated in your chart. Any person who foolishly believes marriage will solve all of their psychological or environmental problems is headed for disaster. Attraction may be fate—compatibility is the result of effort.

Compassionate understanding is the greatest asset in any relationship between two people. Many times I have seen the frank analytical casting of two charts open the way for delineation of true motivations, positive discussion, and potentially successful reconciliation of problems.

One of the strongest human tendencies is to evaluate others in terms of one's own motivations, drives and hopes; and, of course, this can lead to violent disagreements. Even more often, people either evaluate themselves on the basis of what they would like to be rather than what they are; or they refuse to acknowledge their strengths because of guilt or anxiety. They are willing to forgive others, but refuse to forgive themselves.

Astrology can open up perhaps the first real channel of communication that has ever been available to some people. Astrology that is to be of any real value must, like psychology or psychiatry, take an amoral viewpoint. Astrology exists not to please, to titillate, or to censure, but to state facts, facts based upon the premise that man, no matter what his problems, must exist with others and with himself, and with the concept of a Higher Self.

Astrology has grown more sophisticated, yet it has not changed fundamentally, even in the face of changing morals, viewpoints, and sexual standards. The problems which face men today are little different than those of thousands of years ago.

Love after Forty

Men and women today are generally more youthful at forty than they ever have been. As life expectancy has increased, so have the age brackets of middle-age and old-age. The idea that life ends at forty has become outmoded.

A concomitant of better health, more leisure time, and greater prosperity is an increased awareness of emotional and sexual needs. Yet, there are two diametrically opposed conflicts in this new trend. There is the overestimating of basic drives and needs. In the former, there is often devastating results when they realize they truly are not a match for a twenty year old. And there are those who feel silly or inadequate when they discover, to their amazement, they have fallen in love with the same intensity generally only ascribed to youth. The following cases illustrate instances where love and romance were a thing of the past. In these cases I am describing relationships with real depth of emotion— not transitory infatuations.

The first case is about a man I shall call Pat, who was fifty years old when he first had his horoscope cast. Pat was born March 27, 1910; his Sun is in Aries.

Pat had enjoyed a happy marriage for some years and was the father of four children. He had married at nineteen, because, as he bluntly put it: "I had a terrific sex need early in life. Sometimes it was frightening because I had close calls with girls I didn't particularly want to marry."

His late wife had been the kind of romantic with whom he could fall deeply in love: "I felt marriage would be the best solution for all my problems and I intended to be a good husband, fair and honest." Pat's Moon is in Libra, the sign of justice.

The four children came quickly. Though Pat was very happy with his wife, he found he was still attracted to many pretty young women he met along the way. He had affairs, some of which he wanted to excuse by reminding me he had undergone periodic restraint because his wife was indisposed for long periods during their years of marriage. "I had an ungovernable sex need," he wrote, "and I still have."

Pat's Mars is in Gemini, where Mars is usually unpredictable and erratic, and gives the male a need to reaffirm what he considers the strongest evidence of his masculinity. His Venus is direct in Aquarius, which shows that his personality must have constant expression. It was natural that when he "played around," as he called it, he would use his affairs to buttress his ego. Several of his mistresses became status symbols for him. He was quick to let me know that one of his girlfriends had been the wife of his boss and another had been the daughter of a business competitor.

He is a reasonably good father and a good provider. He sent three of his children to college (one of them had married right after high school). All four of his children were grown when he wrote to me. The oldest was thirty and married, the youngest was twenty-five. It was this youngest son who, indirectly, had prompted Pat to write for advice. The boy had fallen in love with an eighteen-year-old college "beatnik" named Diane. Pat had disliked what he had heard about the girl. She was a bright, ultraliberal teenager. "I hated to see my son," he wrote, "a quiet, good boy, get mixed up with a young radical like she is."

Then Pat met Diane. He wrote me his reaction: "She was really beautiful; not ill-kept like I thought she would be, but attractive in her individualism. She wore her hair long and was dressed in a simple, carefree manner. If she hadn't been my son's steady, I would have indicated my attraction right away. What really intrigued me was that she gave me the impression she liked me. But then I remembered I was fifty and she was eighteen. Even so, I secretly hoped she and my boy would break up so I could at least ask for a date."

The problem was that Pat had not waited. His son's firm sent the boy on the road for three months, and in a semi-fatherly gesture, Pat promised to see the girl now and then. She refused Pat's first invitation to dinner, and his second invitation to luncheon a few weeks later. Then, on the spur of the moment one night, she called to let Pat know that she had a letter from his son and that the boy hoped to be home in two weeks. She suggested that Pat meet her at a jazz joint of her selection.

Halfway through the evening, Diane let Pat know that she was not in love with his son. She thought the boy as "sweet," but that was all. Pat was convinced that their romance so far had been innocent. Diane, however, intimated that other romances along the way had not been so innocent.

It was a hot summer night and Diane complained about the heat in her apartment. Teasingly, she said she envied Pat his suburban air conditioning. Pat promptly told her she was free to make use of one of the three empty bedrooms in the house. She accepted the offer, and as she did, Pat saw the old familiar sign around her mouth and eyes. He related what had happened.

"I drove her home, made her a drink, and hated myself. Yet I was fascinated, because I knew what would happen. Well, it did. When a man of fifty possesses a young girl of eighteen, there's a sense of being reborn again. What made it exhilarating for me was that she went for it in a big way. She was newer at the game than I would have thought. She had a lot to learn, but she obviously enjoyed learning from me. We stayed in the house all day and night, and by then I wanted her for good. She said she loved me, that she had never known it could be like that. I planned on a genuine, long-term love affair."

A comparison of Pat's and Diane's horoscope showed that they could have a very successful marriage. There was, however, the problem of breaking the news to the son. Pat and Diane conducted a secret love affair during the next six months, but Pat wanted something more permanent: "When I first suggested marriage to Diane, she was against it. However, there were other times when she very much wanted to be my wife, and to let the whole business out into the open."

Pat's son soon became interested in another girl, so there was no longer any need for secrecy. During the next year, Diane's parents learned that she was in love with an older man and they vehemently opposed any thought of marriage. Diane's father was one year younger than Pat. All of Diane's friends told her that even though Pat was handsome, successful and likeable, they were sure that a marriage between a man of fifty-one and a girl of nineteen would be a failure.

Diane was a junior in college when she tried to break off her two and one-half-year-old liaison with Pat. She dated other men and urged Pat to date other women. But they couldn't find in others what they had together.

"Sometimes," Pat wrote, "after a date with a fellow her own age, she would call me up and ask if she could come to my place. It was just as bad with me. I would have a heavy date with some woman and spend the whole evening thinking about Diane, then I'd try to stop by her place on the way home."

Finally, they gave in to their need and love and were married when Pat was fifty-three and Diane twenty-one. They had a large formal church wedding with all of their friends present. Diane's father gave the bride away.

The last time I heard from Pat they had two boys. Both he and Diane were gloriously happy together. What will happen when Pat is sixty, seventy, and Diane is twenty-eight, thirty-eight? It is obvious that Pat will not be an old man at seventy. At any rate, they both have great faith in each other. Furthermore, they overcame the obstacles placed in the way of their marriage. There is no reason to believe that they will be unable to handle whatever further difficulties might arise.

The pattern of a much older man marrying a young girl is actually somewhat of a tradition in this country, particularly in the Middle and Western states during the 1800s and early 1900s. For the most part, many of the men who settled this area were unable financially or emotionally to establish themselves until their late thirties or early forties, when they could finally afford to marry.

However, there is a tremendous potential for disaster in the marriage of an older man and young woman when their liaison is simply the expression of severe neuroses.

Alice, born April 30, 1920, when the Sun was in Taurus, was an only daughter who had nursed her parents all her life. She was a schoolteacher and had had no opportunity to lead a life of her own until after her parents' death. She was forty-one when she first wrote to me.

She had fallen in love, for the first time in her life, with a boy who was only twenty-six years old. They had met overseas while working for the Peace Corps. Their romance had created a scandal. Alice and the boy, Len, were too little experienced in such matters to be surreptitious, and the ensuing gossip resulted in their discharge from the Peace Corps.

It was at this point that Alice wrote to me. She was very much in love with Len and he with her, but she was frightened of ruining his future by marrying him. "He is the first man in my life," she wrote, "and he wants to marry me." I might add here that, from her photograph, Alice did not look forty-one. She was attractive, though not beautiful, and well groomed; she could have passed for any age between twenty-seven and thirty-five.

I made a comparison chart for Len and Alice. Her Moon was in Libra, the sign of justice. Her Venus was in Aries, making her rather bold and pioneering in her outlook. It was evident from her chart that Alice was willing to take chances, but her Jupiter was in Leo and her Saturn in Virgo, and this indicated she responded strongly to the rules of the game and to the opinion of society. She was in a state of total self-conflict.

Len's Mars was in Gemini, in favorable sextile aspect to Alice's Venus, which is one of the classical omens for happiness in marriage. There was, however, a possibility that Len saw Alice as a mother image. He was responsive to that kind of motherly attraction. I was not surprised to learn that his mother had died when he was six years of age, nor that he had been abandoned by his father. Like Alice, he was an only child.

There was absolutely nothing in their horoscopes to indicate trouble, separation or divorce. Since both of them were well educated they would have little trouble finding jobs wherever they settled. I urged them to pull up stakes, settle in another part of the country, and go ahead with their marriage.

They went to Alaska. Immediately after their marriage they adopted a child; then after another two months Alice was pregnant. She successfully delivered a healthy son. They never discuss their age difference with friends or neighbors, but on official documents, Alice admits she is thirteen years older than her husband. Their marriage is a great success.

The following bizarre case of love after forty had much more than just a difference of ages working against it. It is, in fact, the only case of a polyandrous marriage that I have had direct contact with in all my experience.

Jane, born June 13, 1937, was the daughter of migrant workers who followed the crop seasons up and down the West Coast. Grubbing for a living, forgotten by the government and despised by society in general, Jane's family lived a haphazard life. Then Jane was raped by her stepfather when she was thirteen years old. Quite readily Jane admitted that she had loved her stepfather as a father—then, as a husband; for when Jane's mother died two years later, he married her.

When Jane was eighteen she was caring for three of her half-brothers and her own little daughter. It was then that they left the road and settled down in a share-cropper's farmhouse in northern Arkansas. Her husband was doing relatively well, so he invited his youngest brother, Clay, to join them. Clay, according to Jane, had been falsely accused of theft, for which he served three years in a state penitentiary. He was then twenty-three years old, handsome, and animallike. From the very first, he tried to make love to Jane. She, frightened that a fight might take place between the two brothers, finally began a secret affair with him. Her second child, she believes, is his.

Of course, her husband learned of her infidelity. His reaction was incredible. He insisted that she and Clay go through a marriage ceremony before a justice of the peace. She was then, in a sense, legally married to two men.

They had to work hard on the farm, but they were so used to a lack of permanence, that they considered themselves lucky to have the chance. Their home life was strangely harmonious. It seemed to Jane that sharing a wife brought the two brothers closer together.

Naturally, one has to allow for the deprived environment in the case of these three persons, but in all three horoscopes there was a nefarious Neptune in an unusual zodiacal configuration with the male Mars and the female Venus. Pluto was depressing Clay's Jupiterian trends, and an erratic Mars-Moon involvement was in the chart of the older brother.

Jane then fell in love with the man who owned the farm on which they worked. He was forty-six and twice divorced from the women of his own social class. Jane—who had never had any choice in the matter of husbands in the past—felt a true emotional awakening. She wanted a divorce, or possibly an annulment, but she was fearful of arousing the brutality of the two brothers. Furthermore, she did not want to get them into trouble, for she felt an almost animalistic loyalty to them.

The older man wanted to marry her; he was, from her account, an exemplar of patience and understanding. Even so, as soon as Jane told the brothers of her desire, violence erupted. The brothers were enraged and they shot and wounded Jane's new protector before they disappeared.

In spite of this, Jane and the man married, and their marriage has been a success. Each had a need for an understanding and tolerance that the other could furnish. My last letter from Jane showed remarkable progress on her part in both education and insight.

Agnes, born July 4, 1909, was fifty-two when she first wrote me. She had been divorced when she was forty-four, had gone through an early menopause, and had settled down to a humdrum, though not unpleasant, life. Both her children were married and living away from home when she met Clement at church services, and found him pleasant to be with. Like her, Clement was lonely; his wife had died a year earlier. They went to dinner together, and to the theater several times a month. They became more friendly and Clement got into the habit of phoning her at least once a day from his office.

"My son and daughter teased me unmercifully about Clement," Agnes wrote, "but I never really took the whole thing seriously. I found him rather old for me, which was strange, because he was only three years older than I." At the end of the fourth month of their friendship, Clement proposed marriage.

Agnes was rather unnerved. She wavered between yes and no for the balance of the year, in spite of the fact that both her children were urging her to accept Clement's proposal. "I felt like a fool," she wrote. "I liked him, respected his success, but he had habits I couldn't really get used to, such as pulling on his lips when he talked. Still, it was a wonderful opportunity to be provided for the rest of my life, and to have a companion. I decided to talk it over with our minister, but when I got to the parsonage, I learned he was out of town and that his new assistant was doing his work. I didn't know this man and I figured he wouldn't be able to help me."

But the new minister encouraged Agnes to talk. He mentioned that he, too, had recently lost his spouse in death.

"He was forty-nine years old, very handsome, and much younger looking. The first thing I knew, I was telling him everything, even things I never thought I would breathe to a soul. I told him how I had not been happy in my marriage, how my husband made all the decisions when I felt that I was capable of making a few myself. I fell in love with him. I was actually frightened because I dreamed about him romantically, like a young girl."

These dreams came true—Agnes and the minister were married shortly after their meeting. In her last letter to me she wrote from a new city where her husband had received a pastoral appointment. Agnes called her marriage the marriage of her heart. It was, she said, much more exciting and romantic than her first marriage over thirty years earlier.

Marjorie, at fifty, was one of the town's successful lawyers. She had been married, when she was a much younger woman, to a judge who was her senior by 30 years. After her first husband died she married a military officer; but this had lasted less than three months. It was Marjorie who sought the divorce. She swore she would never marry again.

She was very well off with a beautiful home, servants, and would travel at least a month out of every year. She would have passing love affairs while in Europe, but at home she paid strict attention to the traditional moral conventions. She wrote that she was very lonely and she filled her few leisure hours with charitable works.

When her town made plans for celebrating its centennial, she was appointed in charge of the planning and that was how she met Kevin. He was a newcomer to the town, a widower with a grown daughter, and he had just opened a small electrical business.

"He was charming, handsome, and obviously unimpressed with the fact that I was a leading lawyer and from an old and important family," Marjorie wrote. "I found myself making excuses for checking with him about the lighting arrangements for the centennial. I fell in love with him even before he asked me for a formal date. I wondered what everyone would think if they learned that I was in love with a man who hadn't even been to high school and who was, moreover, four years younger."

There was also a difference in religion. "But we were really in love. We even did silly things like swimming at midnight, and riding a roller coaster at a fair. Kevin held out for marriage. He is rather puritanical in his ideas about love affairs. Finally I did marry him. My friends were scandalized at first, but not anymore. Everybody loves Kevin and I think I'm a good mother to his daughter and to the small boy we adopted recently. We are very, very happy together."

These are only a few of the many cases I have in my files of love after forty. In these situations, as in all others, astrology can advise, but does not compel. There are some astrological generalities which can be made, but keep in mind that these observations are subject to various interpretations depending on individual horoscopes.

Roughly, one can say that Scorpio men and women never cease to expect love. Long before changing conventions permitted a new look at the idea of love after forty or fifty, Scorpios were taking the plunge. The same can be said for Sagittarians. The opposite is true, however, for Capricorns. These people are strongly tied to old conventions, and often quite shocked when they fall in love after forty. They need a lot of understanding on the part of relatives and friends if they are to make the right decision.

Aquarians have the knack of being alerted to all golden opportunities in the field of romance. They have often defied conventions, but they face difficulties at times because they must remain individuals. They all too often bring the trappings of an earlier marriage to their new romances. Strong Neptunian trends in a Pisces can result in abject loneliness in old age. This is often a good reason for making a second or third marriage long after youth has faded. Pisces women have married as late as seventy-five, according to my files. A great many Pisces widows marry for companionship after forty, only to fall in love with their husbands to an extent they never dreamed possible.

It is well to keep in mind, however, that no matter what sign one is born under, a great romance is never impossible—regardless of age. If there is any message which is truly implicit in astrology, it is that a person's state of mind is one of the most influential factors in finding happiness.

Any person over forty or less who accepts defeat, loneliness, and despair as their lot in life chokes off all the potential of their spirit, mind and body to reach out for happiness. Doctors are in full accord that one of the most vital factors in illness is the positive attitude of the patient. Eminently successful men have proved that successes are simply failures who wouldn't give up.

As you judge any couple whose ages are very different, it is very easy to include one's own prejudices or frustrations in the judgment. The two most vital factors in any such case as these mentioned is the sincerity of the individuals and the desire and willingness to face the problems which will arise with independence and understanding. Any adult person within reasonable limits has the absolute right to live their own life when they are willing to meet the problems and responsibilities of their actions. Often one of the most important measures of the validity of their decision is their refusal to insist others accept and give approbation to their actions—knowing time will prove their sincerity and good judgment.

Astrology does show that people's needs and personal expression of love and romance vary, but nowhere in any chart is there pictured the death of the ability to love. In fact, in any person's chart the potential for deep love actually increases with each passing year.

Some Parting Thoughts

Here we are again at the end of yet another journey!

There is so much more I could say about my favorite subject—love—but ultimately it is up to you, the reader, wherever you may be living, to take this guidance and apply it in your life.

Remember always that the stars do not compel. They never have. They never can. You have free will to mold your life as you wish.

But also remember, as it is written in the ancient Chinese oracle, the *I Ching*, there are pigs and fishes. Just as we would be surprised to find a pig swimming in the ocean or a fish by the barn, so must we accept the Divine Will in regard to the basic nature of the various signs of the Zodiac.

While people always have the ability to change, they may not wish to do so. Hence, a good, lasting relationship may not be possible. When this circumstance arises in our own life, we have a decision to make: Shall we stay and "burn" or shall we lick our wounds and move on down the road?

In the finality, it seems to Zolar that we don't "go" through relationships but rather "grow" through them. No doubt at one time or another in our life we have all said, "I don't want to live if I can't be with . . ." But when all is said and done, we *do* live. We go on with our lives and find happiness with others.

Isn't living *and* loving what it's all about?